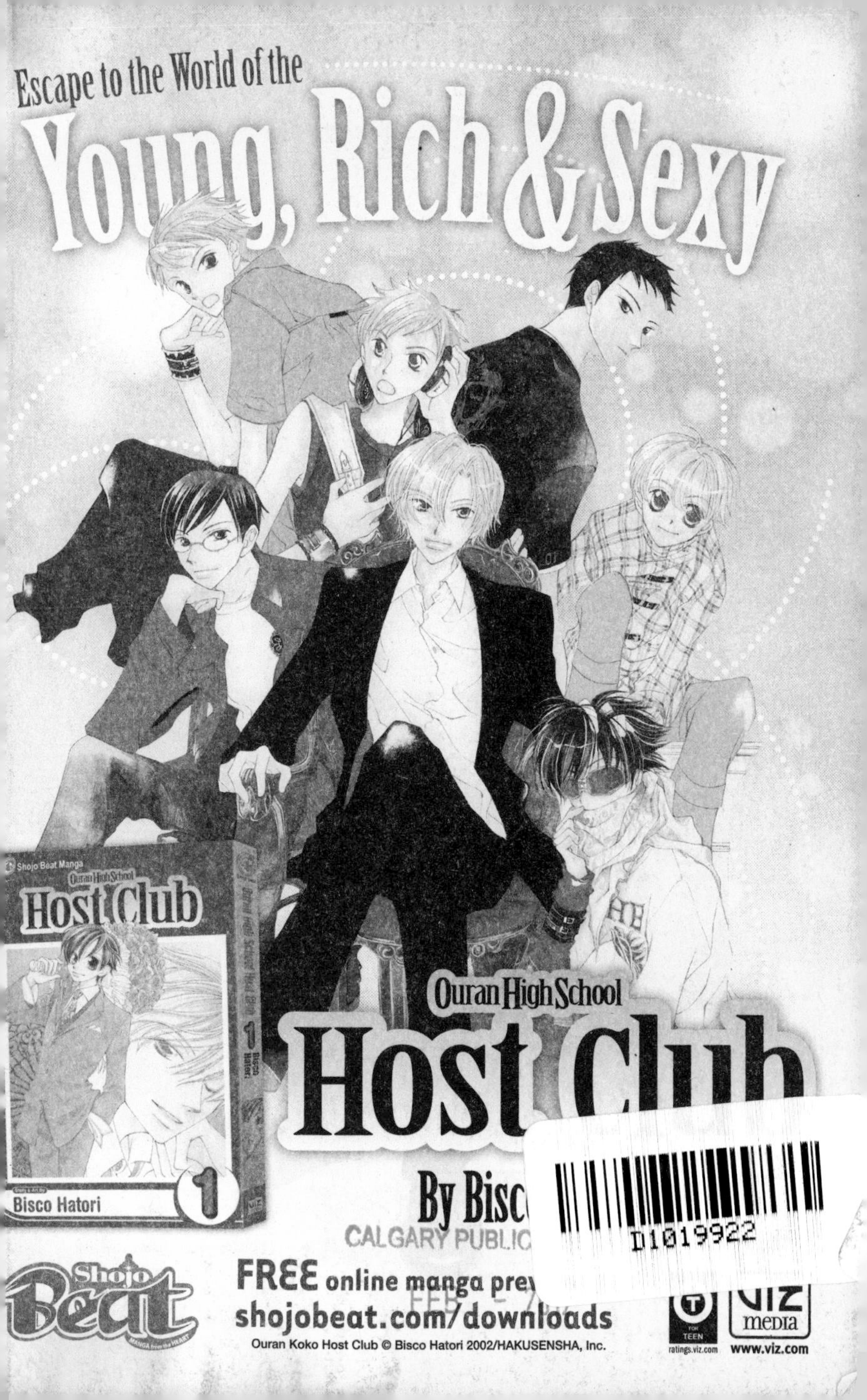
Escape to the World of the
Young, Rich & Sexy
Shojo Beat Manga
Ouran High School
Host Club
Ouran High School Host Club
1
Bisco Hatori
Bisco Hatori
Ouran High School
Host Club
By Bisc
CALGARY PUBLIC
D1019922
Shojo Beat
FREE online manga prev
shojobeat.com/downloads
Ouran Koko Host Club © Bisco Hatori 2002/HAKUSENSHA, Inc.
T
TEEN
ratings.viz.com
VIZ media
www.viz.com

OTOMEN
Vol. 12
Shojo Beat Edition

Story and Art by | **AYA KANNO**

Translation & Adaptation | **JN Productions**
Touch-up Art & Lettering | **Mark McMurray**
Design | **Fawn Lau**
Editor | **Amy Yu**

Otomen by Aya Kanno © Aya Kanno 2011
All rights reserved. First published in Japan in 2011 by HAKUSENSHA, Inc., Tokyo.
English language translation rights arranged with HAKUSENSHA, Inc., Tokyo.

The rights of the author(s) of the work(s) in this publication to be so identified
have been asserted in accordance with the Copyright, Designs and Patents Act 1988.
A CIP catalogue record for this book is available from the British Library.

Printed in the U.S.A.

Published by VIZ Media, LLC
P.O. Box 77010
San Francisco, CA 94107

10 9 8 7 6 5 4 3 2 1
First printing, February 2012

www.viz.com

www.shojobeat.com

STORY

Kiyomi, Asuka's anti-*otomen* mother, has taken control of Ginyuri Academy and is making it difficult for Asuka to live his *otomen* lifestyle. Asuka joins a dessert-making class for men taught by Hiromi, the chef at Patisserie Violet, and starts to feel better again. But Kiyomi is starting to suspect Asuka of hiding something…

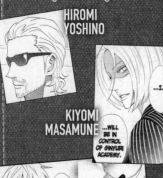

HIROMI YOSHINO

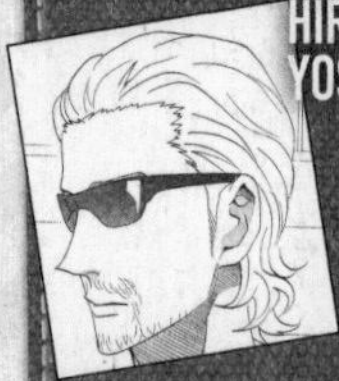

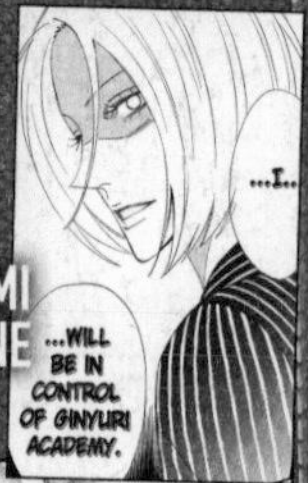
…I…
…WILL BE IN CONTROL OF GINYURI ACADEMY.

KIYOMI MASAMUNE

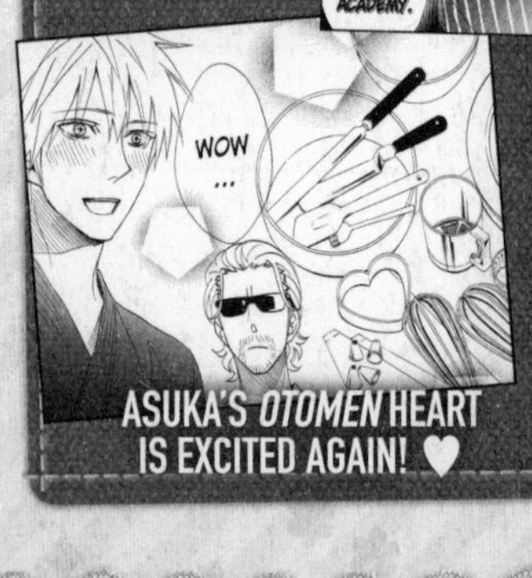
WOW …

ASUKA'S *OTOMEN* HEART IS EXCITED AGAIN! ♥

OTHER OTOMEN

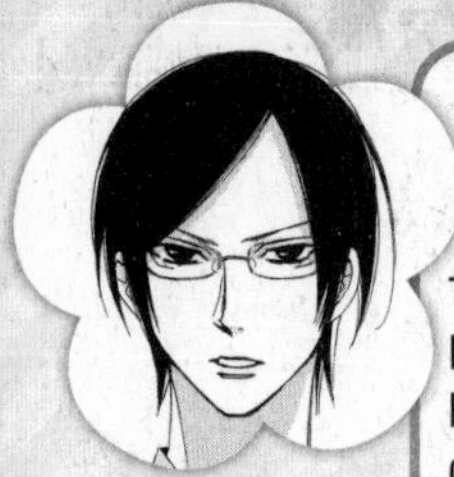

Hajime Tonomine

The captain of the Kinbara High School kendo team, he considers Asuka his sworn rival. He is actually an *otomen* who is good with cosmetics.

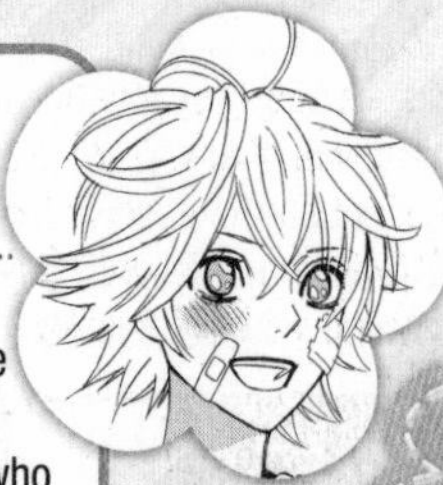

Yamato Ariake

He is younger than Asuka and looks like a cute girl. He is a delusional *otomen* who admires manliness.

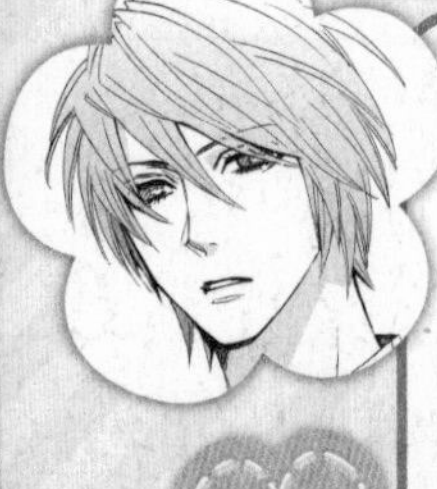

Kitora Kurokawa

Asuka's classmate. A man who is captivated by the beauty of flowers. He is an obsessed *otomen* who wants to cover the world in flowers.

OTOMEN

volume 12
CONTENTS

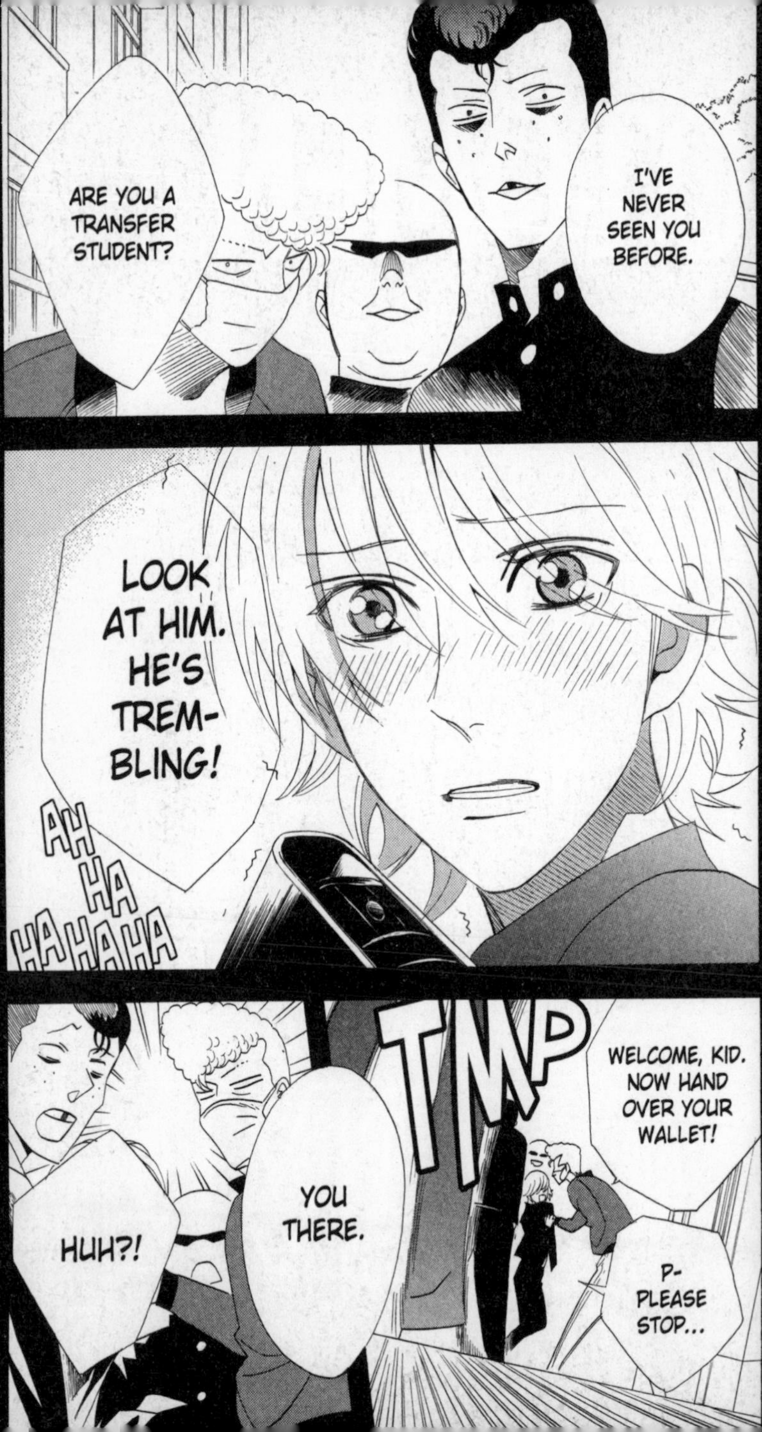
I'VE NEVER SEEN YOU BEFORE.
ARE YOU A TRANSFER STUDENT?
LOOK AT HIM. HE'S TREM-BLING!
AH HA HAHAHAHA
WELCOME, KID. NOW HAND OVER YOUR WALLET!
TMP
P-PLEASE STOP...
YOU THERE.
HUH?!

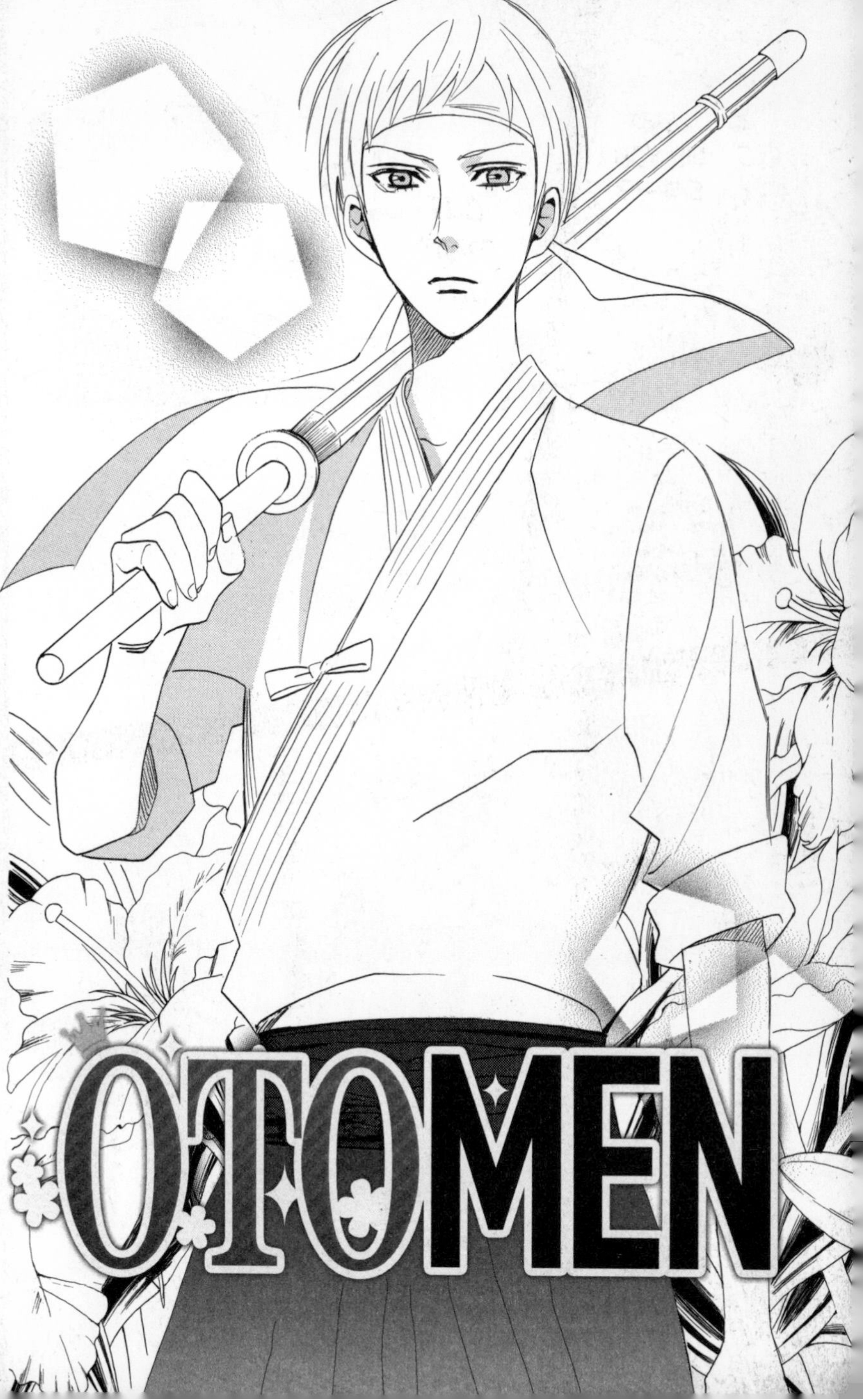
OTOMEN

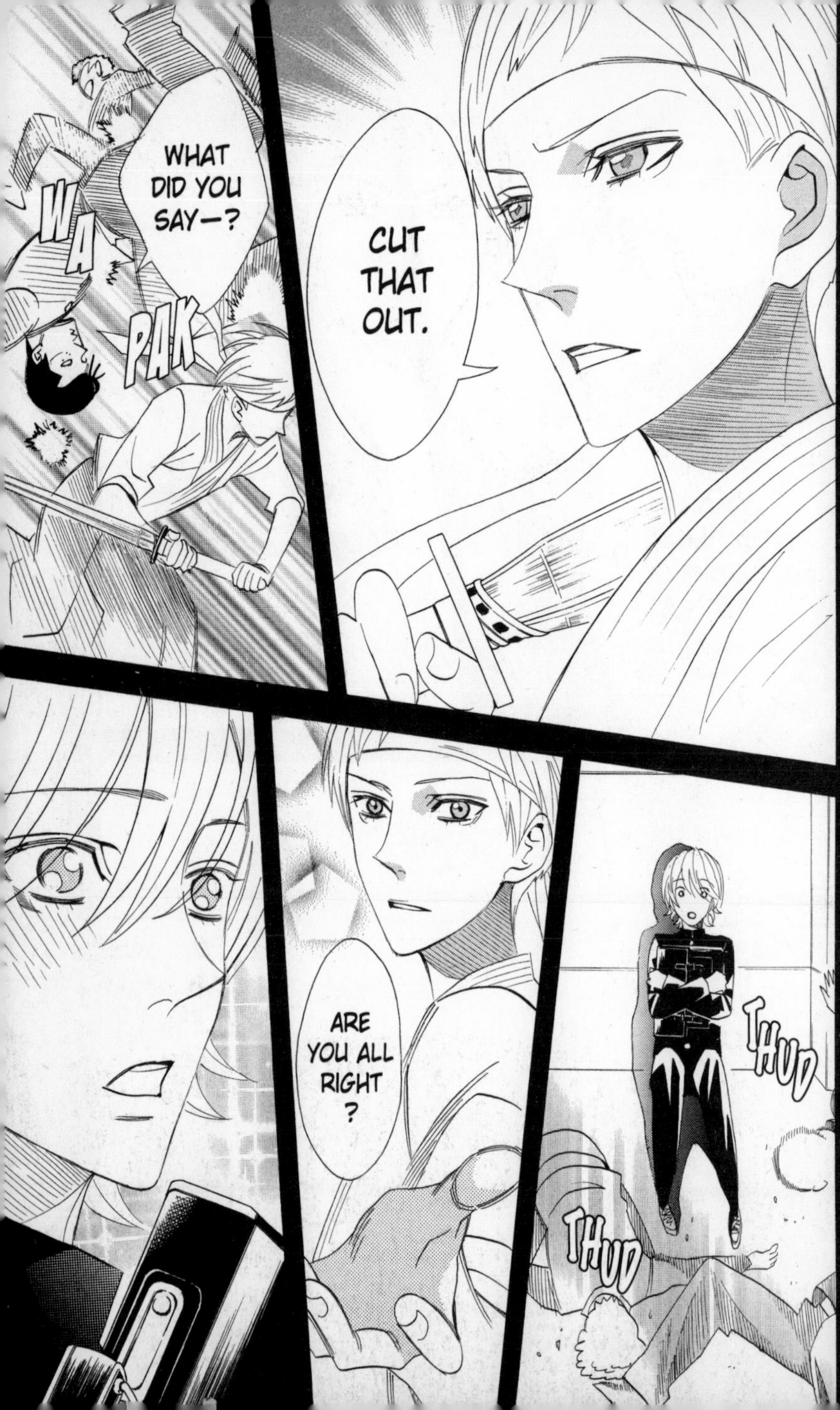
CUT THAT OUT.
WHAT DID YOU SAY—?
WA
PAK
THUD
THUD
ARE YOU ALL RIGHT?

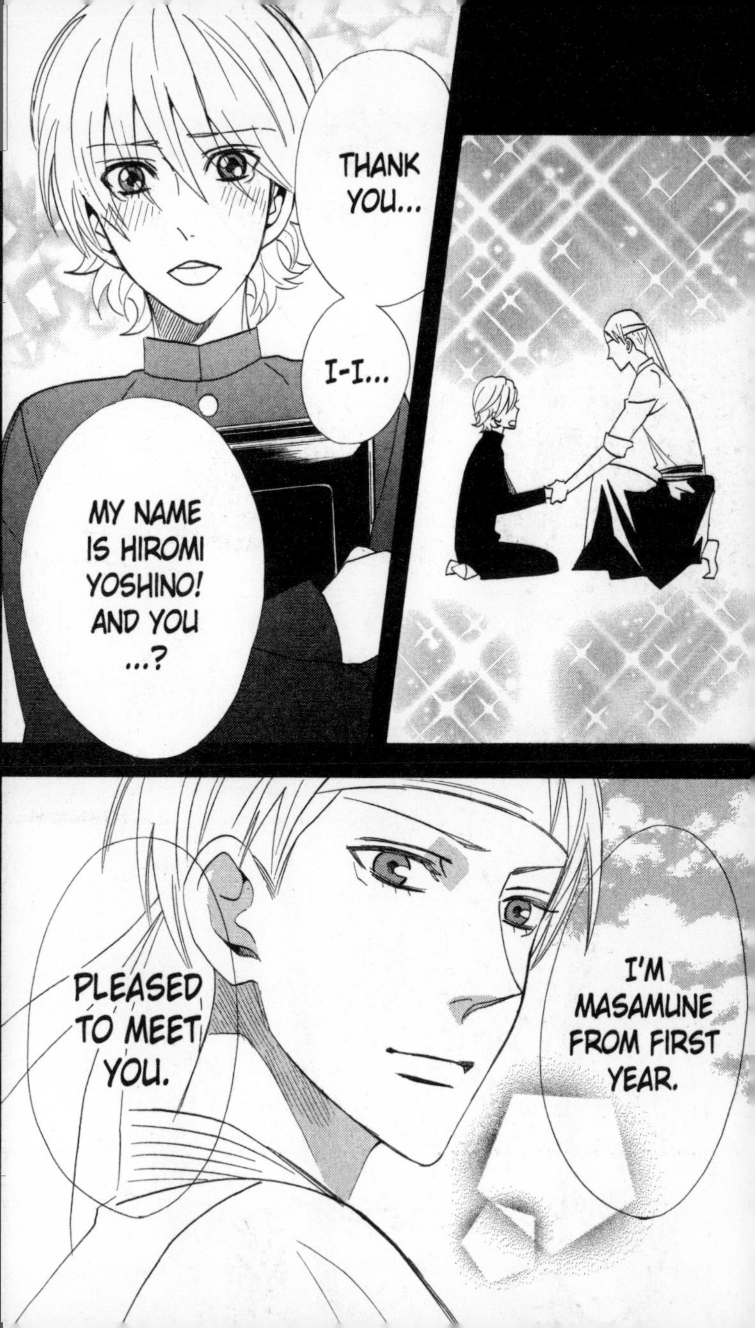
THANK YOU...
I-I...
MY NAME IS HIROMI YOSHINO! AND YOU ...?
I'M MASAMUNE FROM FIRST YEAR.
PLEASED TO MEET YOU.

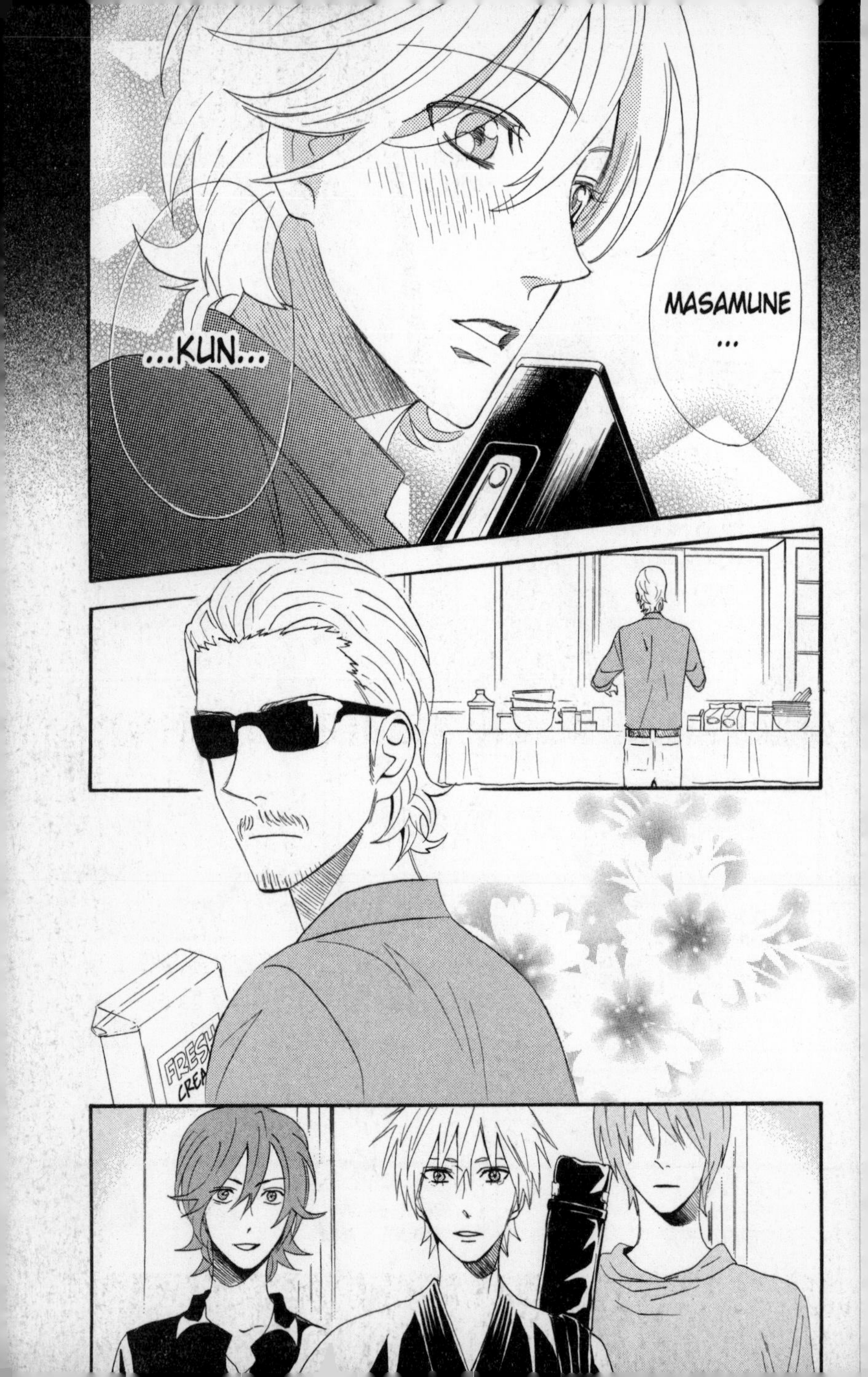
MASAMUNE
...
...KUN...

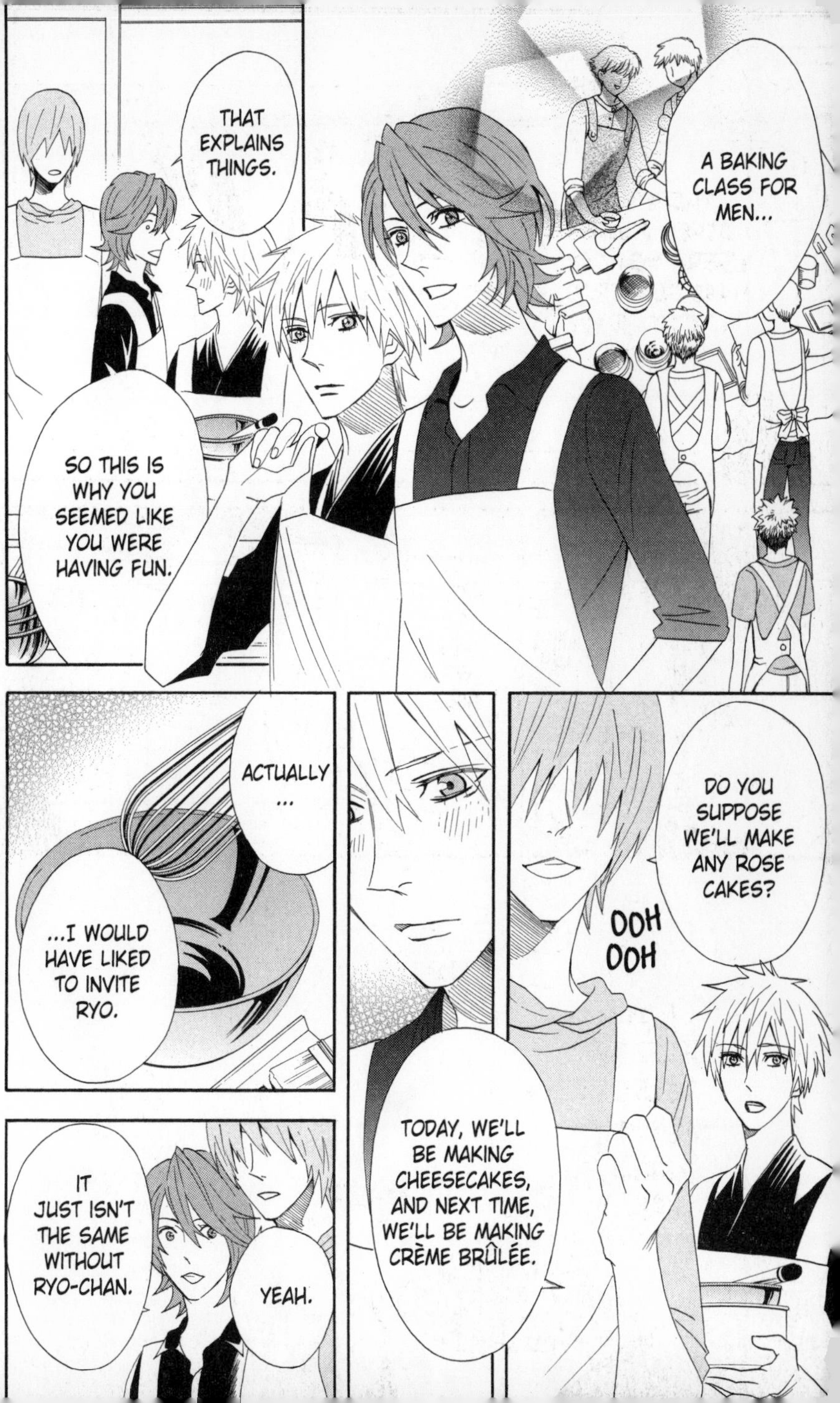
A BAKING CLASS FOR MEN...
THAT EXPLAINS THINGS.
SO THIS IS WHY YOU SEEMED LIKE YOU WERE HAVING FUN.
DO YOU SUPPOSE WE'LL MAKE ANY ROSE CAKES?
OOH OOH
TODAY, WE'LL BE MAKING CHEESECAKES, AND NEXT TIME, WE'LL BE MAKING CRÈME BRÛLÉE.
ACTUALLY ...
...I WOULD HAVE LIKED TO INVITE RYO.
IT JUST ISN'T THE SAME WITHOUT RYO-CHAN.
YEAH.

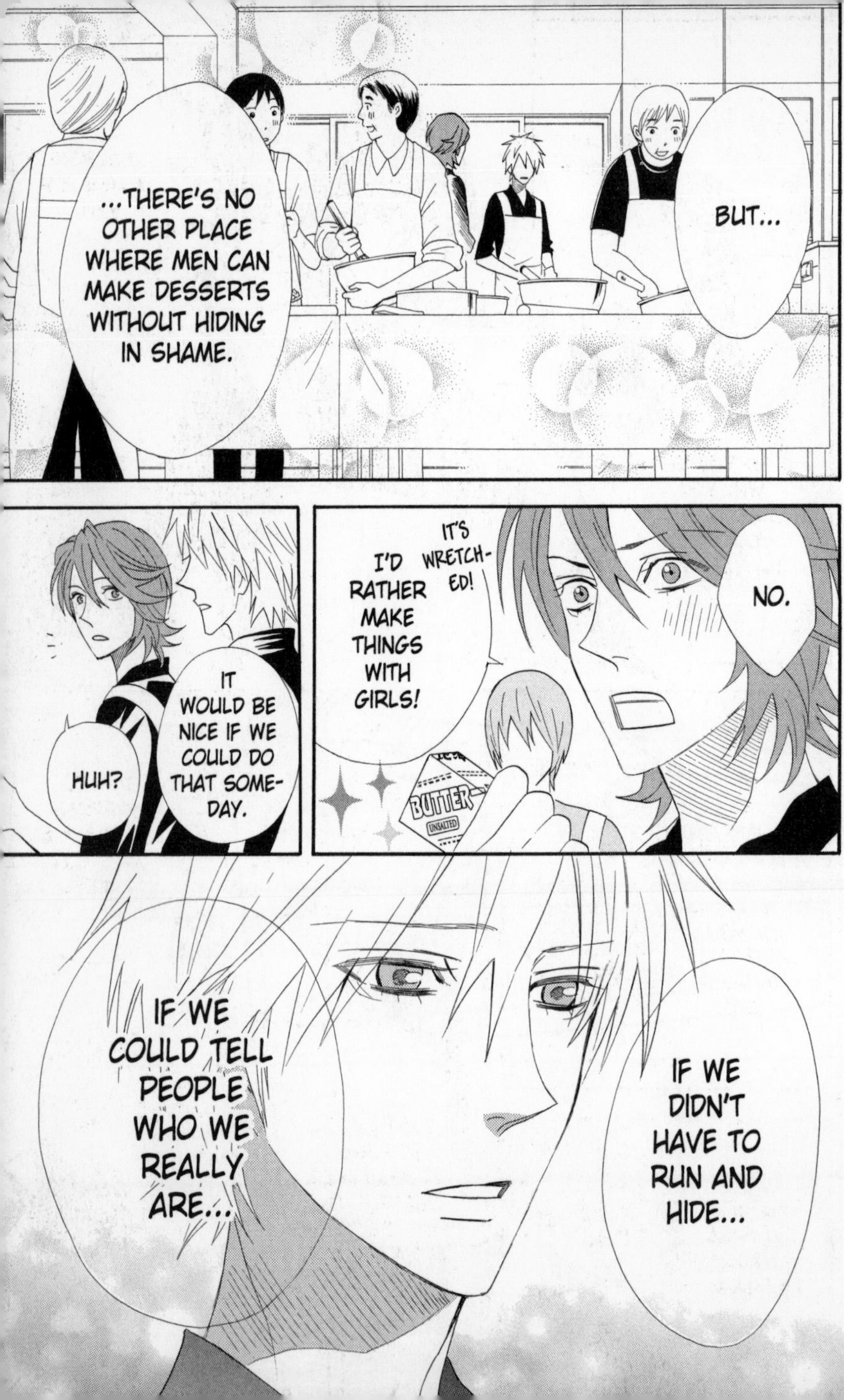
BUT...
...THERE'S NO OTHER PLACE WHERE MEN CAN MAKE DESSERTS WITHOUT HIDING IN SHAME.
NO.
IT'S WRETCH-ED!
I'D RATHER MAKE THINGS WITH GIRLS!
BUTTER
UNSALTED
IT WOULD BE NICE IF WE COULD DO THAT SOME-DAY.
HUH?
IF WE DIDN'T HAVE TO RUN AND HIDE...
IF WE COULD TELL PEOPLE WHO WE REALLY ARE...

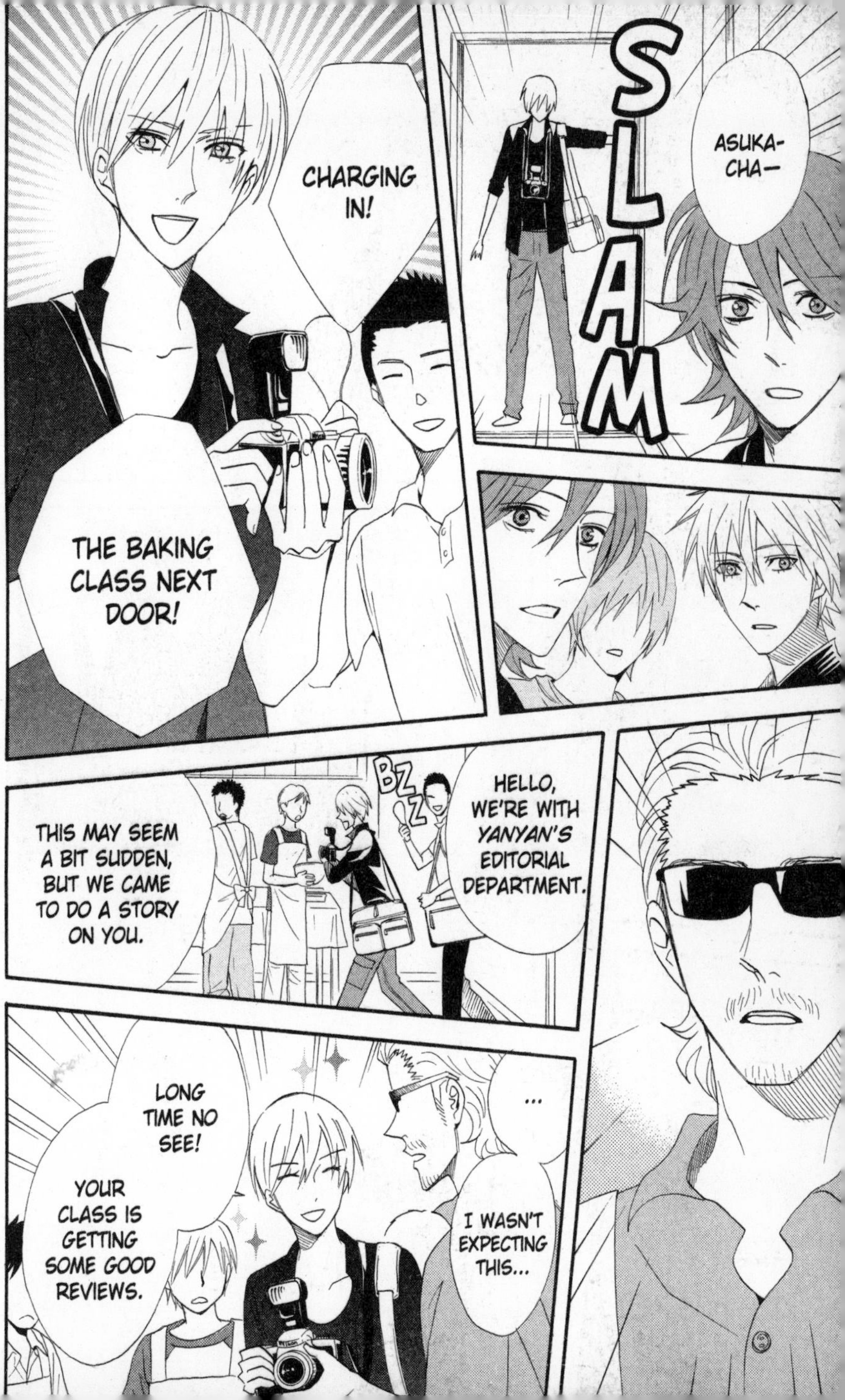
SLAM
ASUKA-CHA—
CHARGING IN!
THE BAKING CLASS NEXT DOOR!
BZZ
HELLO, WE'RE WITH *YANYAN'S* EDITORIAL DEPARTMENT.
THIS MAY SEEM A BIT SUDDEN, BUT WE CAME TO DO A STORY ON YOU.
...
LONG TIME NO SEE!
YOUR CLASS IS GETTING SOME GOOD REVIEWS.
I WASN'T EXPECTING THIS...

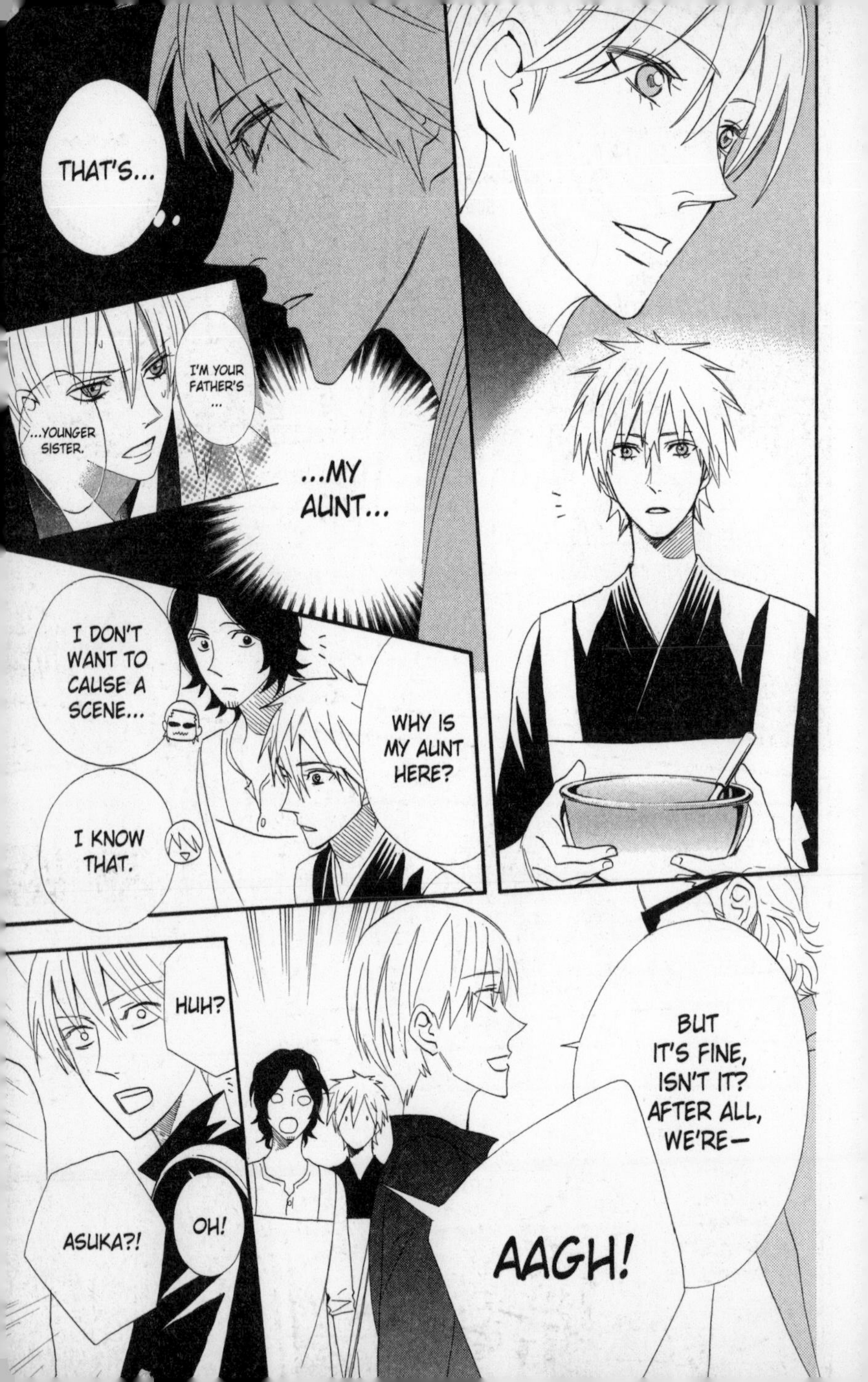
THAT'S...
I'M YOUR FATHER'S ...
...YOUNGER SISTER.
...MY AUNT...
WHY IS MY AUNT HERE?
I DON'T WANT TO CAUSE A SCENE...
I KNOW THAT.
BUT IT'S FINE, ISN'T IT? AFTER ALL, WE'RE—
AAGH!
HUH?
OH!
ASUKA?!

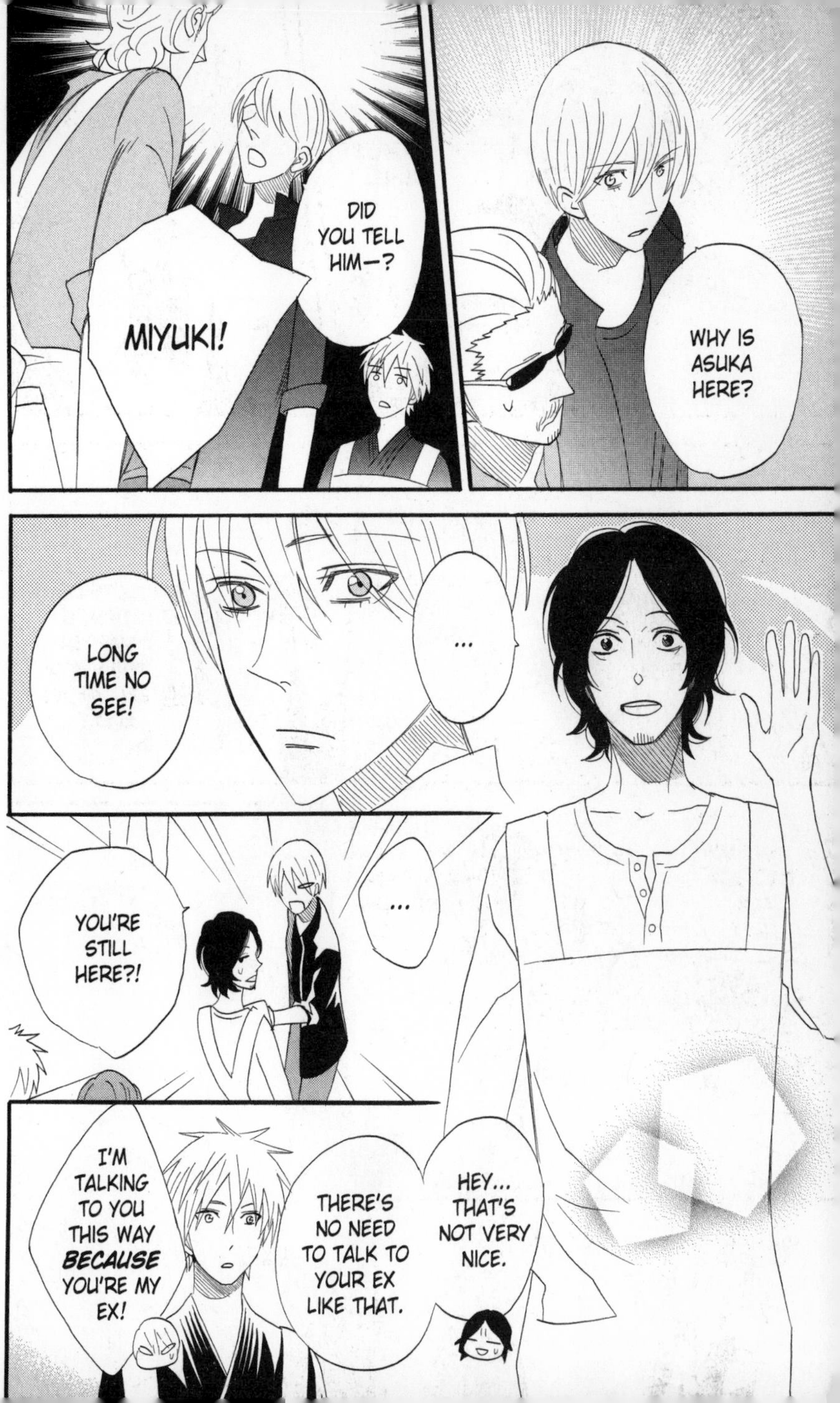
WHY IS ASUKA HERE?
DID YOU TELL HIM—?
MIYUKI!
...
LONG TIME NO SEE!
...
YOU'RE STILL HERE?!
HEY... THAT'S NOT VERY NICE.
THERE'S NO NEED TO TALK TO YOUR EX LIKE THAT.
I'M TALKING TO YOU THIS WAY ***BECAUSE*** YOU'RE MY EX!

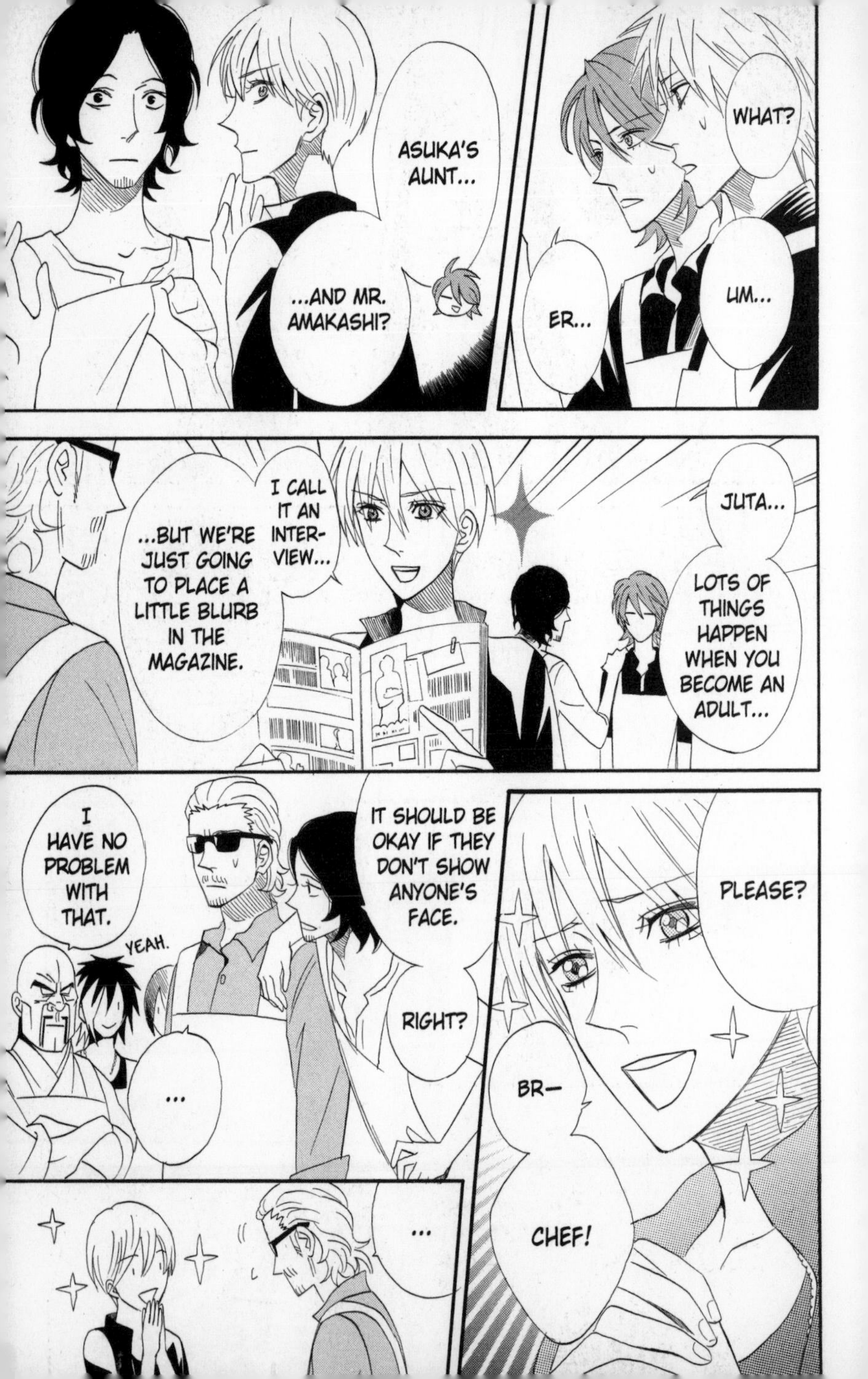
WHAT?
UM...
ER...
ASUKA'S AUNT...
...AND MR. AMAKASHI?
JUTA...
LOTS OF THINGS HAPPEN WHEN YOU BECOME AN ADULT...
I CALL IT AN INTER-VIEW...
...BUT WE'RE JUST GOING TO PLACE A LITTLE BLURB IN THE MAGAZINE.
PLEASE?
BR—
CHEF!
IT SHOULD BE OKAY IF THEY DON'T SHOW ANYONE'S FACE.
RIGHT?
I HAVE NO PROBLEM WITH THAT.
YEAH.
...
...

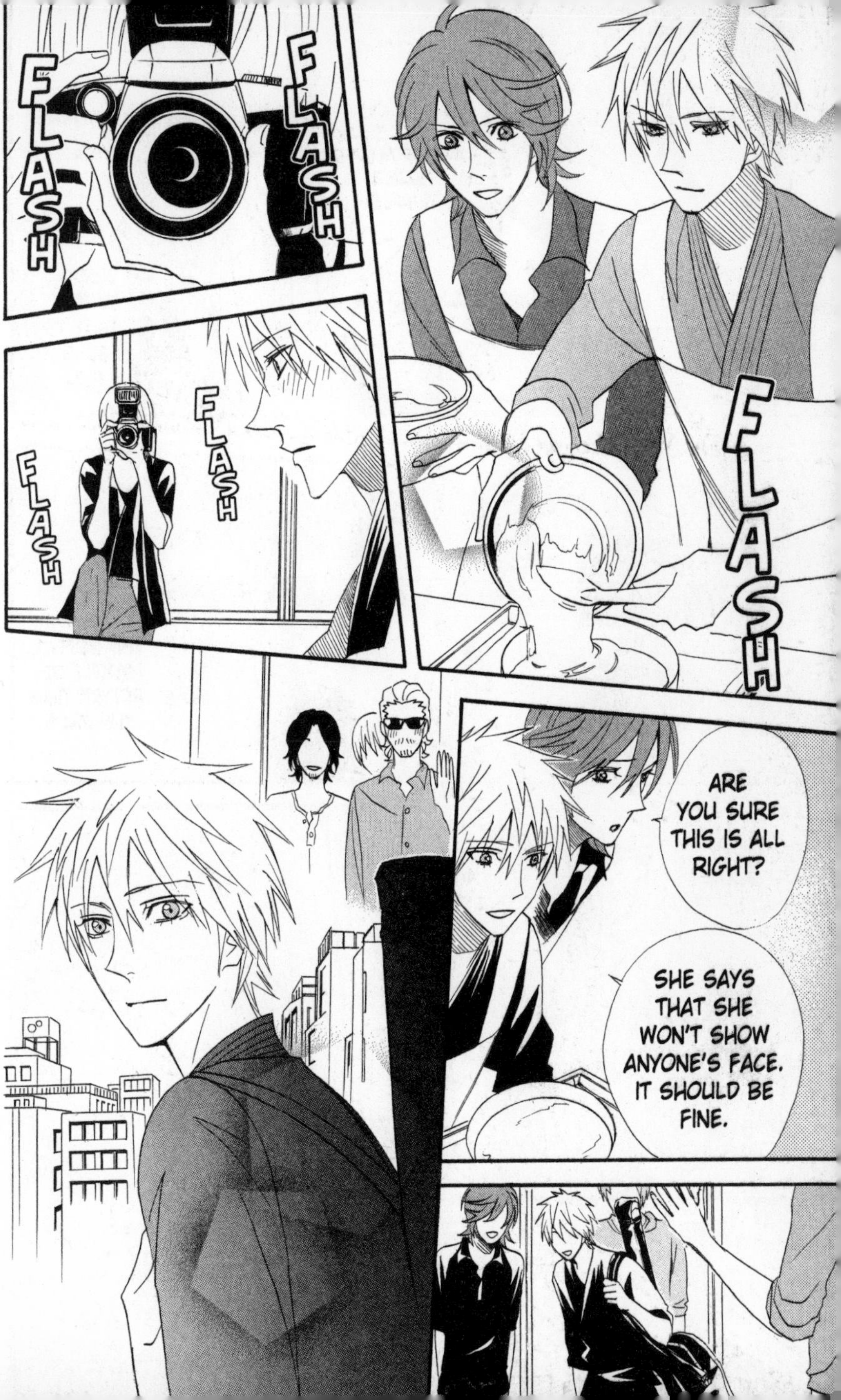
FLASH
FLASH
FLASH
FLASH
FLASH
ARE YOU SURE THIS IS ALL RIGHT?
SHE SAYS THAT SHE WON'T SHOW ANYONE'S FACE. IT SHOULD BE FINE.

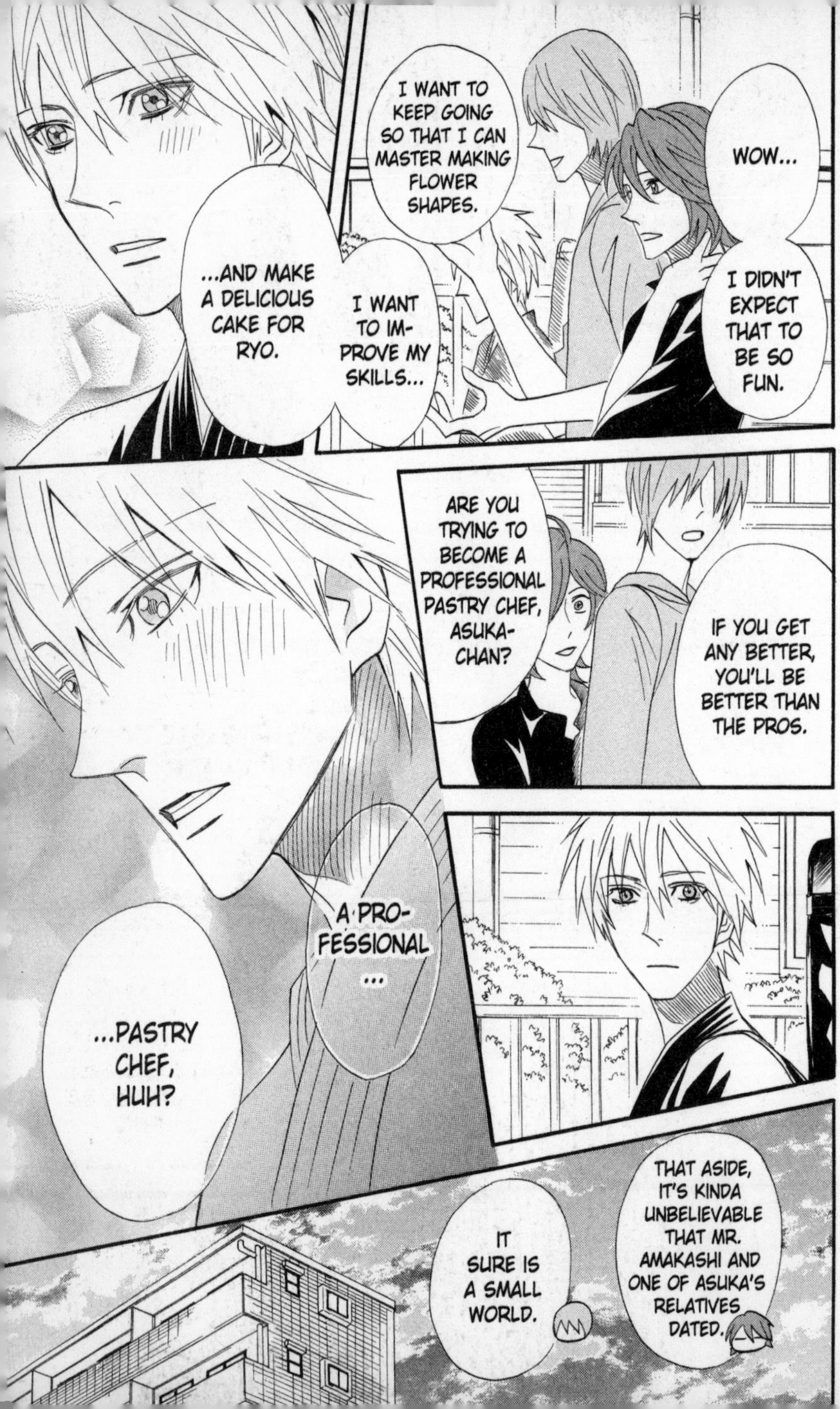

WOW...
I DIDN'T EXPECT THAT TO BE SO FUN.
I WANT TO KEEP GOING SO THAT I CAN MASTER MAKING FLOWER SHAPES.
I WANT TO IM-PROVE MY SKILLS...
...AND MAKE A DELICIOUS CAKE FOR RYO.
IF YOU GET ANY BETTER, YOU'LL BE BETTER THAN THE PROS.
ARE YOU TRYING TO BECOME A PROFESSIONAL PASTRY CHEF, ASUKA-CHAN?
A PRO-FESSIONAL ...
...PASTRY CHEF, HUH?
THAT ASIDE, IT'S KINDA UNBELIEVABLE THAT MR. AMAKASHI AND ONE OF ASUKA'S RELATIVES DATED.
IT SURE IS A SMALL WORLD.

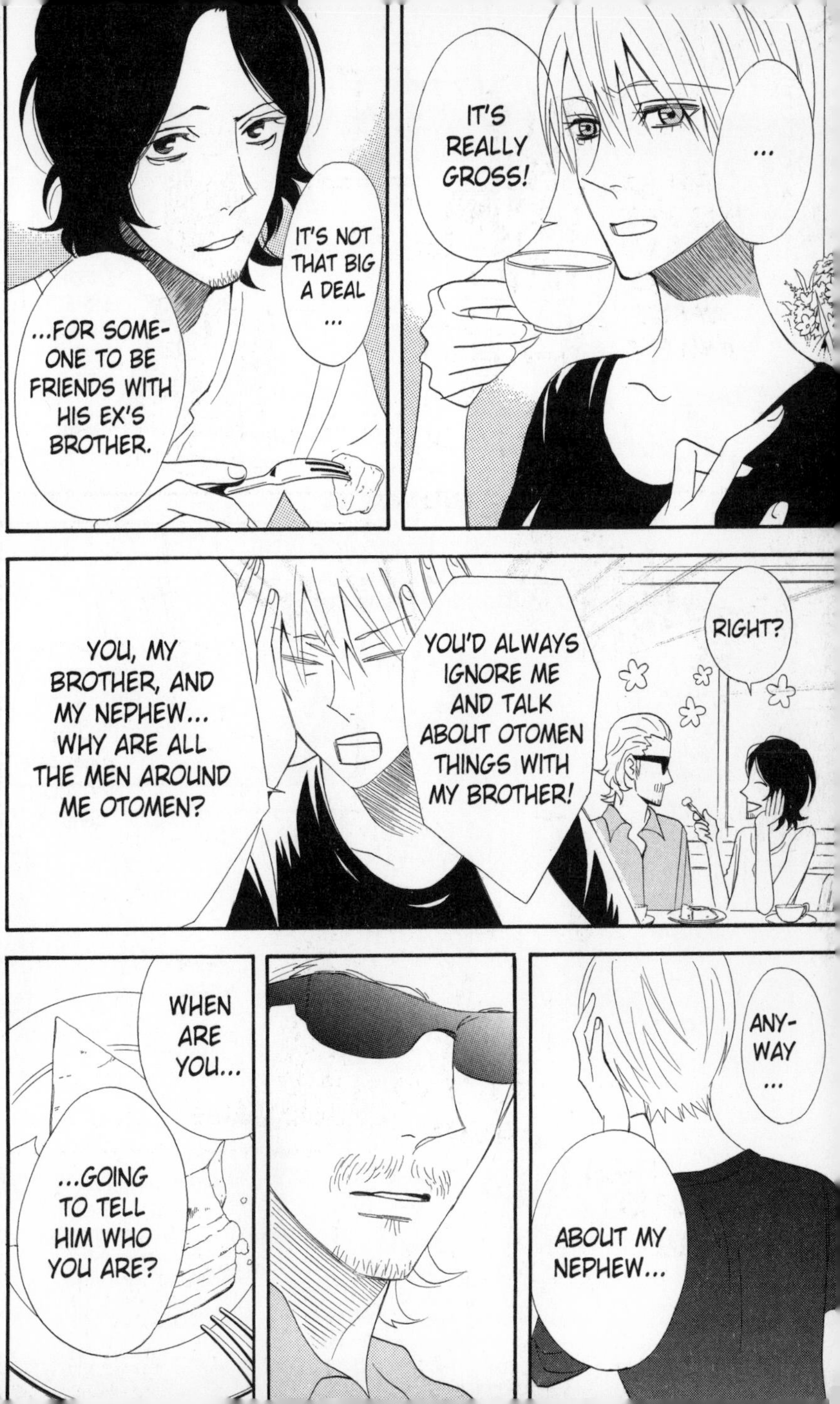
...
IT'S REALLY GROSS!
IT'S NOT THAT BIG A DEAL ...
...FOR SOME-ONE TO BE FRIENDS WITH HIS EX'S BROTHER.
RIGHT?
YOU'D ALWAYS IGNORE ME AND TALK ABOUT OTOMEN THINGS WITH MY BROTHER!
YOU, MY BROTHER, AND MY NEPHEW... WHY ARE ALL THE MEN AROUND ME OTOMEN?
ANY-WAY ...
ABOUT MY NEPHEW...
WHEN ARE YOU...
...GOING TO TELL HIM WHO YOU ARE?

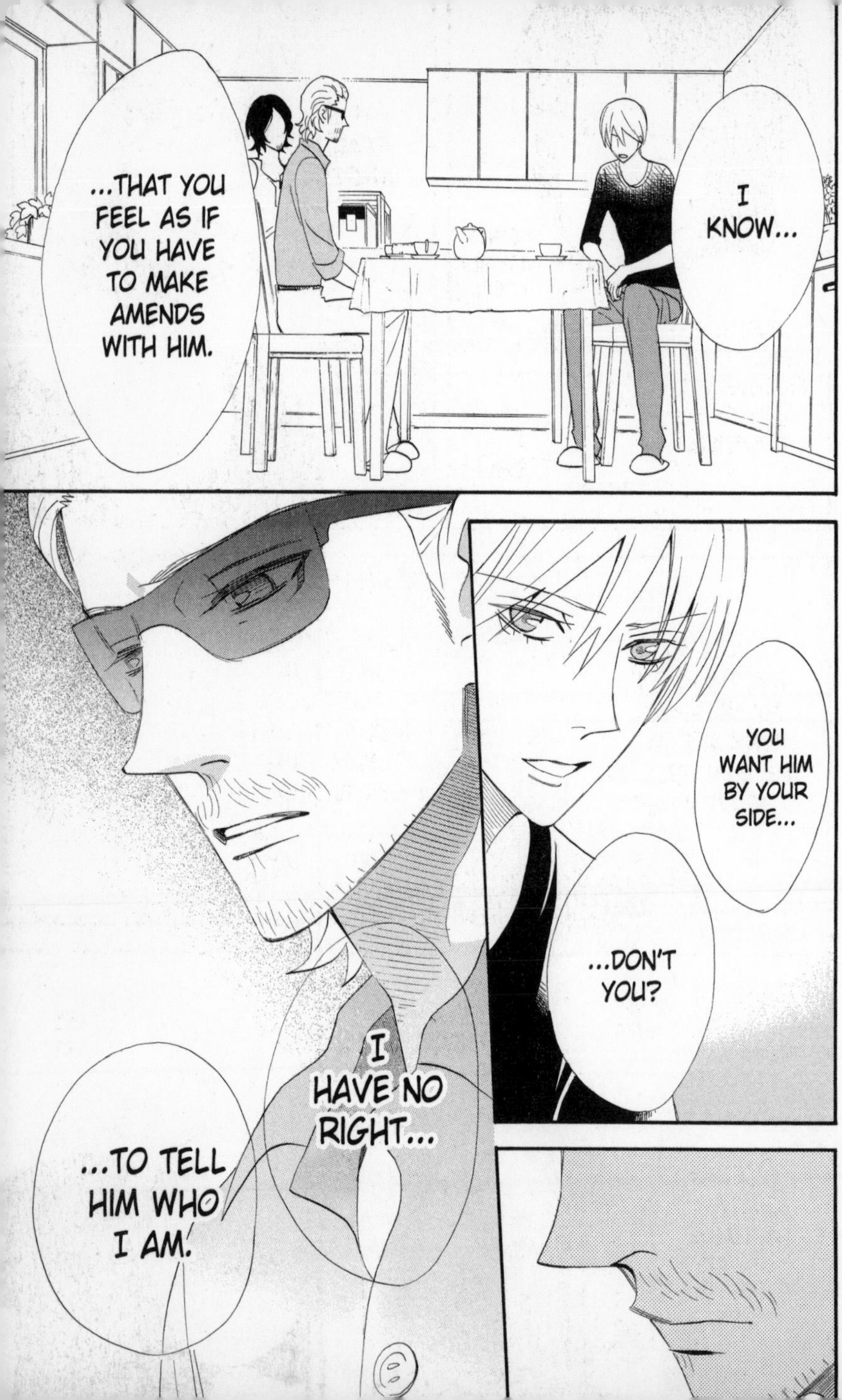
I KNOW...
...THAT YOU FEEL AS IF YOU HAVE TO MAKE AMENDS WITH HIM.
YOU WANT HIM BY YOUR SIDE...
...DON'T YOU?
I HAVE NO RIGHT...
...TO TELL HIM WHO I AM.

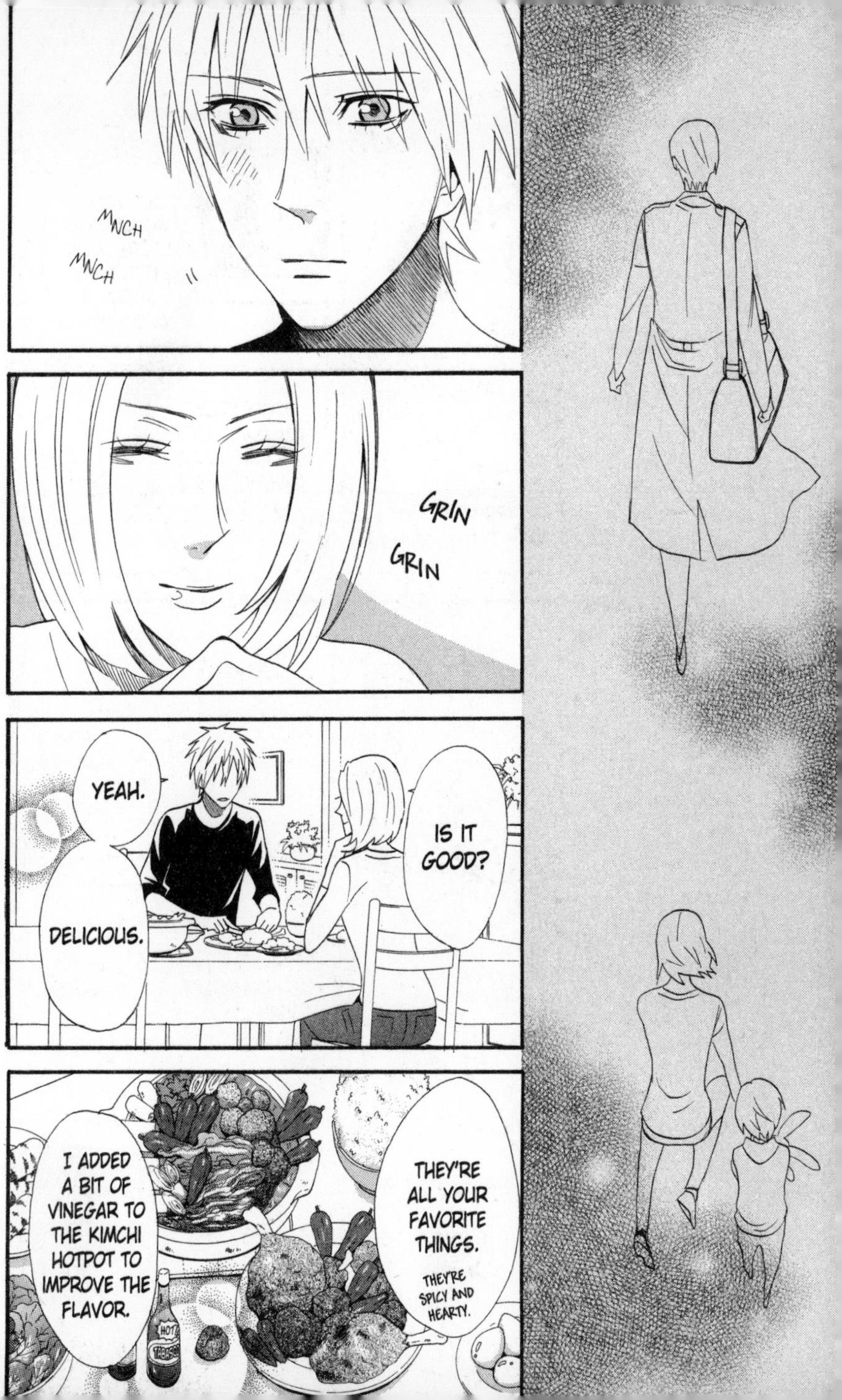
MNCH
MNCH
GRIN
GRIN
IS IT GOOD?
YEAH.
DELICIOUS.
THEY'RE ALL YOUR FAVORITE THINGS.
THEY'RE SPICY AND HEARTY.
I ADDED A BIT OF VINEGAR TO THE KIMCHI HOTPOT TO IMPROVE THE FLAVOR.

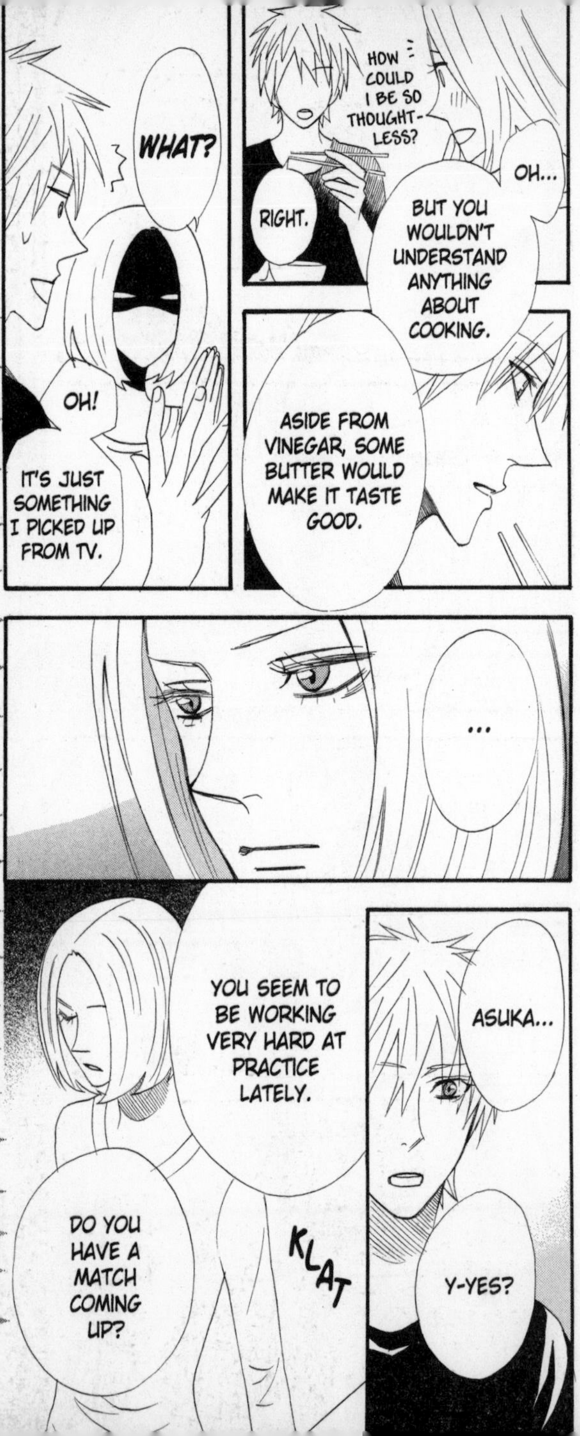
HOW COULD I BE SO THOUGHTLESS?
RIGHT.
OH...
BUT YOU WOULDN'T UNDERSTAND ANYTHING ABOUT COOKING.
ASIDE FROM VINEGAR, SOME BUTTER WOULD MAKE IT TASTE GOOD.
WHAT?
OH!
IT'S JUST SOMETHING I PICKED UP FROM TV.
...
ASUKA...
Y-YES?
YOU SEEM TO BE WORKING VERY HARD AT PRACTICE LATELY.
KLAT
DO YOU HAVE A MATCH COMING UP?

It's volume 12!

Time flies by so quickly. I was just celebrating volume 10, and now, we're already at volume 12. I've been writing about otomen for quite a long time.

In volume 12, we finally finish up the story of Asuka and his father. I'm planning on slowly bringing *Otomen* to its climax.

I hope you stay with me until the end.

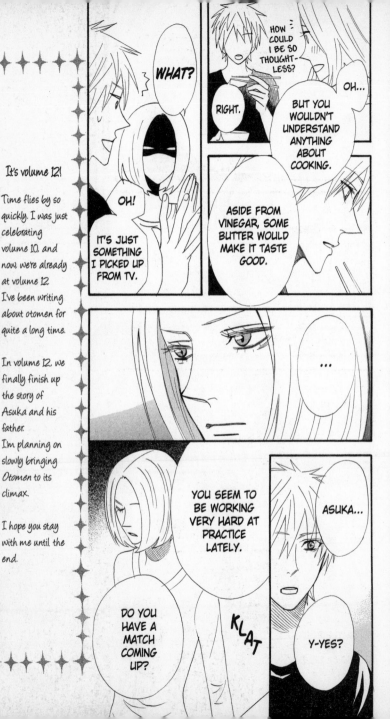

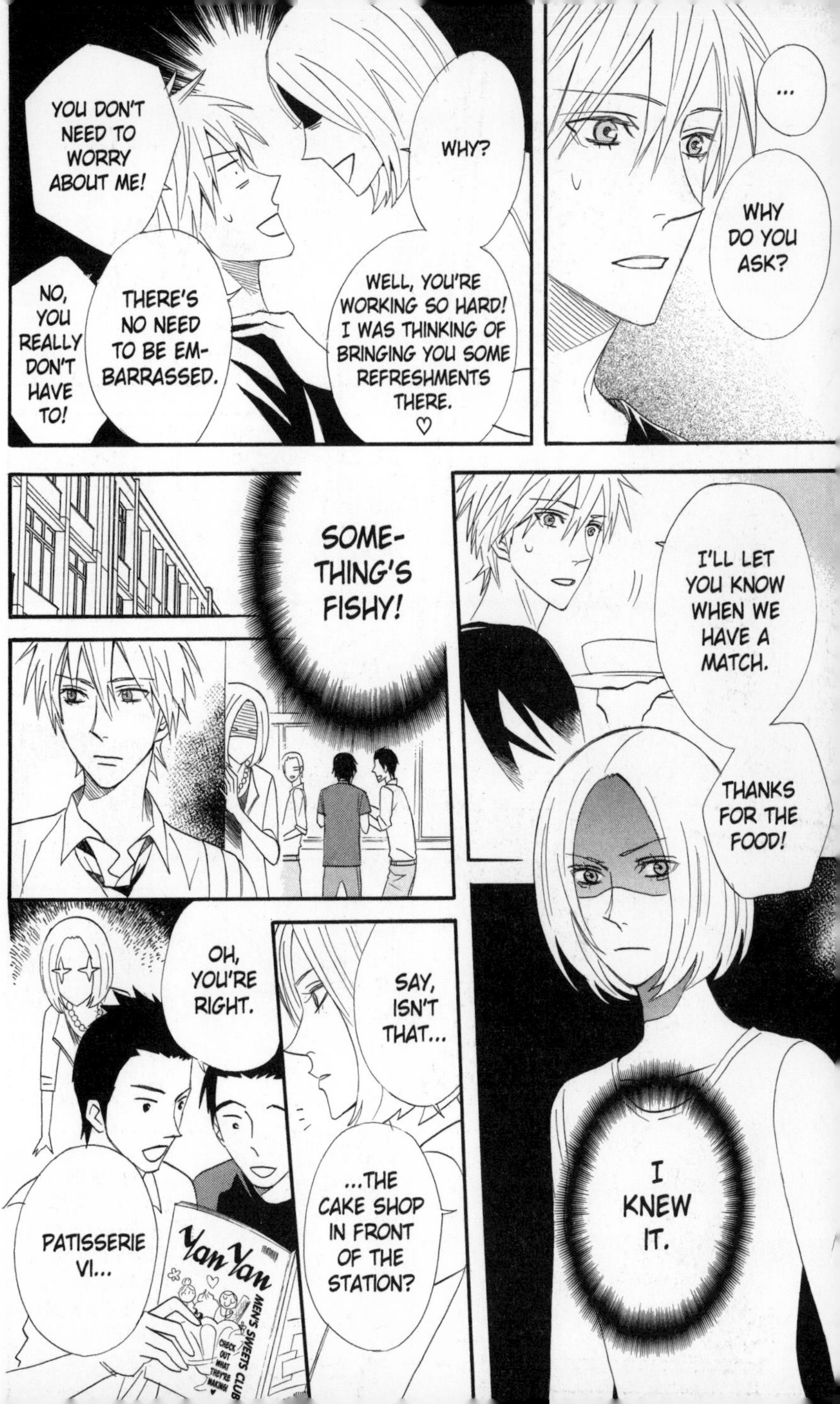
...
WHY DO YOU ASK?
WHY?
YOU DON'T NEED TO WORRY ABOUT ME!
WELL, YOU'RE WORKING SO HARD! I WAS THINKING OF BRINGING YOU SOME REFRESHMENTS THERE. ♡
THERE'S NO NEED TO BE EM-BARRASSED.
NO, YOU REALLY DON'T HAVE TO!
I'LL LET YOU KNOW WHEN WE HAVE A MATCH.
THANKS FOR THE FOOD!
I KNEW IT.
SOME-THING'S FISHY!
SAY, ISN'T THAT...
...THE CAKE SHOP IN FRONT OF THE STATION?
OH, YOU'RE RIGHT.
PATISSERIE VI...
Yan Yan
MEN'S SWEETS CLUB
CHECK OUT WHAT THEY'RE MAKING!

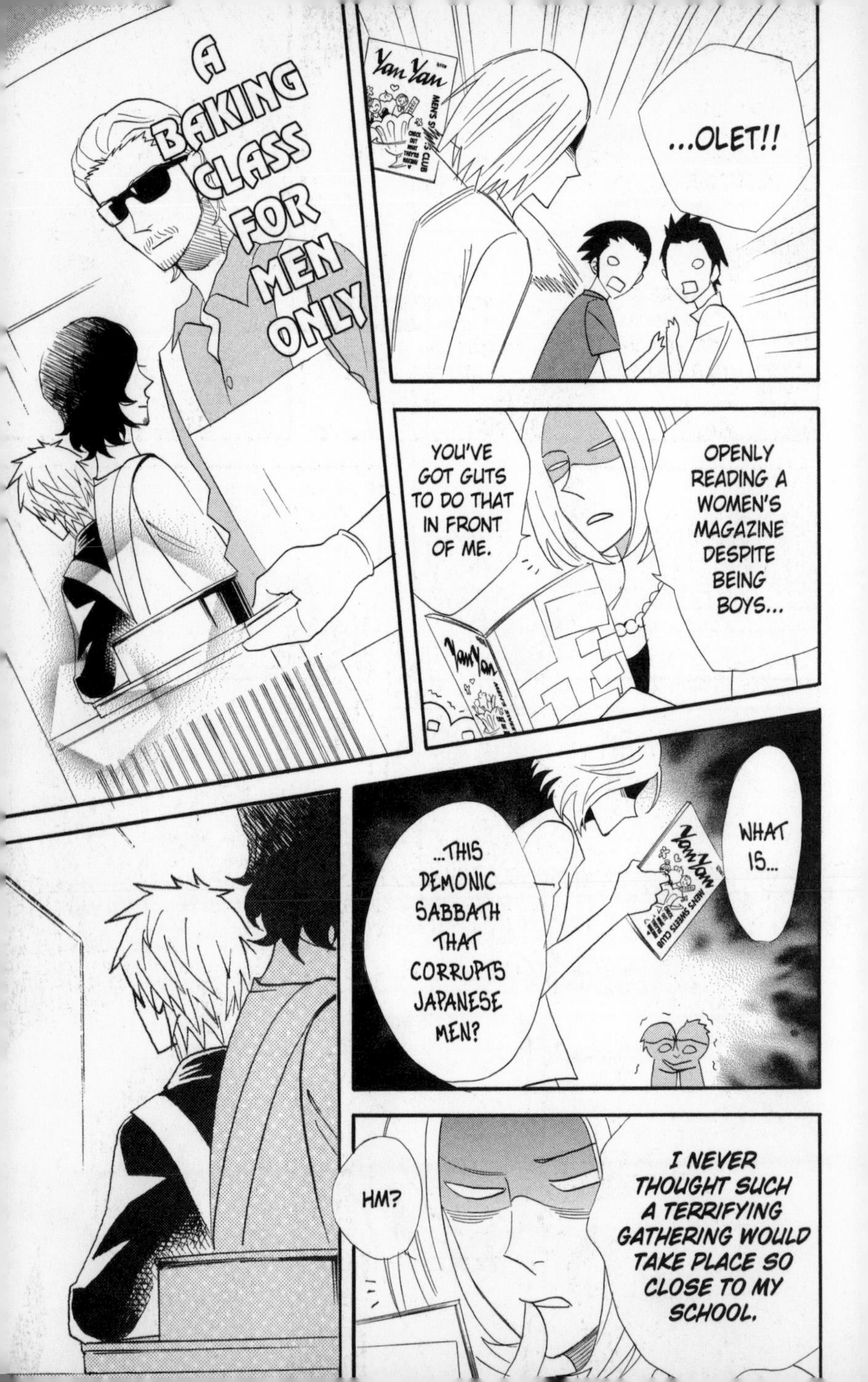
...OLET!!
OPENLY READING A WOMEN'S MAGAZINE DESPITE BEING BOYS...
YOU'VE GOT GUTS TO DO THAT IN FRONT OF ME.
A BAKING CLASS FOR MEN ONLY
WHAT IS...
Yam Yam
MEN'S SWEETS CLUB
...THIS DEMONIC SABBATH THAT CORRUPTS JAPANESE MEN?
I NEVER THOUGHT SUCH A TERRIFYING GATHERING WOULD TAKE PLACE SO CLOSE TO MY SCHOOL.
HM?

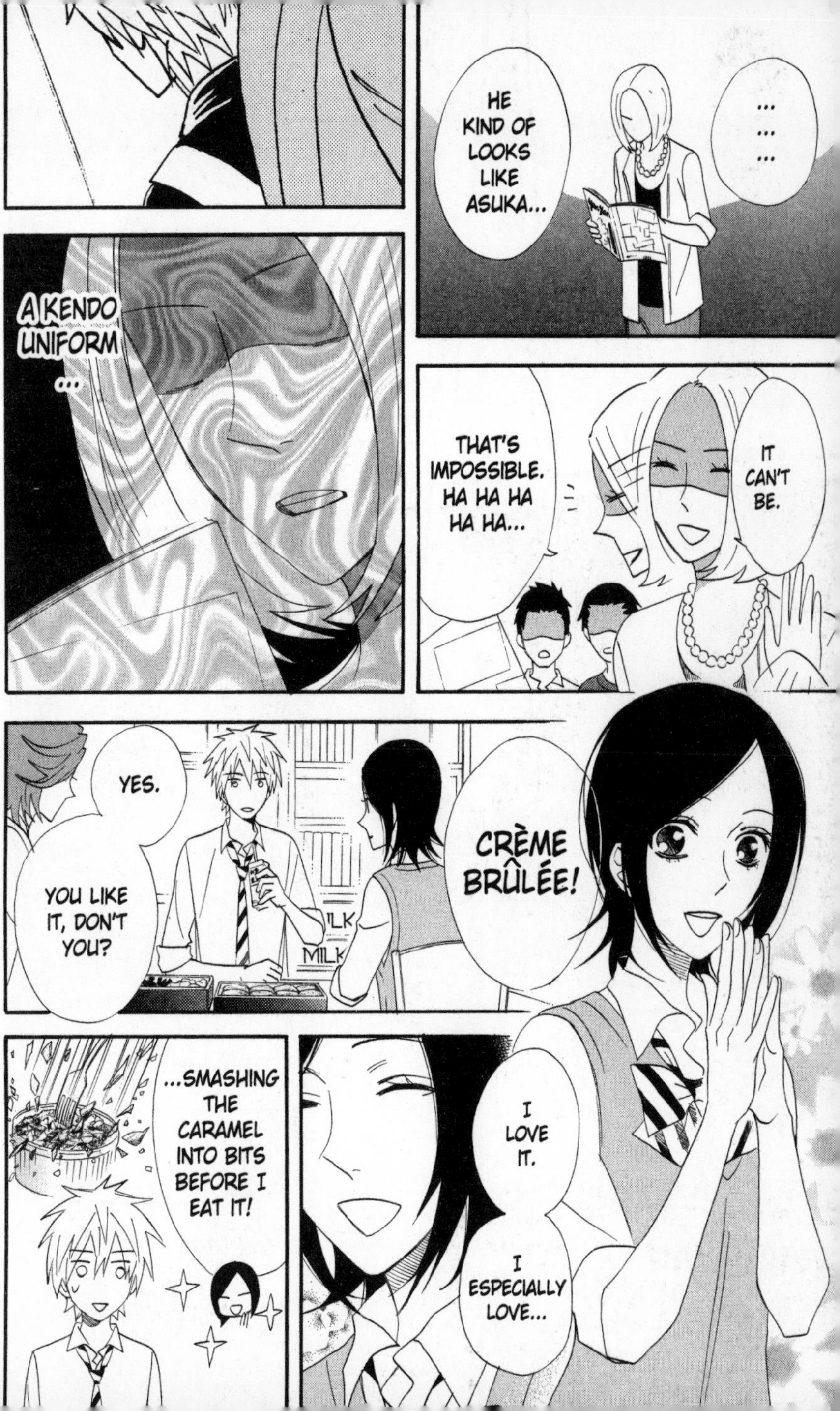

... ...
HE KIND OF LOOKS LIKE ASUKA...
IT CAN'T BE.
THAT'S IMPOSSIBLE. HA HA HA HA HA...
A KENDO UNIFORM ...
CRÈME BRÛLÉE!
I LOVE IT.
I ESPECIALLY LOVE...
YES.
YOU LIKE IT, DON'T YOU?
MILK
...SMASHING THE CARAMEL INTO BITS BEFORE I EAT IT!

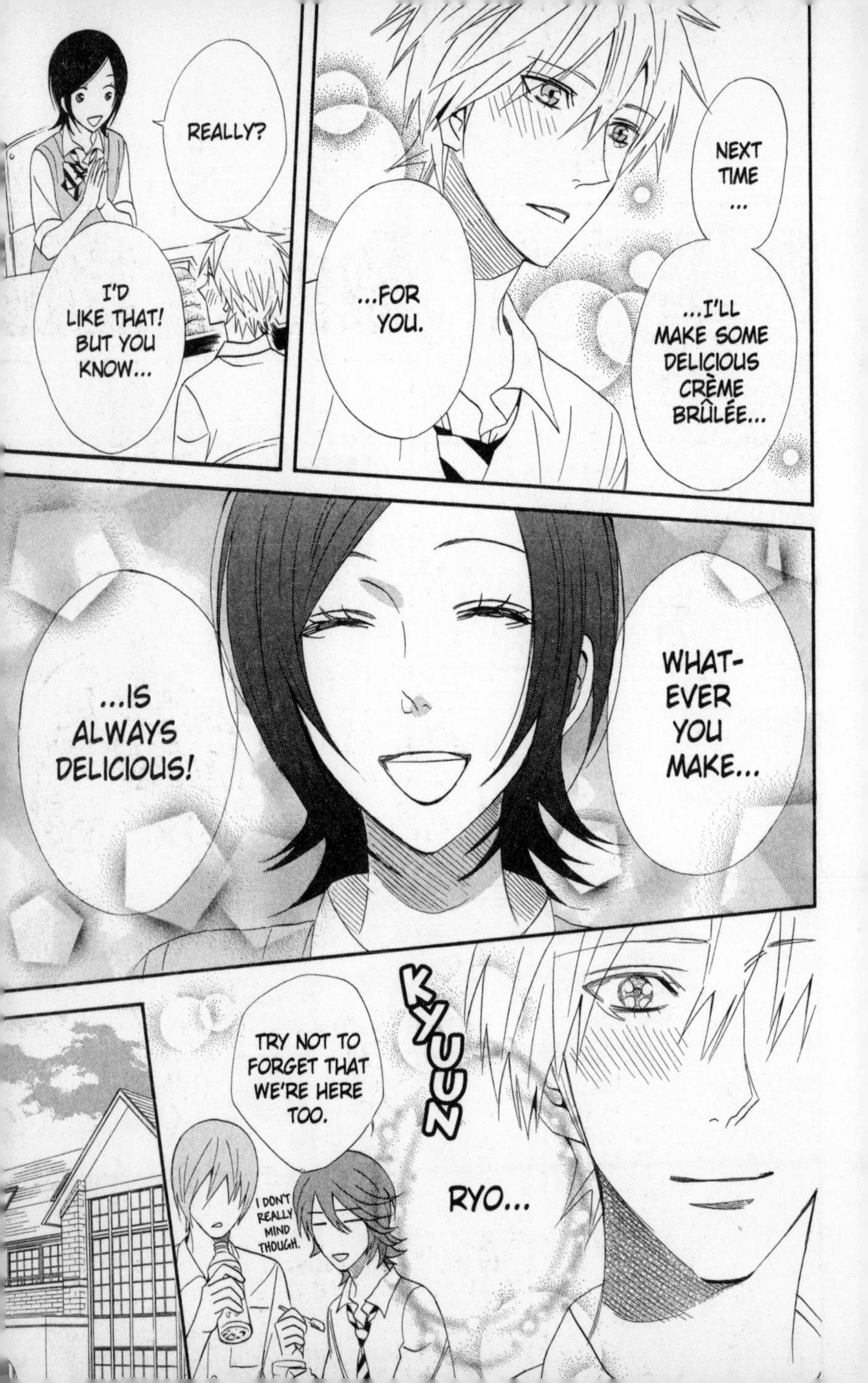
NEXT TIME ...
...I'LL MAKE SOME DELICIOUS CRÈME BRÛLÉE...
...FOR YOU.
REALLY?
I'D LIKE THAT! BUT YOU KNOW...
WHAT-EVER YOU MAKE...
...IS ALWAYS DELICIOUS!
RYO...
KYUUN
TRY NOT TO FORGET THAT WE'RE HERE TOO.
I DON'T REALLY MIND THOUGH.

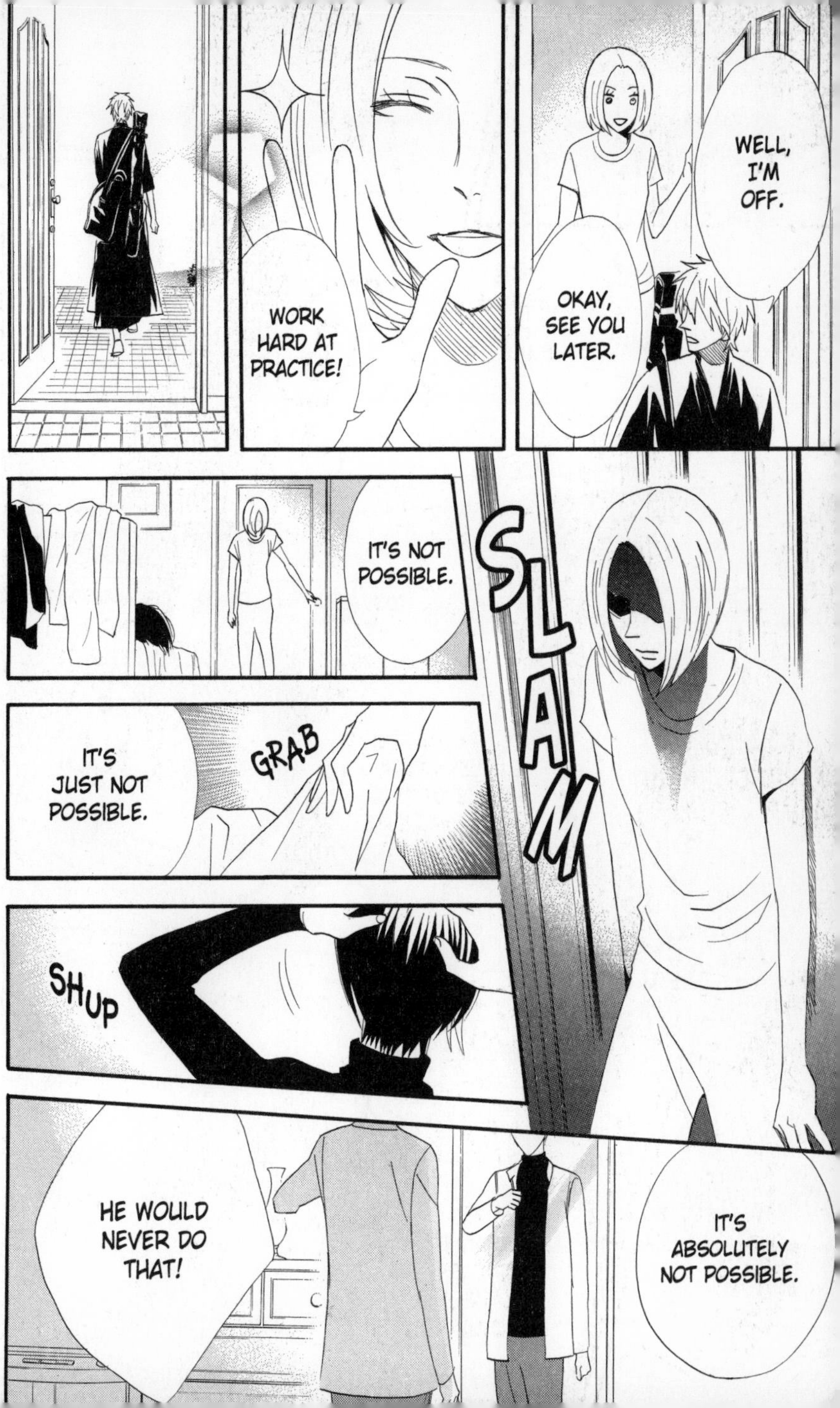
WELL, I'M OFF.
OKAY, SEE YOU LATER.
WORK HARD AT PRACTICE!
SLAM
IT'S NOT POSSIBLE.
GRAB
IT'S JUST NOT POSSIBLE.
SHUP
IT'S ABSOLUTELY NOT POSSIBLE.
HE WOULD NEVER DO THAT!

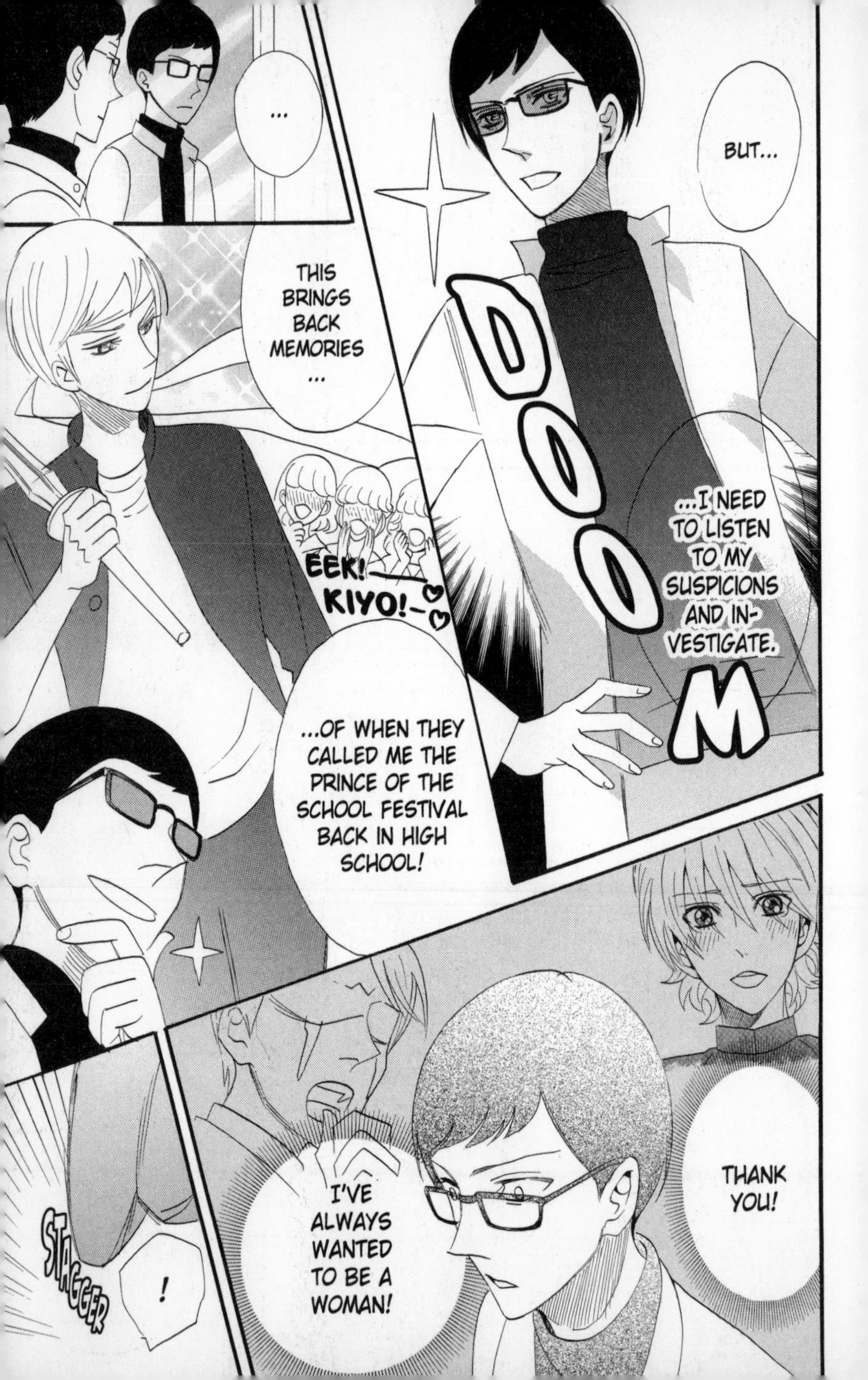
BUT...
DOOOM
...I NEED TO LISTEN TO MY SUSPICIONS AND IN-VESTIGATE.
...
THIS BRINGS BACK MEMORIES...
EEK!
KIYO!
...OF WHEN THEY CALLED ME THE PRINCE OF THE SCHOOL FESTIVAL BACK IN HIGH SCHOOL!
THANK YOU!
I'VE ALWAYS WANTED TO BE A WOMAN!
STAGGER
!

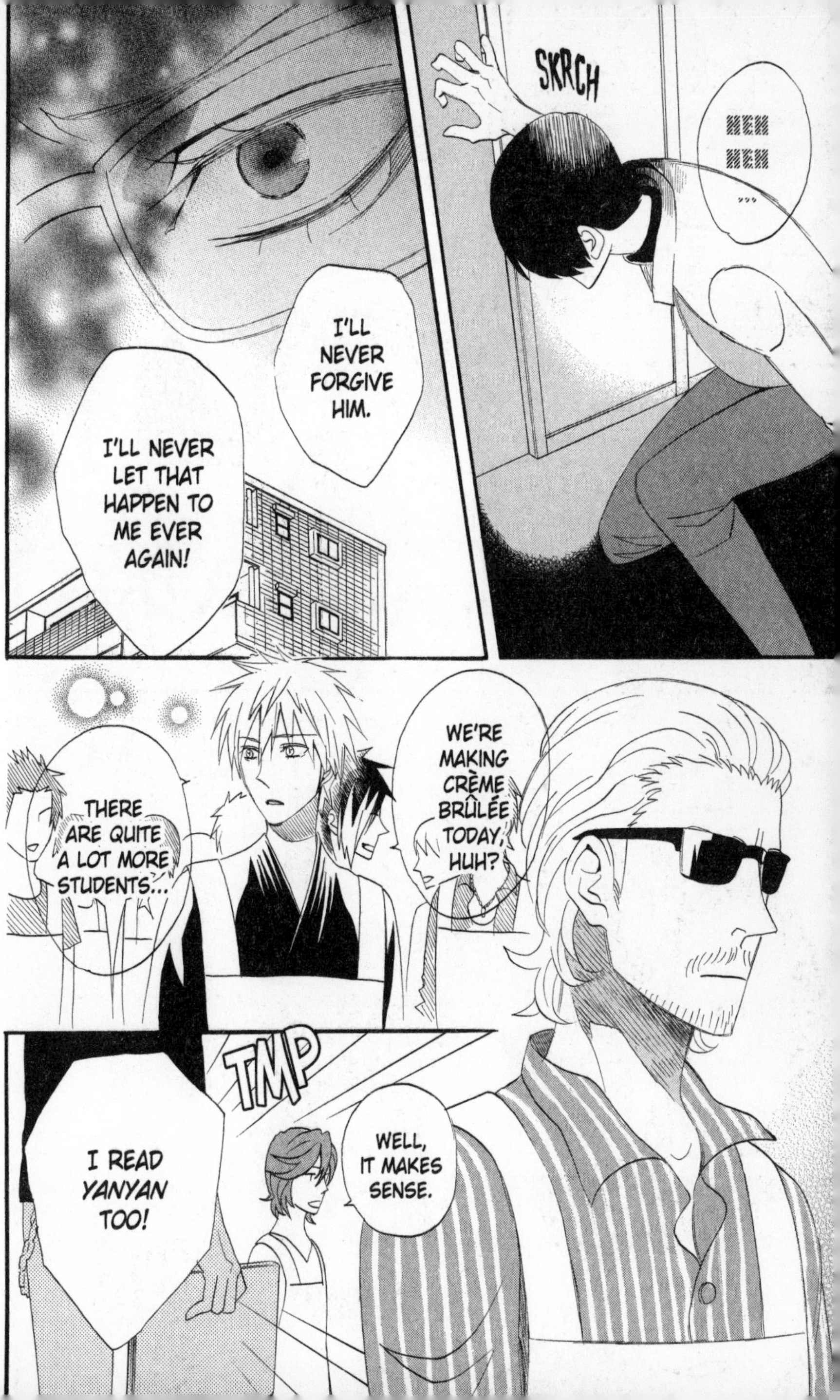
SKRCH
HEH HEH...
I'LL NEVER FORGIVE HIM.
I'LL NEVER LET THAT HAPPEN TO ME EVER AGAIN!
WE'RE MAKING CRÈME BRÛLÉE TODAY, HUH?
THERE ARE QUITE A LOT MORE STUDENTS...
TMP
WELL, IT MAKES SENSE.
I READ *YANYAN* TOO!

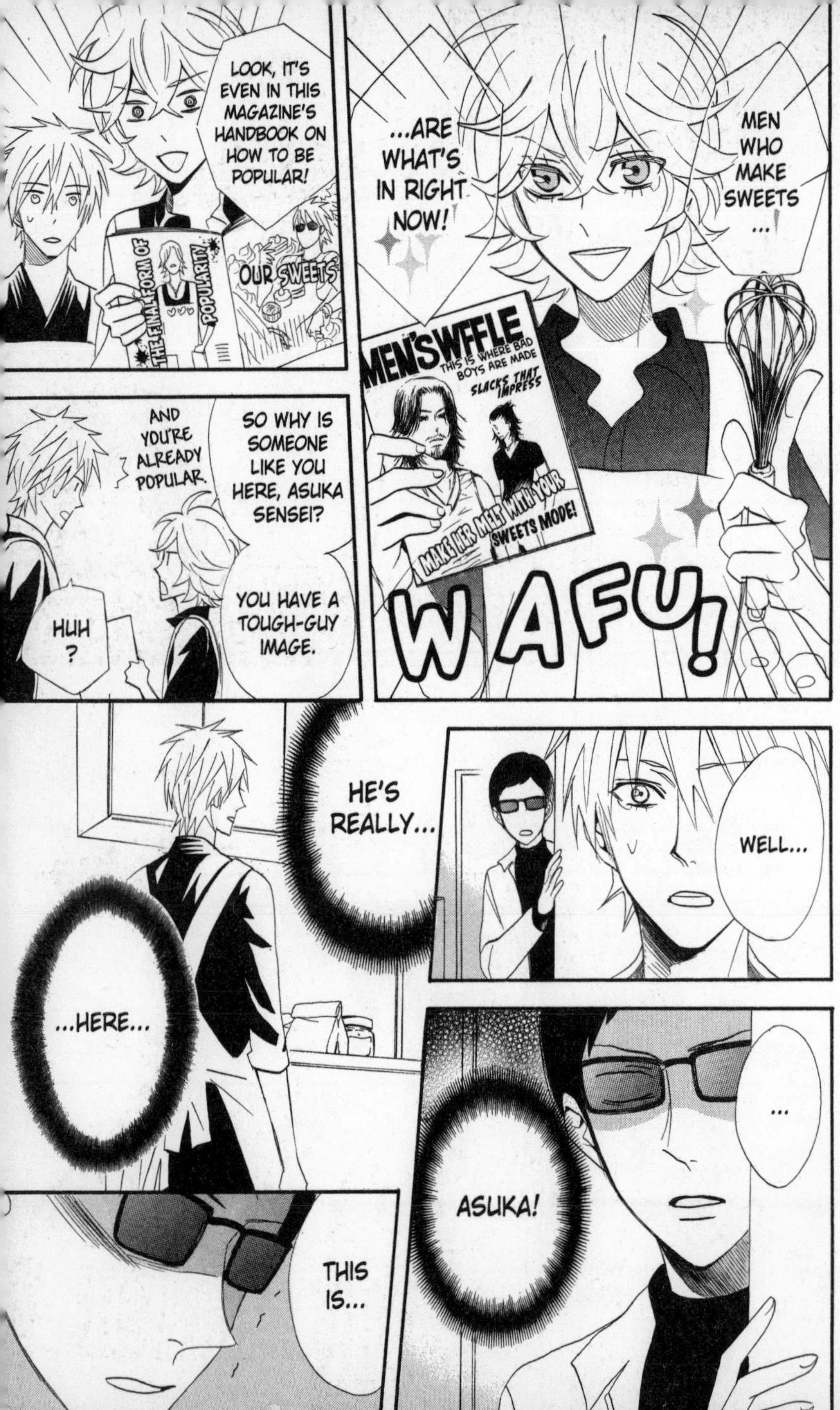
MEN WHO MAKE SWEETS...
...ARE WHAT'S IN RIGHT NOW!
MEN'SWFFLE
THIS IS WHERE BAD BOYS ARE MADE
SLACKS THAT IMPRESS
MAKE HER MELT WITH YOUR SWEETS MODE!
WAFU!
LOOK, IT'S EVEN IN THIS MAGAZINE'S HANDBOOK ON HOW TO BE POPULAR!
THE FINAL FORM OF POPULARITY
OUR SWEETS
SO WHY IS SOMEONE LIKE YOU HERE, ASUKA SENSEI?
AND YOU'RE ALREADY POPULAR.
YOU HAVE A TOUGH-GUY IMAGE.
HUH?
WELL...
HE'S REALLY...
...HERE...
...
ASUKA!
THIS IS...

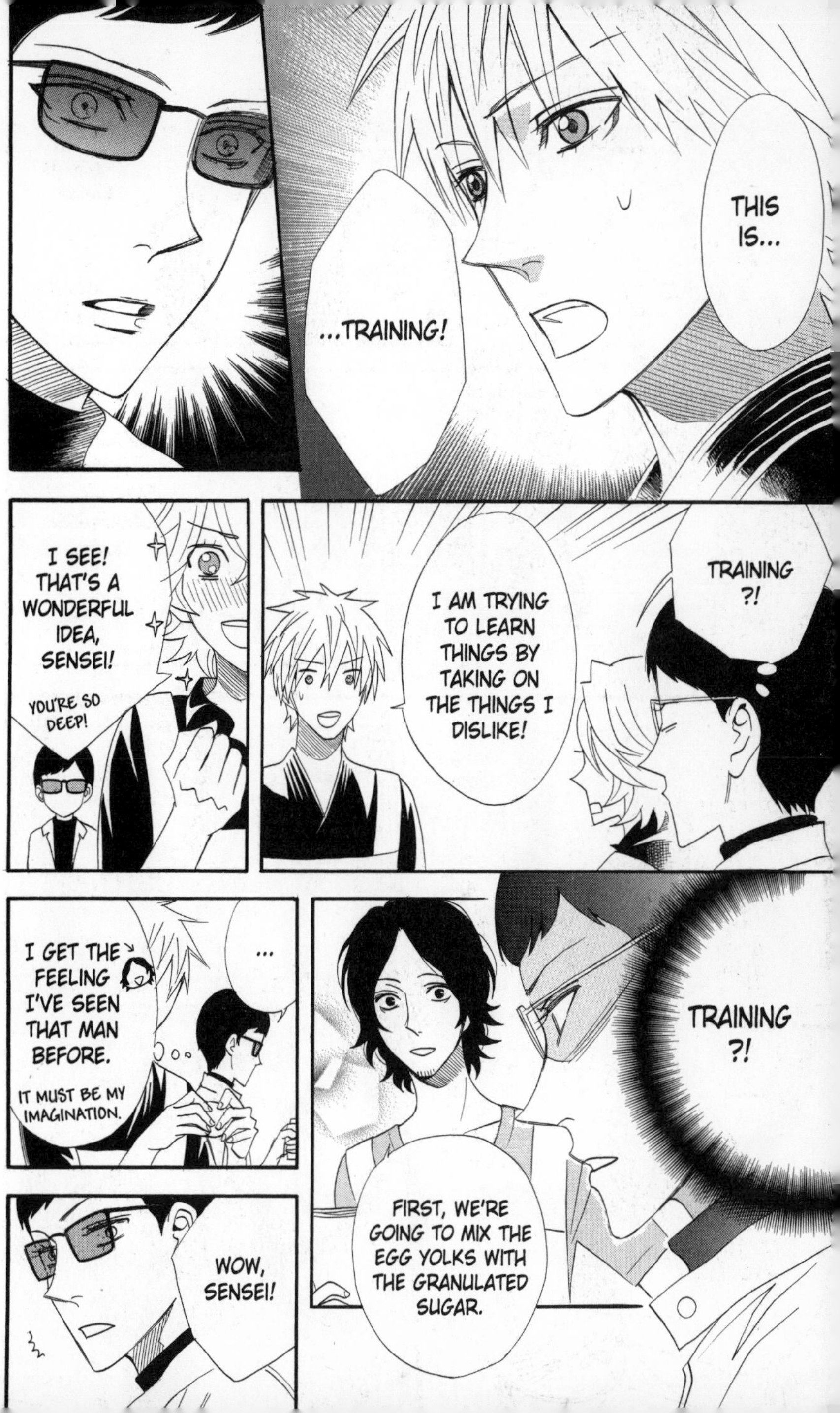
THIS IS...
...TRAINING!
TRAINING ?!
I AM TRYING TO LEARN THINGS BY TAKING ON THE THINGS I DISLIKE!
I SEE! THAT'S A WONDERFUL IDEA, SENSEI!
YOU'RE SO DEEP!
TRAINING ?!
FIRST, WE'RE GOING TO MIX THE EGG YOLKS WITH THE GRANULATED SUGAR.
...
I GET THE FEELING I'VE SEEN THAT MAN BEFORE.
IT MUST BE MY IMAGINATION.
WOW, SENSEI!

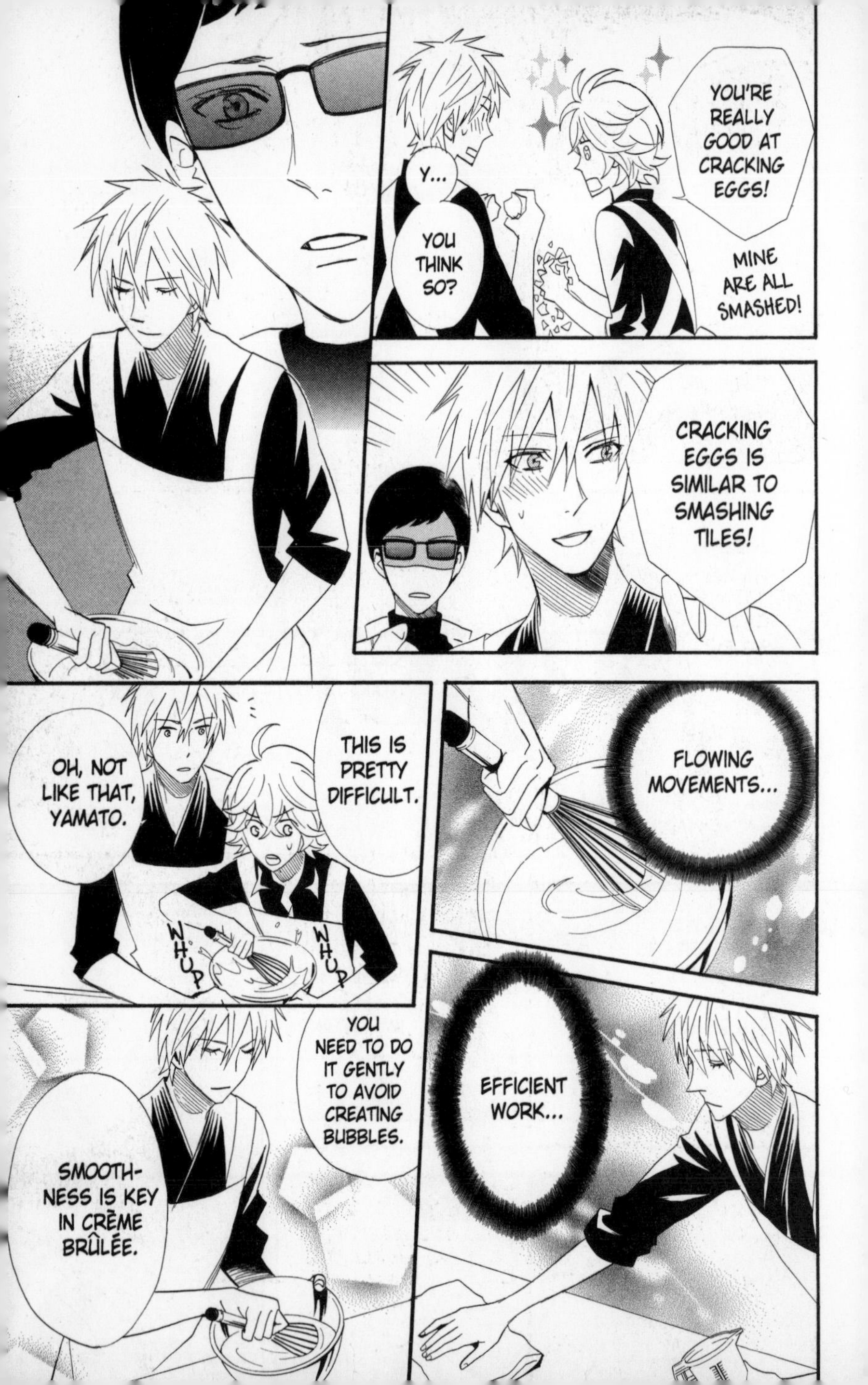
YOU'RE REALLY GOOD AT CRACKING EGGS!
MINE ARE ALL SMASHED!
Y...
YOU THINK SO?
CRACKING EGGS IS SIMILAR TO SMASHING TILES!
FLOWING MOVEMENTS...
THIS IS PRETTY DIFFICULT.
OH, NOT LIKE THAT, YAMATO.
WHUP
WHUP
EFFICIENT WORK...
YOU NEED TO DO IT GENTLY TO AVOID CREATING BUBBLES.
SMOOTHNESS IS KEY IN CRÈME BRÛLÉE.

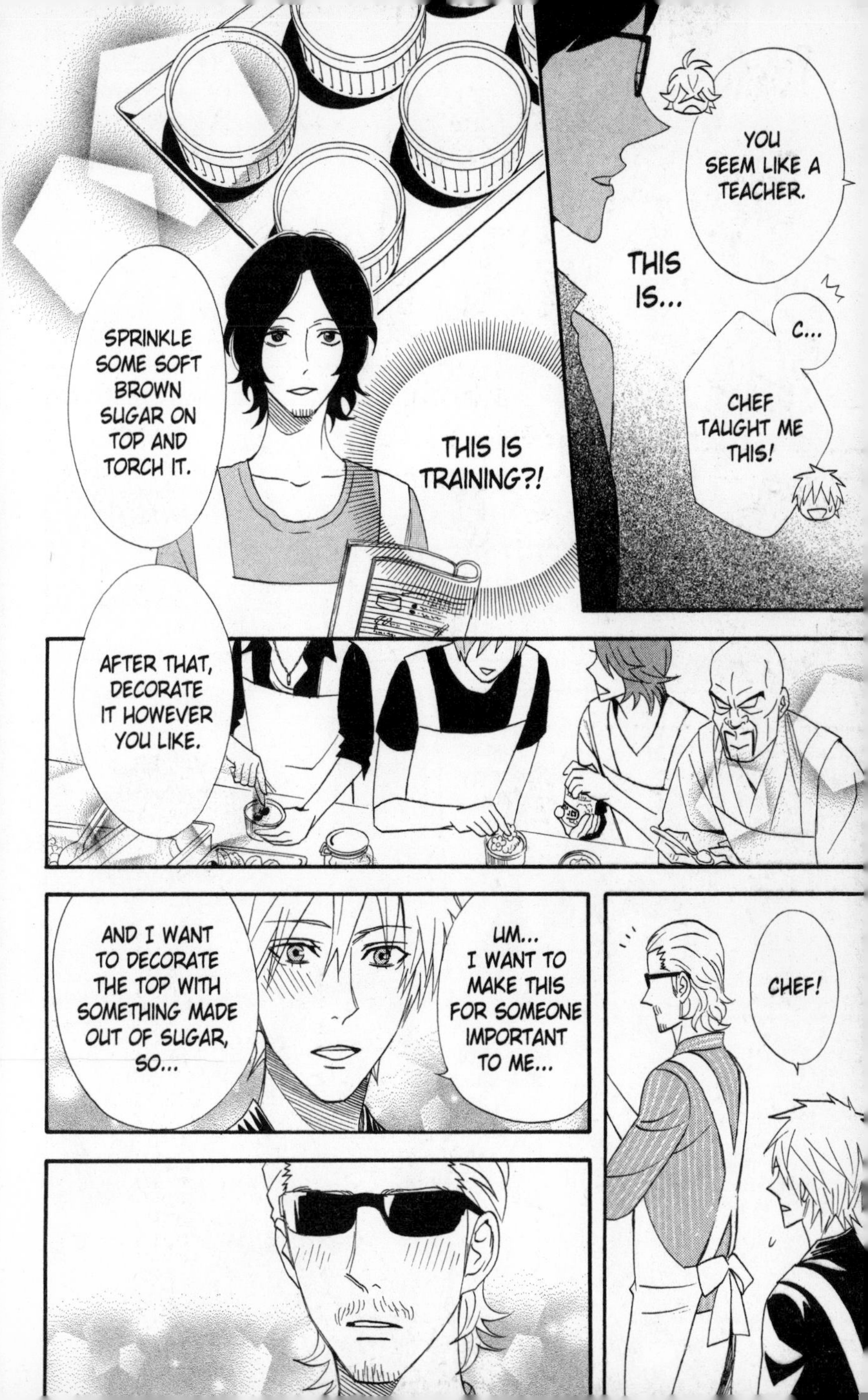
YOU SEEM LIKE A TEACHER.
THIS IS...
C...
CHEF TAUGHT ME THIS!
SPRINKLE SOME SOFT BROWN SUGAR ON TOP AND TORCH IT.
THIS IS TRAINING?!
AFTER THAT, DECORATE IT HOWEVER YOU LIKE.
CHEF!
UM... I WANT TO MAKE THIS FOR SOMEONE IMPORTANT TO ME...
AND I WANT TO DECORATE THE TOP WITH SOMETHING MADE OUT OF SUGAR, SO...

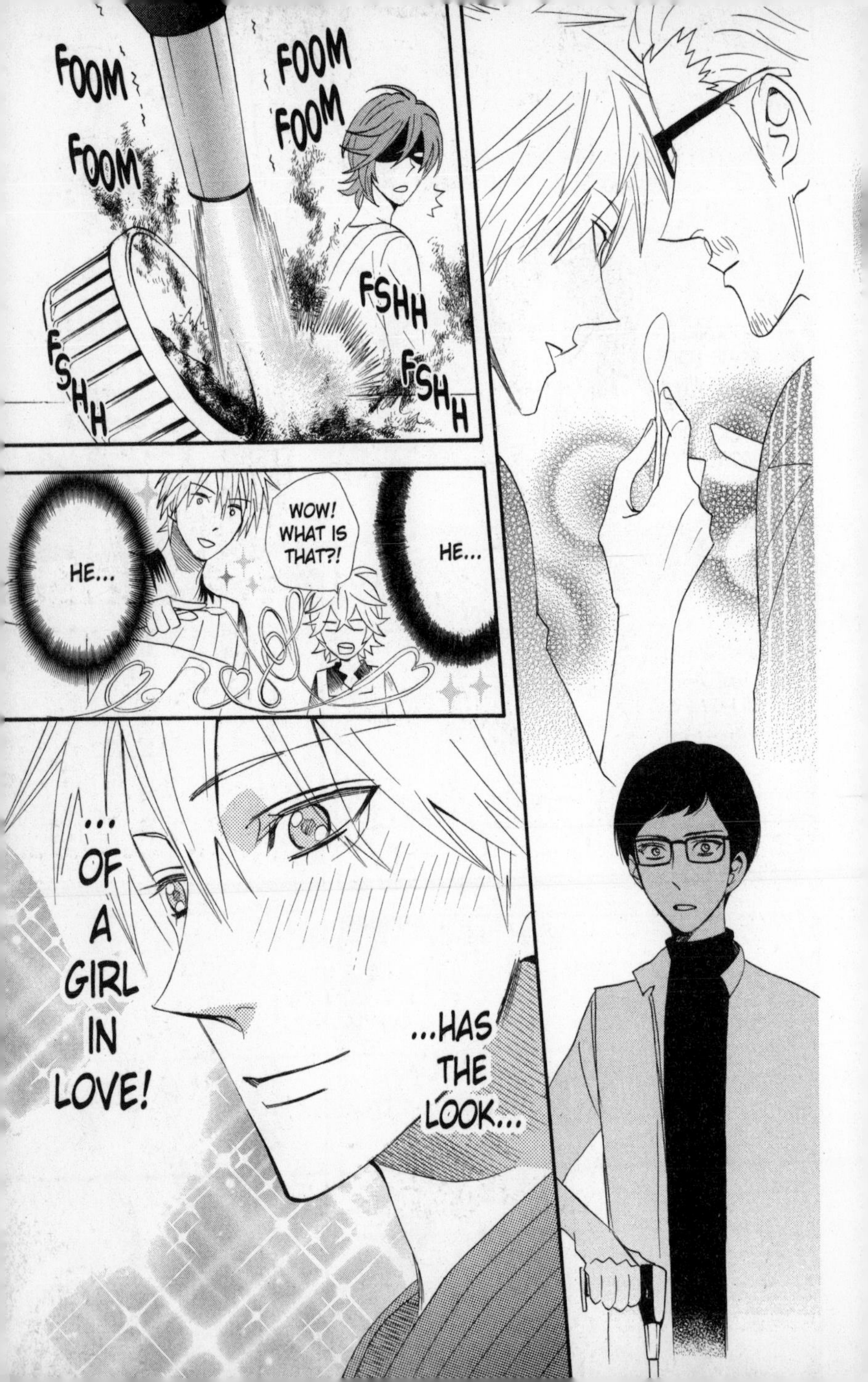
FOOM FOOM
FSHH
FSHH
FOOM
FOOM
FSHH
HE...
WOW! WHAT IS THAT?!
HE...
...HAS THE LOOK...
...OF A GIRL IN LOVE!

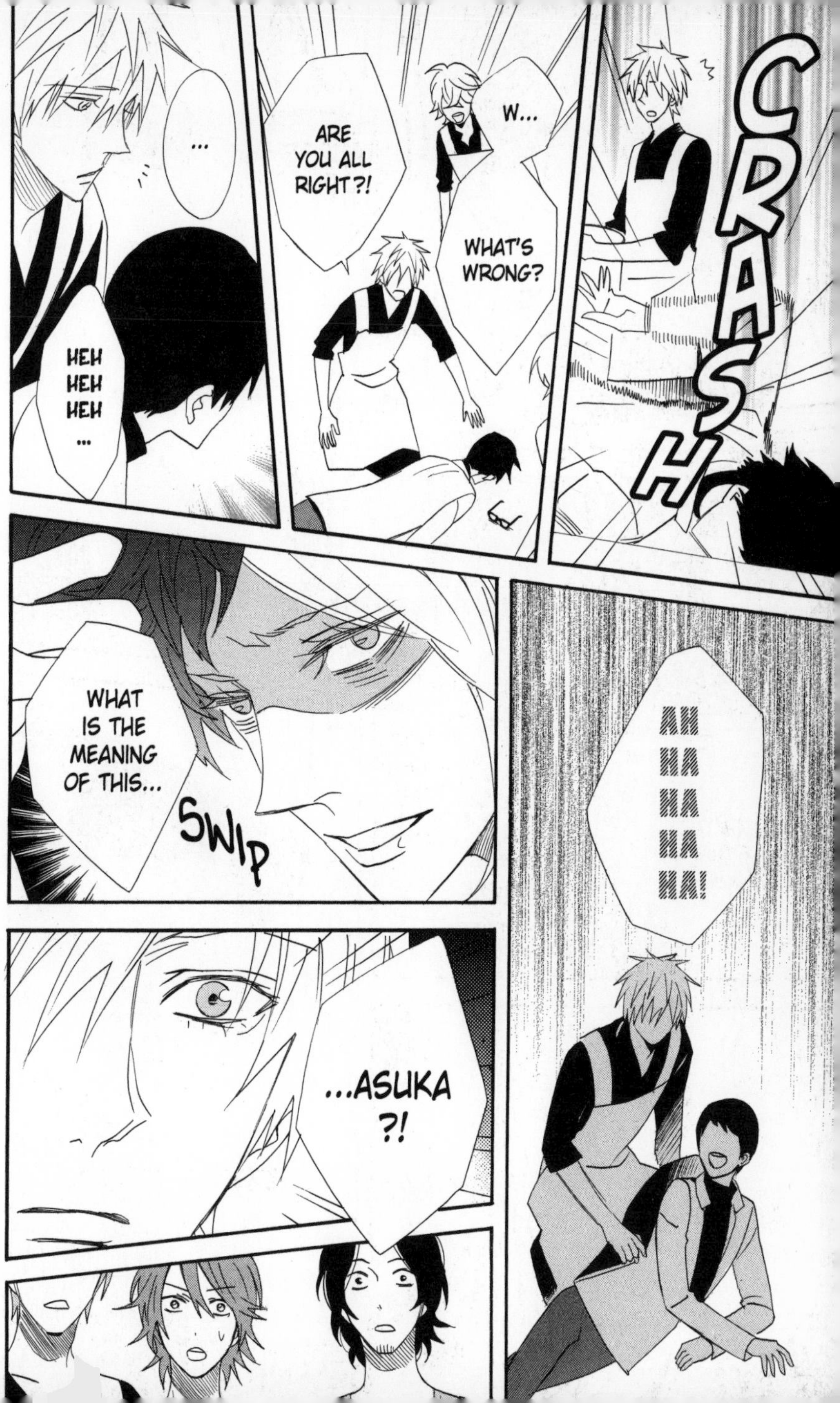
CRASH
W...
WHAT'S WRONG?
ARE YOU ALL RIGHT?!
...
HEH HEH HEH...
AH HA HA HA HA HA!
WHAT IS THE MEANING OF THIS...
SWIP
...ASUKA ?!

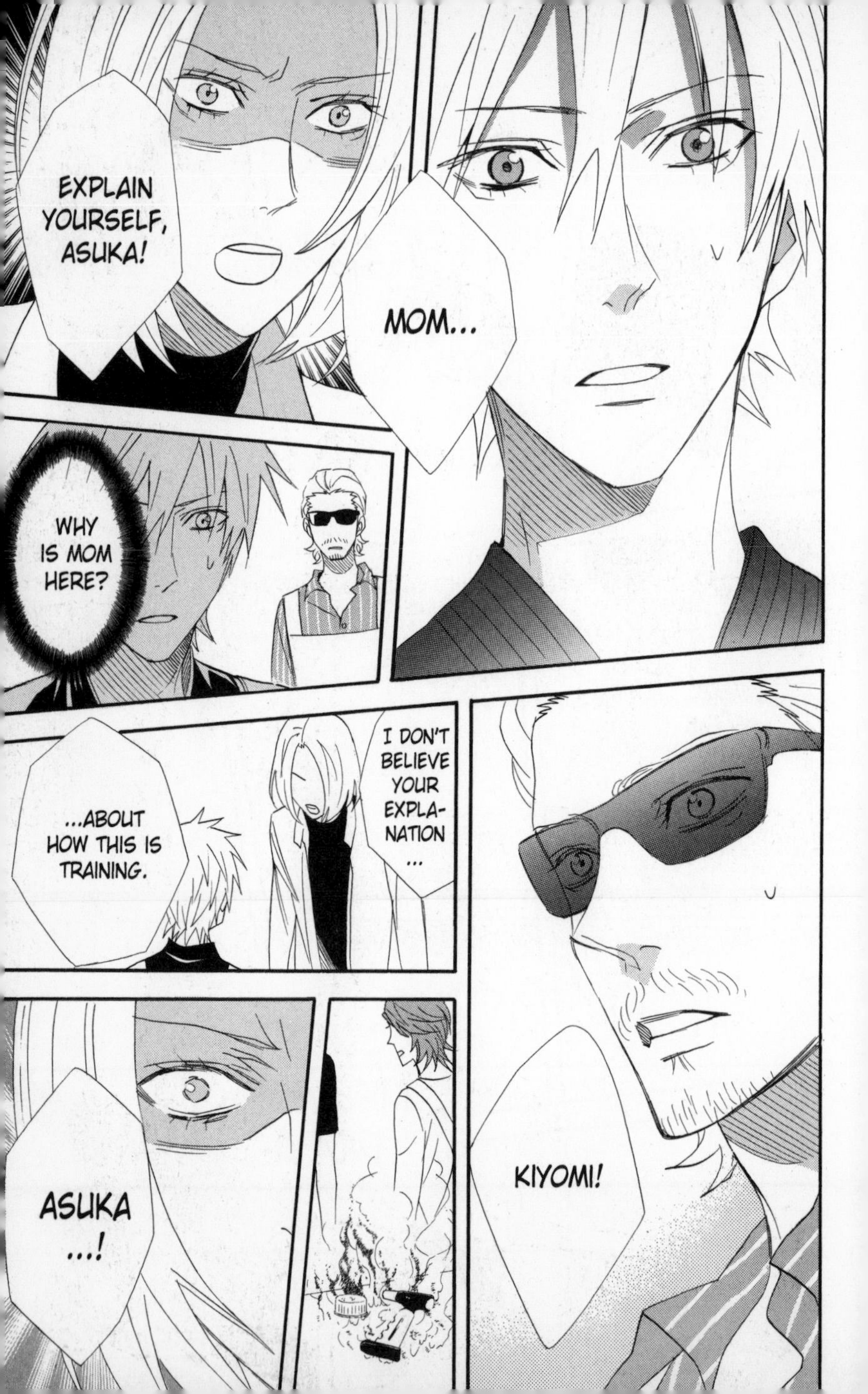
MOM...
EXPLAIN YOURSELF, ASUKA!
WHY IS MOM HERE?
KIYOMI!
I DON'T BELIEVE YOUR EXPLANATION...
...ABOUT HOW THIS IS TRAINING.
ASUKA...!

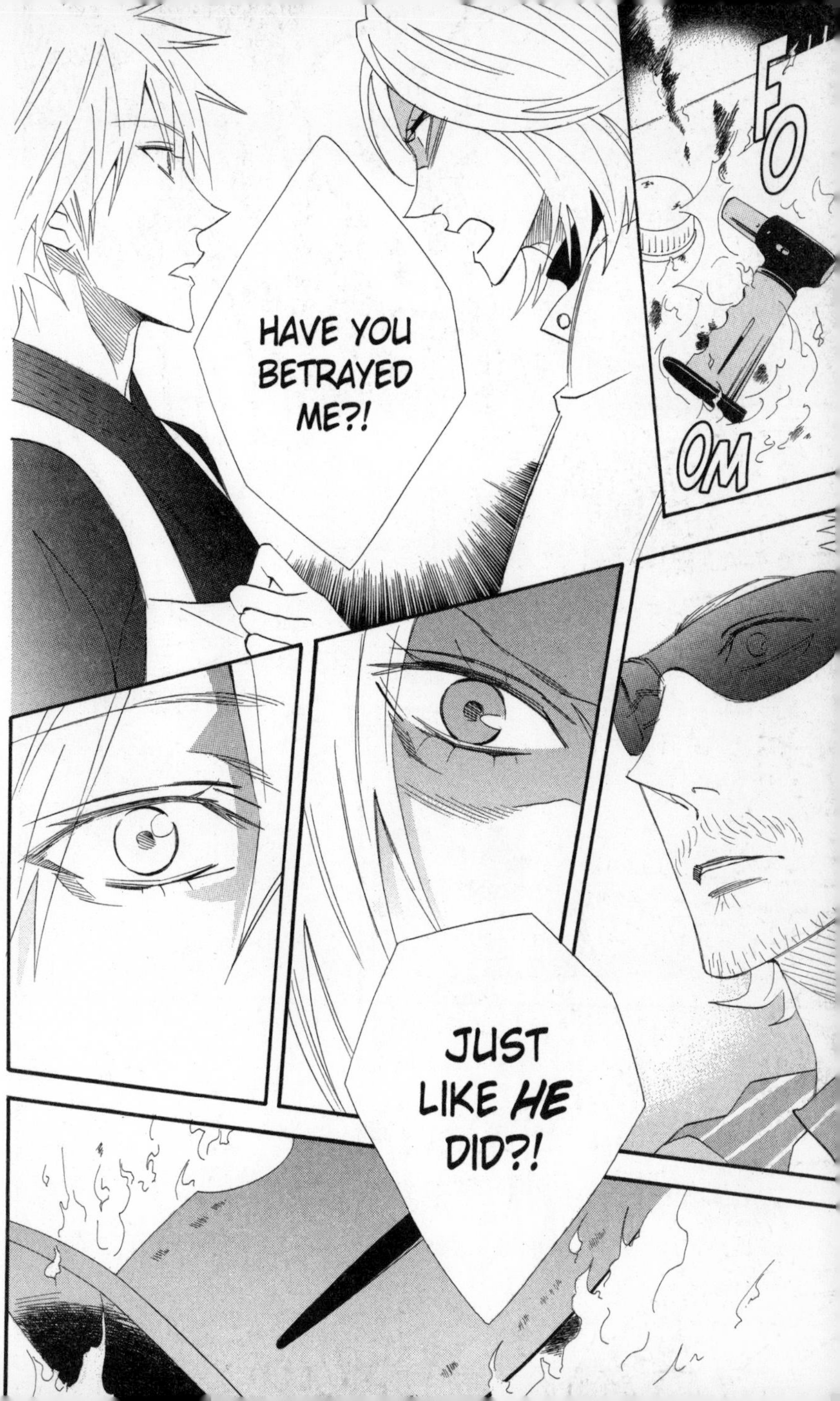
FOOM
HAVE YOU BETRAYED ME?!
JUST LIKE *HE* DID?!

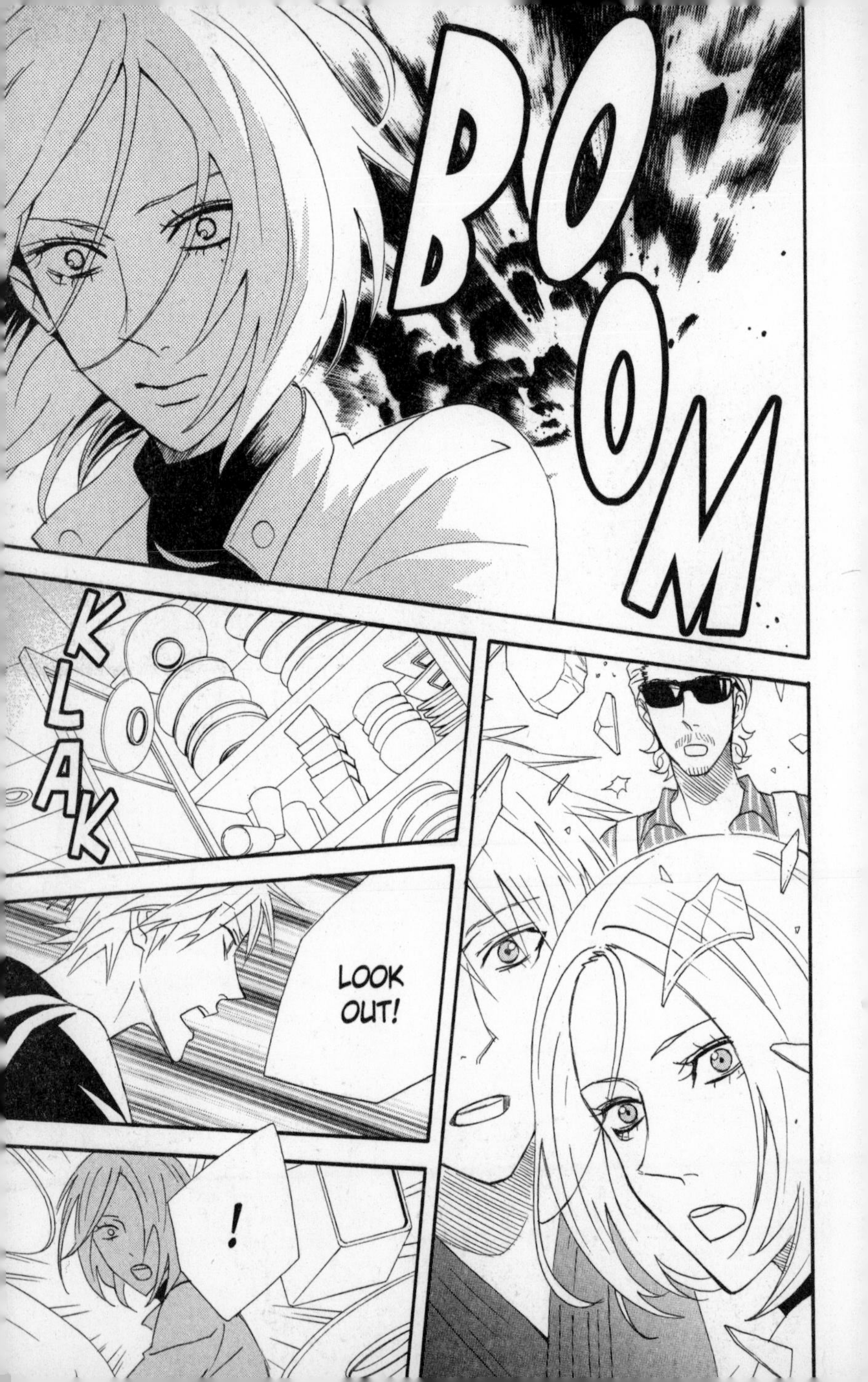
BOOM
KLLAK
LOOK OUT!
!

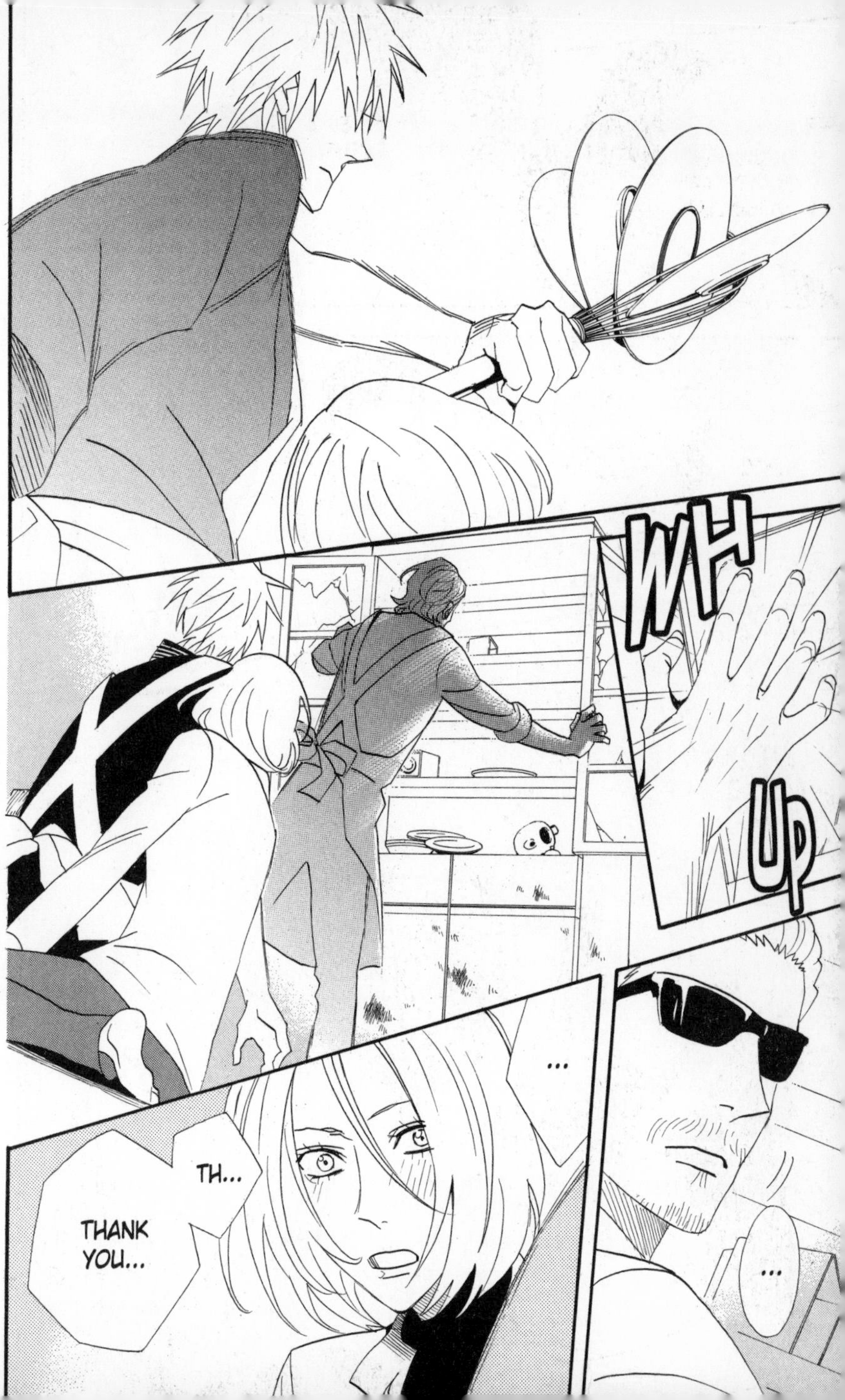

WH
UP
...
...
TH...
THANK YOU...

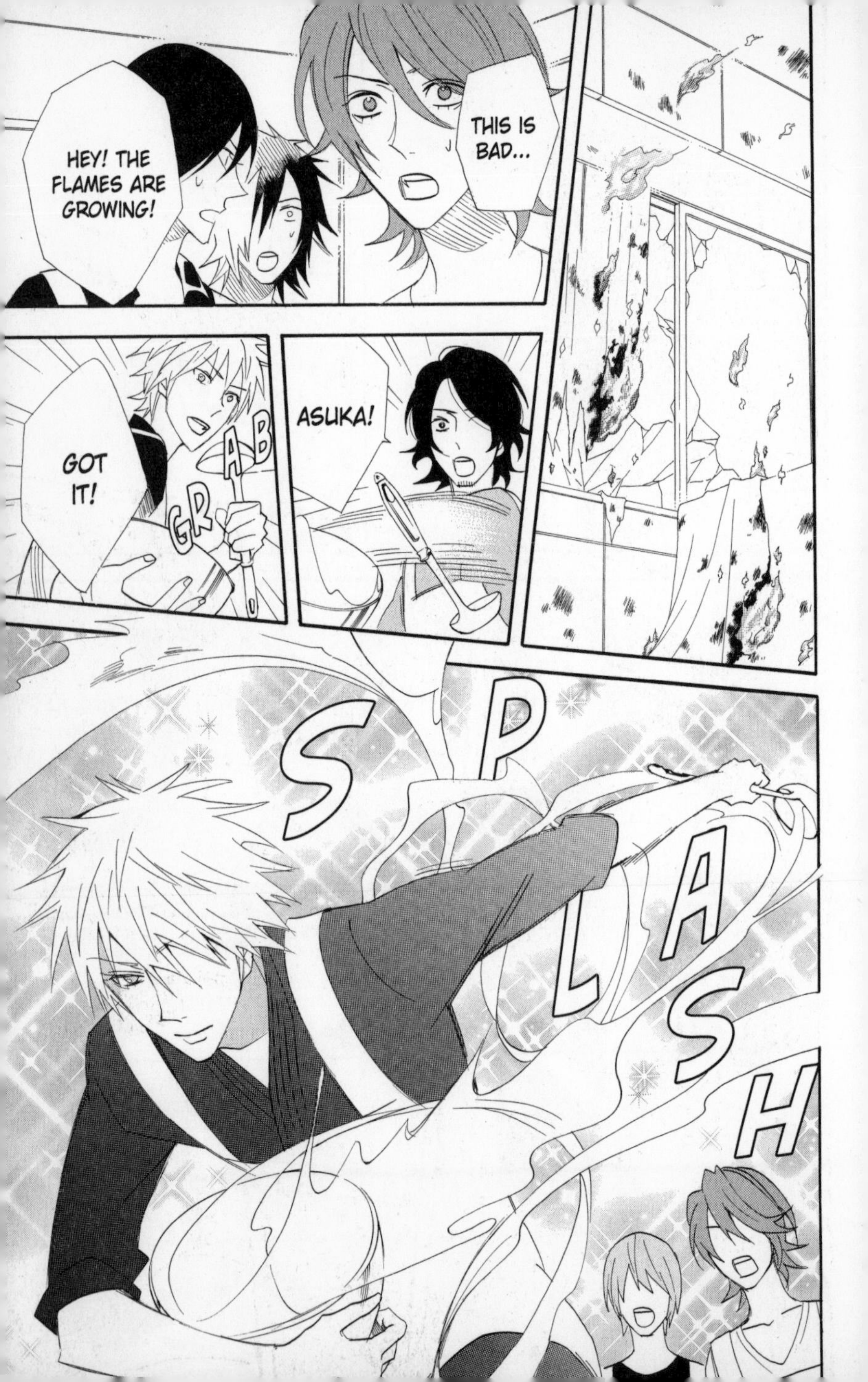
THIS IS BAD...
HEY! THE FLAMES ARE GROWING!
ASUKA!
GRAB
GOT IT!
SPLASH

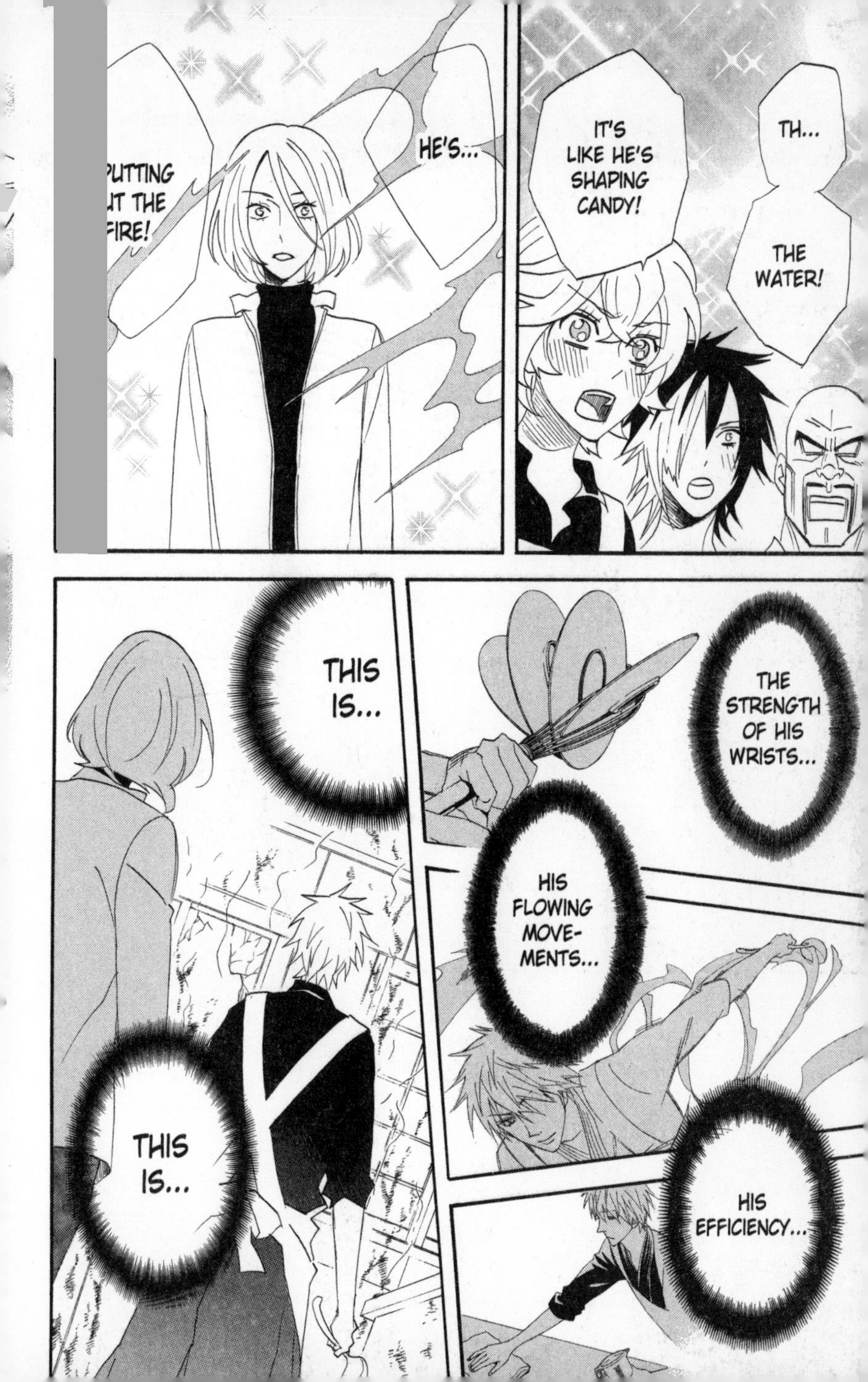
TH... THE WATER!
IT'S LIKE HE'S SHAPING CANDY!
HE'S...
PUTTING UT THE FIRE!
THE STRENGTH OF HIS WRISTS...
HIS FLOWING MOVE-MENTS...
HIS EFFICIENCY...
THIS IS...
THIS IS...

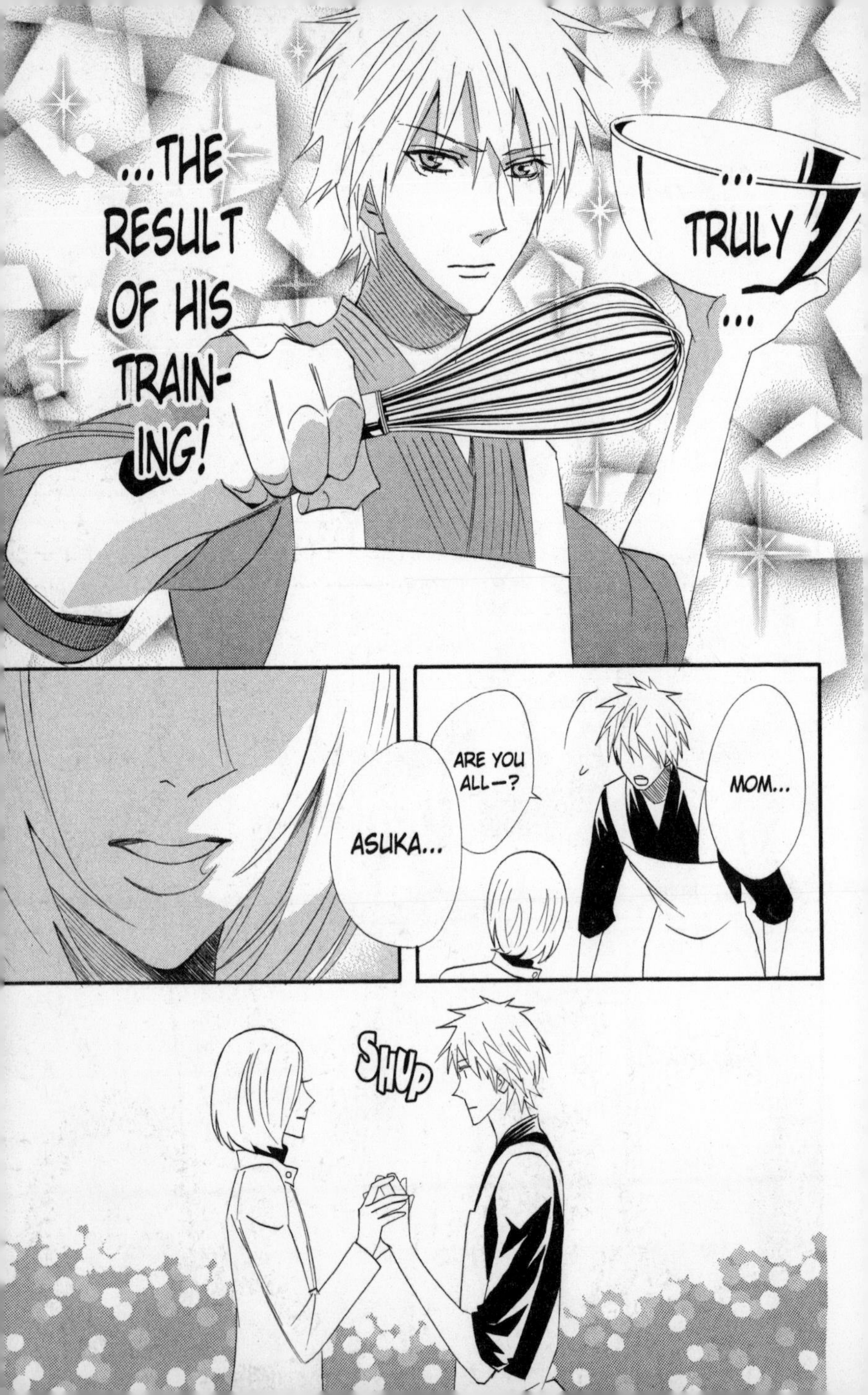
... TRULY ...
...THE RESULT OF HIS TRAIN-ING!
MOM...
ARE YOU ALL—?
ASUKA...
SHUP

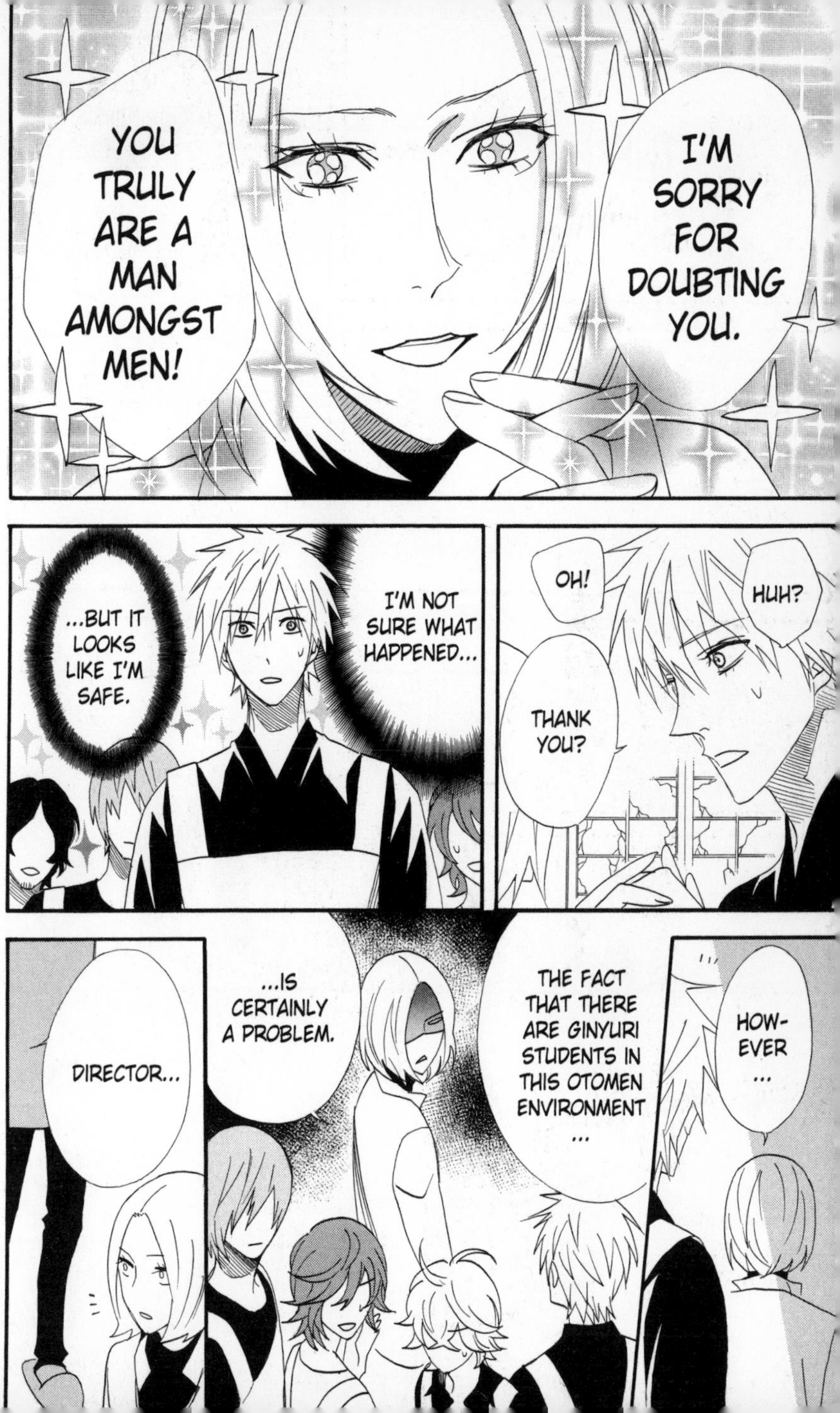
I'M SORRY FOR DOUBTING YOU.
YOU TRULY ARE A MAN AMONGST MEN!
HUH?
OH!
THANK YOU?
I'M NOT SURE WHAT HAPPENED...
...BUT IT LOOKS LIKE I'M SAFE.
HOW-EVER ...
THE FACT THAT THERE ARE GINYURI STUDENTS IN THIS OTOMEN ENVIRONMENT ...
...IS CERTAINLY A PROBLEM.
DIRECTOR...

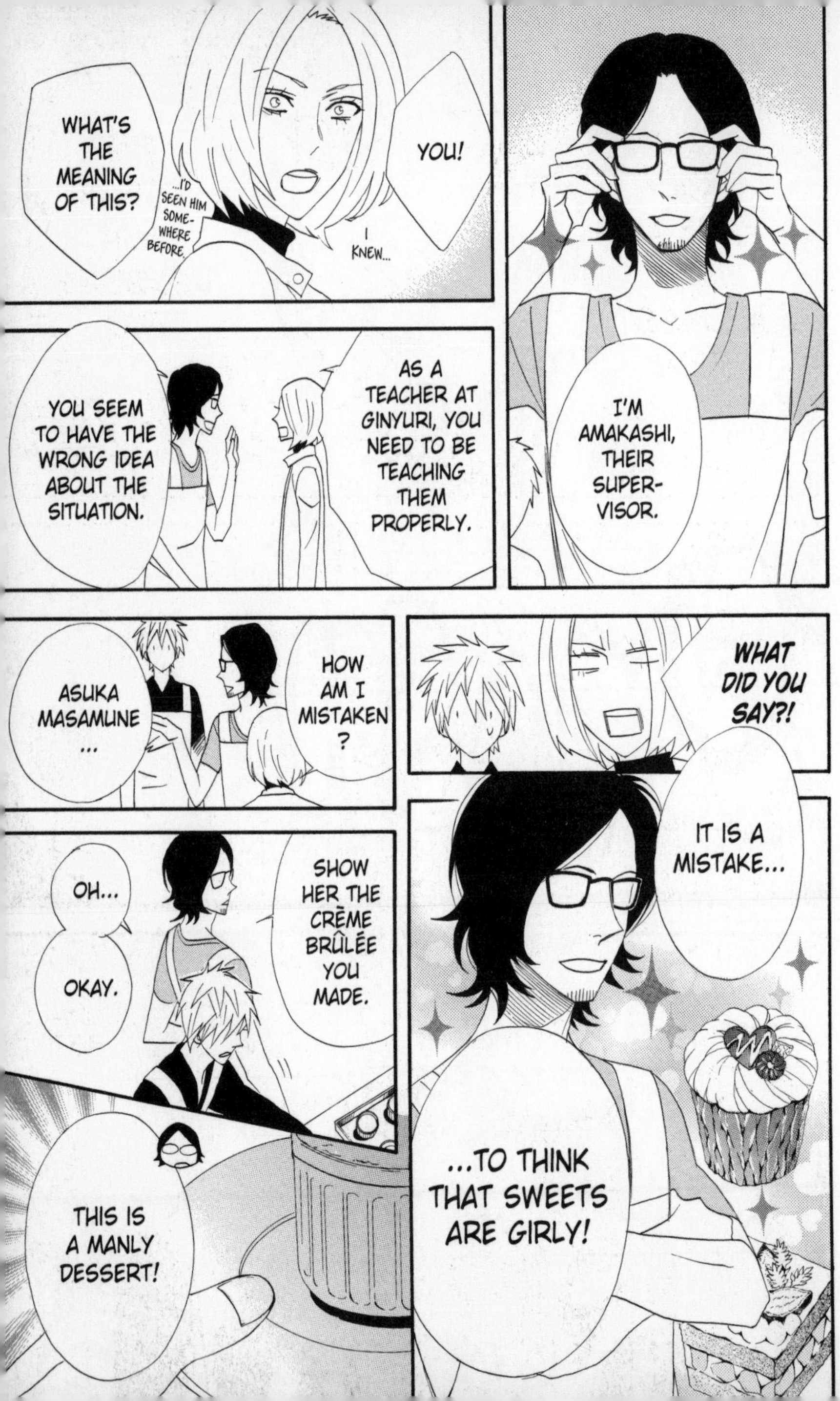
I'M AMAKASHI, THEIR SUPER-VISOR.
YOU!
I KNEW...
...I'D SEEN HIM SOME-WHERE BEFORE.
WHAT'S THE MEANING OF THIS?
AS A TEACHER AT GINYURI, YOU NEED TO BE TEACHING THEM PROPERLY.
YOU SEEM TO HAVE THE WRONG IDEA ABOUT THE SITUATION.
WHAT DID YOU SAY?!
HOW AM I MISTAKEN?
ASUKA MASAMUNE...
IT IS A MISTAKE...
...TO THINK THAT SWEETS ARE GIRLY!
SHOW HER THE CRÈME BRÛLÉE YOU MADE.
OH...
OKAY.
THIS IS A MANLY DESSERT!

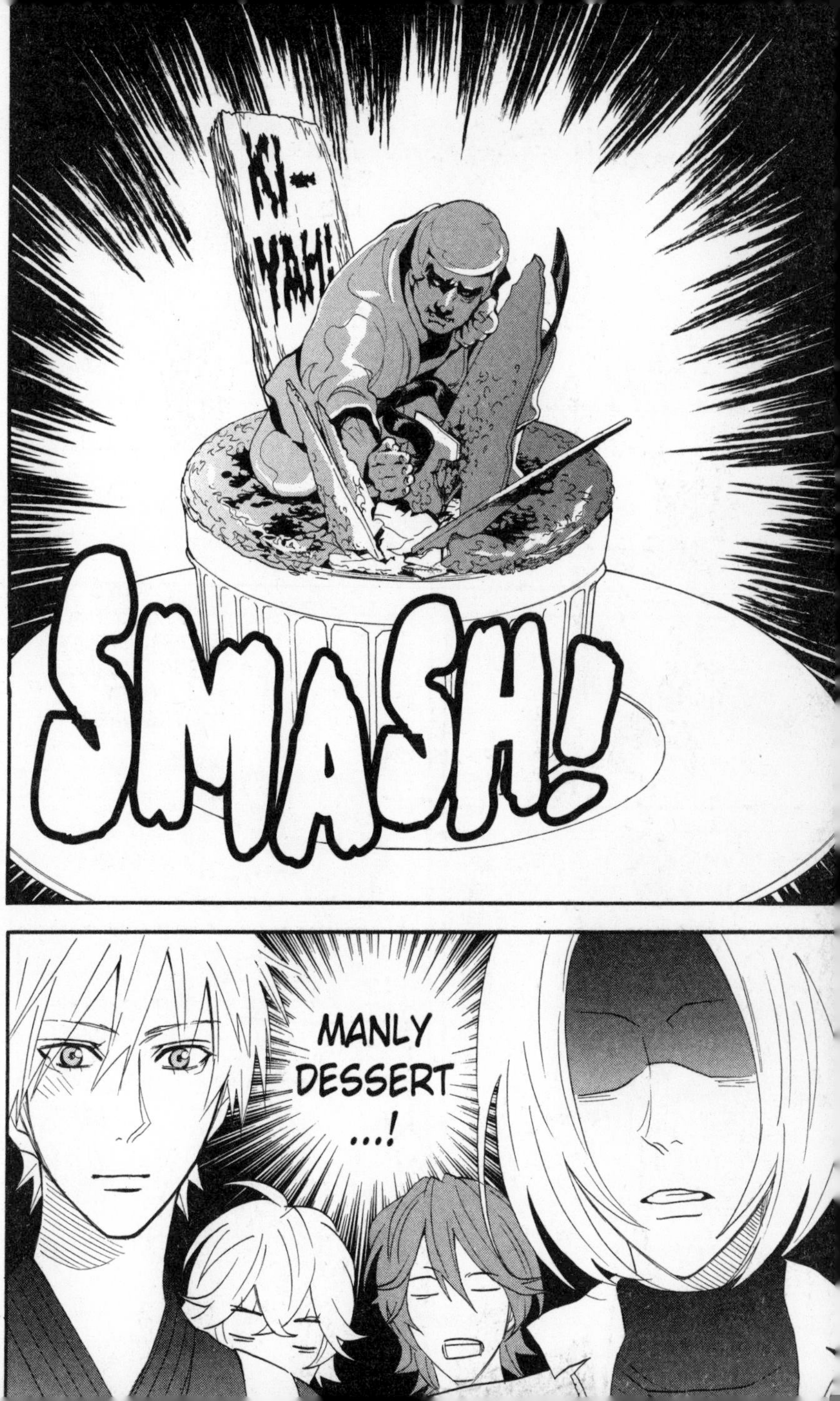
KI-YAH!
SMASH!
MANLY DESSERT ...!

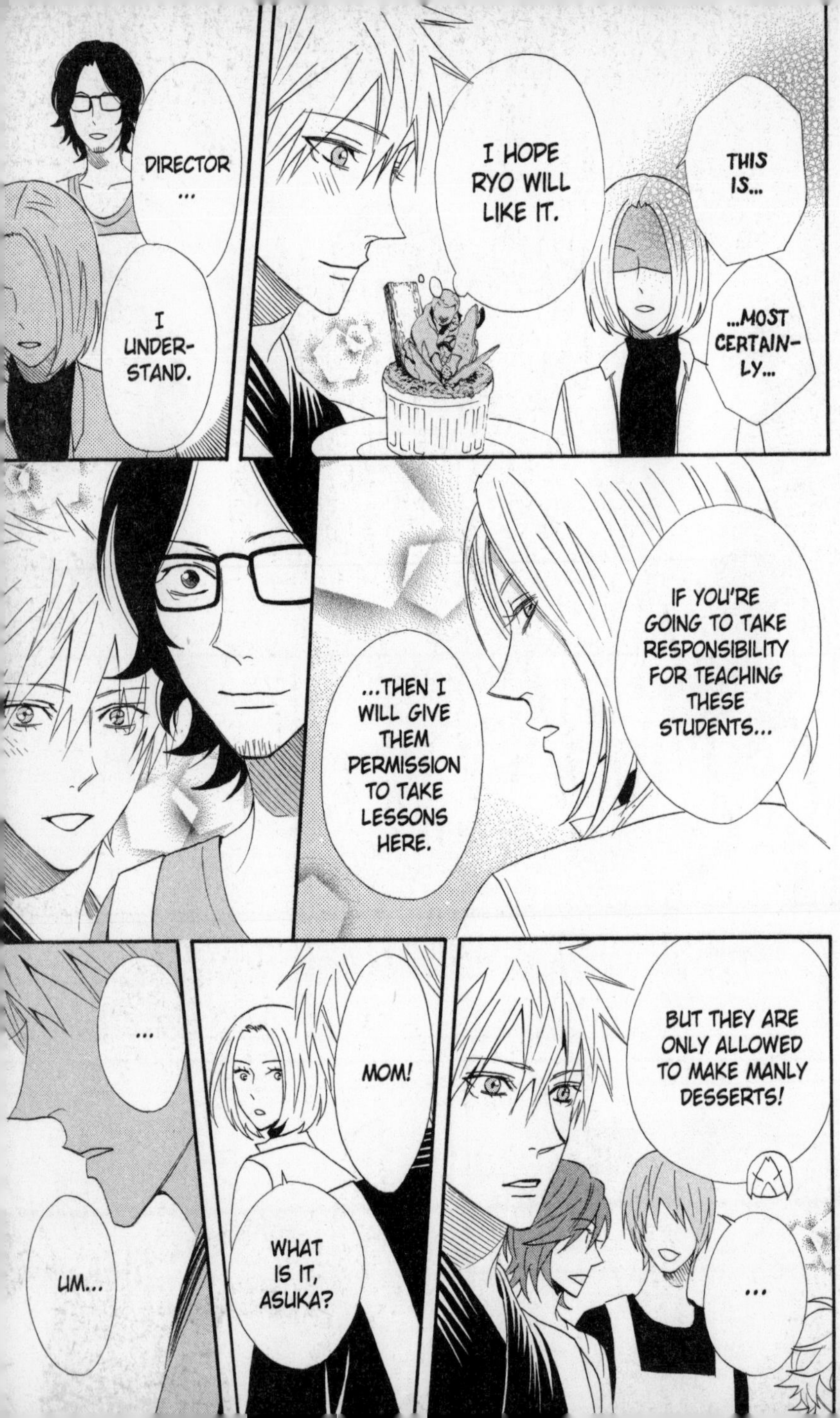
THIS IS...
...MOST CERTAINLY...
I HOPE RYO WILL LIKE IT.
DIRECTOR ...
I UNDERSTAND.
IF YOU'RE GOING TO TAKE RESPONSIBILITY FOR TEACHING THESE STUDENTS...
...THEN I WILL GIVE THEM PERMISSION TO TAKE LESSONS HERE.
BUT THEY ARE ONLY ALLOWED TO MAKE MANLY DESSERTS!
...
MOM!
WHAT IS IT, ASUKA?
...
UM...

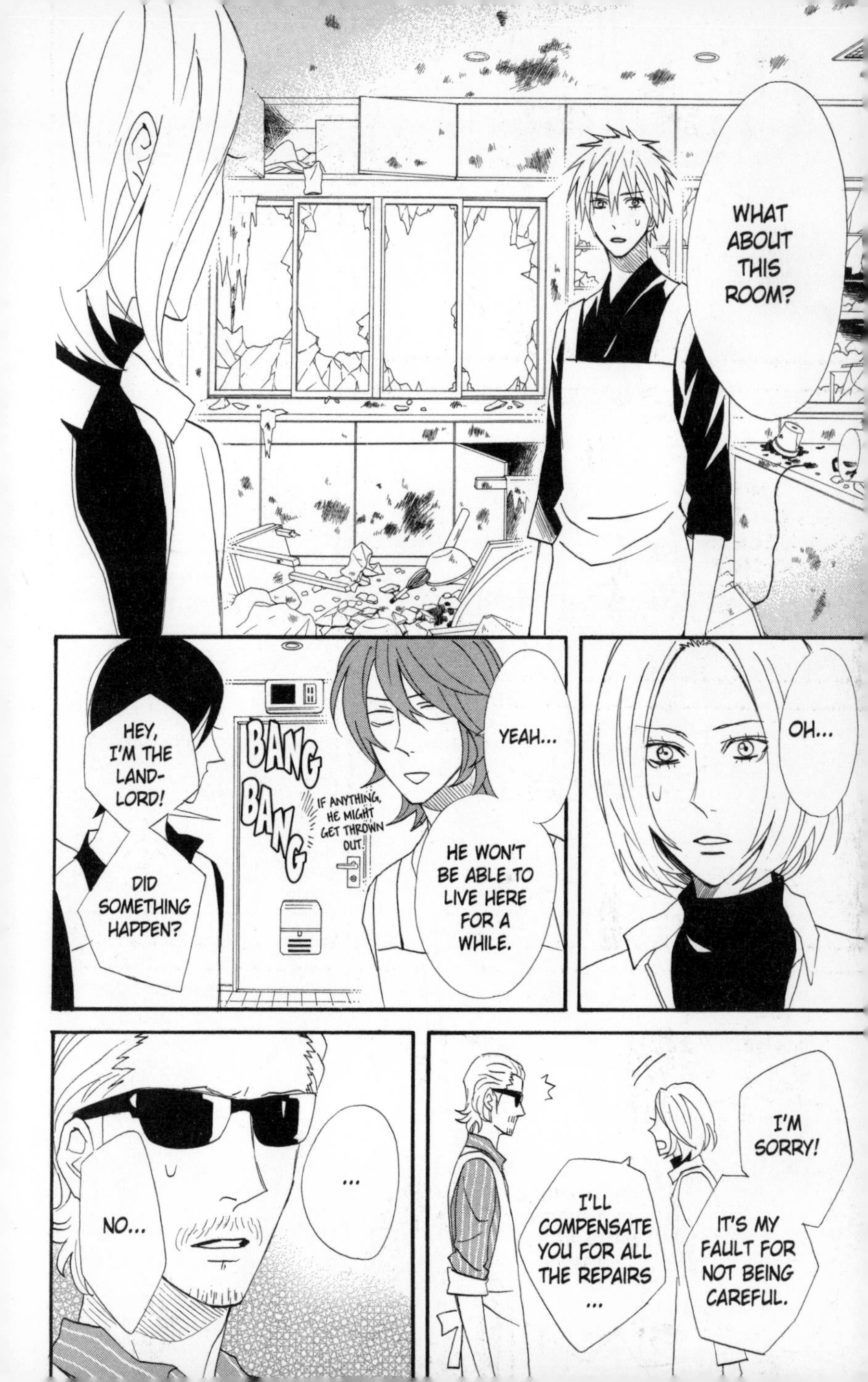
WHAT ABOUT THIS ROOM?
OH...
YEAH...
HE WON'T BE ABLE TO LIVE HERE FOR A WHILE.
IF ANYTHING, HE MIGHT GET THROWN OUT.
BANG BANG
HEY, I'M THE LAND-LORD!
DID SOMETHING HAPPEN?
I'M SORRY!
IT'S MY FAULT FOR NOT BEING CAREFUL.
I'LL COMPENSATE YOU FOR ALL THE REPAIRS ...
...
NO...

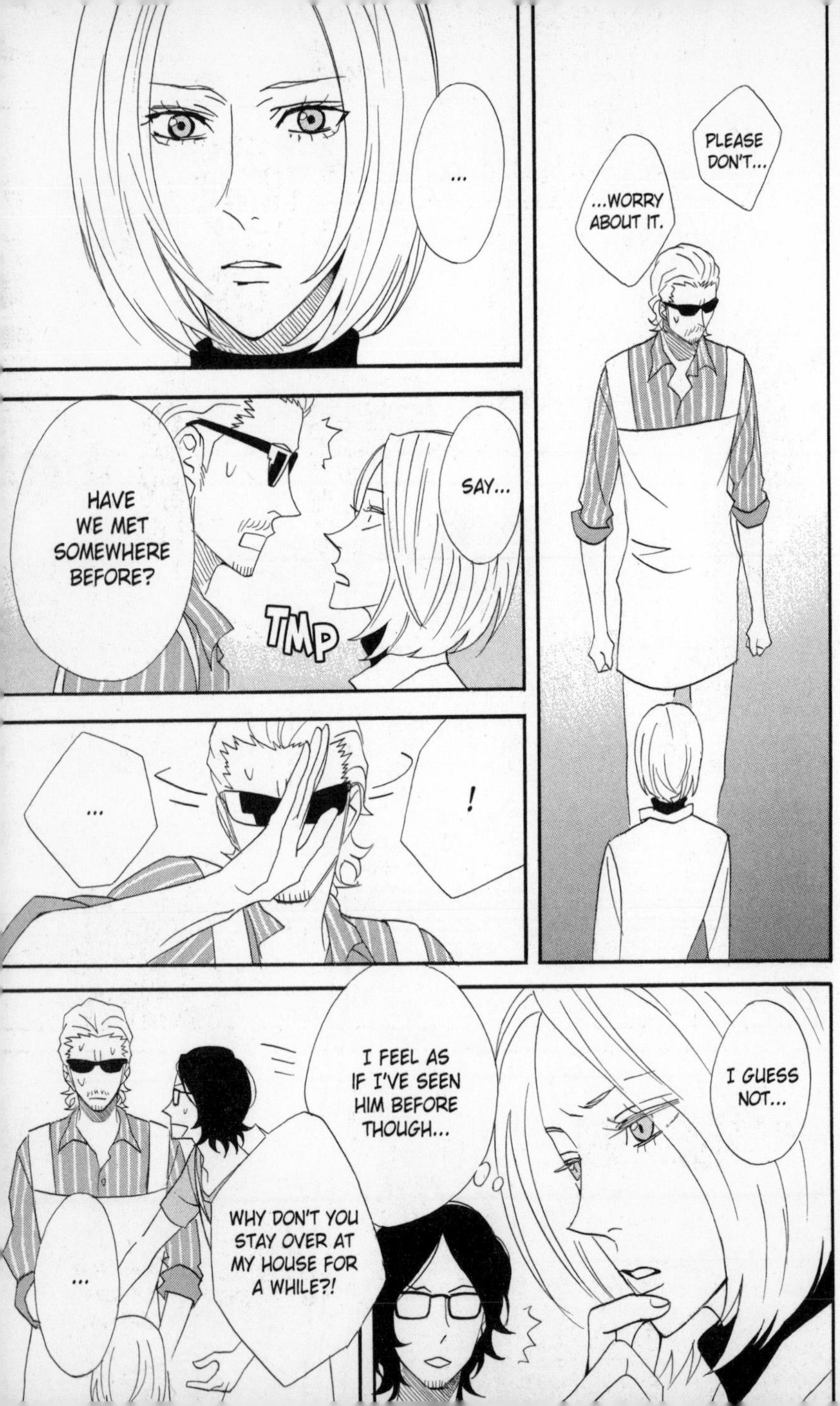
PLEASE DON'T...
...WORRY ABOUT IT.
...
SAY...
HAVE WE MET SOMEWHERE BEFORE?
TMP
!
...
I GUESS NOT...
I FEEL AS IF I'VE SEEN HIM BEFORE THOUGH...
WHY DON'T YOU STAY OVER AT MY HOUSE FOR A WHILE?!
...

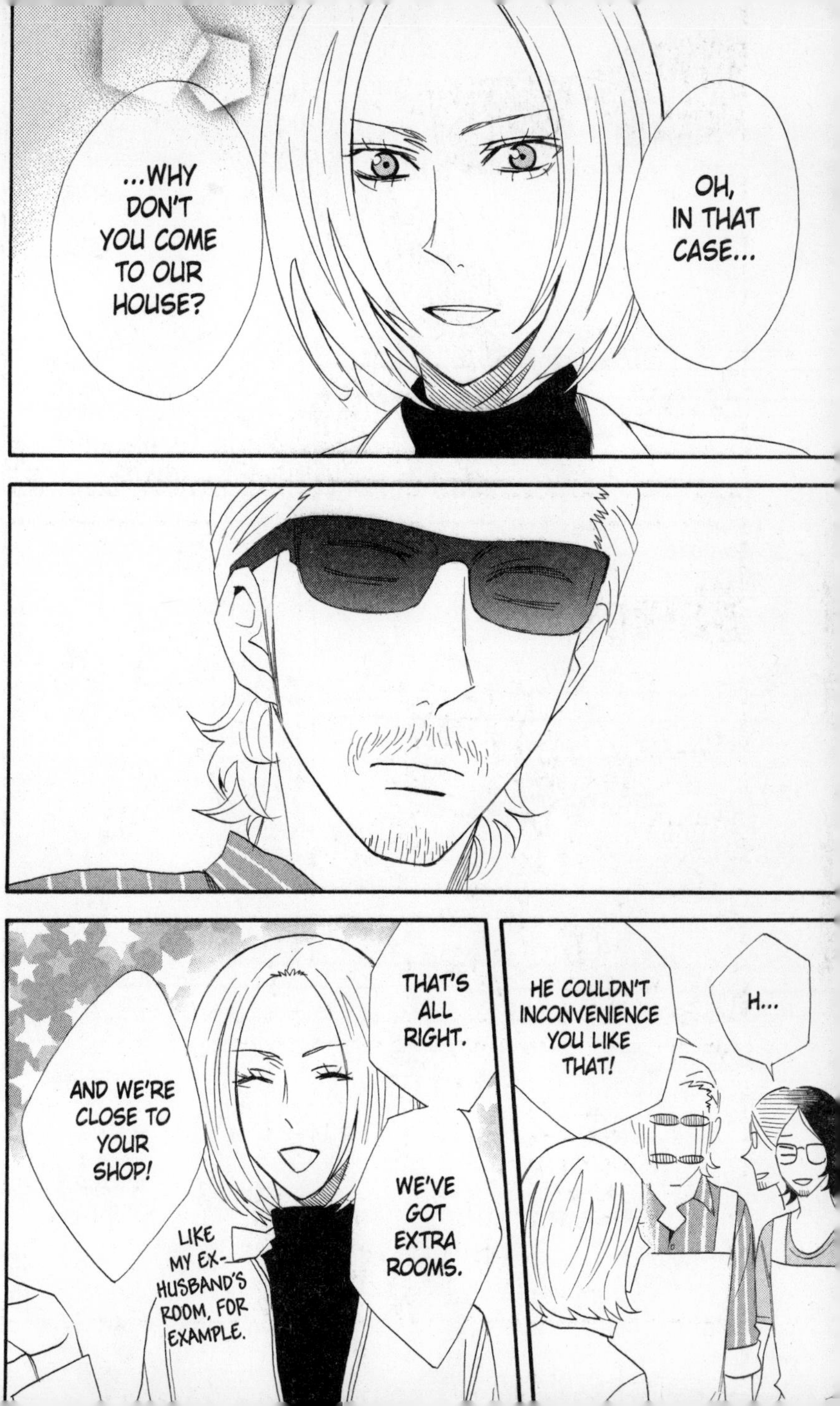
OH, IN THAT CASE...
...WHY DON'T YOU COME TO OUR HOUSE?
H...
HE COULDN'T INCONVENIENCE YOU LIKE THAT!
THAT'S ALL RIGHT.
WE'VE GOT EXTRA ROOMS.
AND WE'RE CLOSE TO YOUR SHOP!
LIKE MY EX-HUSBAND'S ROOM, FOR EXAMPLE.

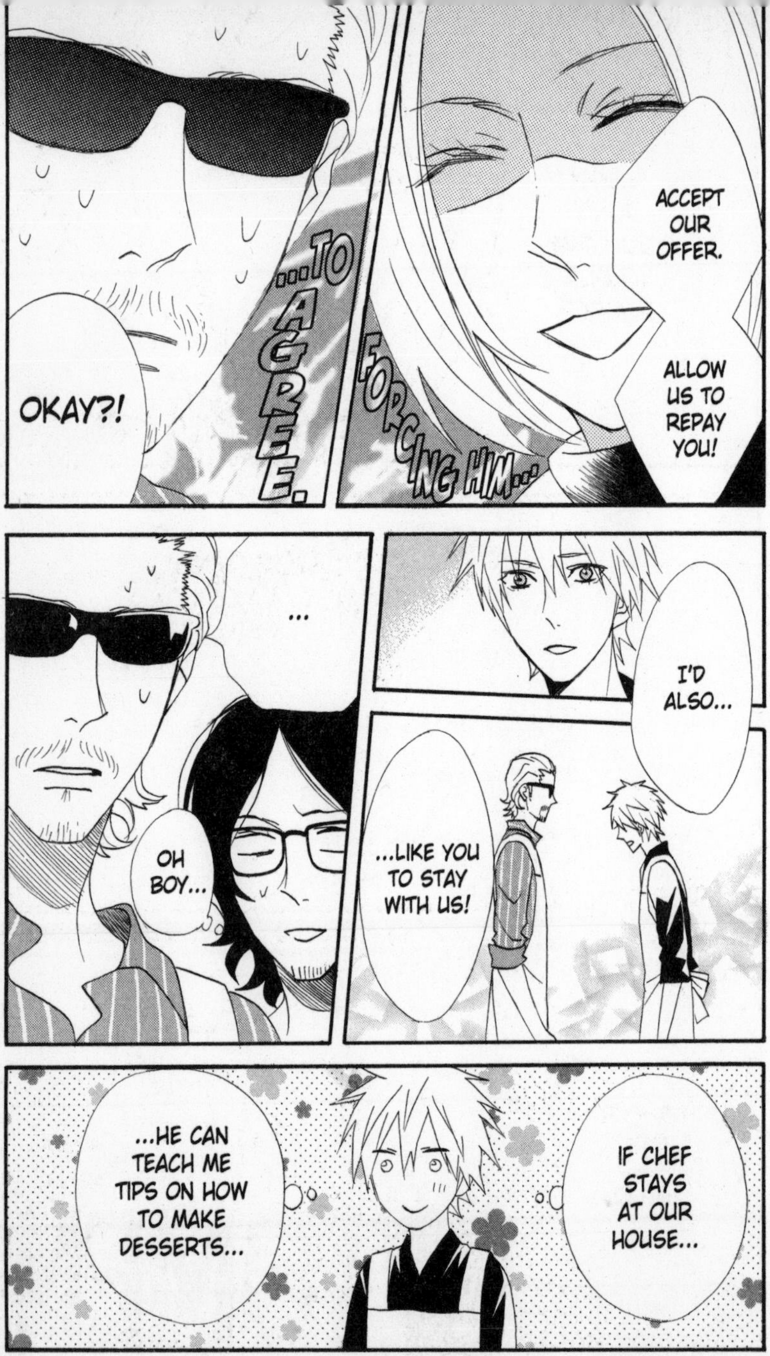
ACCEPT OUR OFFER.
ALLOW US TO REPAY YOU!
FORCING HIM...
...TO AGREE.
OKAY?!
I'D ALSO...
...LIKE YOU TO STAY WITH US!
...
OH BOY...
IF CHEF STAYS AT OUR HOUSE...
...HE CAN TEACH ME TIPS ON HOW TO MAKE DESSERTS...

OTOMEN

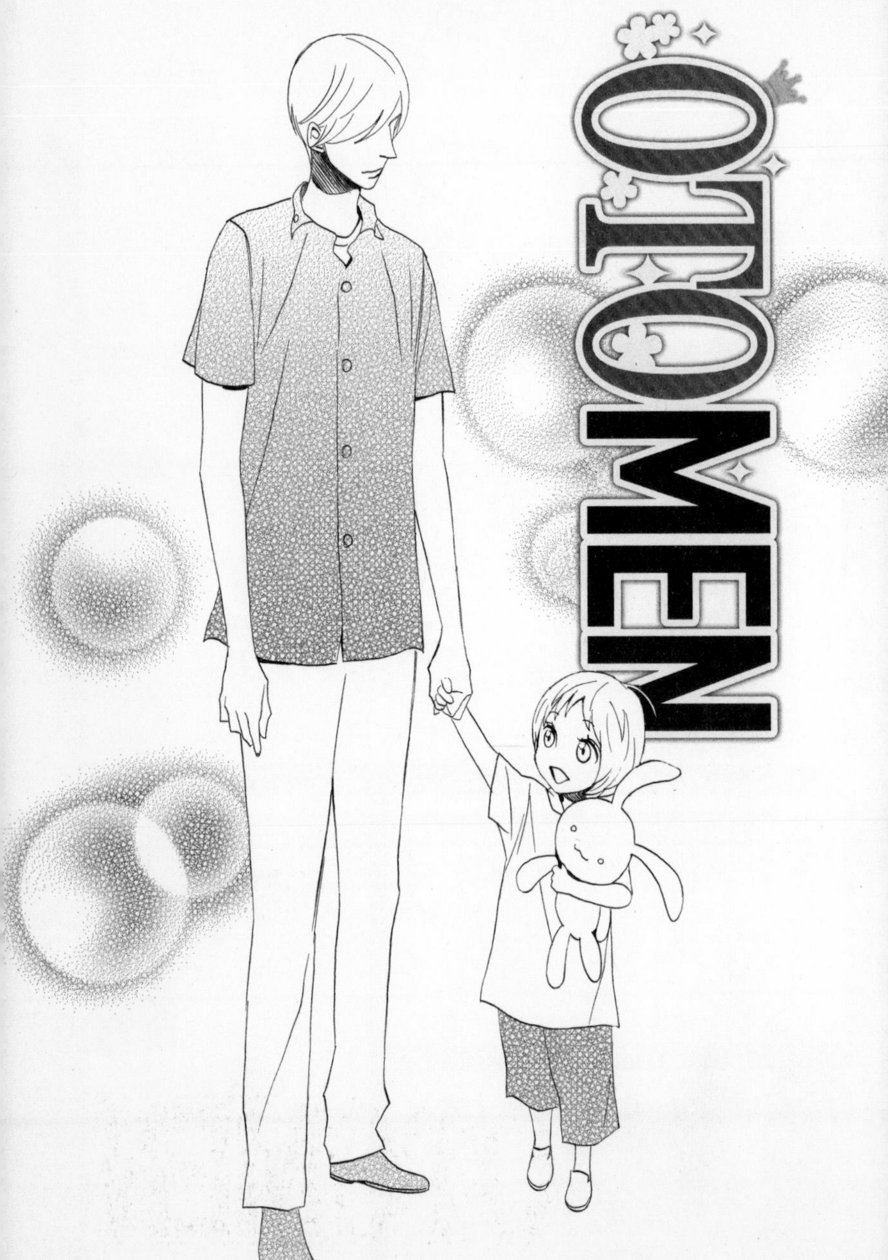
OTOMEN

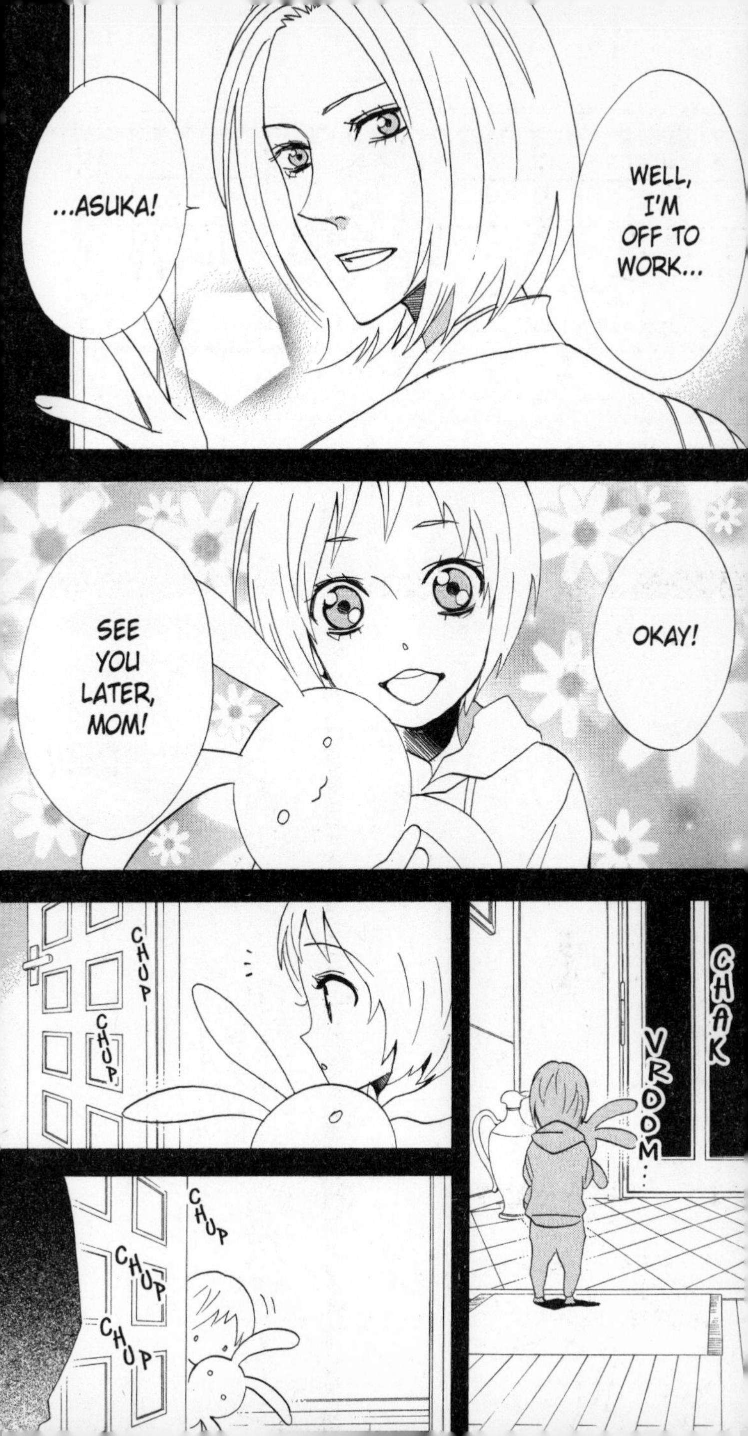
WELL, I'M OFF TO WORK...
...ASUKA!
OKAY!
SEE YOU LATER, MOM!
CHAK
VROOM...
CHUP
CHUP
CHUP
CHUP
CHUP

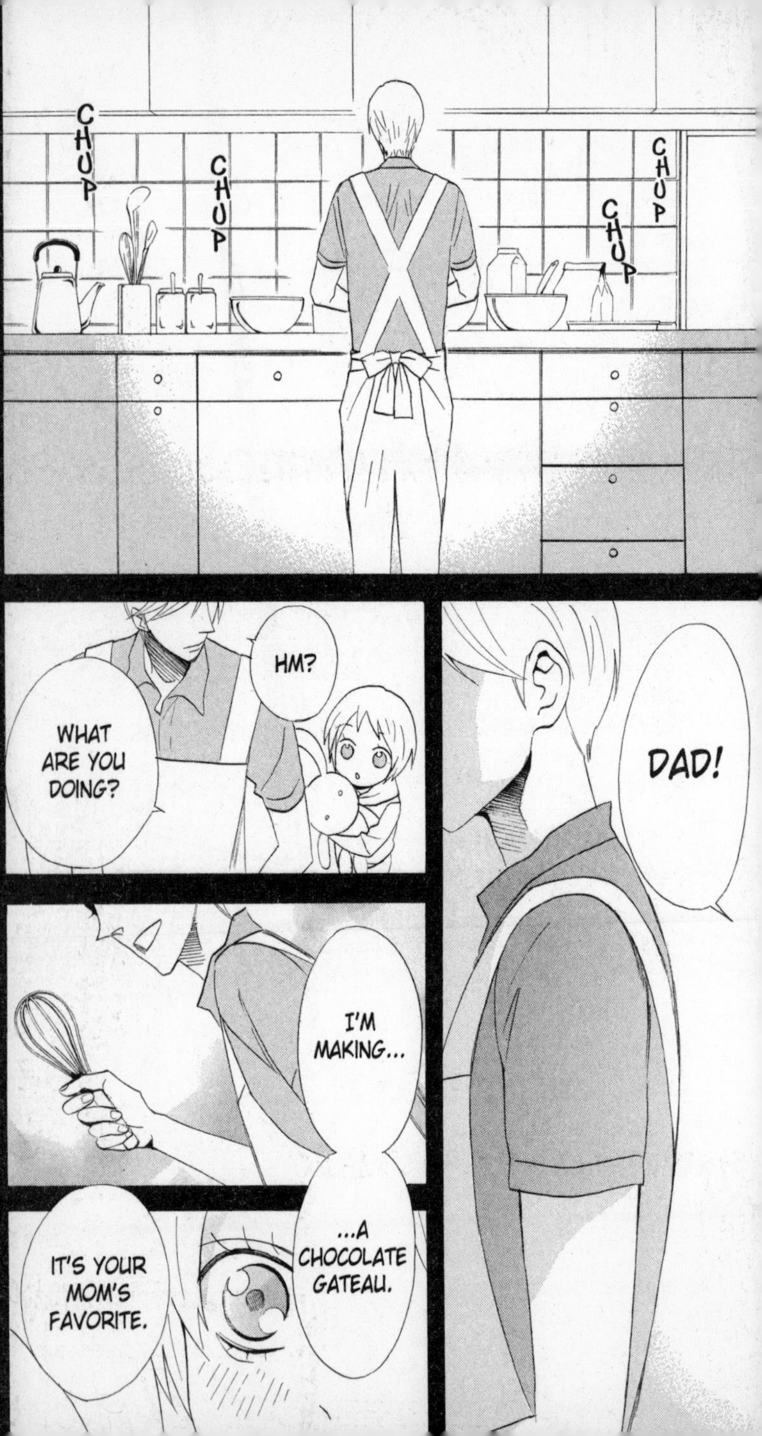
CHUP
CHUP
CHUP
CHUP
DAD!
HM?
WHAT ARE YOU DOING?
I'M MAKING...
...A CHOCOLATE GATEAU.
IT'S YOUR MOM'S FAVORITE.

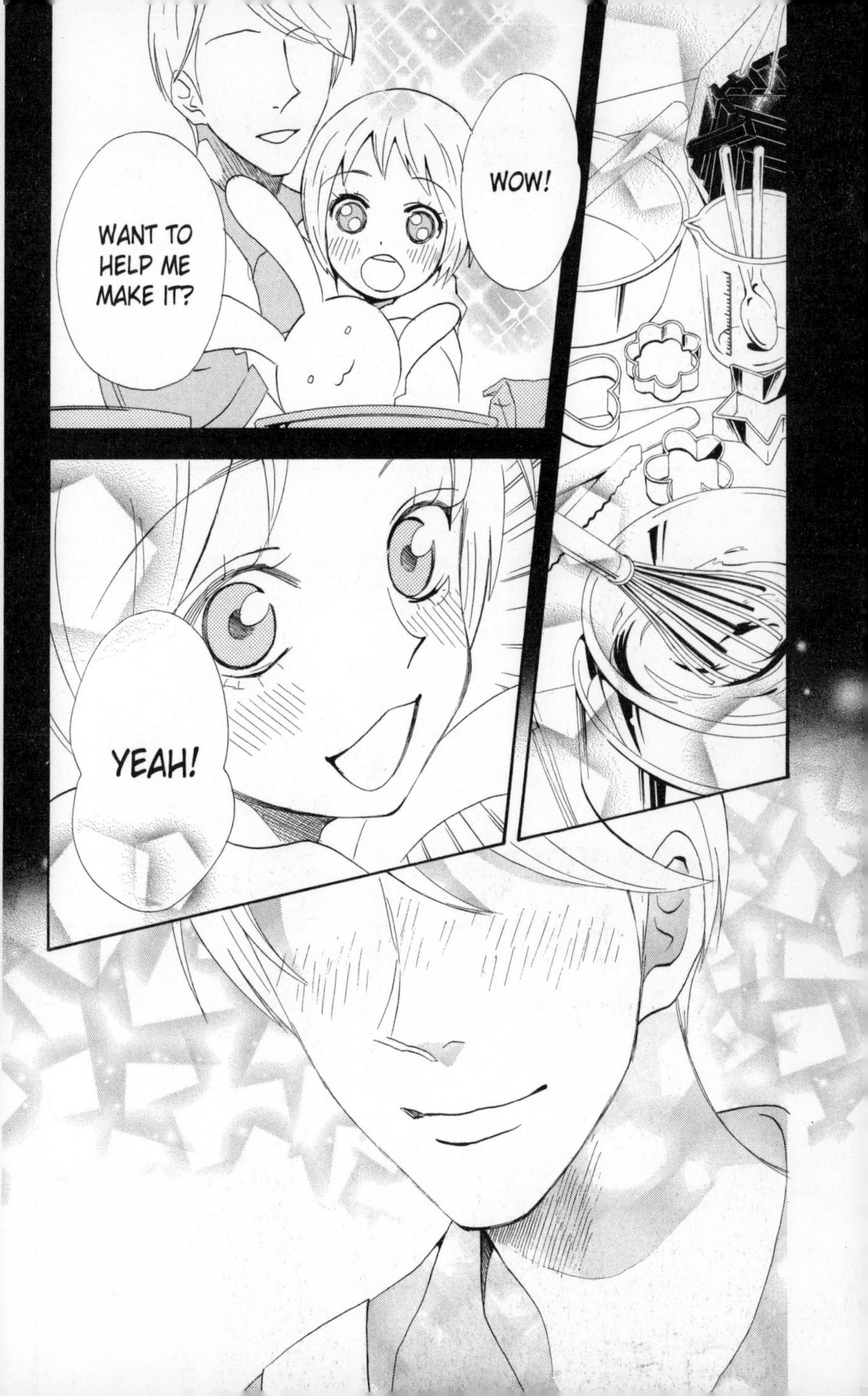
WOW!
WANT TO HELP ME MAKE IT?
YEAH!

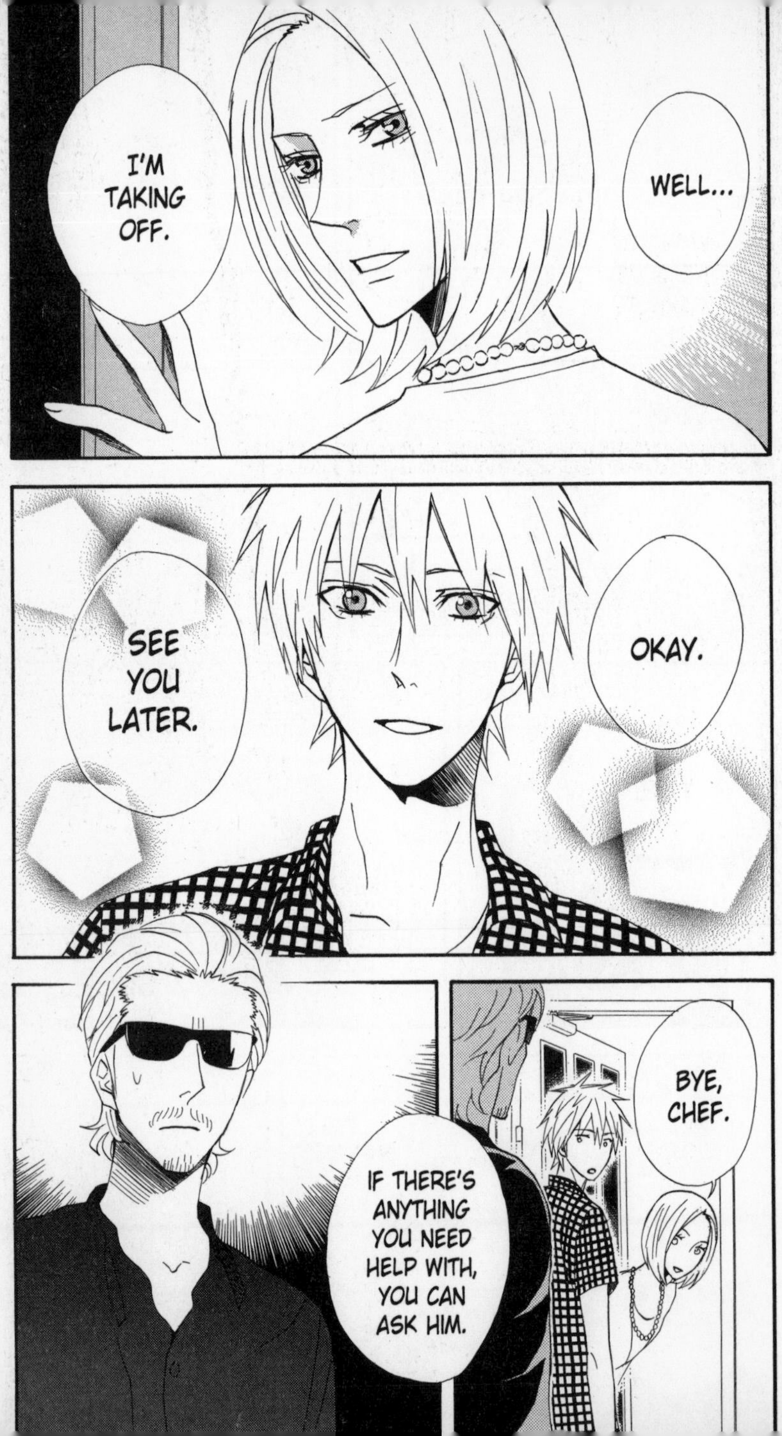
WELL...
I'M TAKING OFF.
OKAY.
SEE YOU LATER.
BYE, CHEF.
IF THERE'S ANYTHING YOU NEED HELP WITH, YOU CAN ASK HIM.

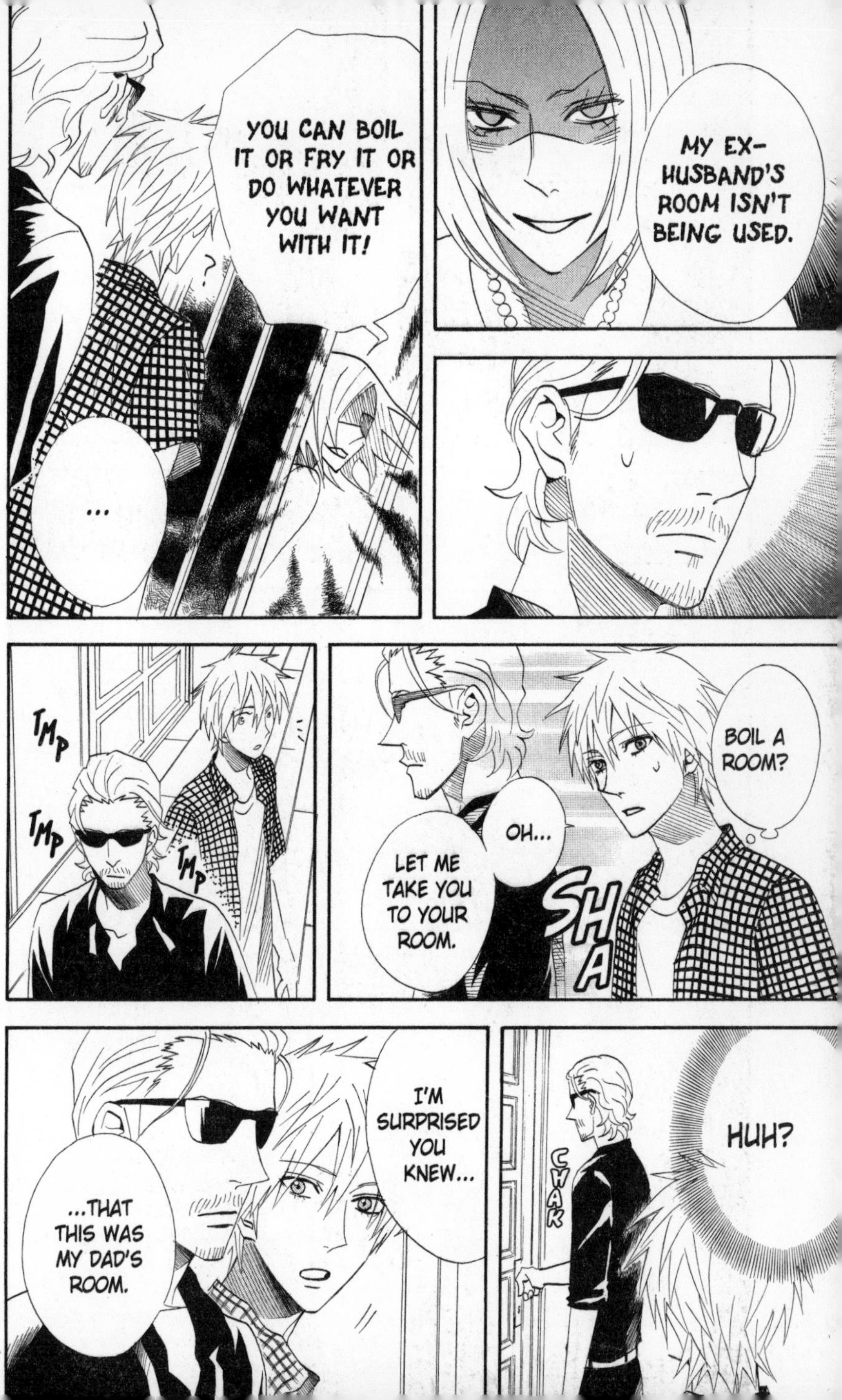
MY EX-HUSBAND'S ROOM ISN'T BEING USED.
YOU CAN BOIL IT OR FRY IT OR DO WHATEVER YOU WANT WITH IT!
?
...
BOIL A ROOM?
OH...
LET ME TAKE YOU TO YOUR ROOM.
SHA
TMP
TMP
TMP
HUH?
CHAK
I'M SURPRISED YOU KNEW...
...THAT THIS WAS MY DAD'S ROOM.

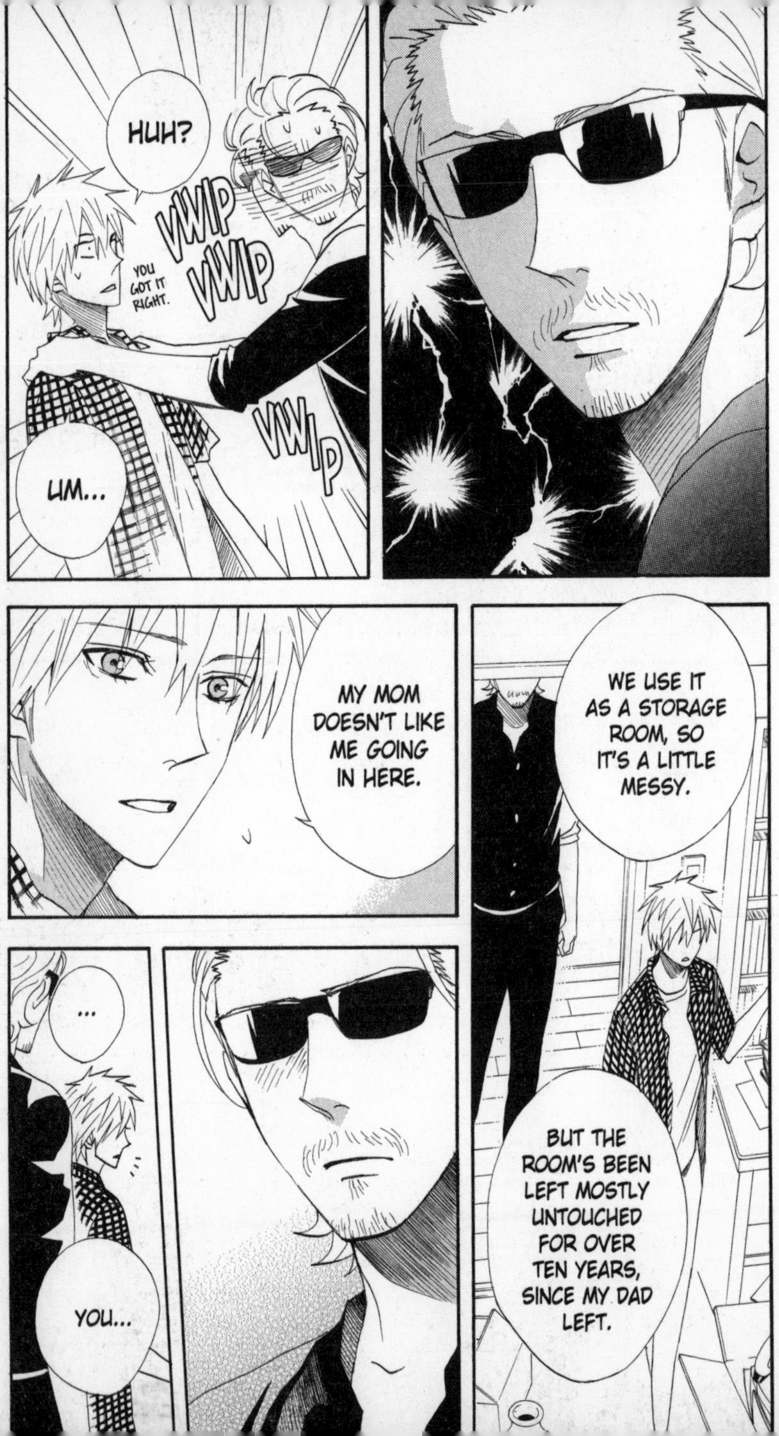
HUH?
VWIP VWIP
YOU GOT IT RIGHT.
VWIP
UM...
WE USE IT AS A STORAGE ROOM, SO IT'S A LITTLE MESSY.
BUT THE ROOM'S BEEN LEFT MOSTLY UNTOUCHED FOR OVER TEN YEARS, SINCE MY DAD LEFT.
MY MOM DOESN'T LIKE ME GOING IN HERE.
...
YOU...

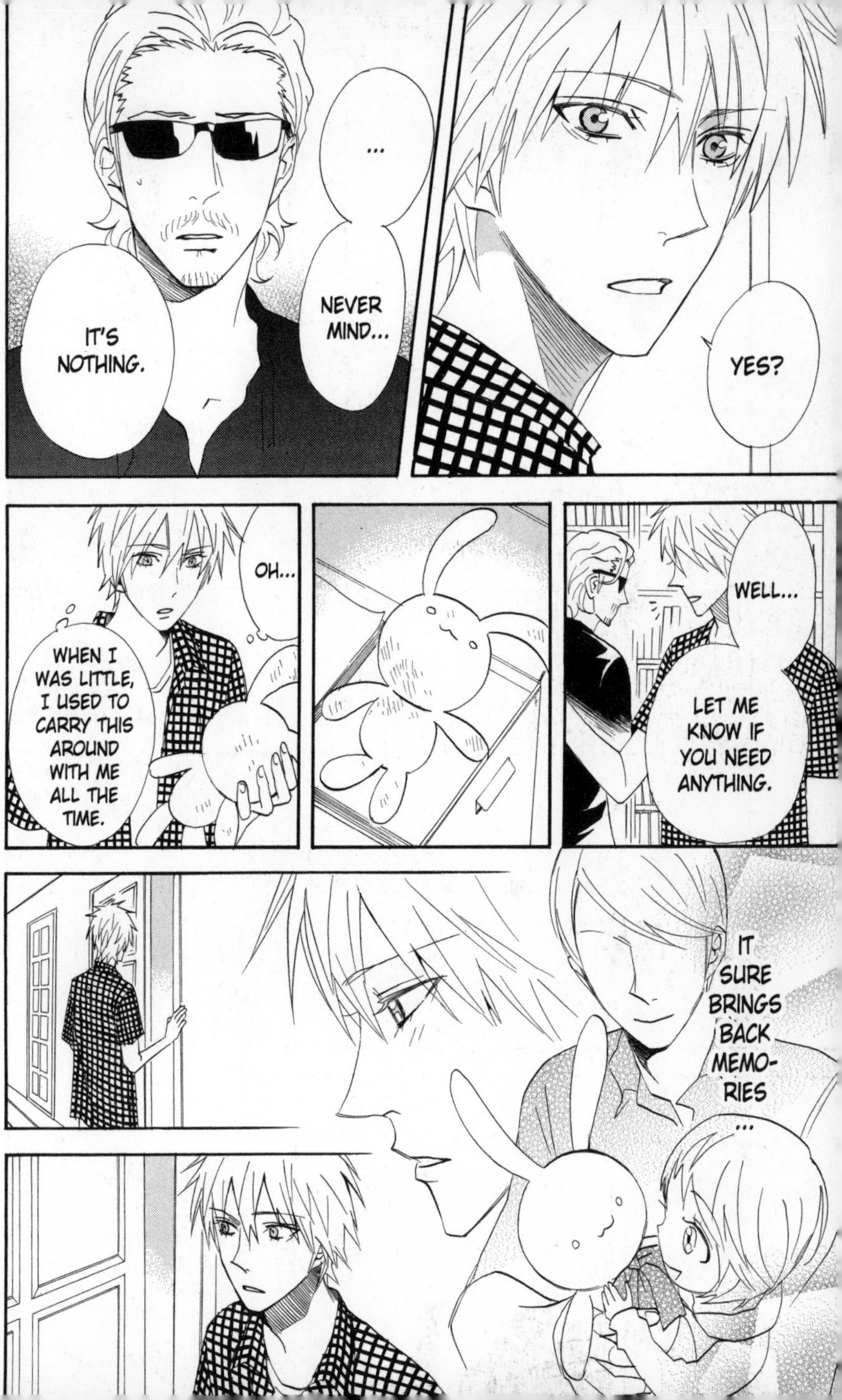
YES?
...
NEVER MIND...
IT'S NOTHING.
WELL...
LET ME KNOW IF YOU NEED ANYTHING.
OH...
WHEN I WAS LITTLE, I USED TO CARRY THIS AROUND WITH ME ALL THE TIME.
IT SURE BRINGS BACK MEMORIES...

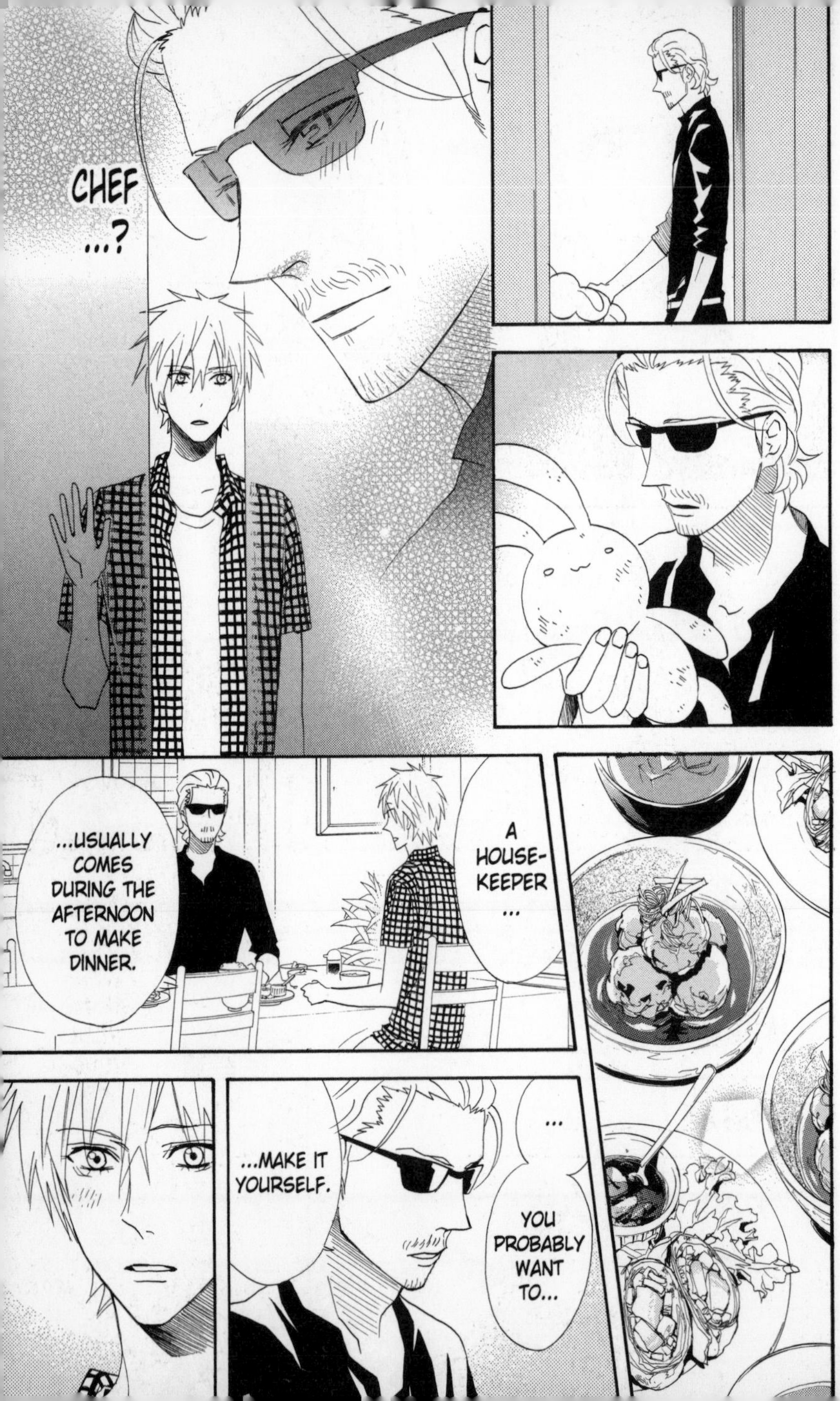
CHEF ...?
A HOUSE-KEEPER ...
...USUALLY COMES DURING THE AFTERNOON TO MAKE DINNER.
...
YOU PROBABLY WANT TO...
...MAKE IT YOURSELF.

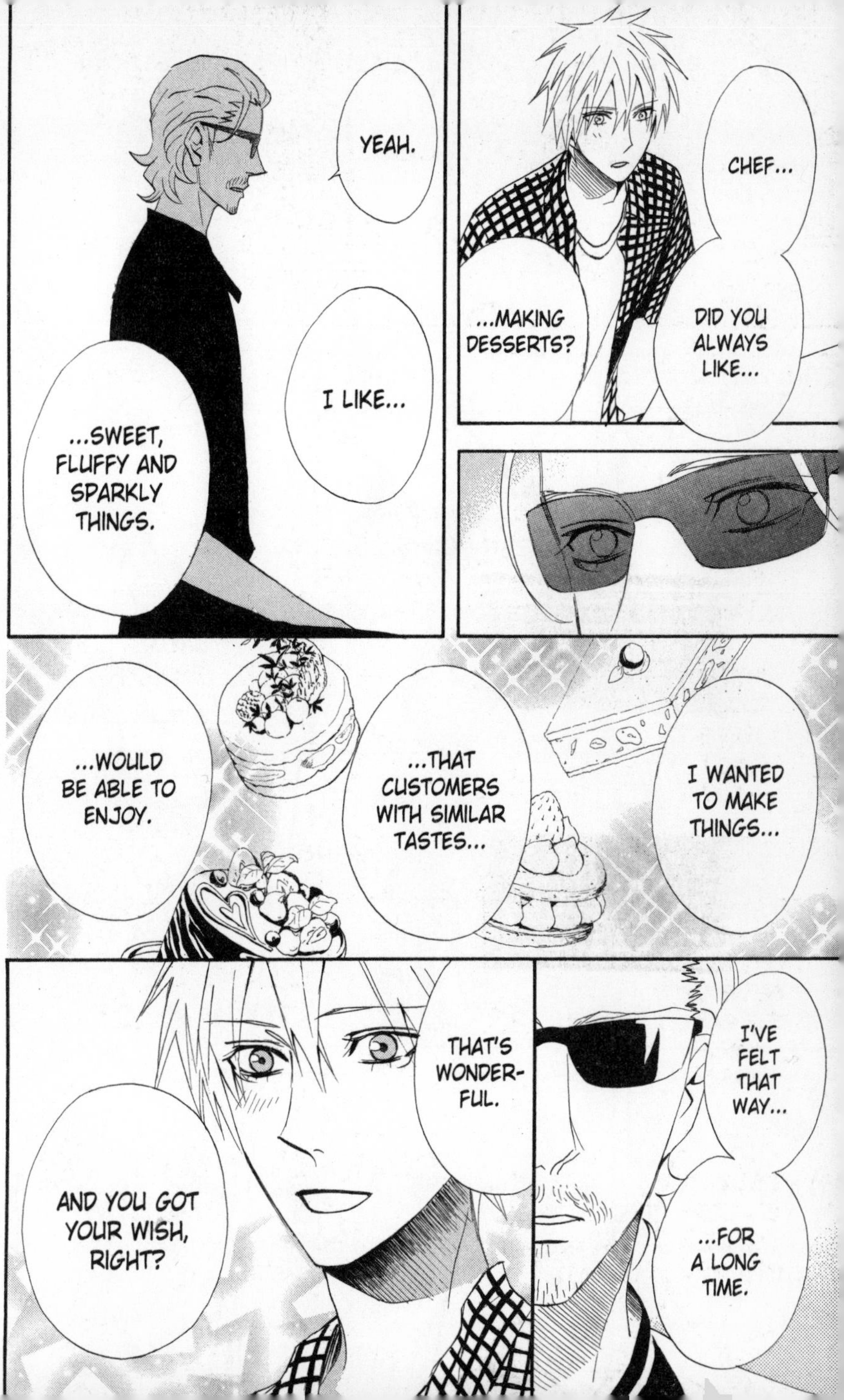
CHEF...
DID YOU ALWAYS LIKE...
...MAKING DESSERTS?
YEAH.
I LIKE...
...SWEET, FLUFFY AND SPARKLY THINGS.
I WANTED TO MAKE THINGS...
...THAT CUSTOMERS WITH SIMILAR TASTES...
...WOULD BE ABLE TO ENJOY.
I'VE FELT THAT WAY...
...FOR A LONG TIME.
THAT'S WONDER-FUL.
AND YOU GOT YOUR WISH, RIGHT?

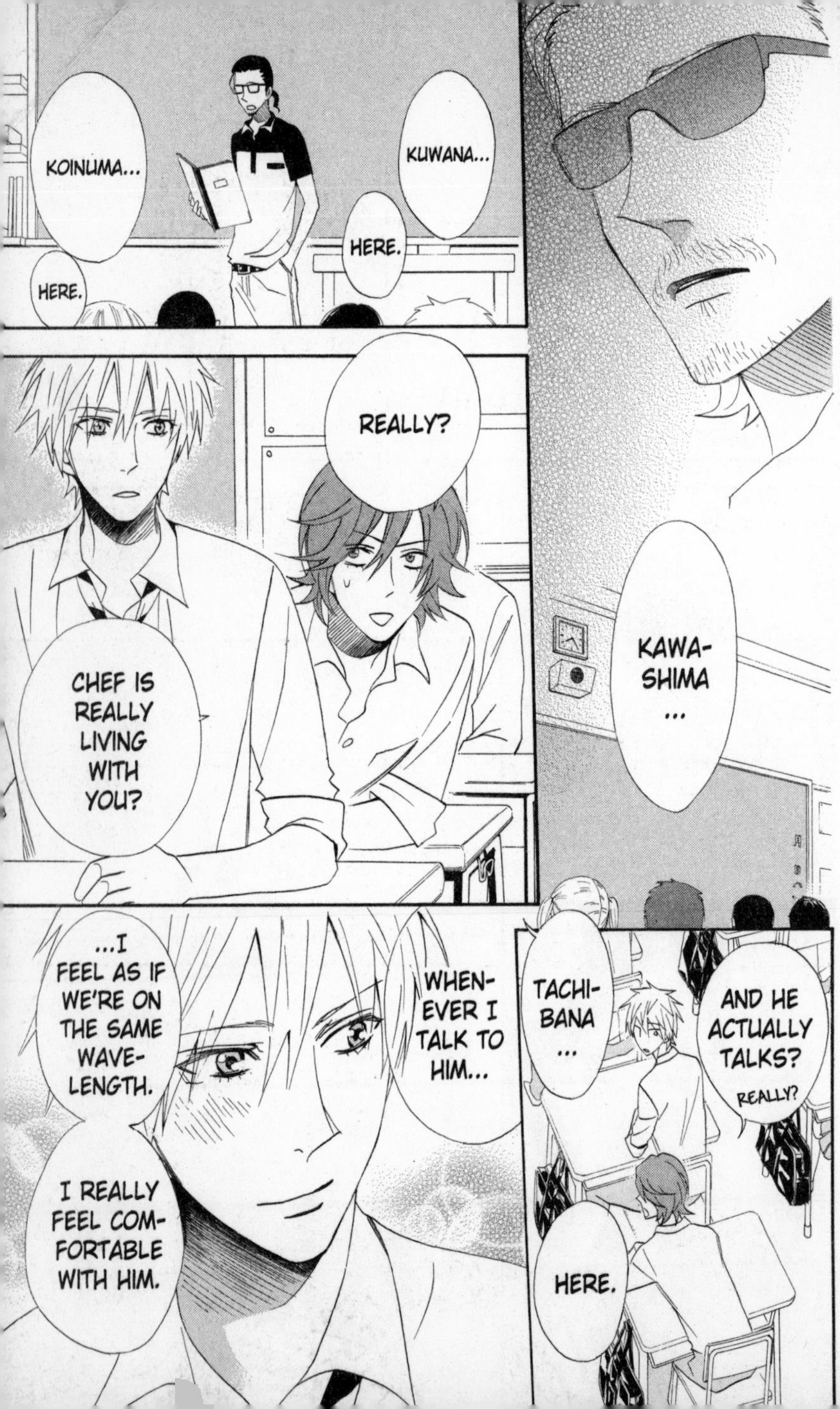
KAWA-SHIMA ...
KUWANA...
HERE.
KOINUMA...
HERE.
REALLY?
CHEF IS REALLY LIVING WITH YOU?
AND HE ACTUALLY TALKS?
REALLY?
TACHI-BANA ...
HERE.
WHEN-EVER I TALK TO HIM...
...I FEEL AS IF WE'RE ON THE SAME WAVE-LENGTH.
I REALLY FEEL COM-FORTABLE WITH HIM.

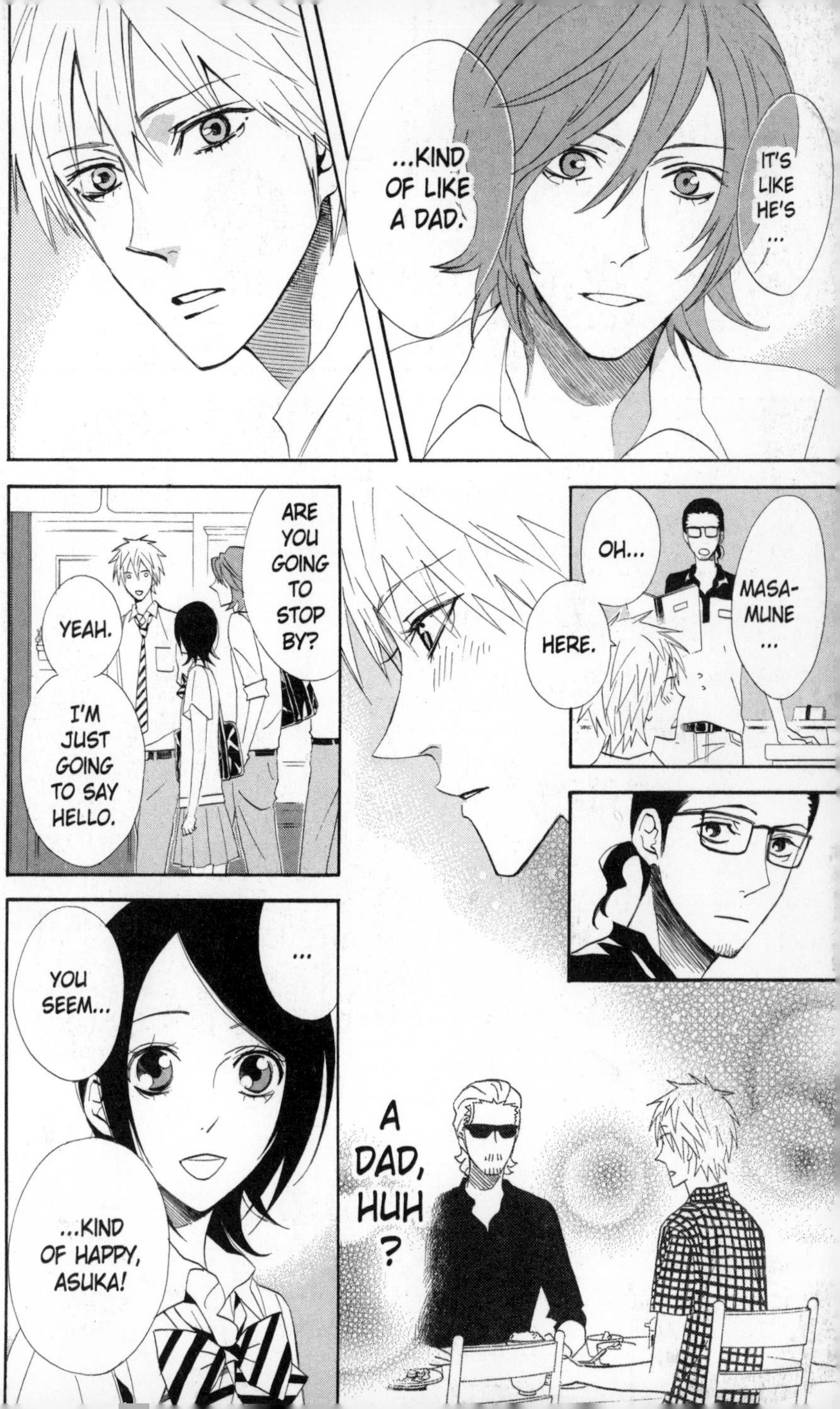
IT'S LIKE HE'S ...
...KIND OF LIKE A DAD.
MASA-MUNE ...
OH...
HERE.
ARE YOU GOING TO STOP BY?
YEAH.
I'M JUST GOING TO SAY HELLO.
A DAD, HUH?
...
YOU SEEM...
...KIND OF HAPPY, ASUKA!

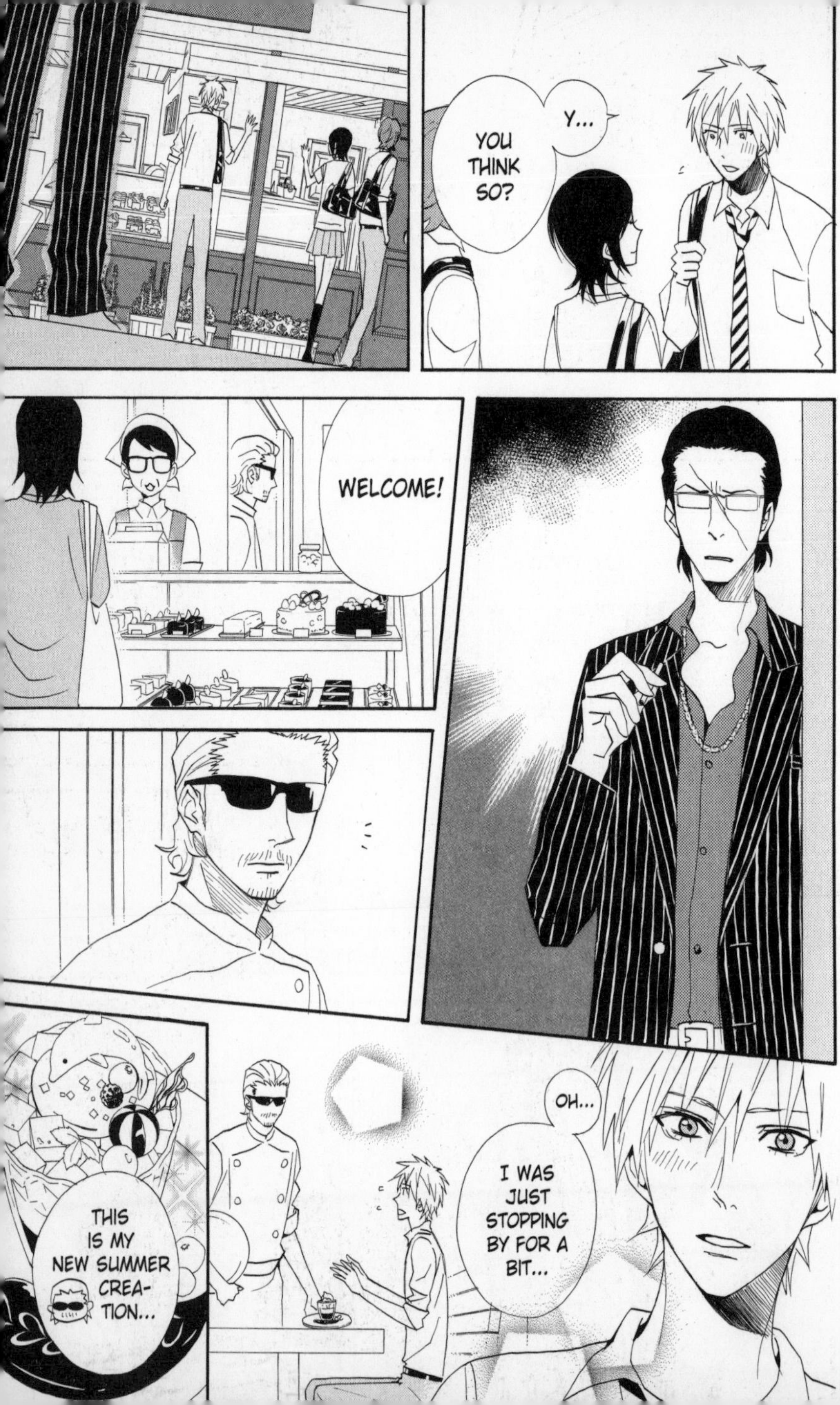
Y...
YOU THINK SO?
WELCOME!
OH...
I WAS JUST STOPPING BY FOR A BIT...
THIS IS MY NEW SUMMER CREA-TION...

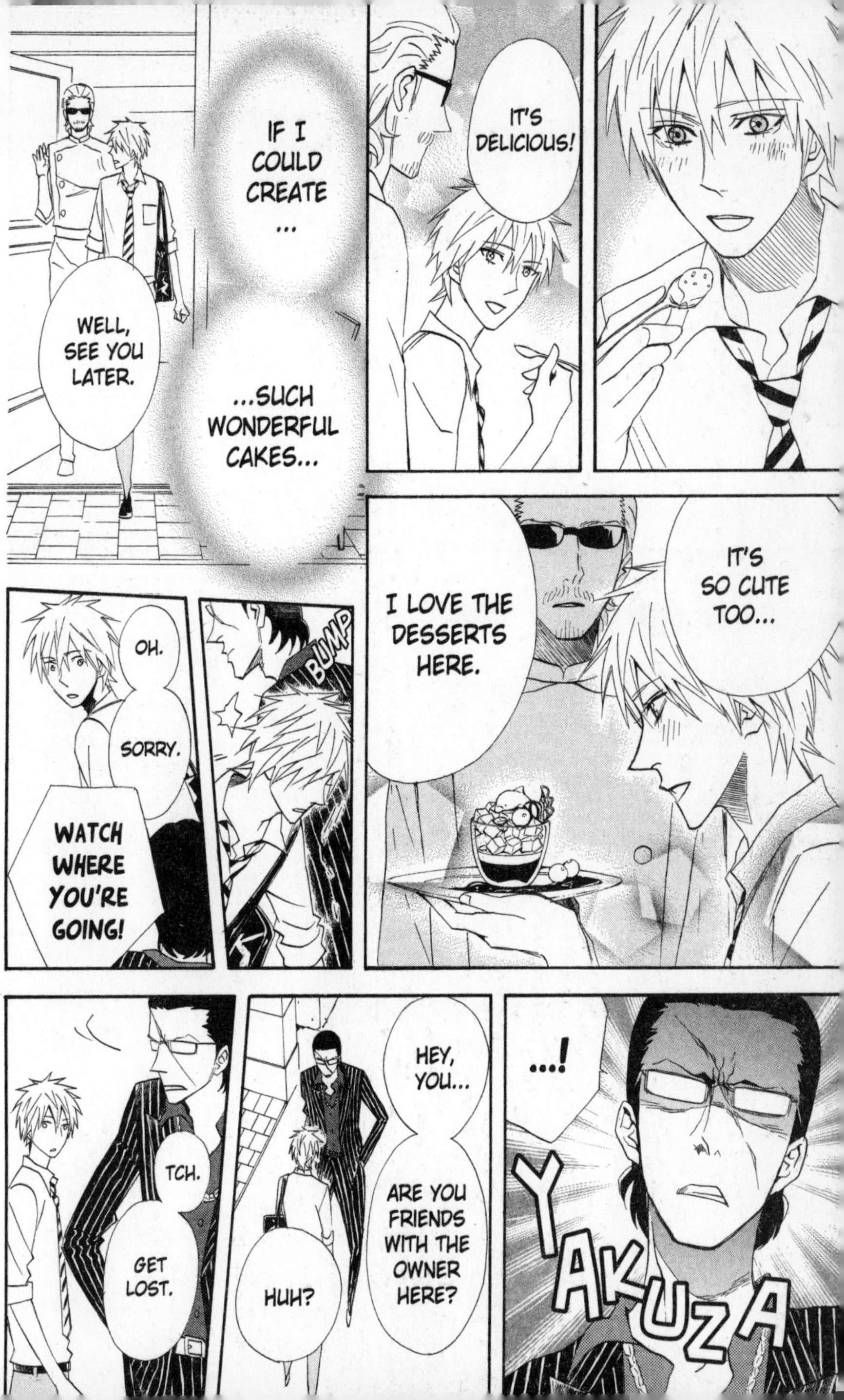
IT'S DELICIOUS!
IF I COULD CREATE ...
...SUCH WONDERFUL CAKES...
WELL, SEE YOU LATER.
IT'S SO CUTE TOO...
I LOVE THE DESSERTS HERE.
BUMP
OH.
SORRY.
WATCH WHERE YOU'RE GOING!
...!
YAKUZA
HEY, YOU...
ARE YOU FRIENDS WITH THE OWNER HERE?
HUH?
TCH.
GET LOST.

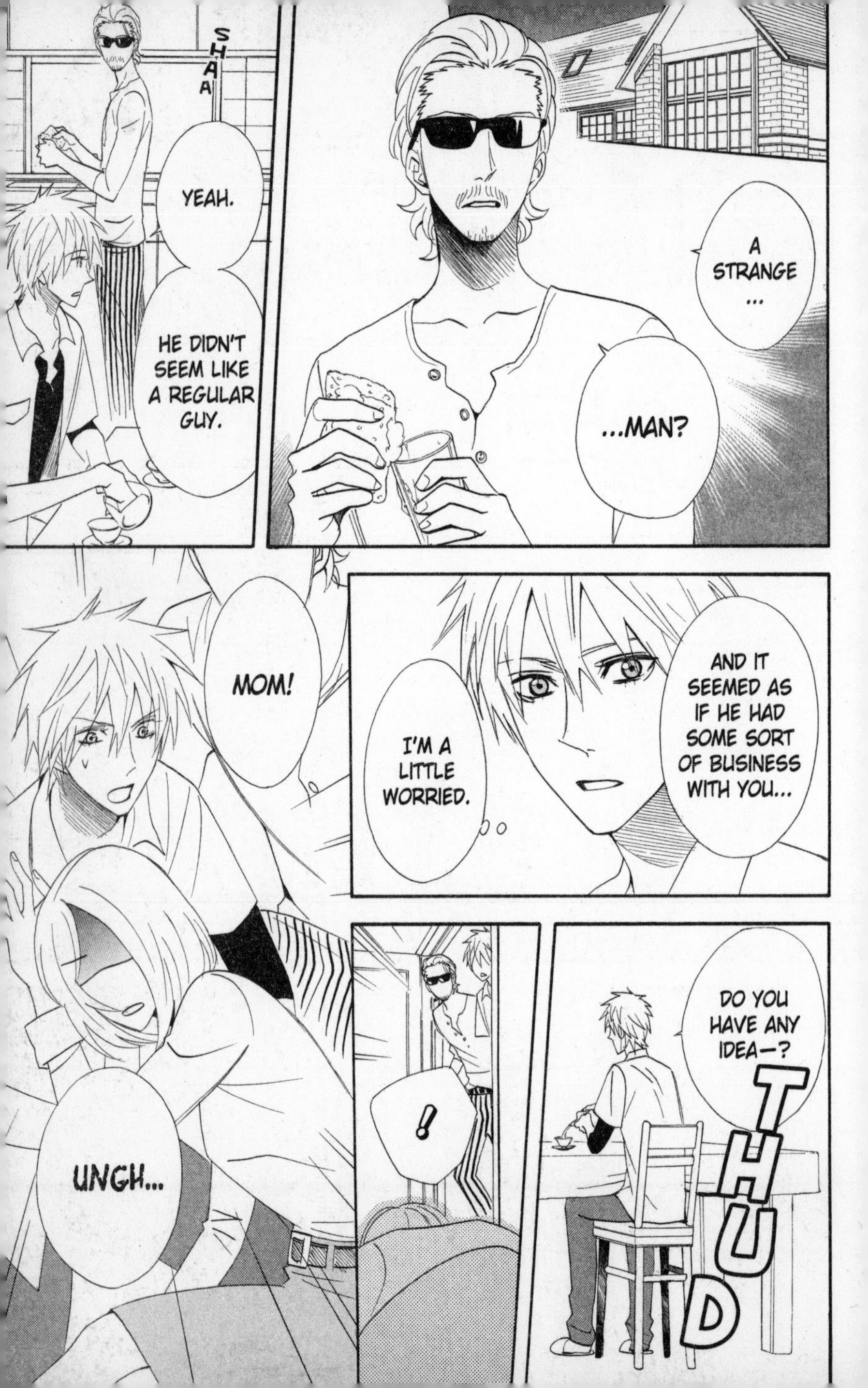
A STRANGE ...
...MAN?
SHAA
YEAH.
HE DIDN'T SEEM LIKE A REGULAR GUY.
AND IT SEEMED AS IF HE HAD SOME SORT OF BUSINESS WITH YOU...
I'M A LITTLE WORRIED.
DO YOU HAVE ANY IDEA—?
THUD
!
MOM!
UNGH...

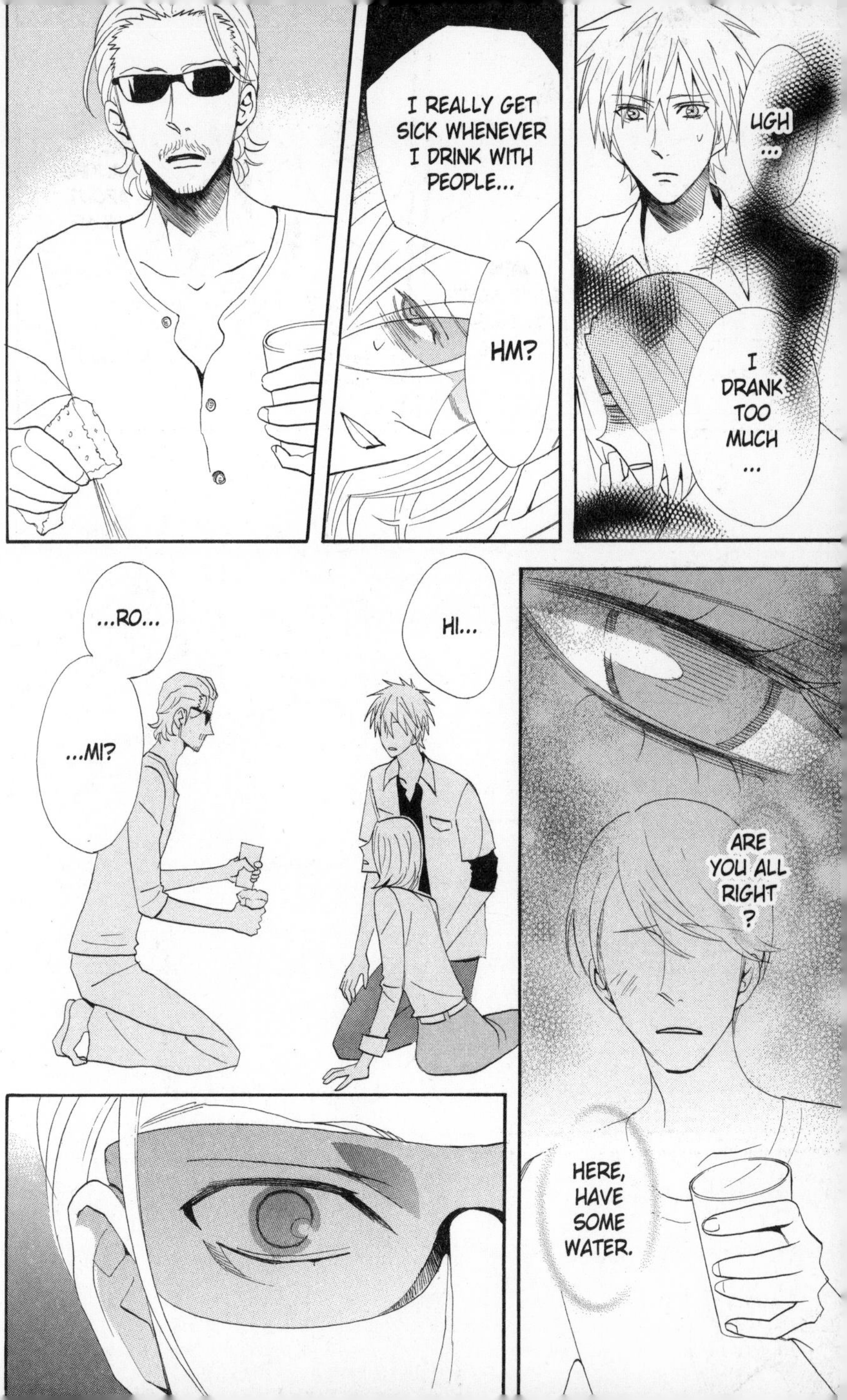
UGH ...
I DRANK TOO MUCH ...
I REALLY GET SICK WHENEVER I DRINK WITH PEOPLE...
HM?
ARE YOU ALL RIGHT ?
HERE, HAVE SOME WATER.
HI...
...RO...
...MI?

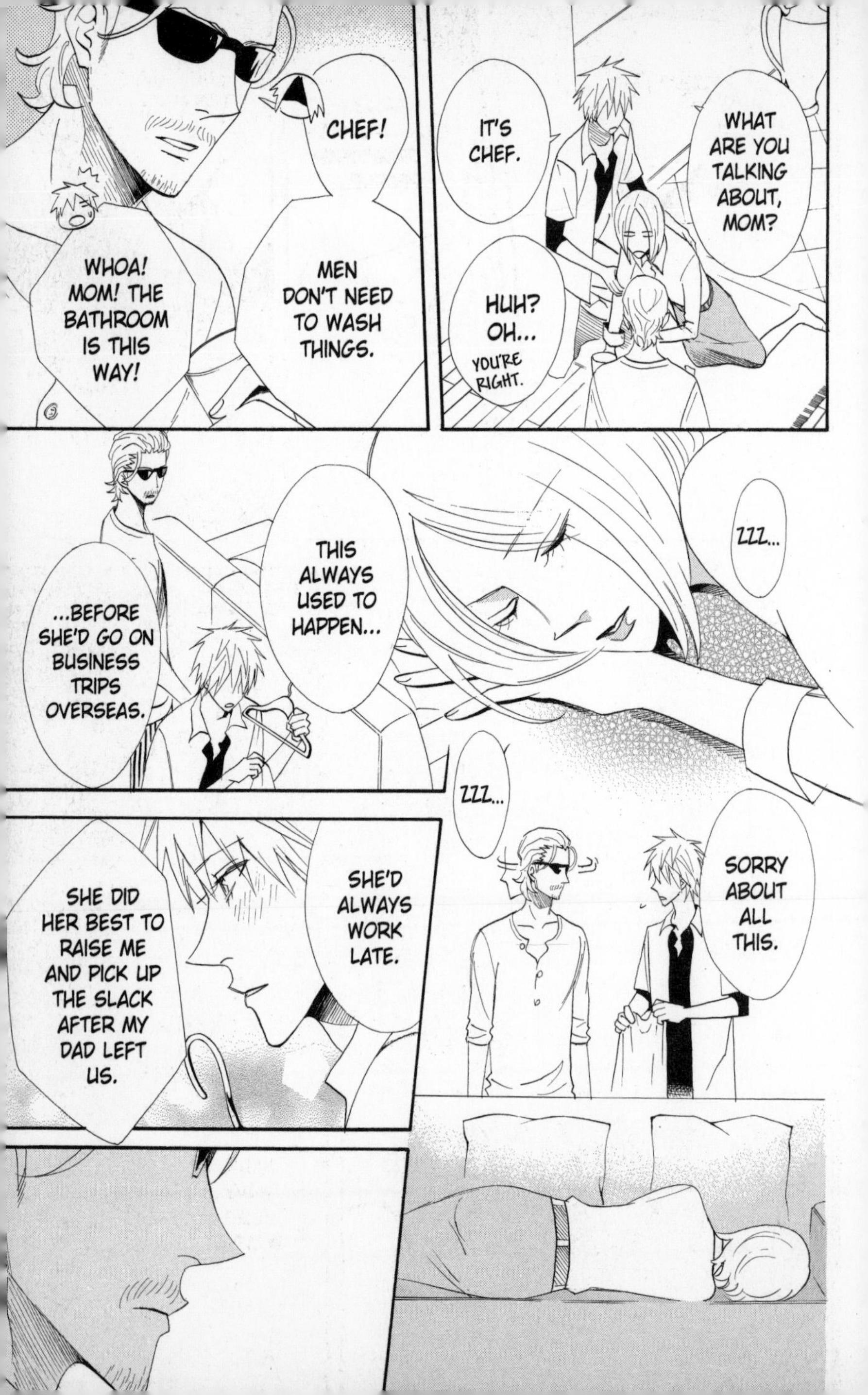
WHAT ARE YOU TALKING ABOUT, MOM?
IT'S CHEF.
HUH? OH... YOU'RE RIGHT.
CHEF!
MEN DON'T NEED TO WASH THINGS.
WHOA! MOM! THE BATHROOM IS THIS WAY!
ZZZ...
ZZZ...
SORRY ABOUT ALL THIS.
THIS ALWAYS USED TO HAPPEN...
...BEFORE SHE'D GO ON BUSINESS TRIPS OVERSEAS.
SHE'D ALWAYS WORK LATE.
SHE DID HER BEST TO RAISE ME AND PICK UP THE SLACK AFTER MY DAD LEFT US.

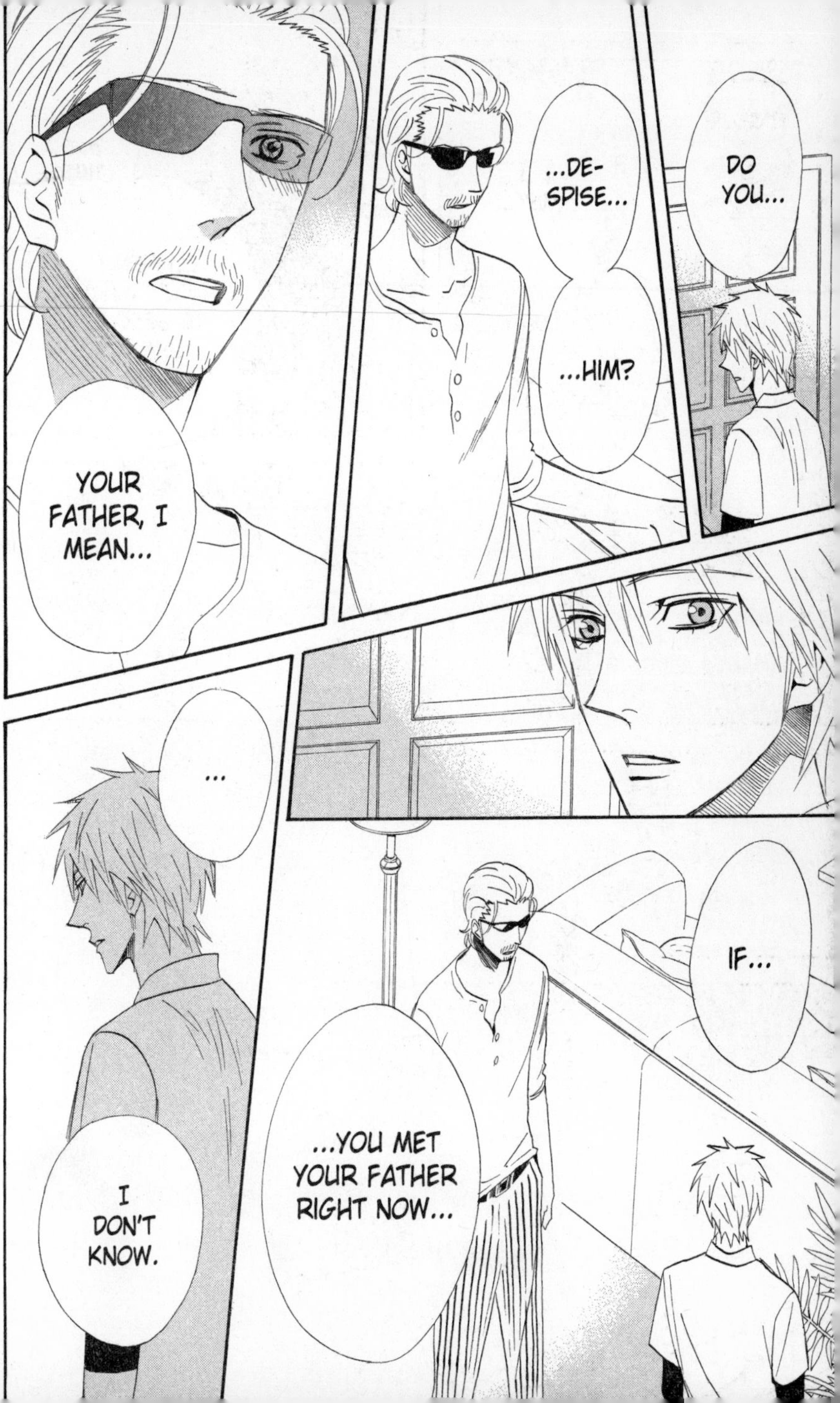
DO YOU...
...DE-SPISE...
...HIM?
YOUR FATHER, I MEAN...
IF...
...YOU MET YOUR FATHER RIGHT NOW...
...
I DON'T KNOW.

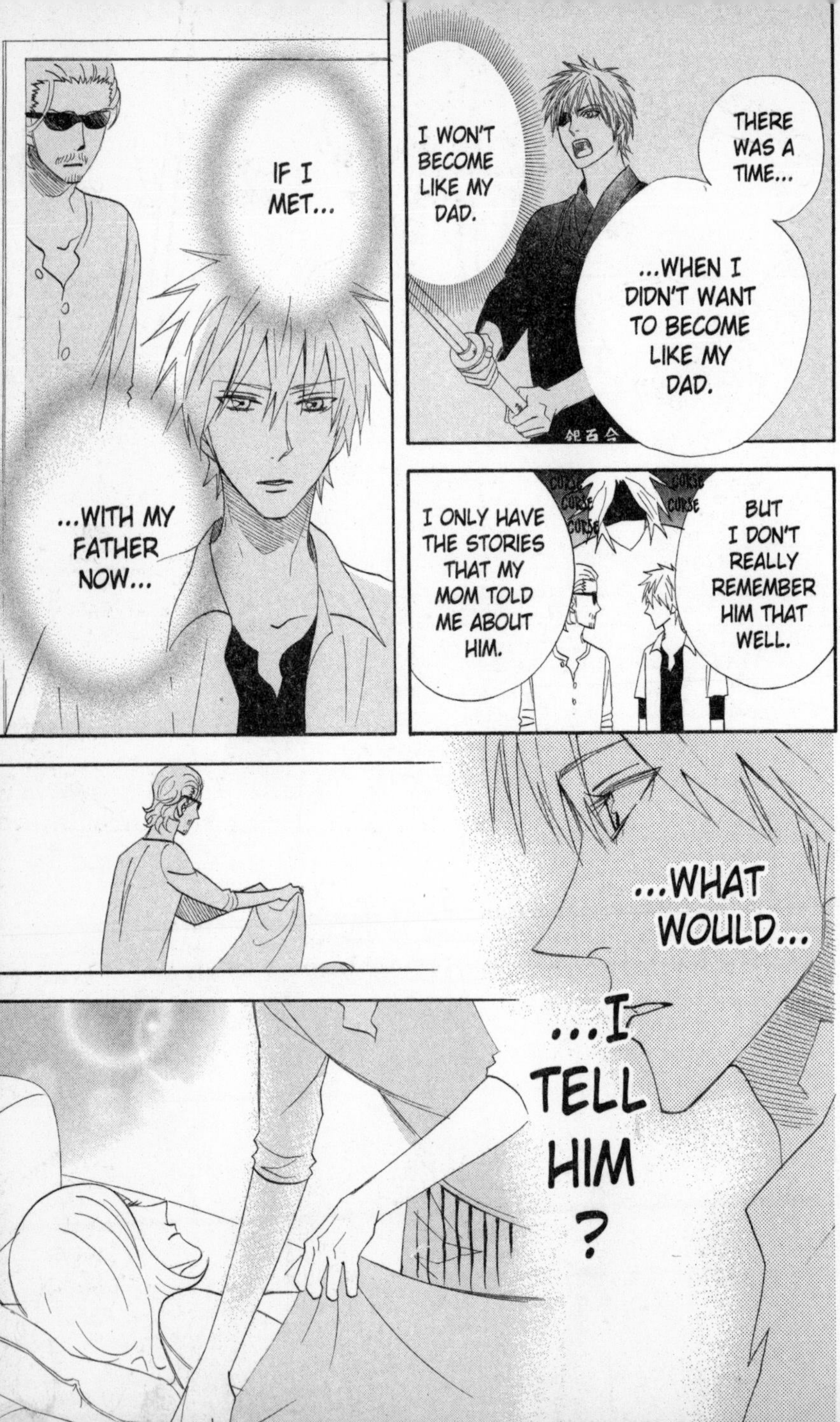
THERE WAS A TIME...
...WHEN I DIDN'T WANT TO BECOME LIKE MY DAD.
I WON'T BECOME LIKE MY DAD.
CURSE CURSE
CURSE CURSE CURSE
BUT I DON'T REALLY REMEMBER HIM THAT WELL.
I ONLY HAVE THE STORIES THAT MY MOM TOLD ME ABOUT HIM.
IF I MET...
...WITH MY FATHER NOW...
...WHAT WOULD...
...I TELL HIM?

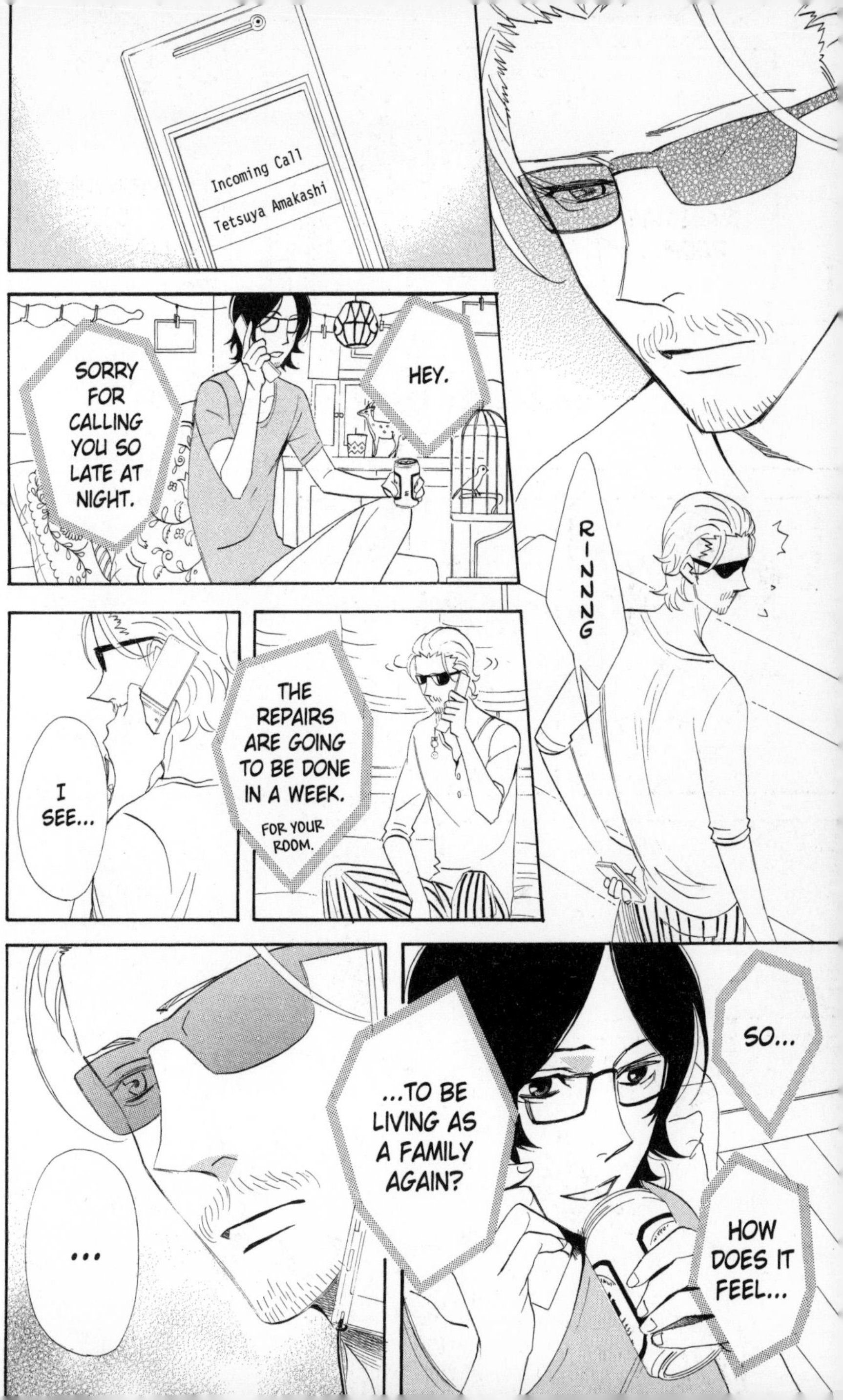
RINNNG
Incoming Call
Tetsuya Amakashi
HEY.
SORRY FOR CALLING YOU SO LATE AT NIGHT.
THE REPAIRS ARE GOING TO BE DONE IN A WEEK.
FOR YOUR ROOM.
I SEE...
SO...
HOW DOES IT FEEL...
...TO BE LIVING AS A FAMILY AGAIN?
...

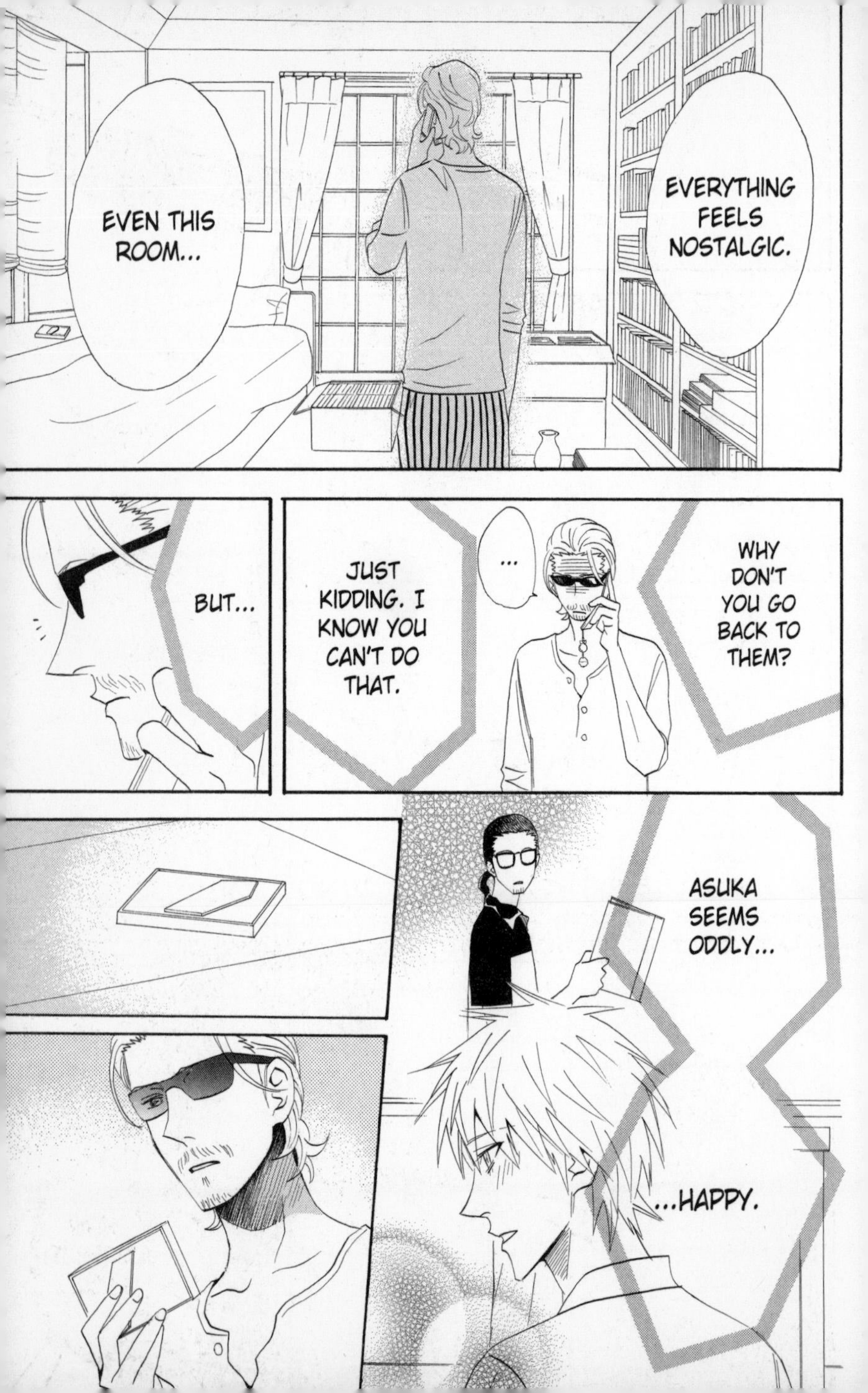
EVERYTHING FEELS NOSTALGIC.
EVEN THIS ROOM...
WHY DON'T YOU GO BACK TO THEM?
...
JUST KIDDING. I KNOW YOU CAN'T DO THAT.
BUT...
ASUKA SEEMS ODDLY...
...HAPPY.

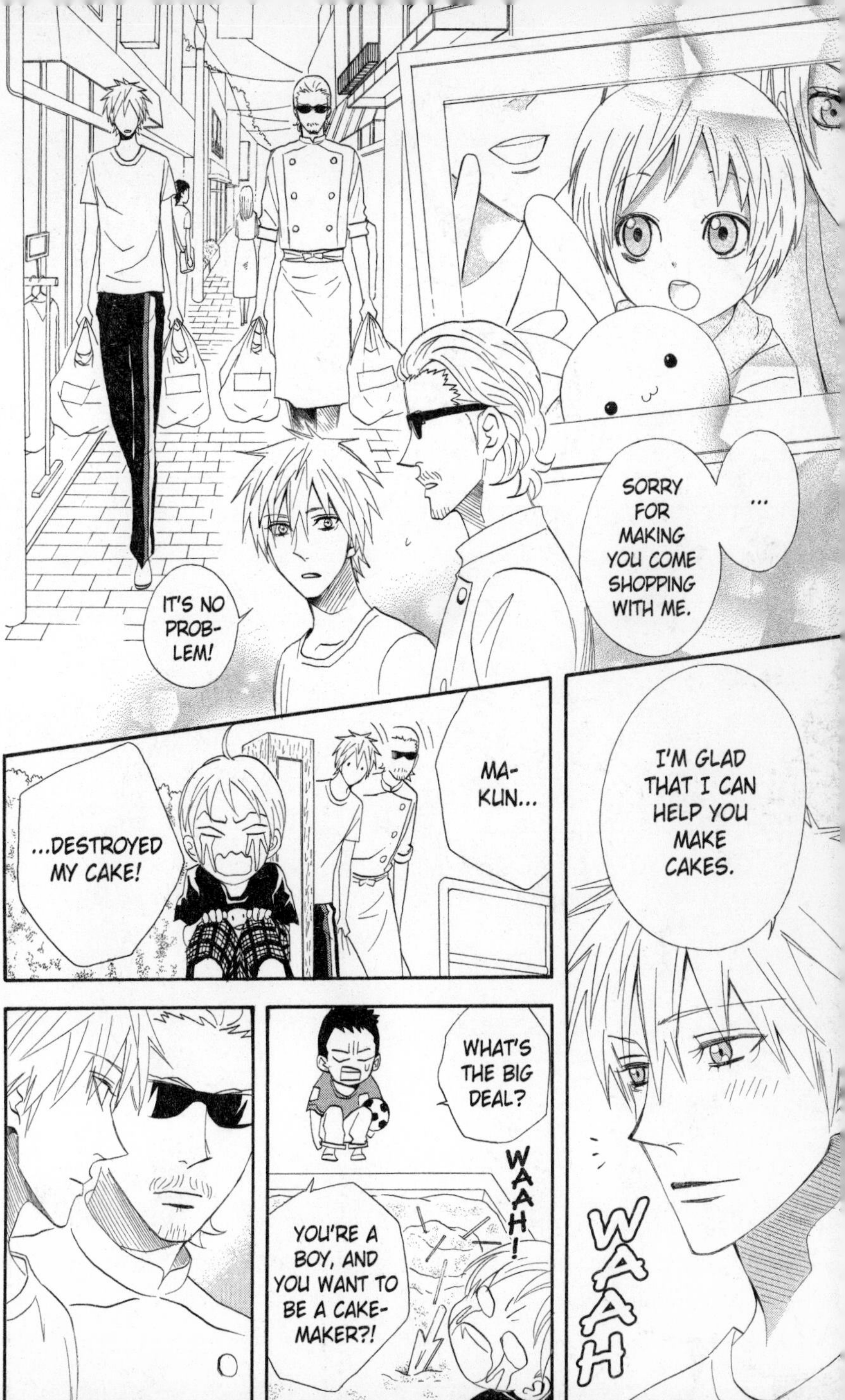
...
SORRY FOR MAKING YOU COME SHOPPING WITH ME.
IT'S NO PROB-LEM!
I'M GLAD THAT I CAN HELP YOU MAKE CAKES.
WAAH
MA-KUN...
...DESTROYED MY CAKE!
WHAT'S THE BIG DEAL?
WAAH!
YOU'RE A BOY, AND YOU WANT TO BE A CAKE-MAKER?!

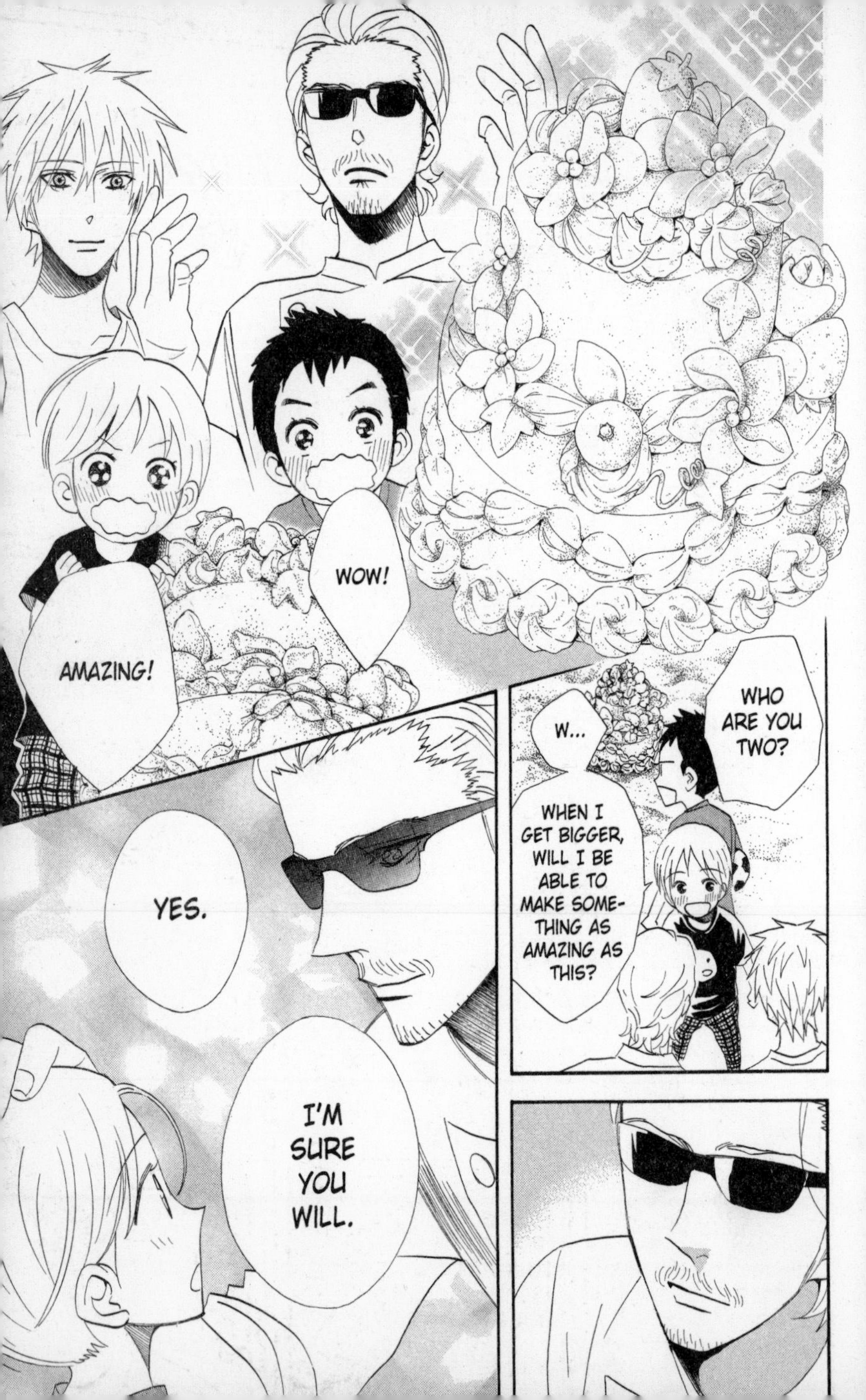
WOW!
AMAZING!
WHO ARE YOU TWO?
W...
WHEN I GET BIGGER, WILL I BE ABLE TO MAKE SOME-THING AS AMAZING AS THIS?
YES.
I'M SURE YOU WILL.

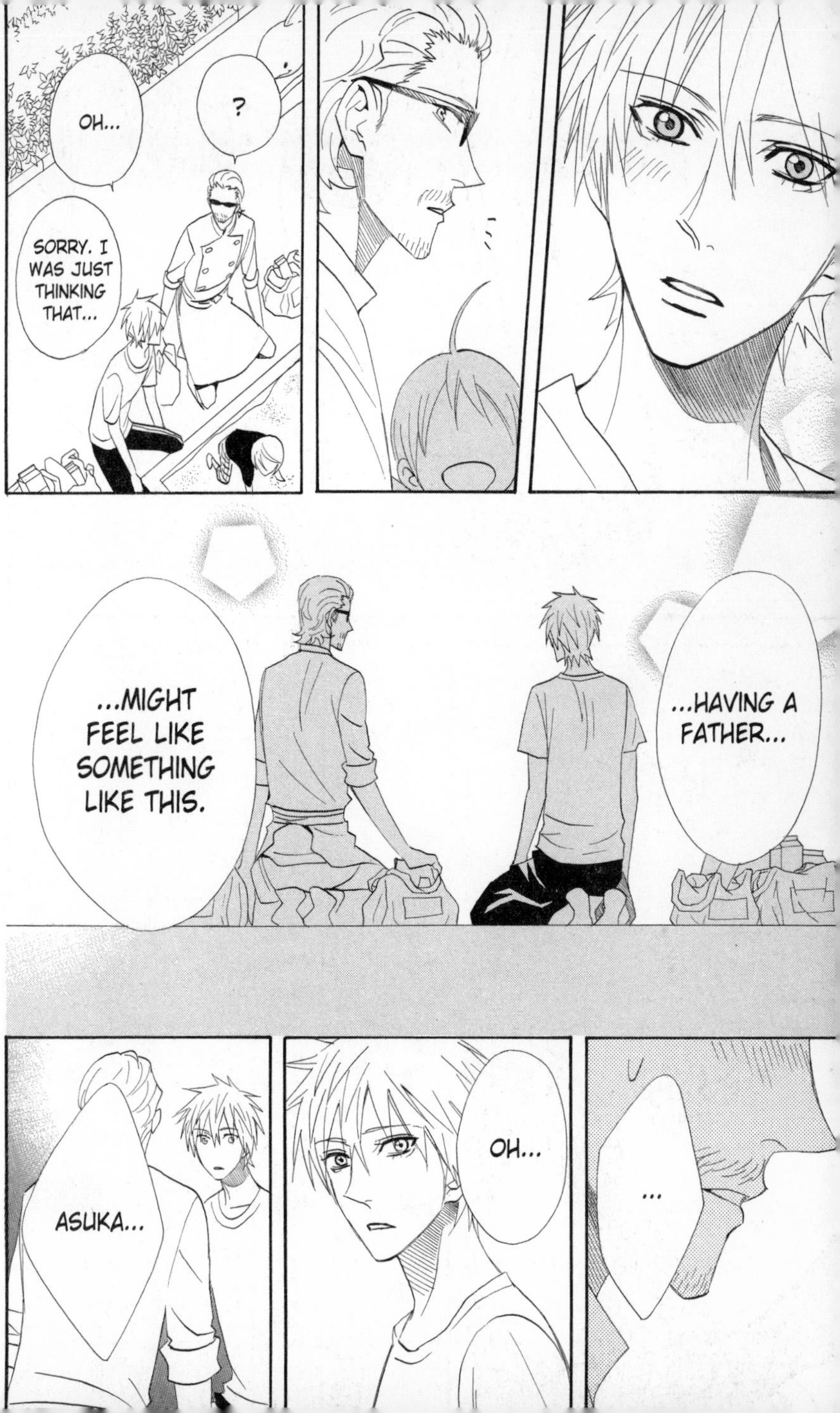
?
OH...
SORRY. I WAS JUST THINKING THAT...
...HAVING A FATHER...
...MIGHT FEEL LIKE SOMETHING LIKE THIS.
...
OH...
ASUKA...

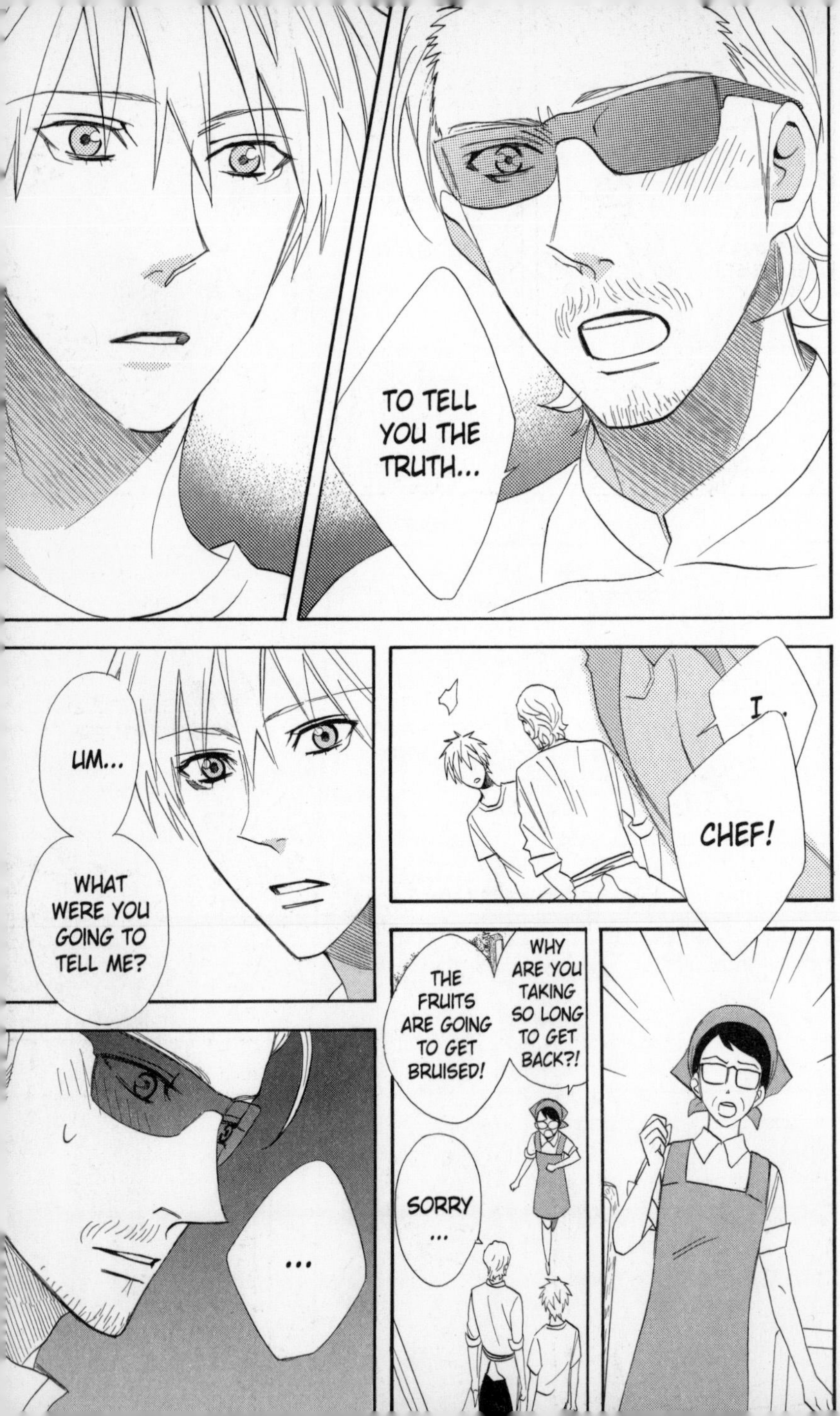
TO TELL YOU THE TRUTH...
I...
CHEF!
UM...
WHAT WERE YOU GOING TO TELL ME?
WHY ARE YOU TAKING SO LONG TO GET BACK?!
THE FRUITS ARE GOING TO GET BRUISED!
SORRY ...
...

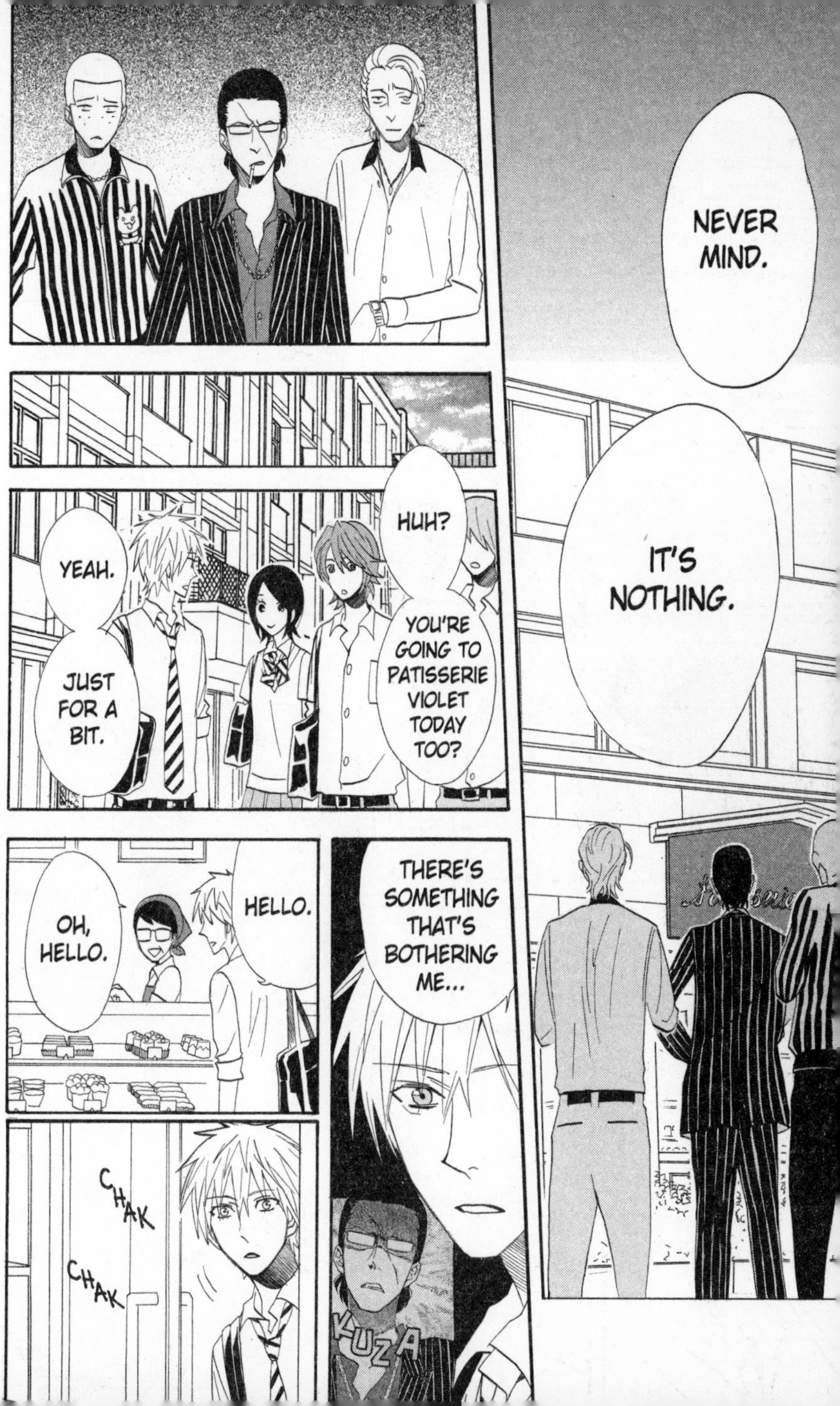
NEVER MIND.
IT'S NOTHING.
HUH?
YOU'RE GOING TO PATISSERIE VIOLET TODAY TOO?
YEAH.
JUST FOR A BIT.
THERE'S SOMETHING THAT'S BOTHERING ME...
HELLO.
OH, HELLO.
CHAK
CHAK

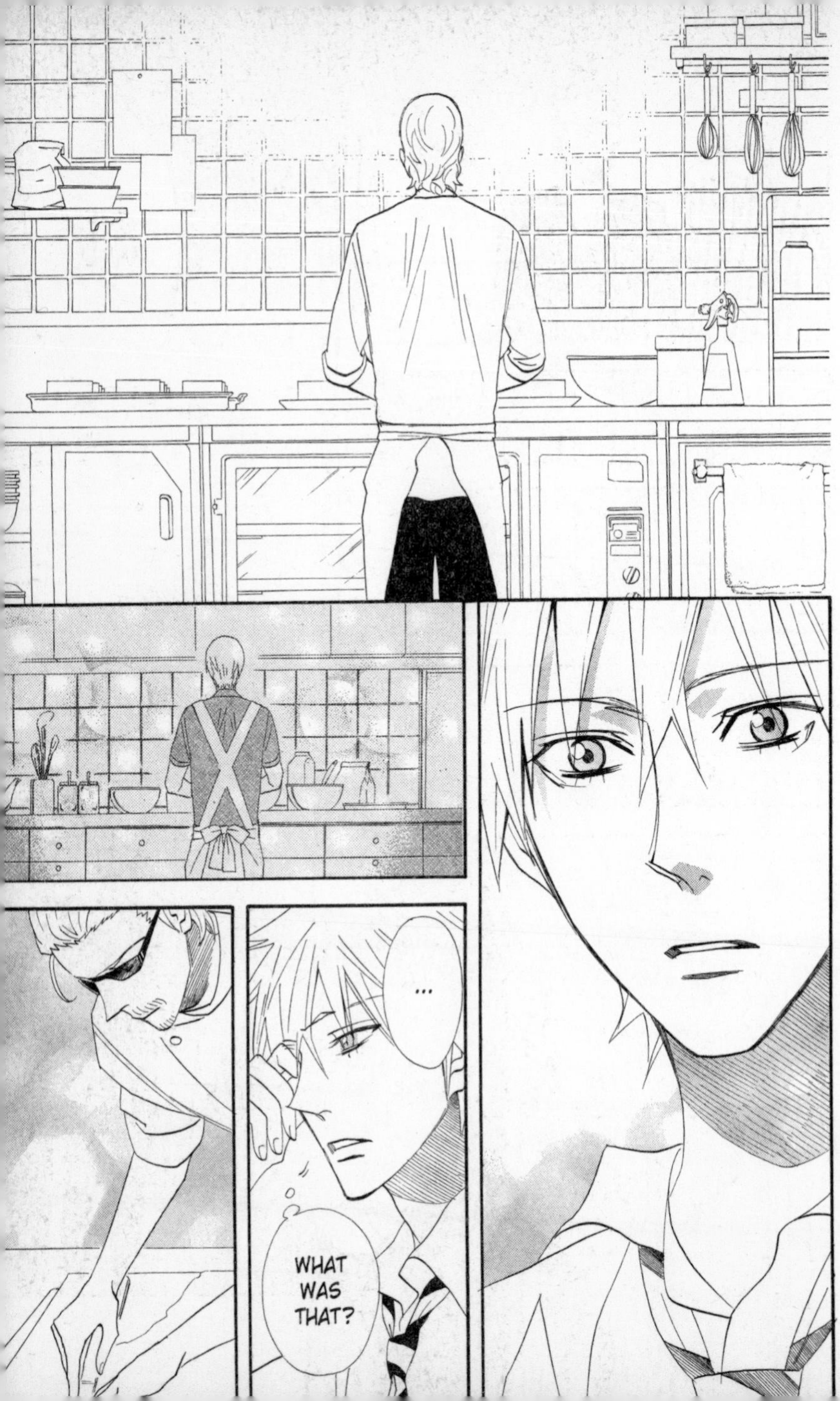
...
WHAT WAS THAT?

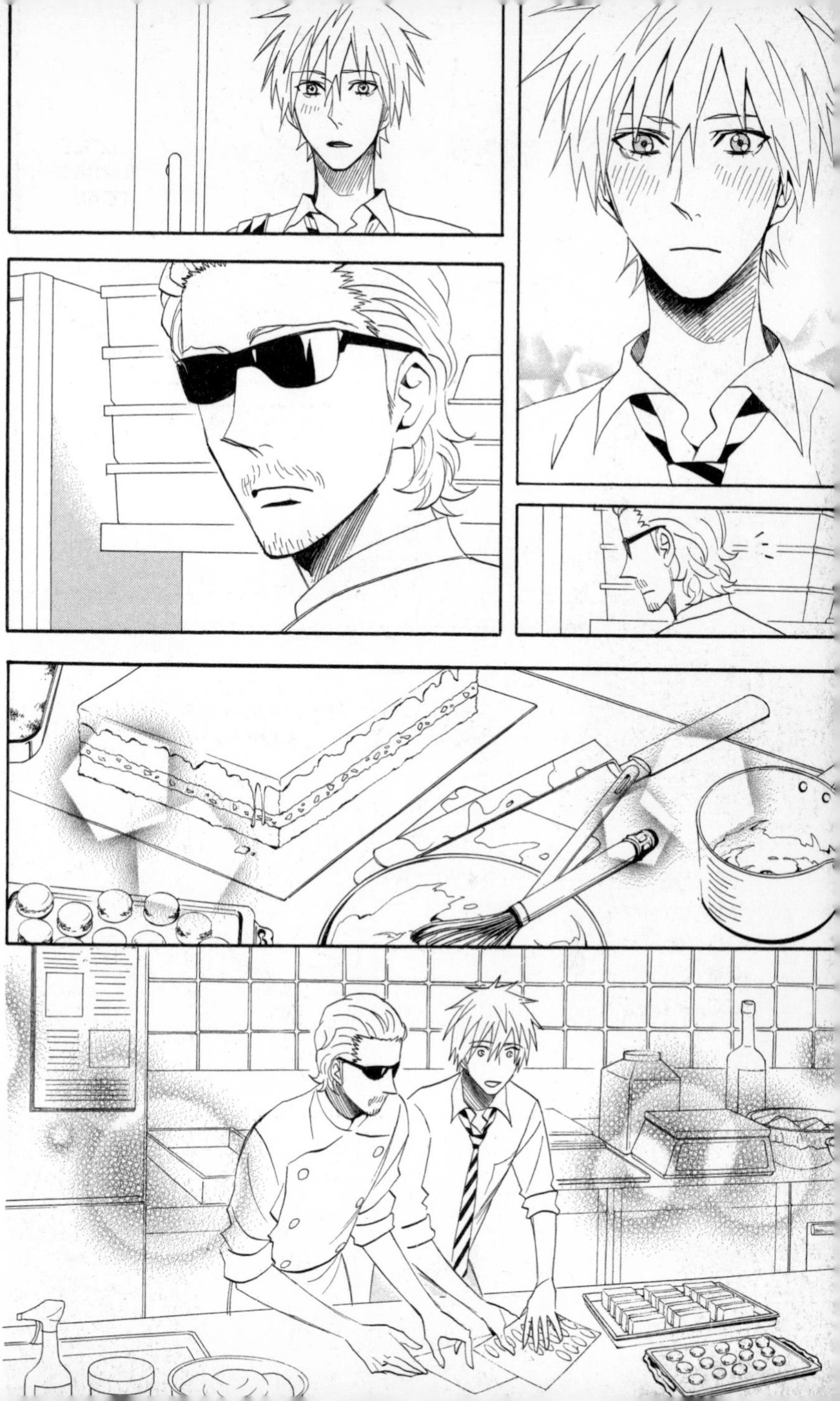

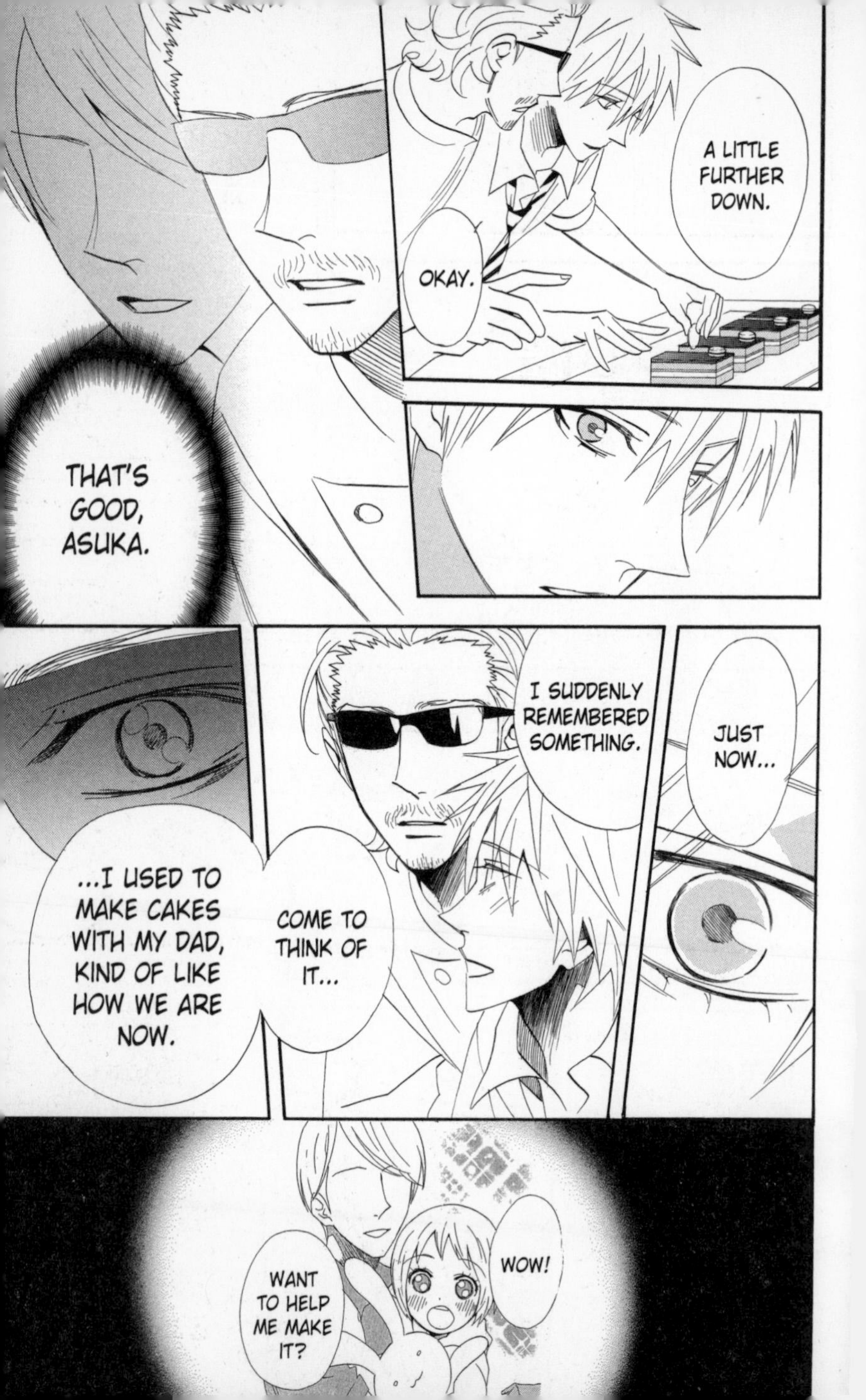
A LITTLE FURTHER DOWN.
OKAY.
THAT'S GOOD, ASUKA.
JUST NOW...
I SUDDENLY REMEMBERED SOMETHING.
COME TO THINK OF IT...
...I USED TO MAKE CAKES WITH MY DAD, KIND OF LIKE HOW WE ARE NOW.
WOW!
WANT TO HELP ME MAKE IT?

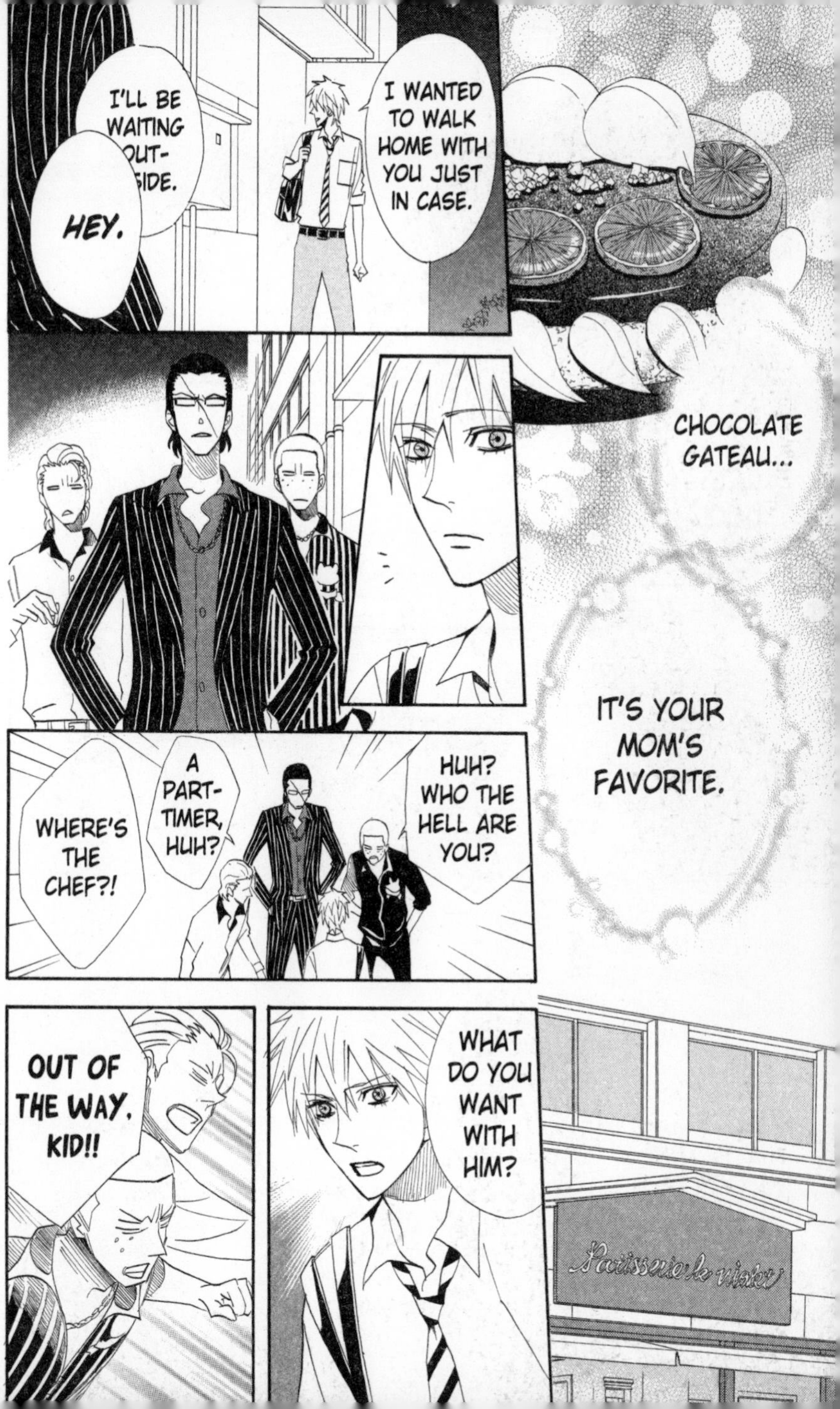
CHOCOLATE GATEAU...
IT'S YOUR MOM'S FAVORITE.
I WANTED TO WALK HOME WITH YOU JUST IN CASE.
I'LL BE WAITING OUTSIDE.
HEY.
HUH? WHO THE HELL ARE YOU?
A PART-TIMER, HUH?
WHERE'S THE CHEF?!
WHAT DO YOU WANT WITH HIM?
OUT OF THE WAY, KID!!

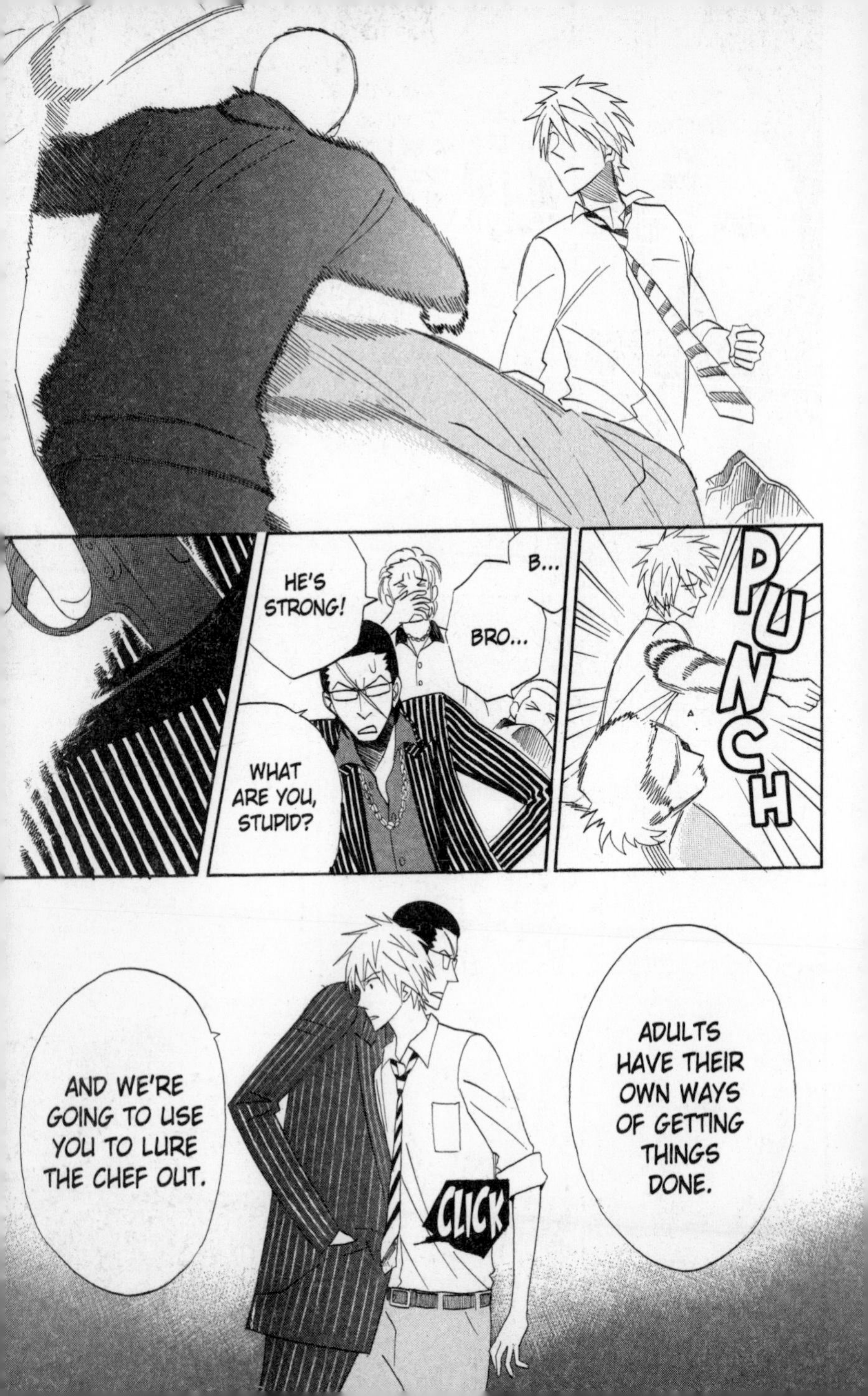
PUNCH
B...
BRO...
HE'S STRONG!
WHAT ARE YOU, STUPID?
ADULTS HAVE THEIR OWN WAYS OF GETTING THINGS DONE.
CLICK
AND WE'RE GOING TO USE YOU TO LURE THE CHEF OUT.

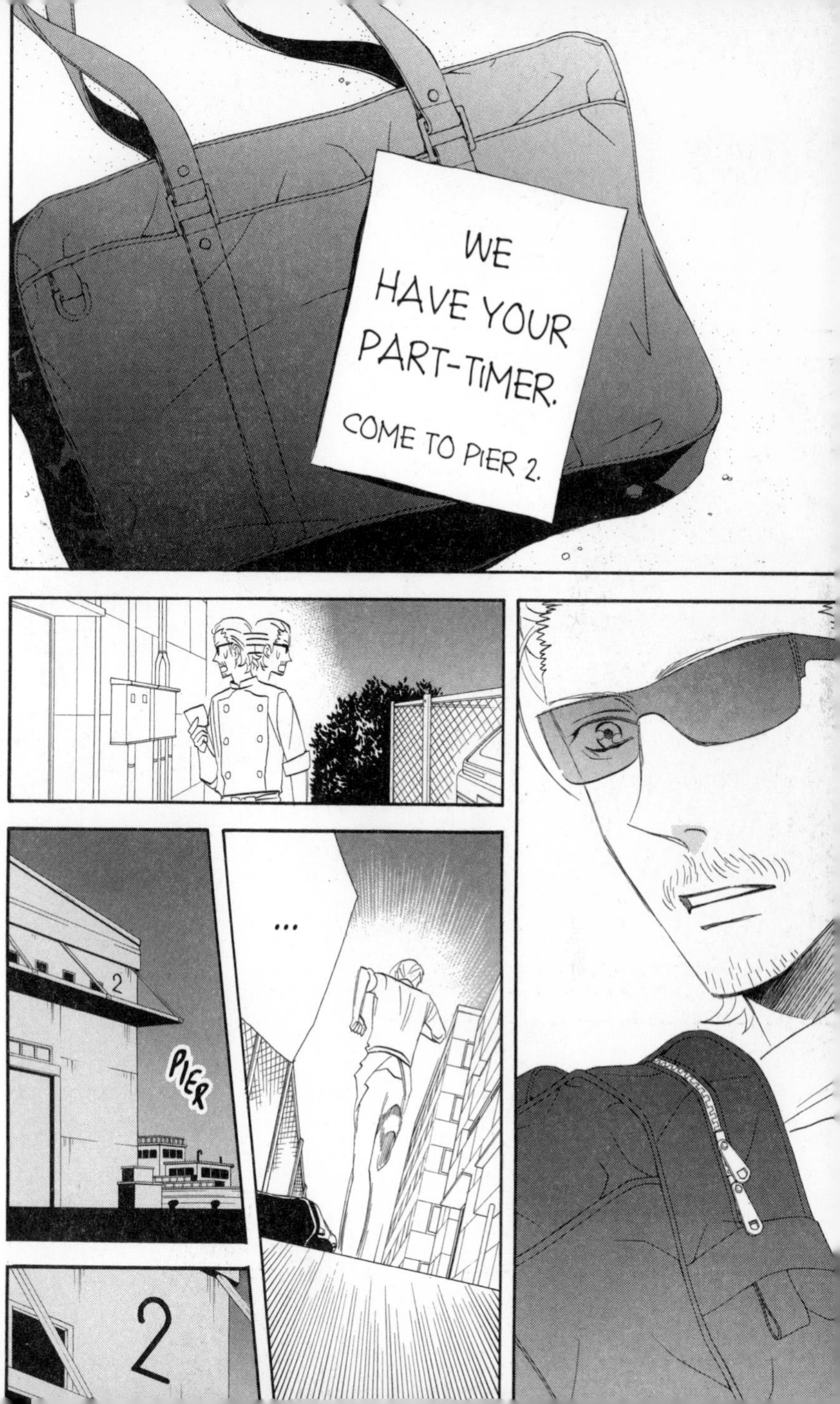
WE HAVE YOUR PART-TIMER.
COME TO PIER 2.
...
PIER

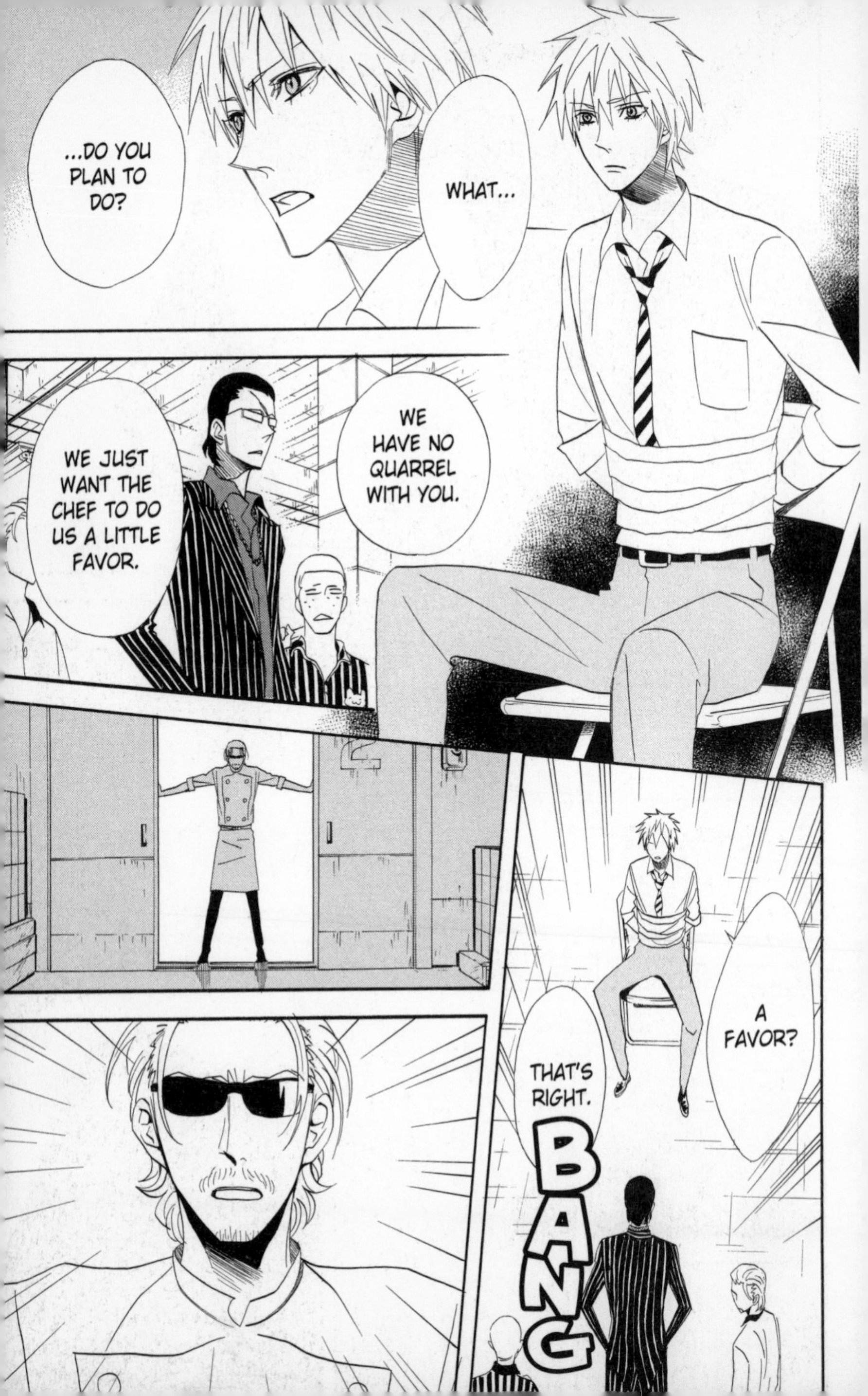
WHAT...
...DO YOU PLAN TO DO?
WE HAVE NO QUARREL WITH YOU.
WE JUST WANT THE CHEF TO DO US A LITTLE FAVOR.
A FAVOR?
THAT'S RIGHT.
BANG

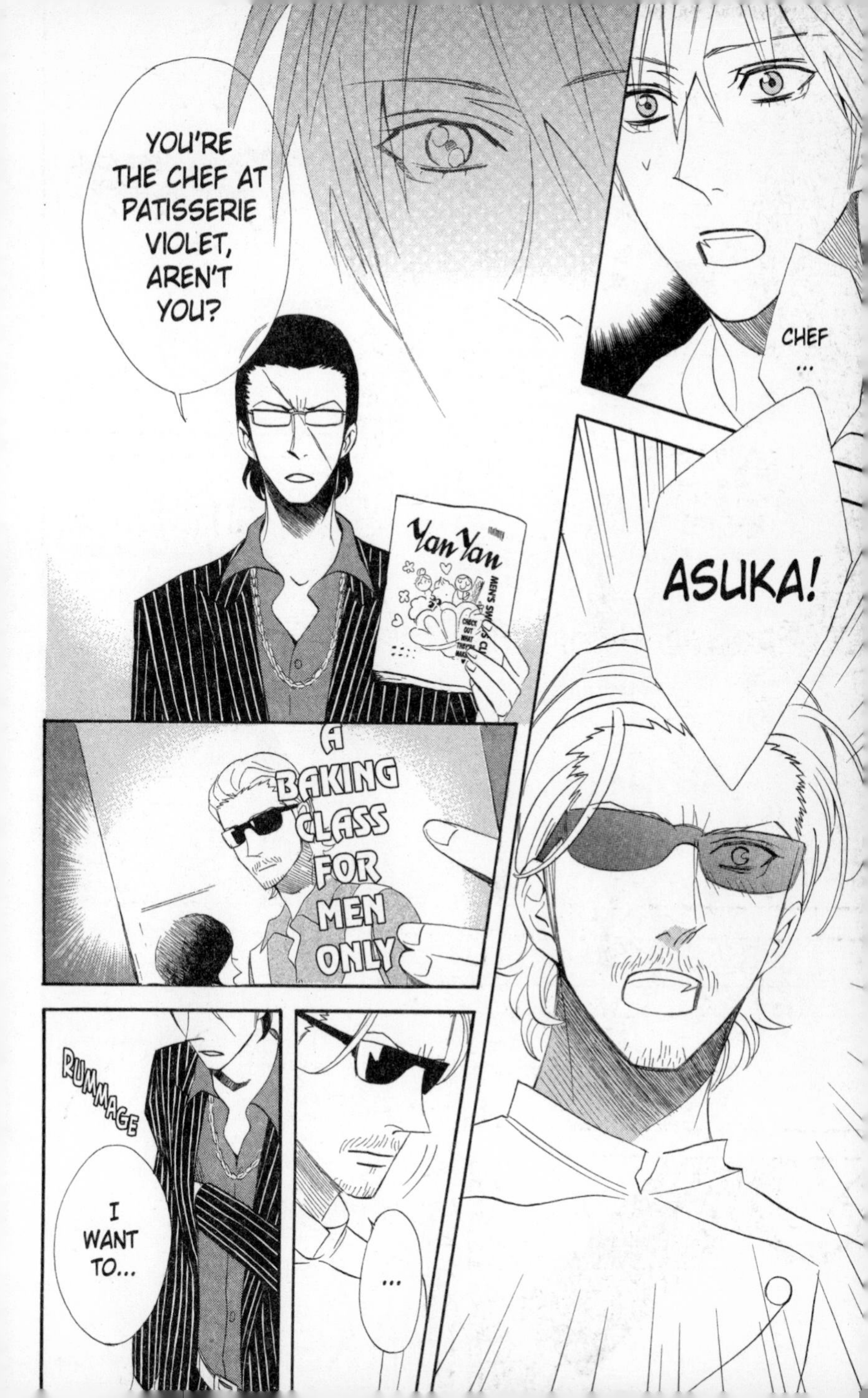
CHEF ...
ASUKA!
YOU'RE THE CHEF AT PATISSERIE VIOLET, AREN'T YOU?
Yan Yan
A BAKING CLASS FOR MEN ONLY
...
RUMMAGE
I WANT TO...

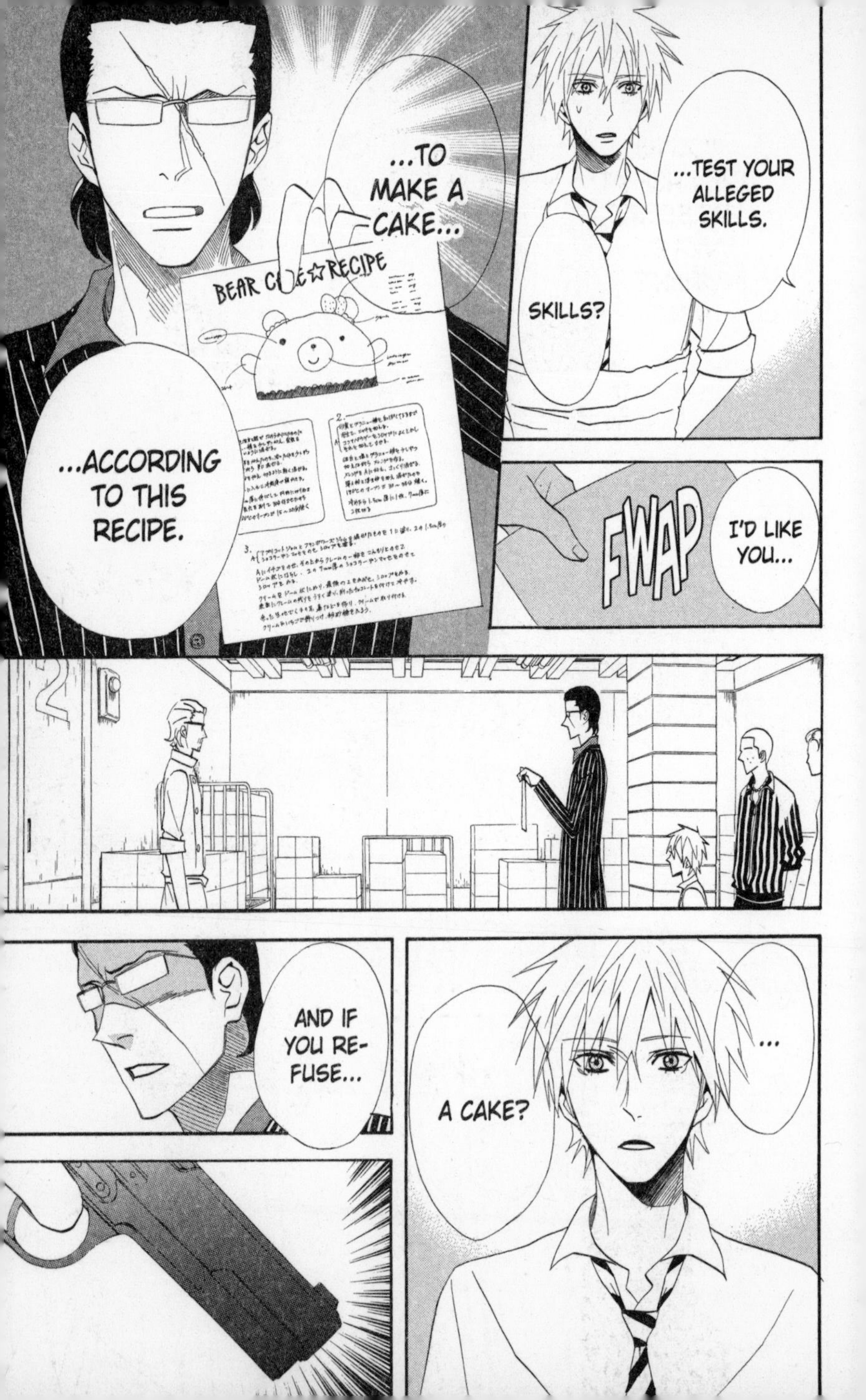
...TEST YOUR ALLEGED SKILLS.
SKILLS?
I'D LIKE YOU...
FWAP
...TO MAKE A CAKE...
BEAR C KE☆RECIPE
...ACCORDING TO THIS RECIPE.
...
A CAKE?
AND IF YOU RE-FUSE...

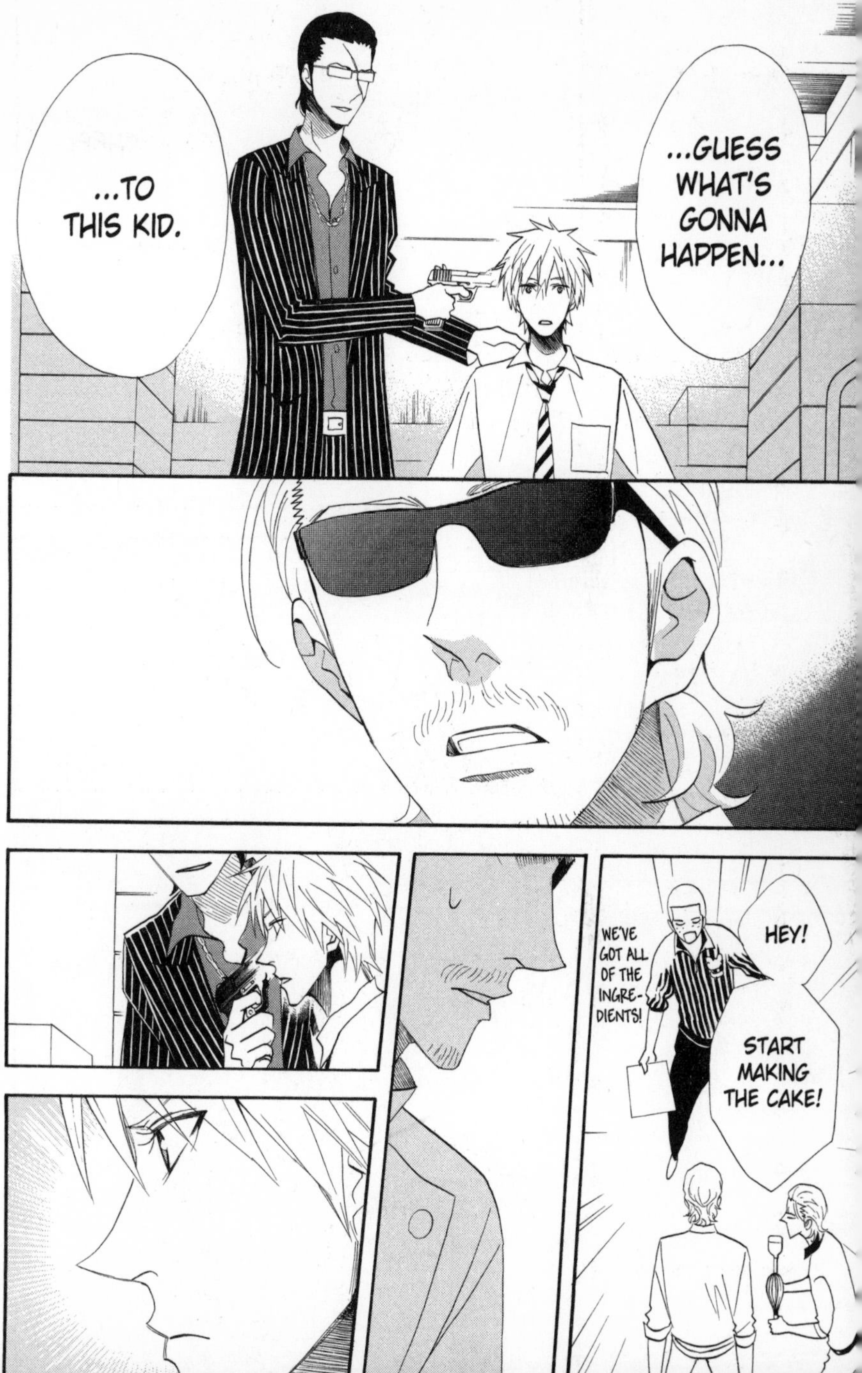
...GUESS WHAT'S GONNA HAPPEN...
...TO THIS KID.
HEY!
WE'VE GOT ALL OF THE INGRE-DIENTS!
START MAKING THE CAKE!

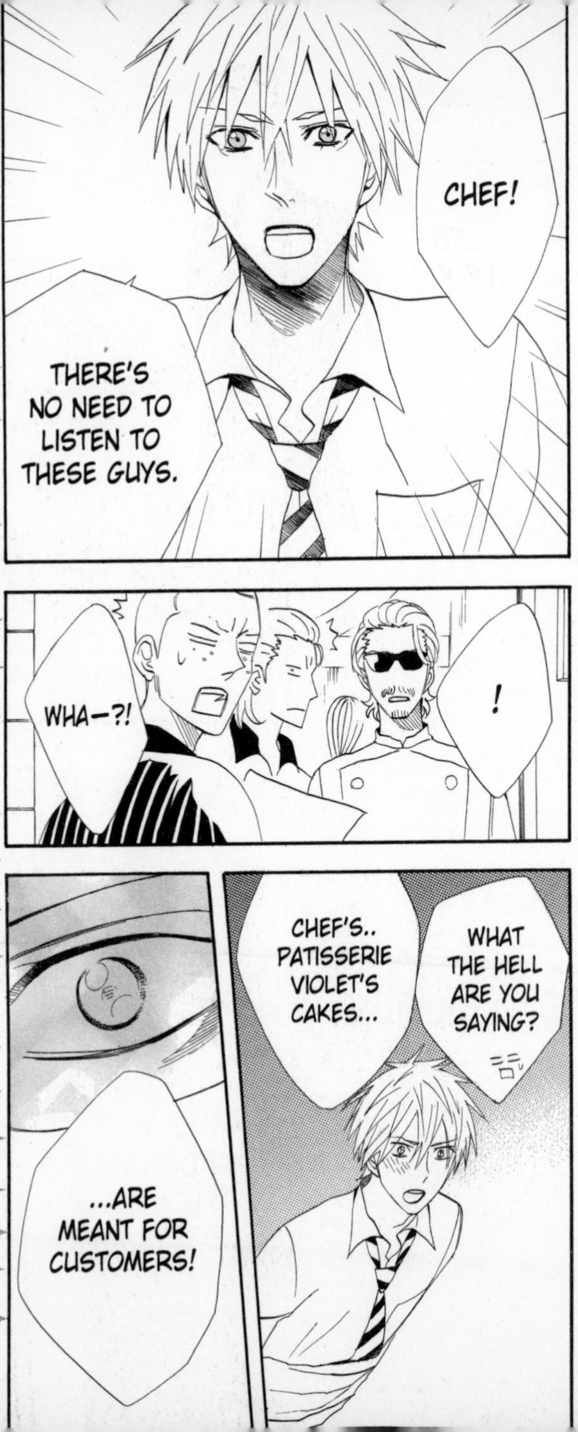
CHEF!
THERE'S NO NEED TO LISTEN TO THESE GUYS.
!
WHA—?!
WHAT THE HELL ARE YOU SAYING?
CHEF'S.. PATISSERIE VIOLET'S CAKES...
...ARE MEANT FOR CUSTOMERS!

Umm...
Whenever I depict criminals, I always create ones full of attitude.

I've wanted to do the story in this chapter and the next chapter for a long time. I had fun doing it.

I'm glad I got to draw Asuka's parents when they were in school.

I even wanted to do an entire chapter about the past, but I resisted the urge.

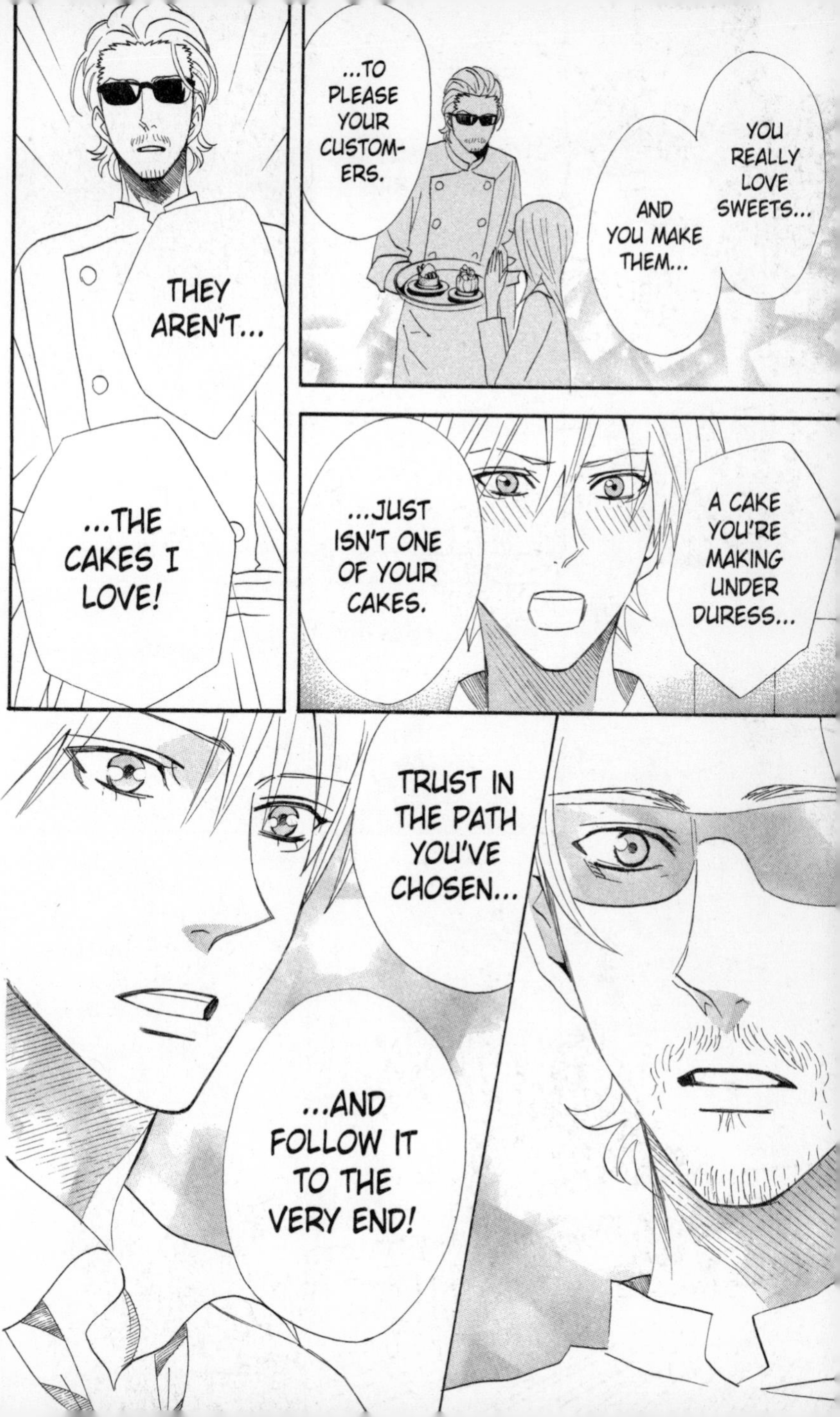
YOU REALLY LOVE SWEETS...
AND YOU MAKE THEM...
...TO PLEASE YOUR CUSTOM-ERS.
A CAKE YOU'RE MAKING UNDER DURESS...
...JUST ISN'T ONE OF YOUR CAKES.
THEY AREN'T...
...THE CAKES I LOVE!
TRUST IN THE PATH YOU'VE CHOSEN...
...AND FOLLOW IT TO THE VERY END!

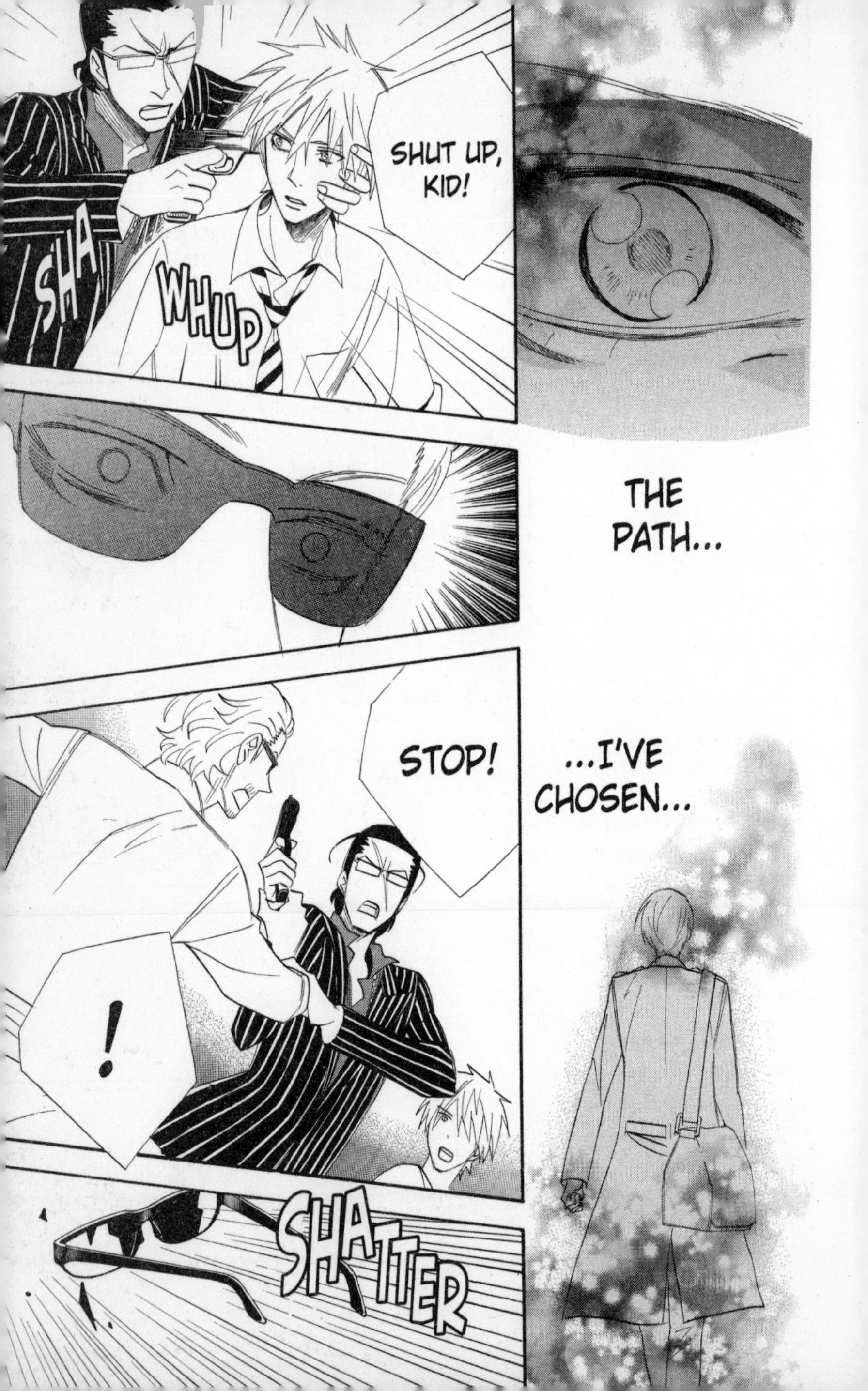
THE PATH...
...I'VE CHOSEN...
SHUT UP, KID!
SHA
WHUP
STOP!
!
SHATTER

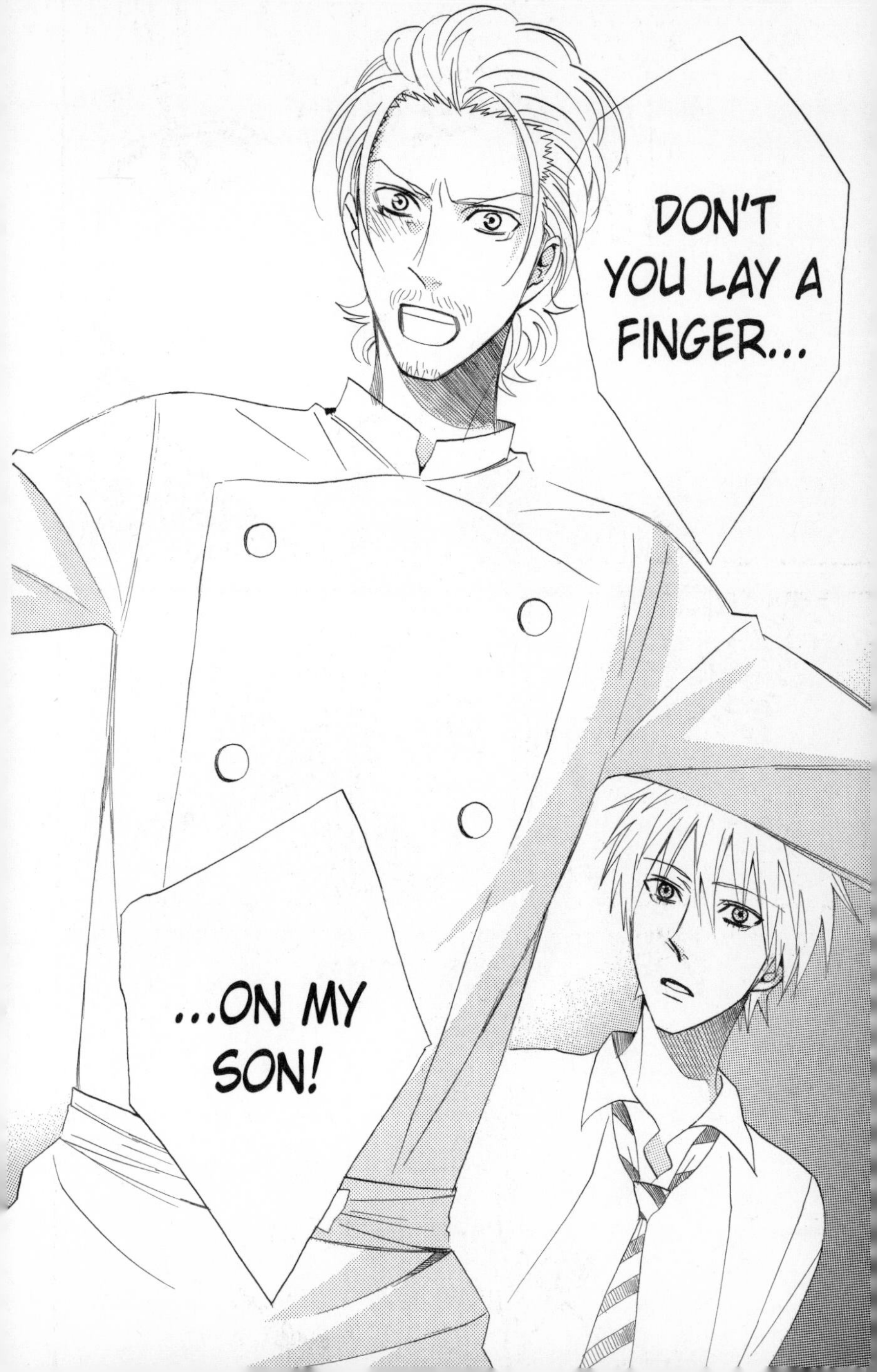
DON'T YOU LAY A FINGER...
...ON MY SON!

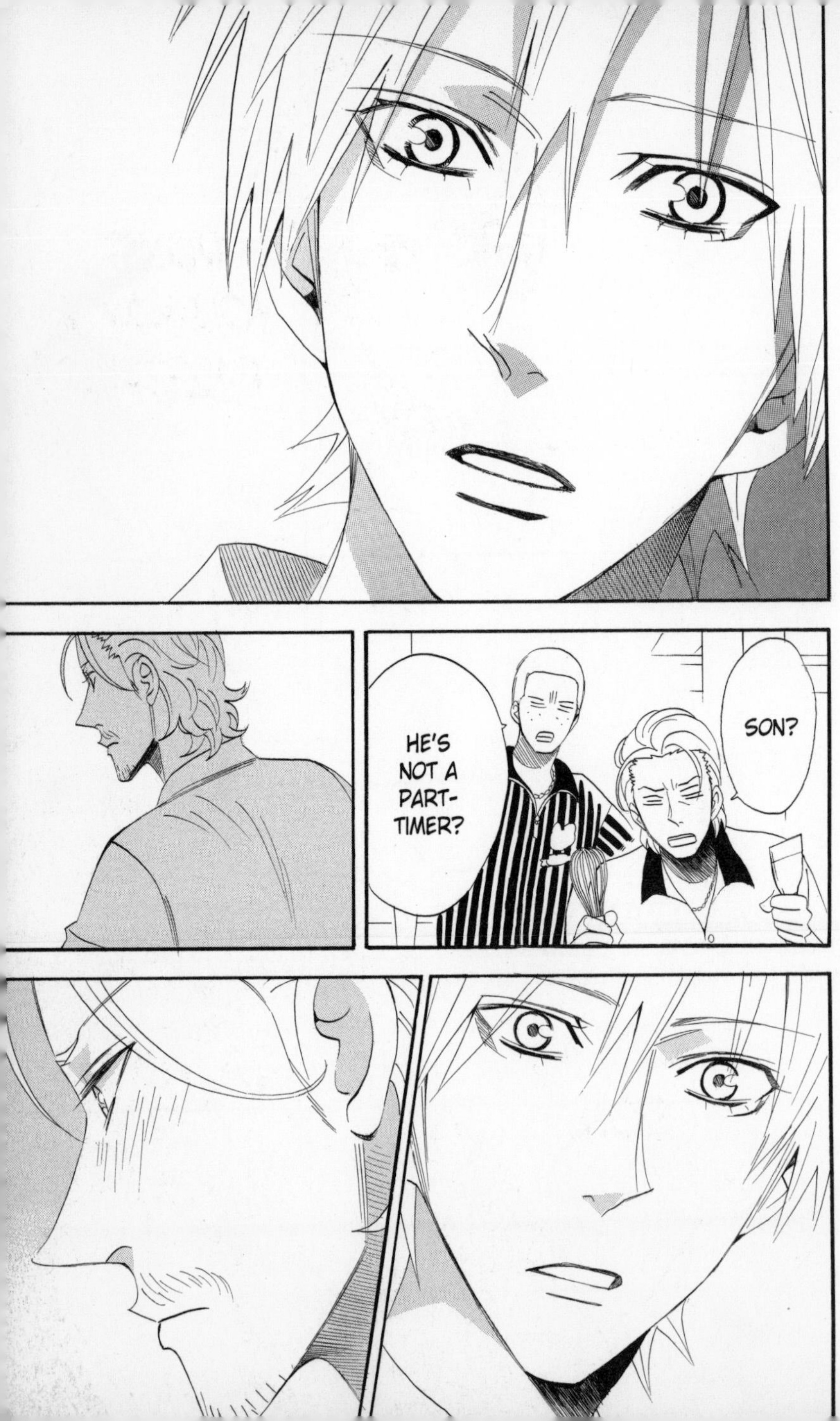
SON?
HE'S NOT A PART-TIMER?

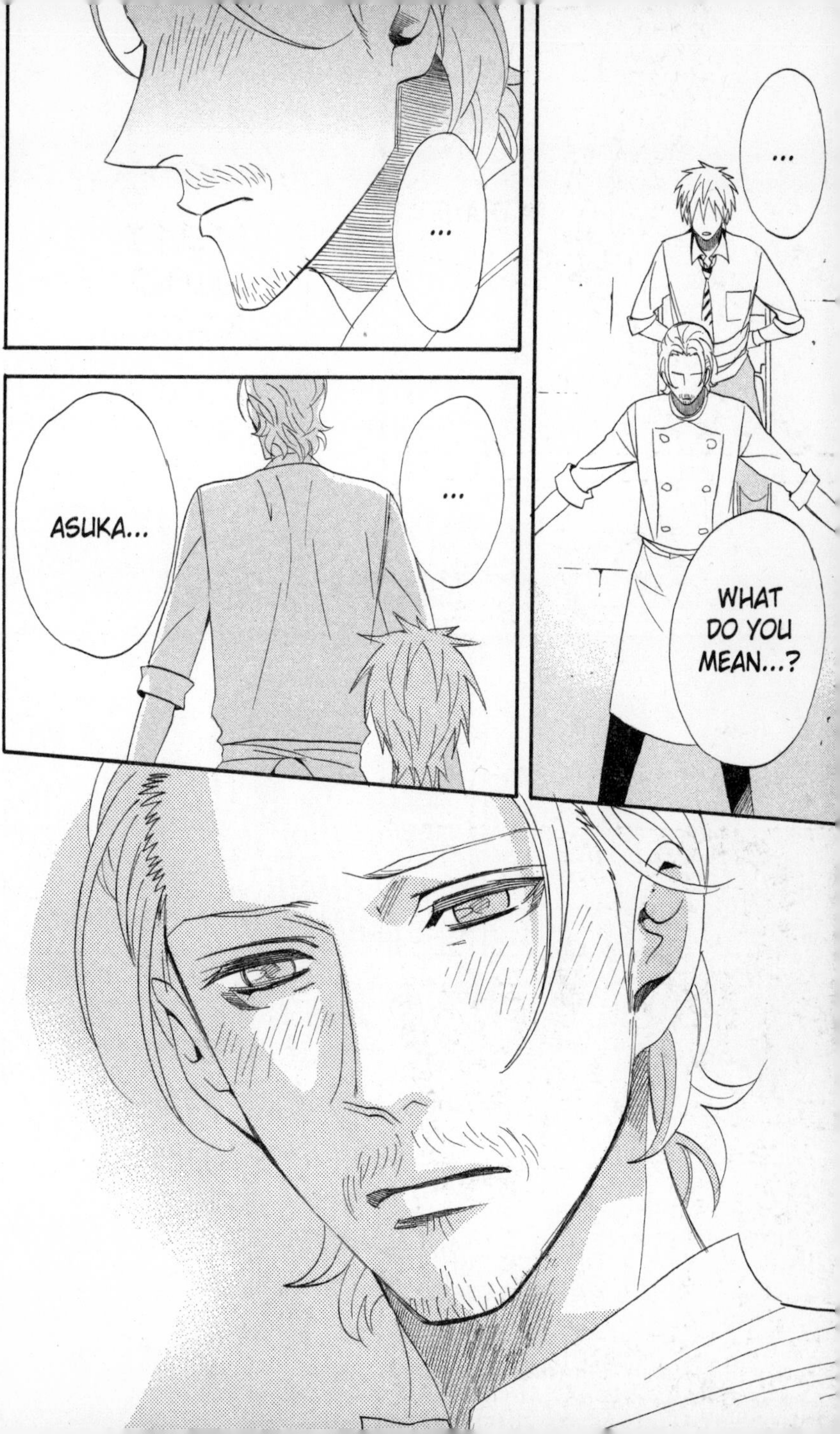
...
WHAT DO YOU MEAN...?
...
...
ASUKA...

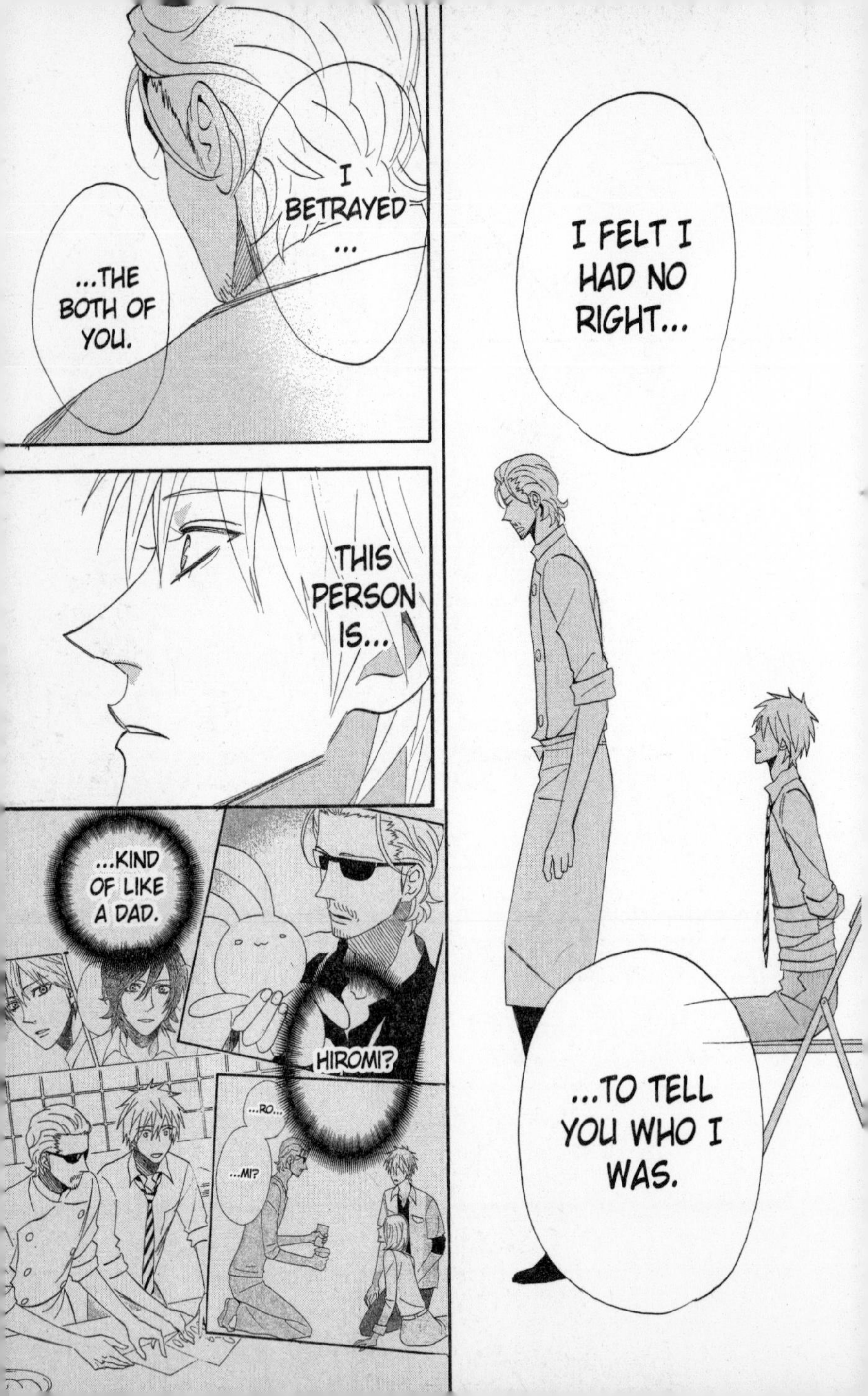
I FELT I HAD NO RIGHT...
...TO TELL YOU WHO I WAS.
I BETRAYED...
...THE BOTH OF YOU.
THIS PERSON IS...
...KIND OF LIKE A DAD.
HIROMI?
...RO...
...MI?

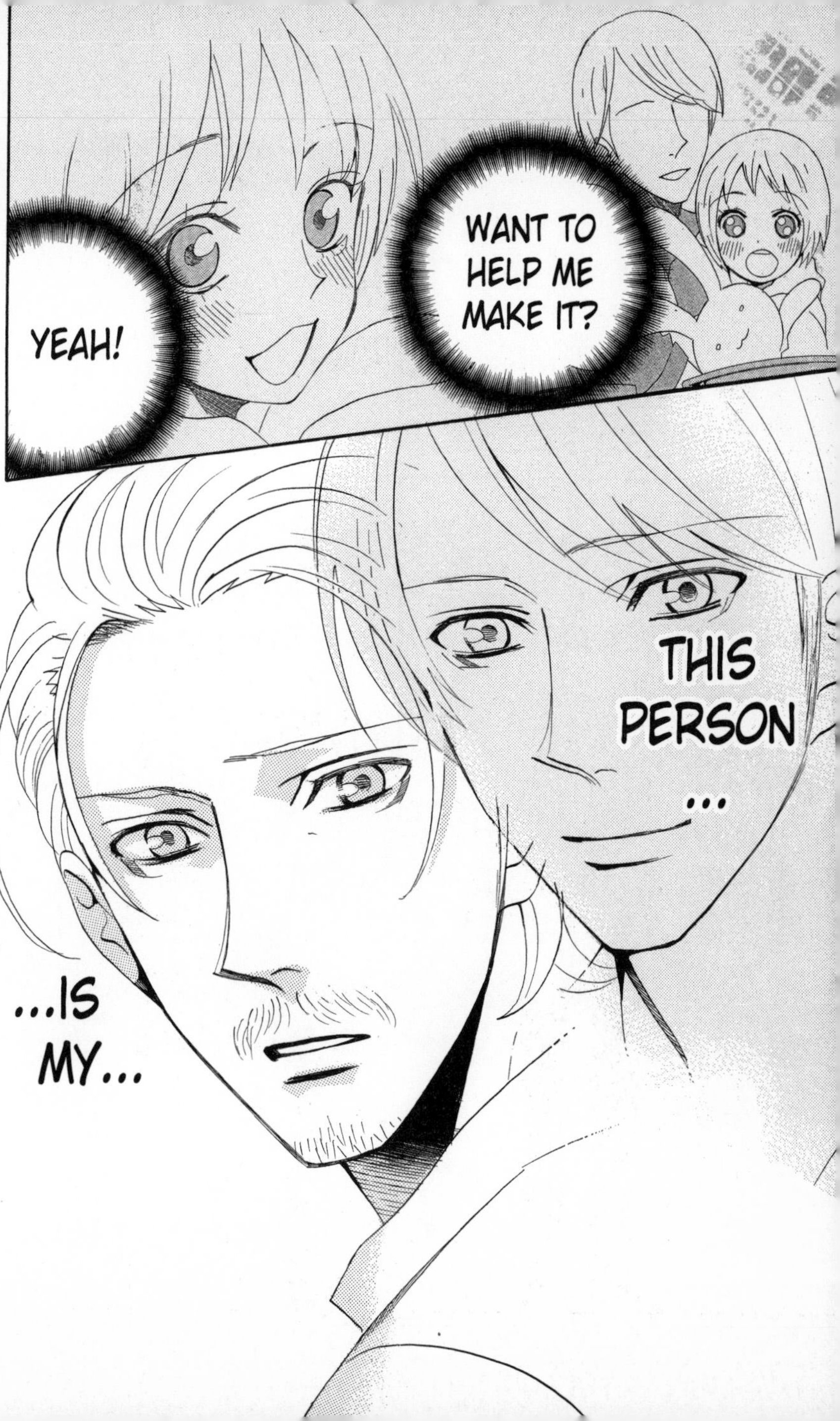
WANT TO HELP ME MAKE IT?
YEAH!
THIS PERSON ...
...IS MY...

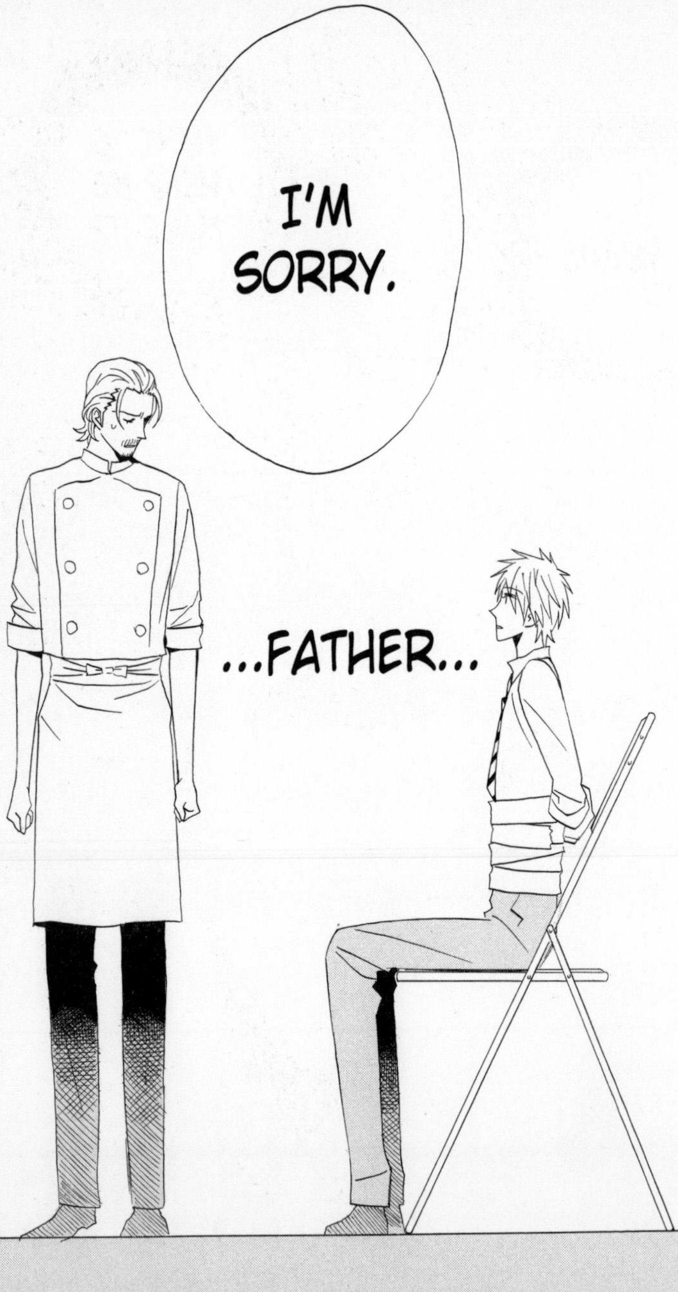
I'M SORRY.
...FATHER...

OTOMEN

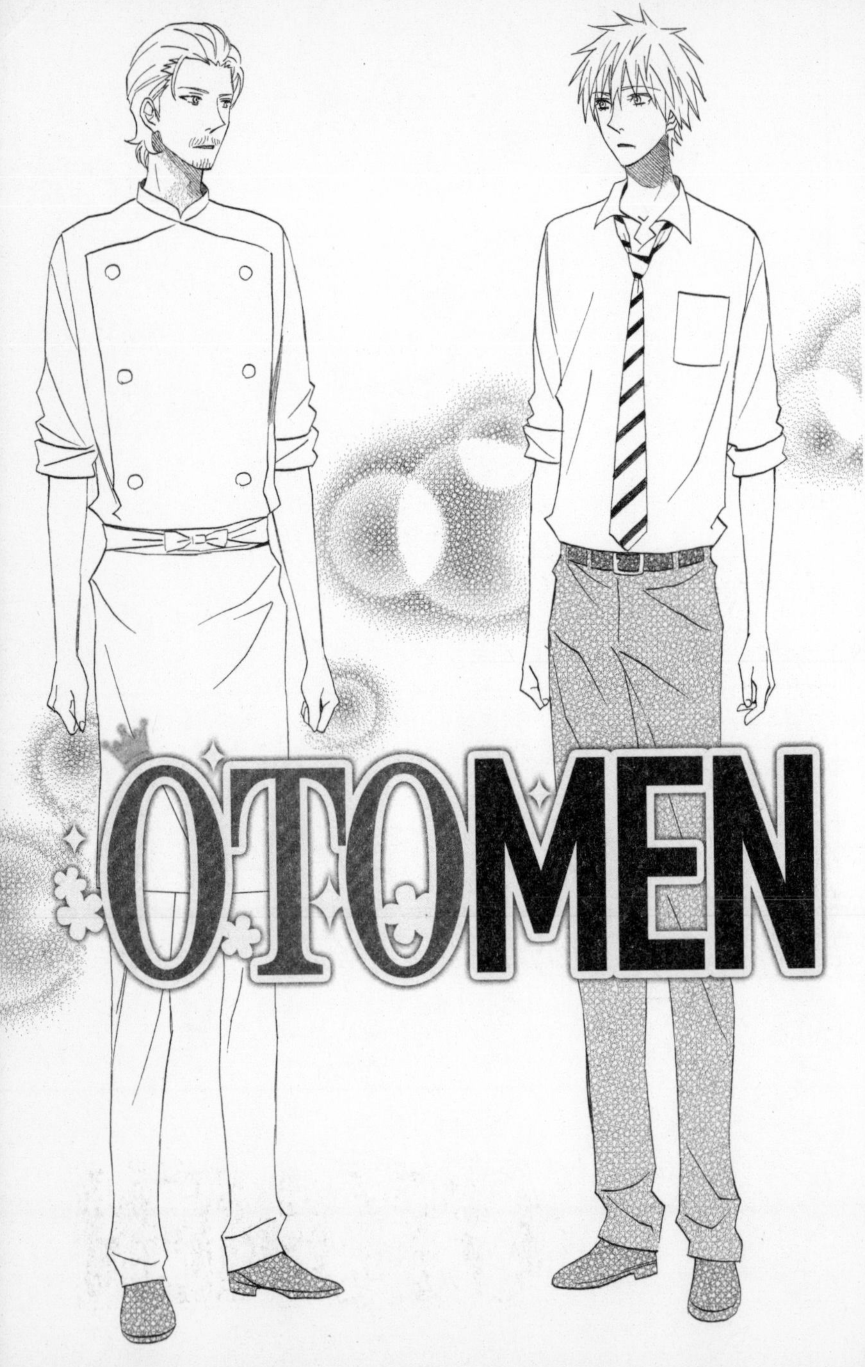
OTOMEN

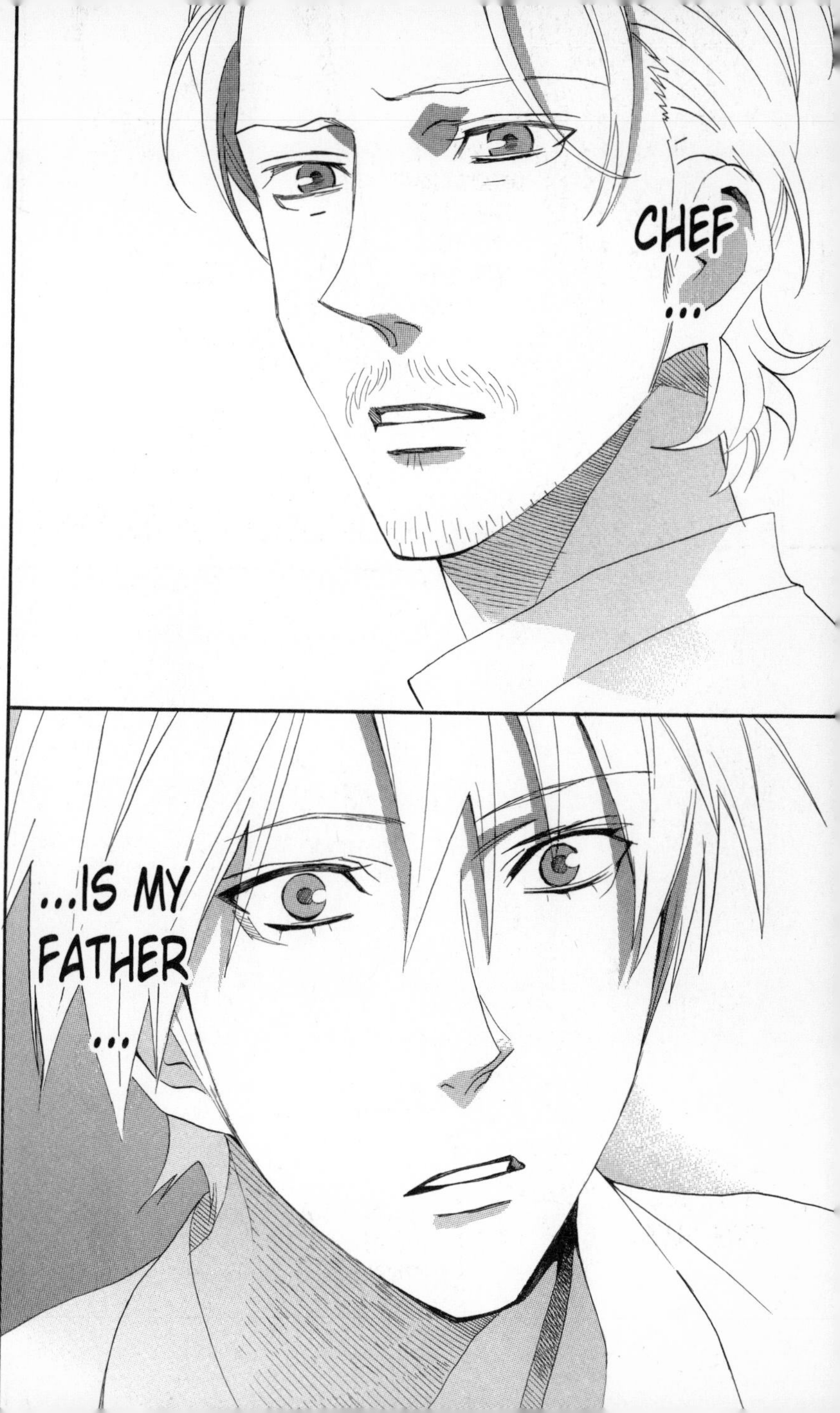
CHEF
...
...IS MY FATHER
...

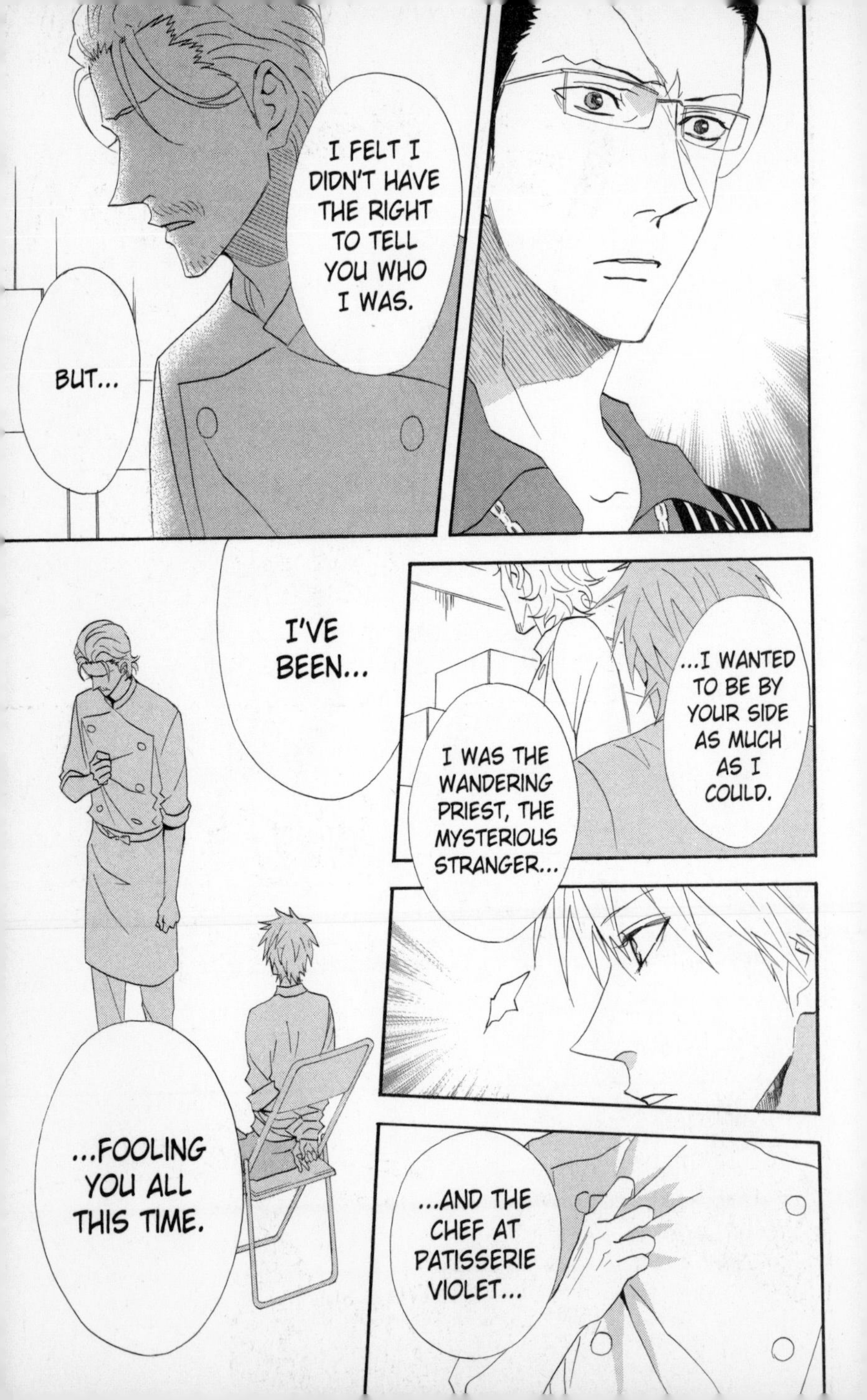
I FELT I DIDN'T HAVE THE RIGHT TO TELL YOU WHO I WAS.
BUT...
...I WANTED TO BE BY YOUR SIDE AS MUCH AS I COULD.
I WAS THE WANDERING PRIEST, THE MYSTERIOUS STRANGER...
...AND THE CHEF AT PATISSERIE VIOLET...
I'VE BEEN...
...FOOLING YOU ALL THIS TIME.

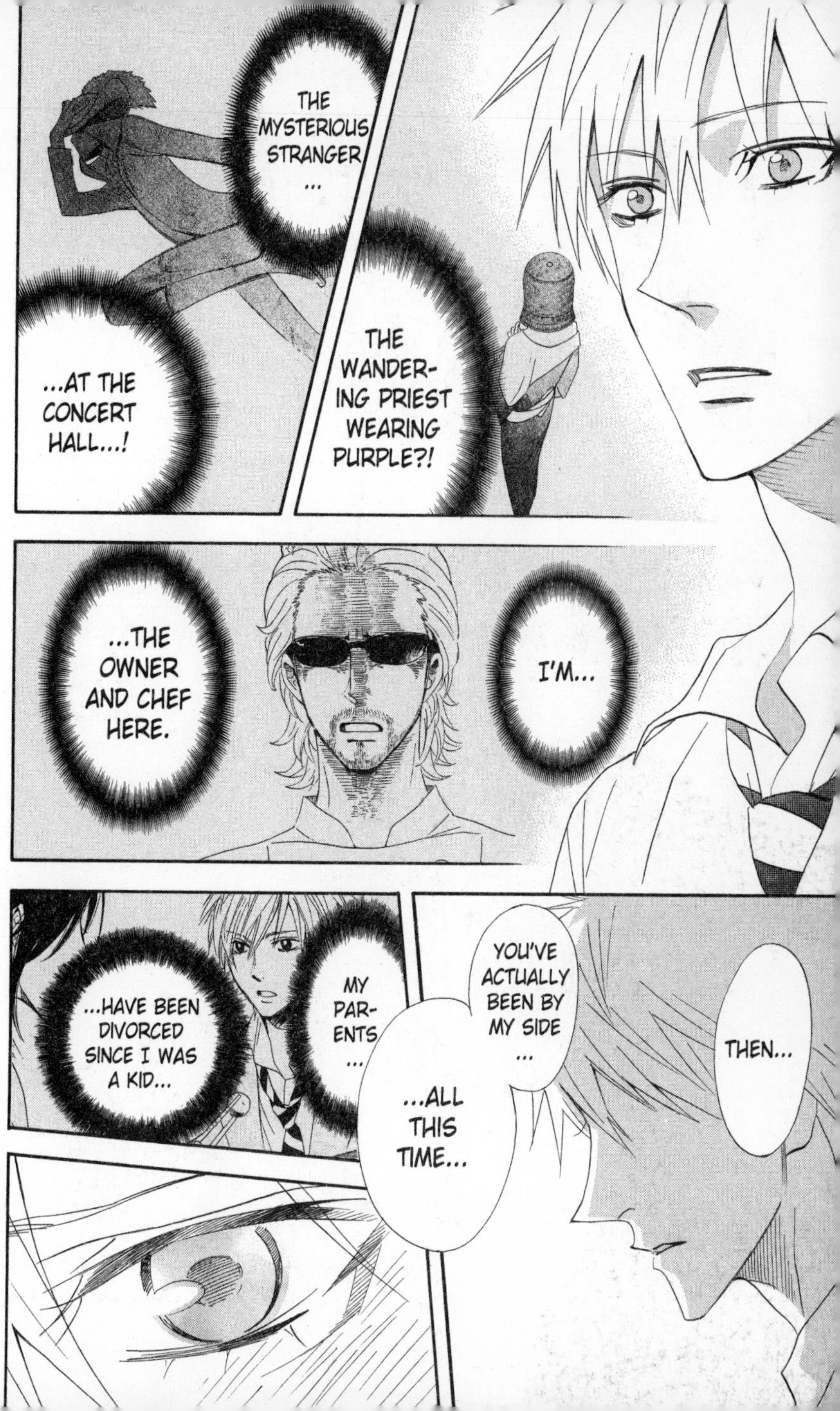
THE WANDER-ING PRIEST WEARING PURPLE?!
THE MYSTERIOUS STRANGER ...
...AT THE CONCERT HALL...!
I'M...
...THE OWNER AND CHEF HERE.
THEN...
YOU'VE ACTUALLY BEEN BY MY SIDE ...
...ALL THIS TIME...
MY PAR-ENTS ...
...HAVE BEEN DIVORCED SINCE I WAS A KID...

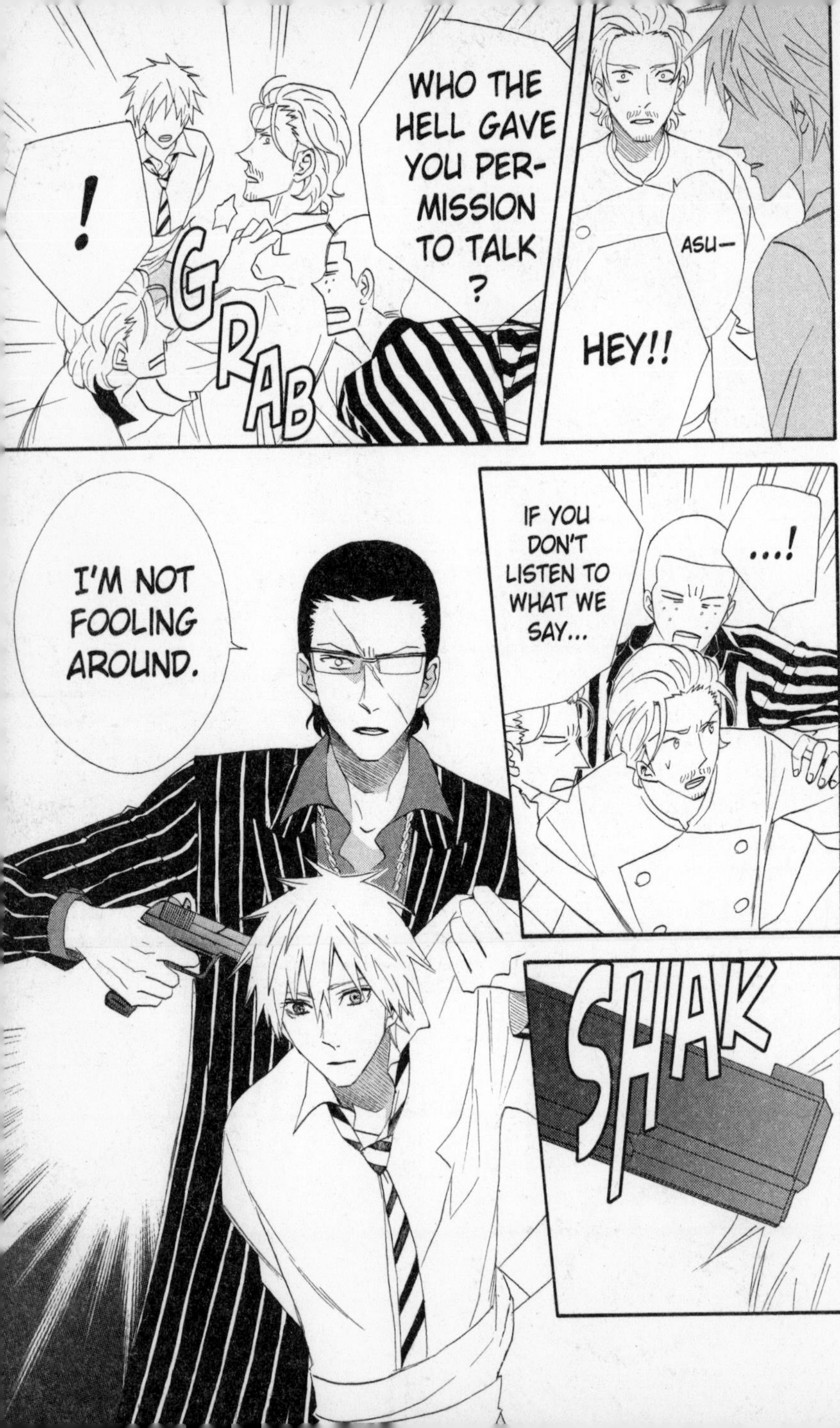
ASU—
HEY!!
WHO THE HELL GAVE YOU PER-MISSION TO TALK?
!
GRAB
...!
IF YOU DON'T LISTEN TO WHAT WE SAY...
SHAK
I'M NOT FOOLING AROUND.

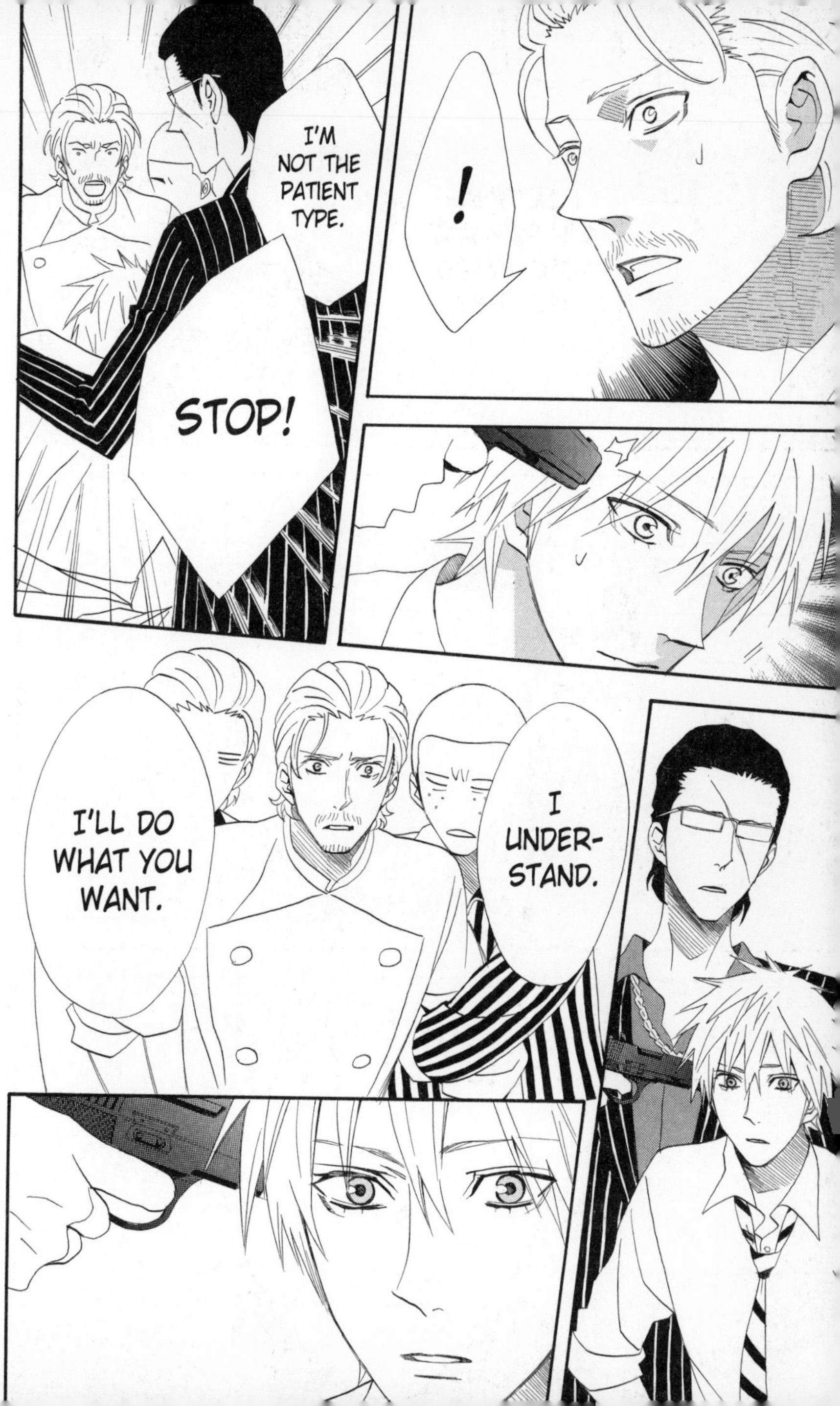
!
I'M NOT THE PATIENT TYPE.
STOP!
I UNDER-STAND.
I'LL DO WHAT YOU WANT.

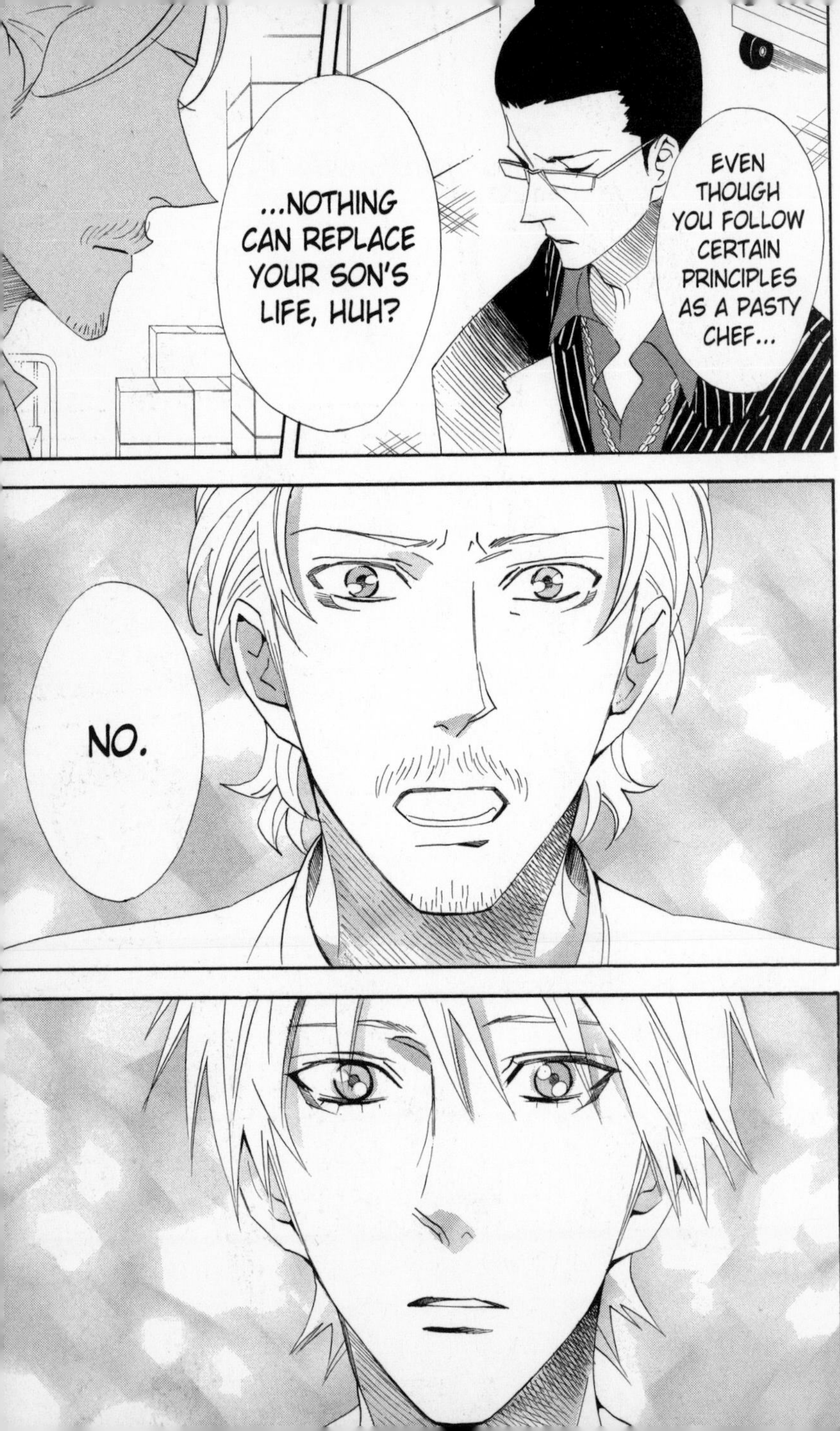
EVEN THOUGH YOU FOLLOW CERTAIN PRINCIPLES AS A PASTY CHEF...
...NOTHING CAN REPLACE YOUR SON'S LIFE, HUH?
NO.

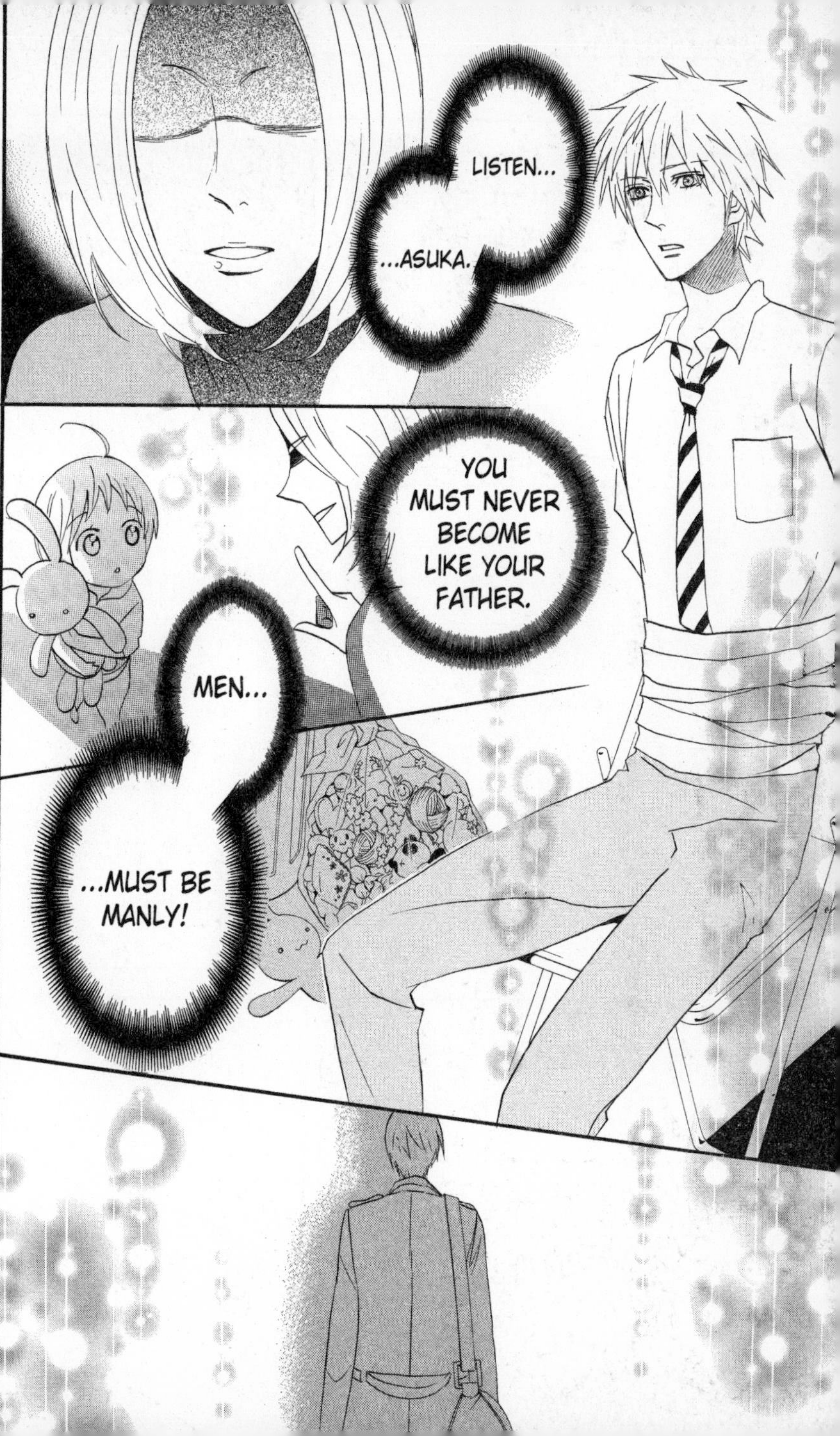
LISTEN...
...ASUKA.
YOU MUST NEVER BECOME LIKE YOUR FATHER.
MEN...
...MUST BE MANLY!

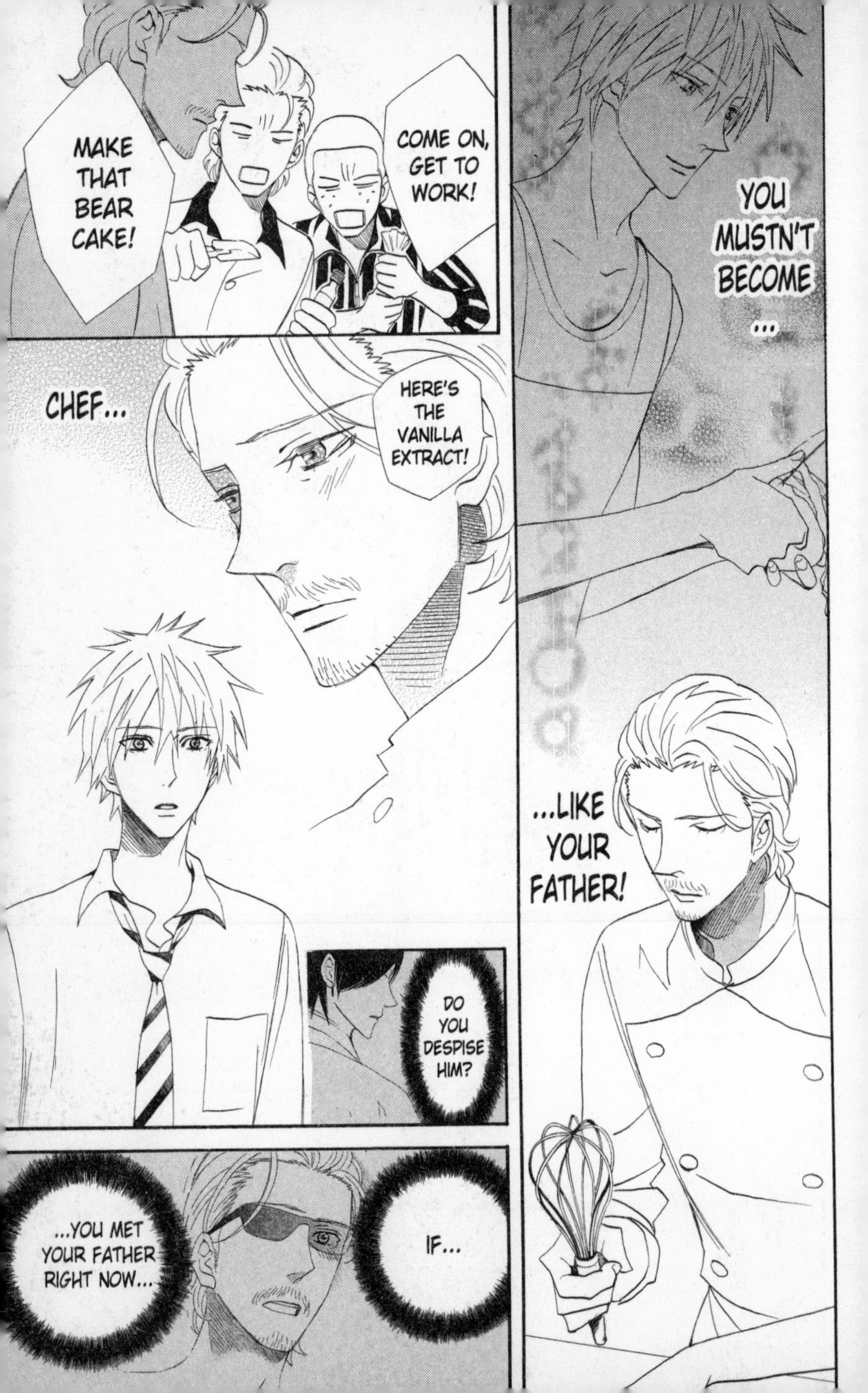
YOU MUSTN'T BECOME ...
...LIKE YOUR FATHER!
COME ON, GET TO WORK!
MAKE THAT BEAR CAKE!
HERE'S THE VANILLA EXTRACT!
CHEF...
DO YOU DESPISE HIM?
IF...
...YOU MET YOUR FATHER RIGHT NOW...

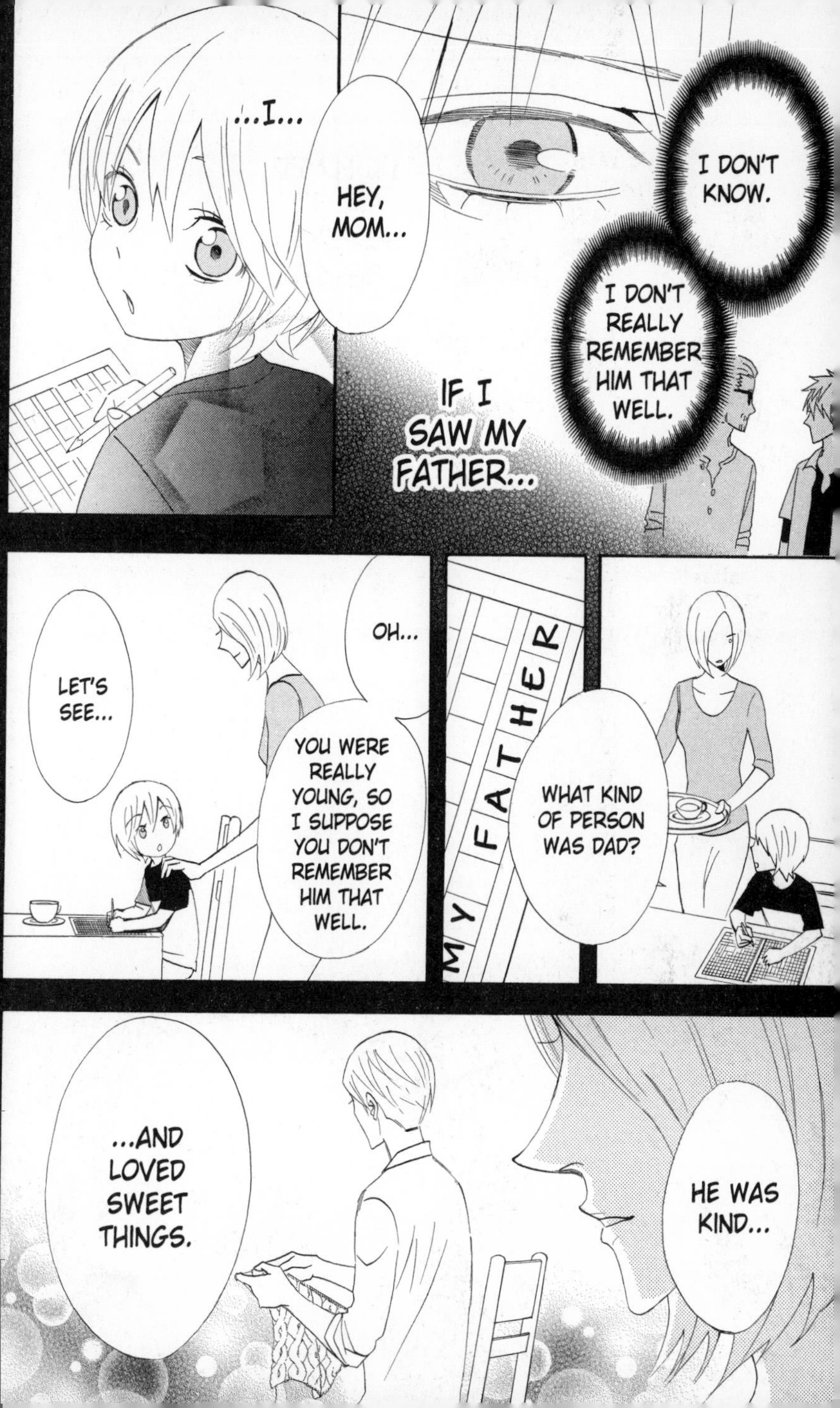
I DON'T KNOW.
I DON'T REALLY REMEMBER HIM THAT WELL.
IF I SAW MY FATHER...
HEY, MOM...
...I...
WHAT KIND OF PERSON WAS DAD?
MY FATHER
OH...
YOU WERE REALLY YOUNG, SO I SUPPOSE YOU DON'T REMEMBER HIM THAT WELL.
LET'S SEE...
HE WAS KIND...
...AND LOVED SWEET THINGS.

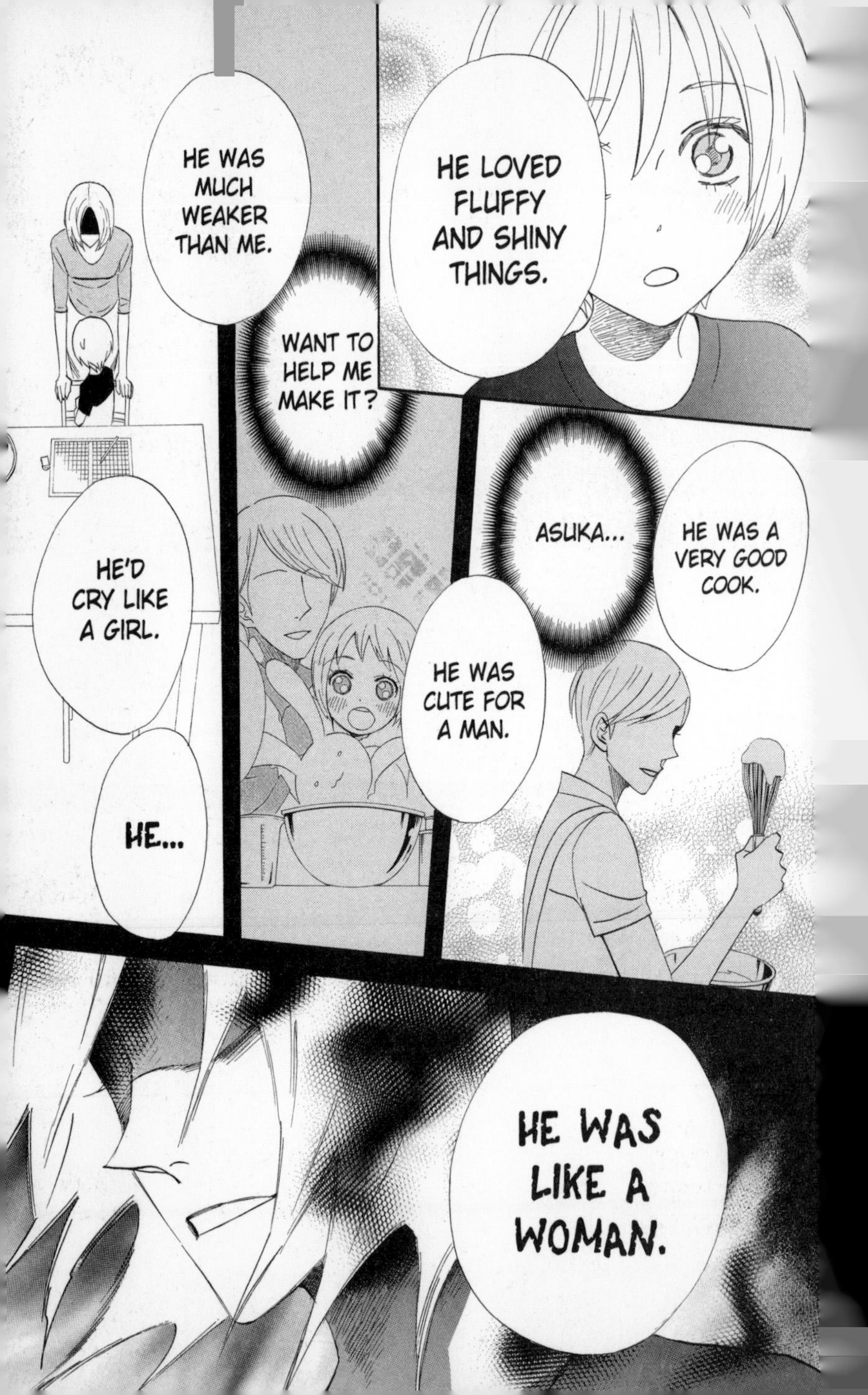
HE LOVED FLUFFY AND SHINY THINGS.
HE WAS A VERY GOOD COOK.
ASUKA...
HE WAS CUTE FOR A MAN.
WANT TO HELP ME MAKE IT?
HE WAS MUCH WEAKER THAN ME.
HE'D CRY LIKE A GIRL.
HE...
HE WAS LIKE A WOMAN.

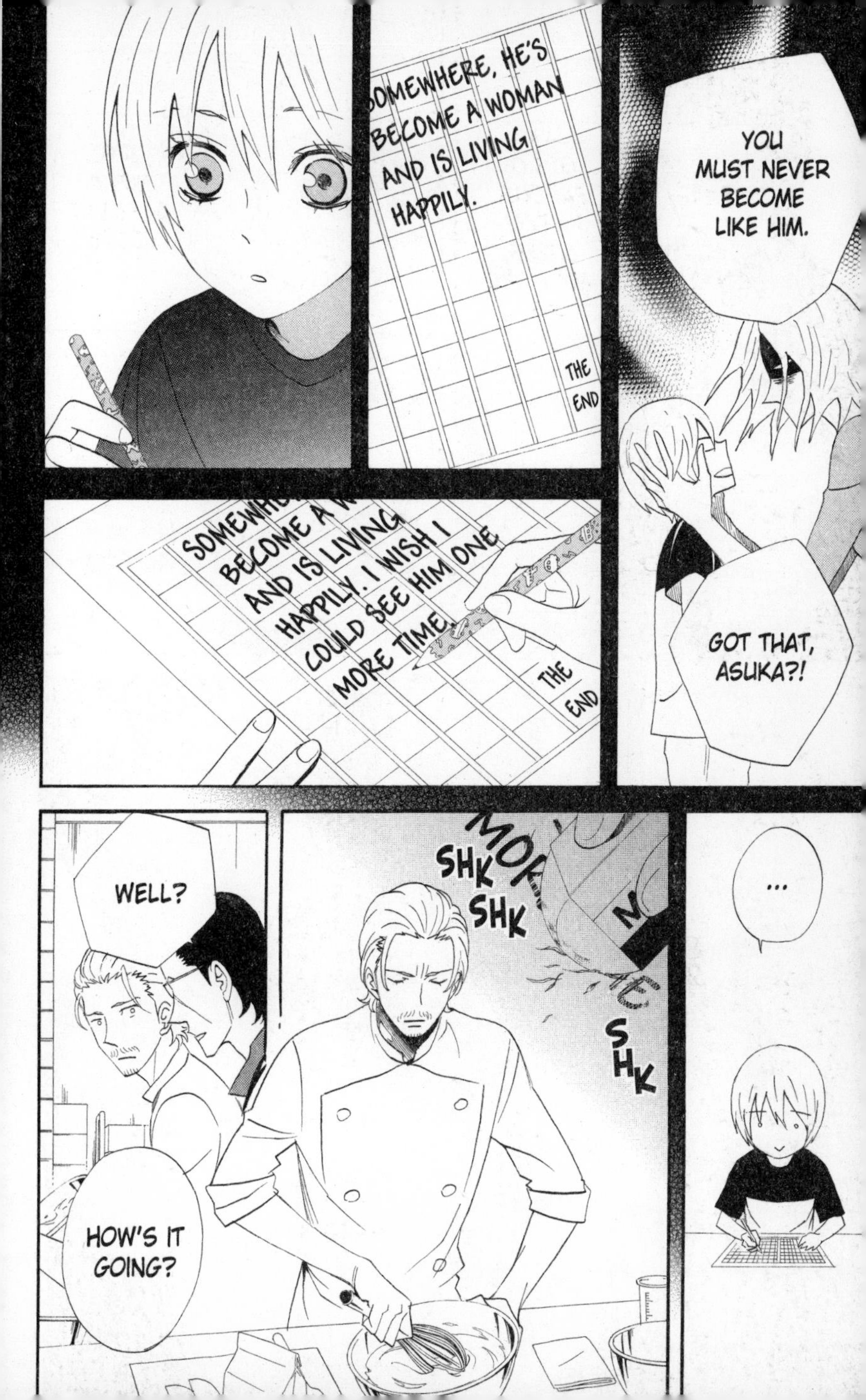
YOU MUST NEVER BECOME LIKE HIM.
GOT THAT, ASUKA?!
SOMEWHERE, HE'S BECOME A WOMAN AND IS LIVING HAPPILY.
THE END
SOMEWH
BECOME A W
AND IS LIVING
HAPPILY. I WISH I
COULD SEE HIM ONE
MORE TIME.
THE END
...
SHK SHK
SHK
WELL?
HOW'S IT GOING?

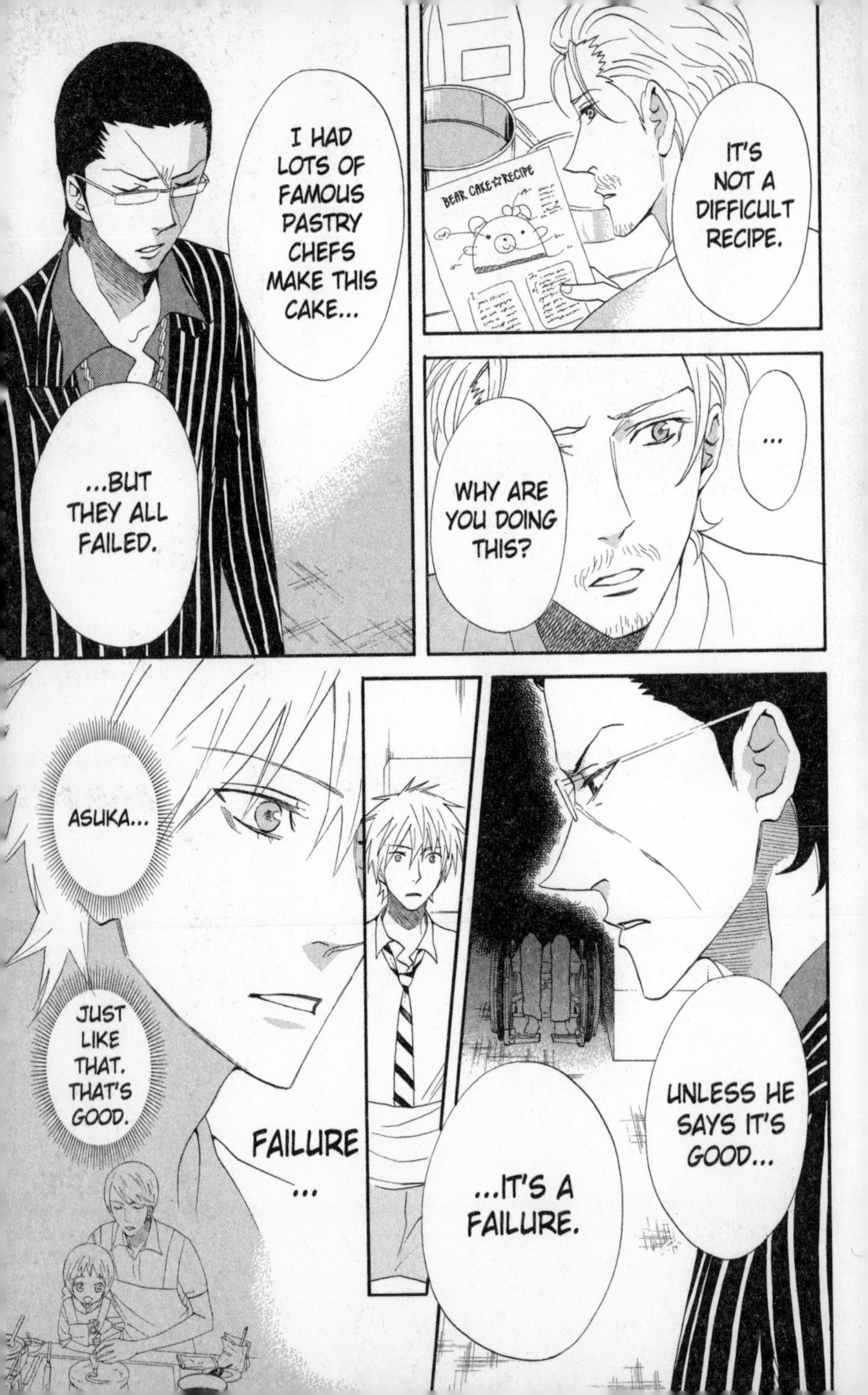
IT'S NOT A DIFFICULT RECIPE.
BEAR CAKE☆RECIPE
...
WHY ARE YOU DOING THIS?
I HAD LOTS OF FAMOUS PASTRY CHEFS MAKE THIS CAKE...
...BUT THEY ALL FAILED.
UNLESS HE SAYS IT'S GOOD...
...IT'S A FAILURE.
ASUKA...
JUST LIKE THAT. THAT'S GOOD.
FAILURE...

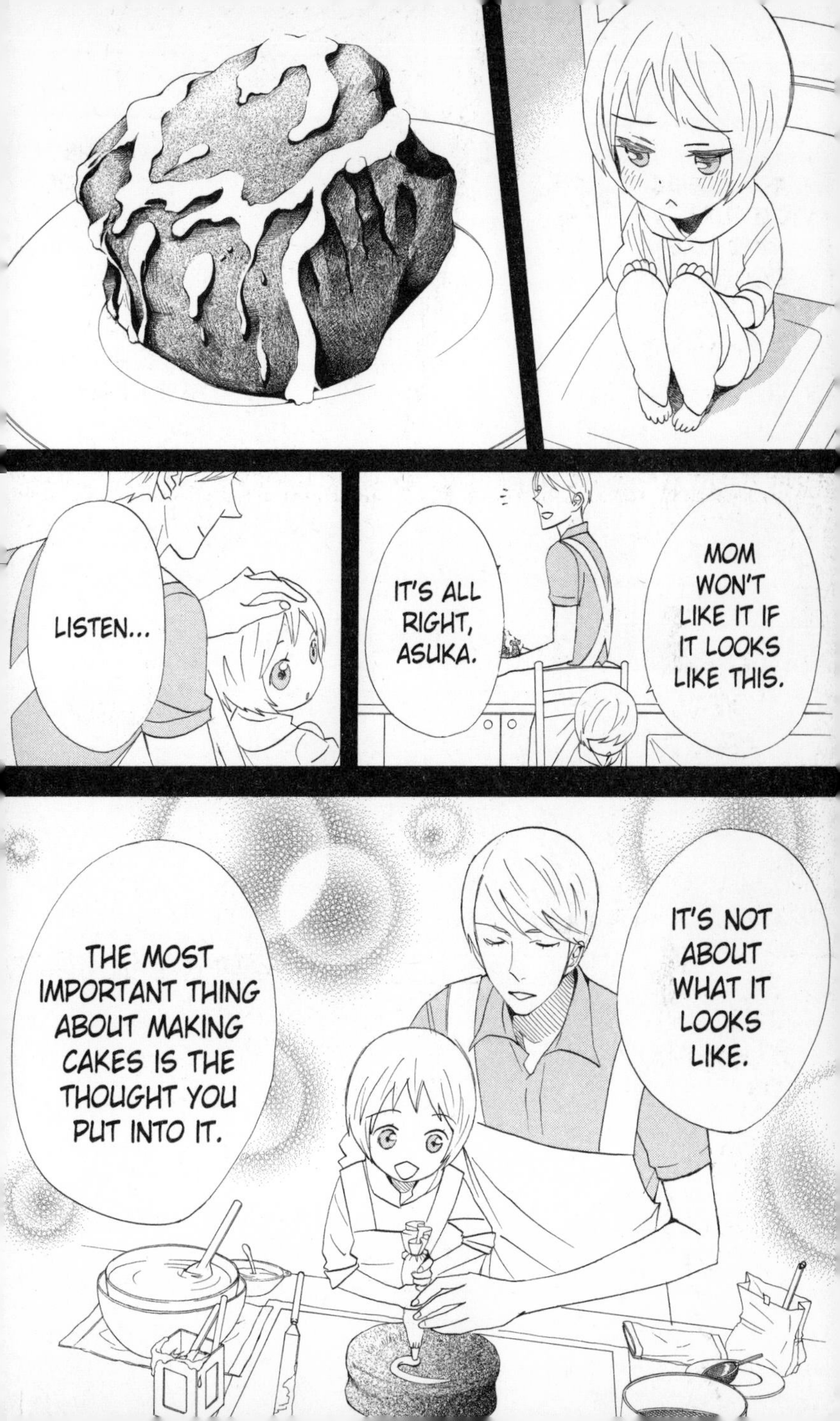
MOM WON'T LIKE IT IF IT LOOKS LIKE THIS.
IT'S ALL RIGHT, ASUKA.
LISTEN...
IT'S NOT ABOUT WHAT IT LOOKS LIKE.
THE MOST IMPORTANT THING ABOUT MAKING CAKES IS THE THOUGHT YOU PUT INTO IT.

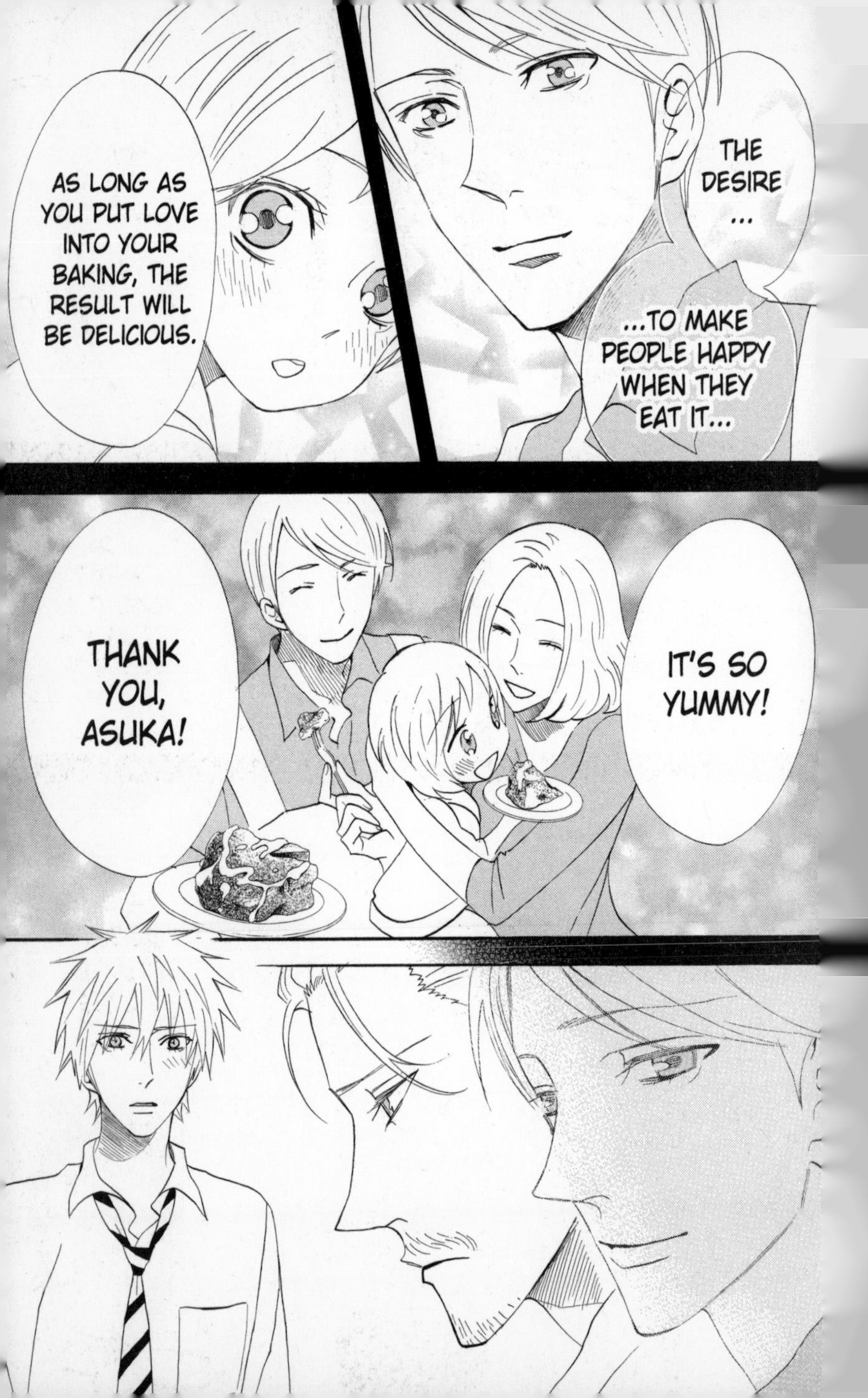
THE DESIRE ...
...TO MAKE PEOPLE HAPPY WHEN THEY EAT IT...
AS LONG AS YOU PUT LOVE INTO YOUR BAKING, THE RESULT WILL BE DELICIOUS.
IT'S SO YUMMY!
THANK YOU, ASUKA!

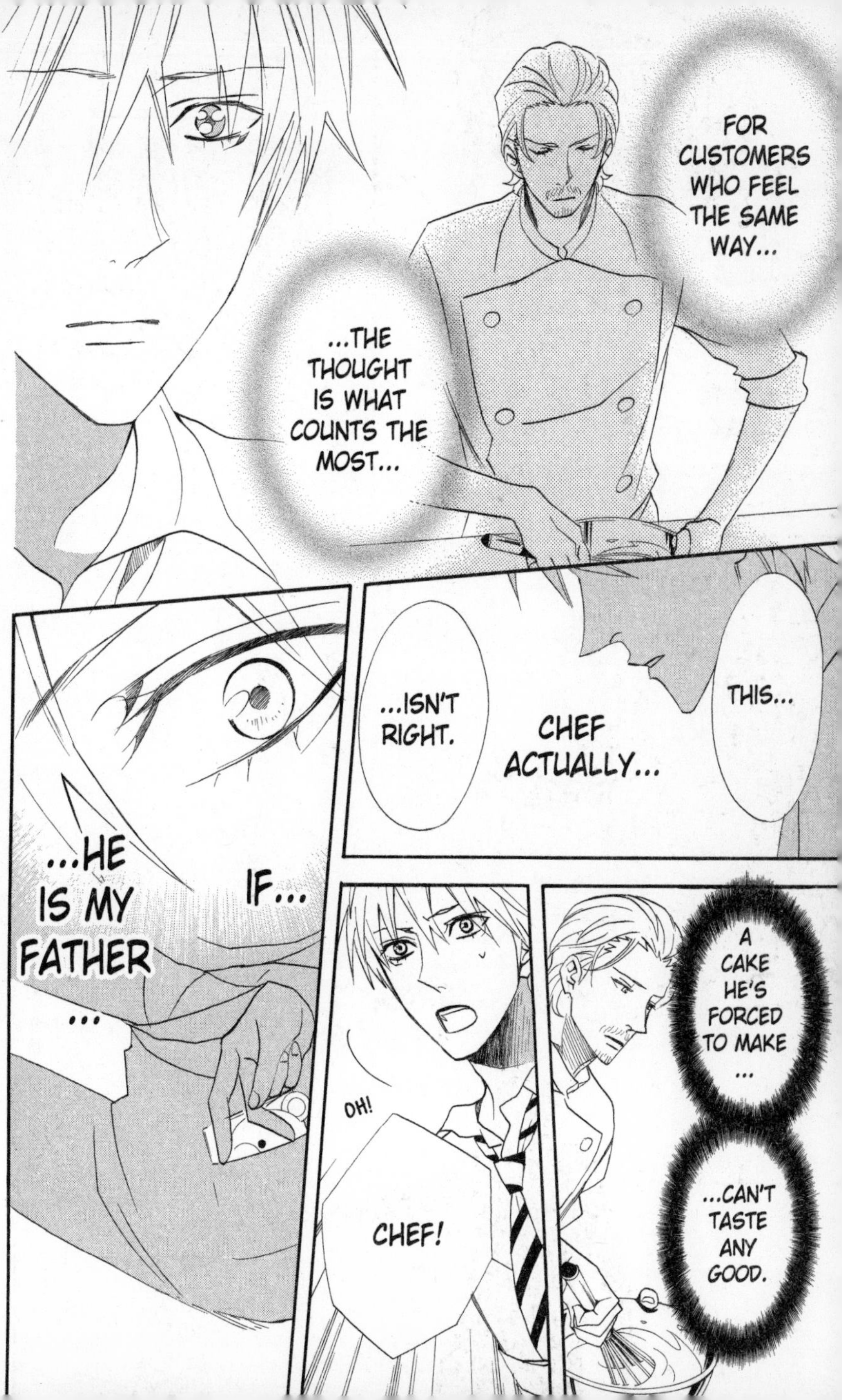
FOR CUSTOMERS WHO FEEL THE SAME WAY...
...THE THOUGHT IS WHAT COUNTS THE MOST...
THIS...
CHEF ACTUALLY...
...ISN'T RIGHT.
A CAKE HE'S FORCED TO MAKE ...
...CAN'T TASTE ANY GOOD.
OH!
CHEF!
IF...
...HE IS MY FATHER ...

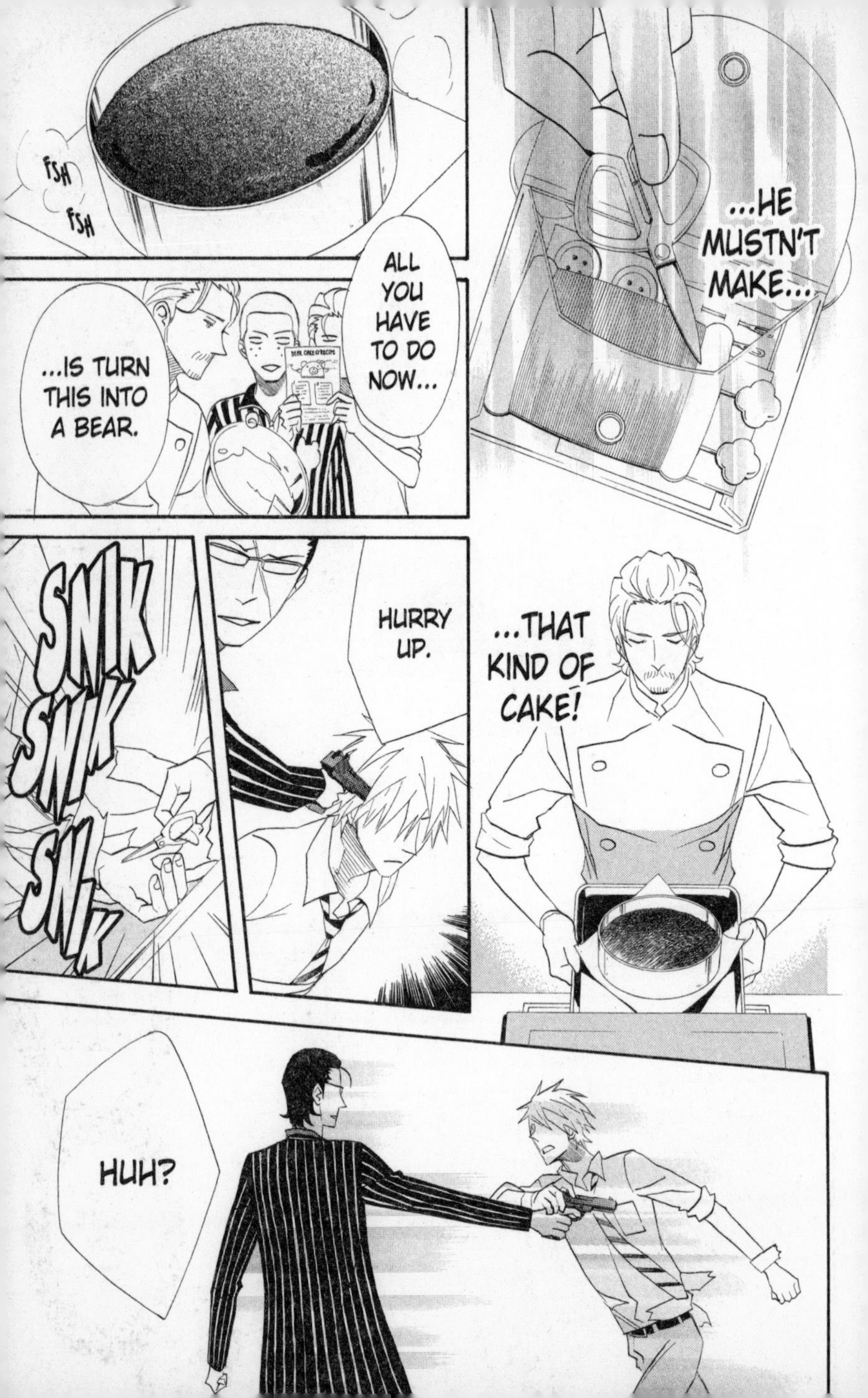
...HE MUSTN'T MAKE...
FSH
FSH
ALL YOU HAVE TO DO NOW...
...IS TURN THIS INTO A BEAR.
...THAT KIND OF CAKE!
HURRY UP.
SNIK
SNIK
SNIK
HUH?

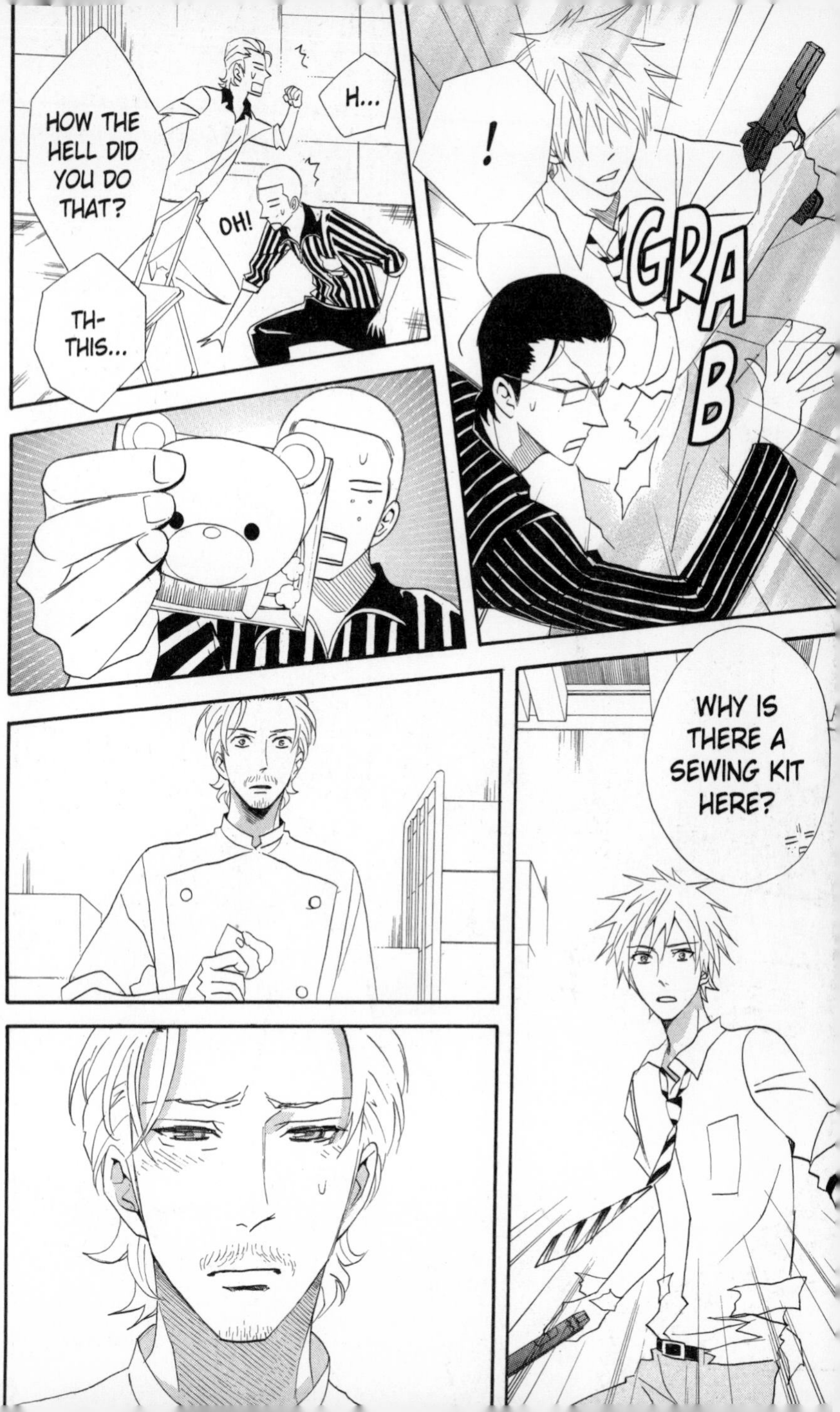
!
GRAB
H...
HOW THE HELL DID YOU DO THAT?
OH!
TH-THIS...
WHY IS THERE A SEWING KIT HERE?

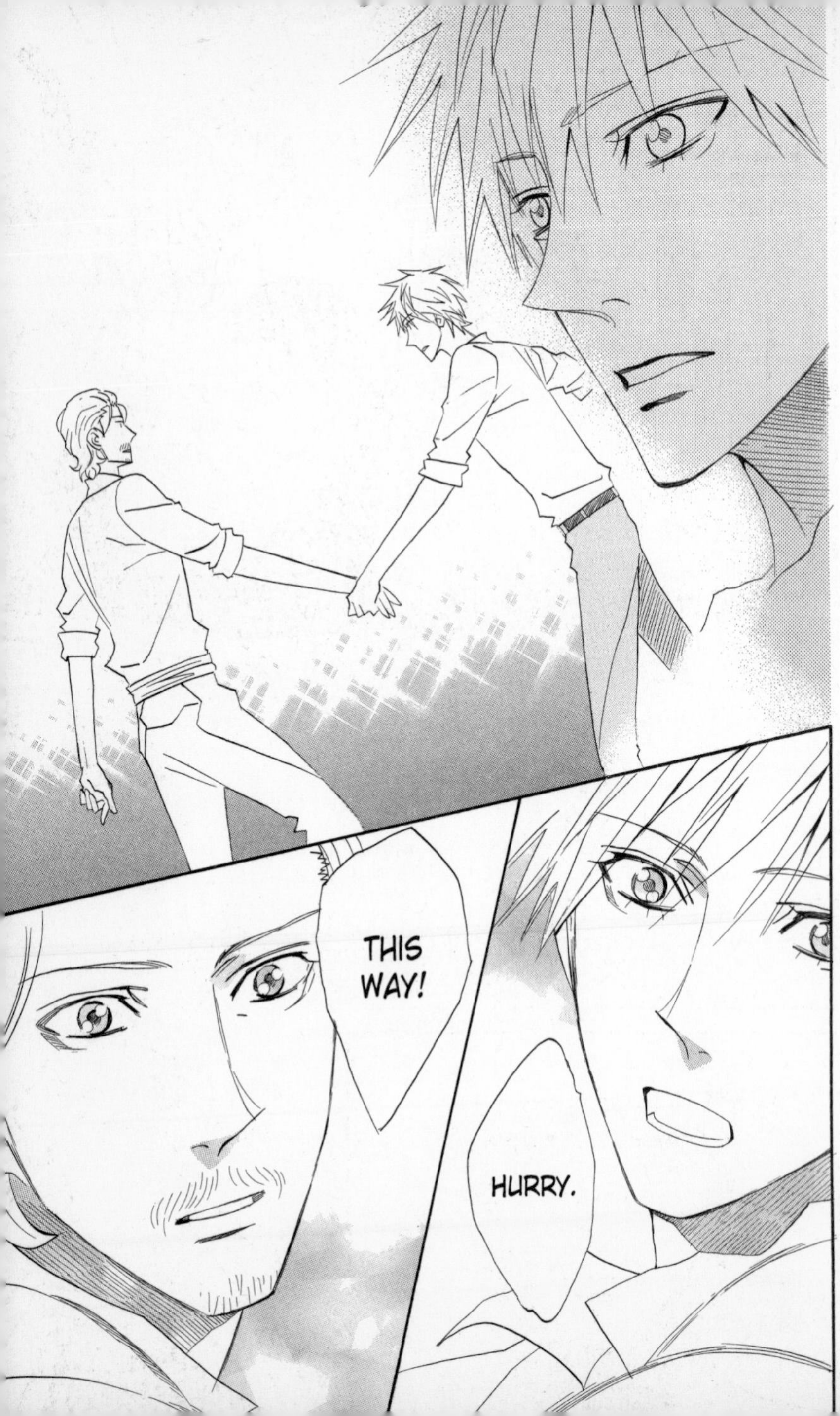
THIS WAY!
HURRY.

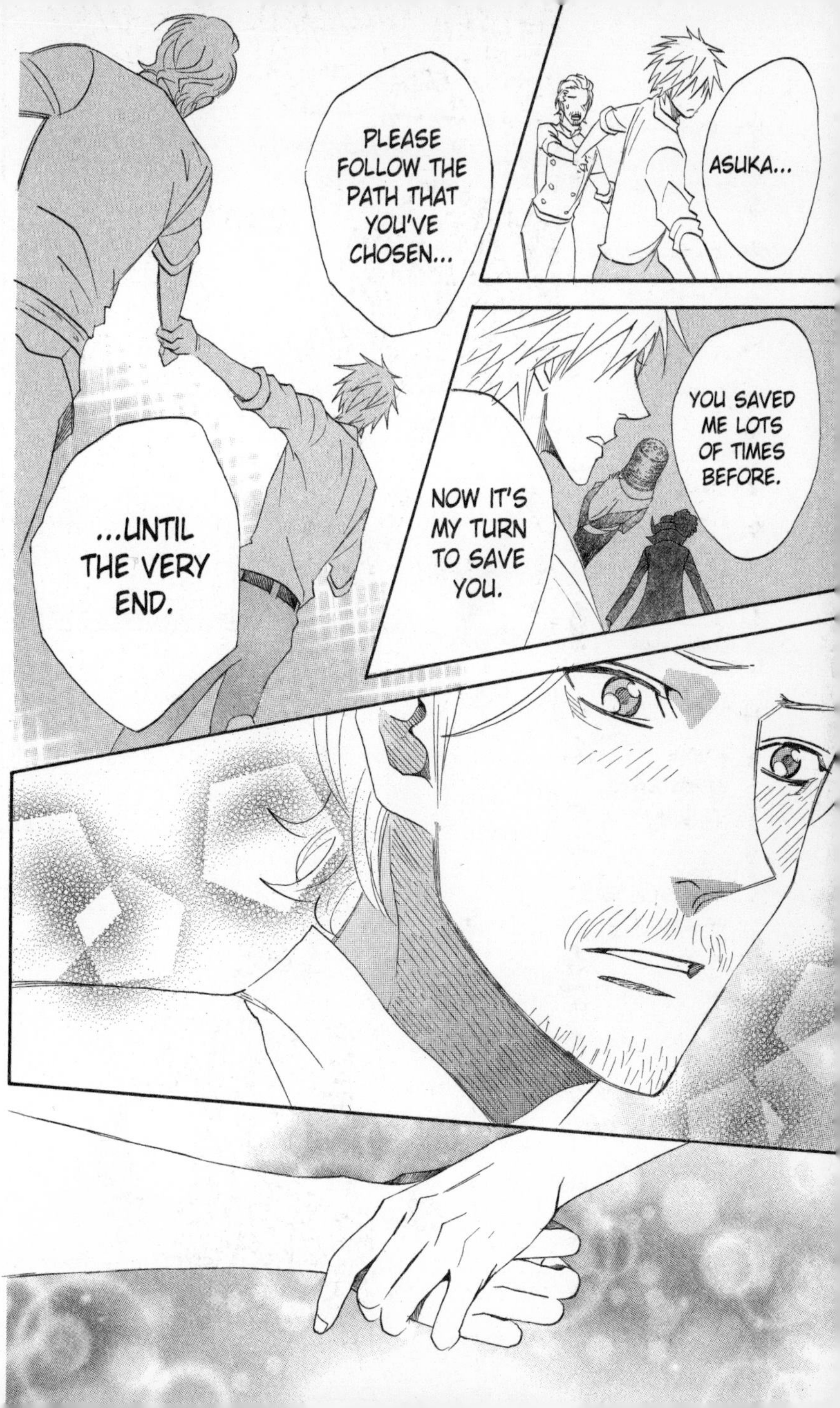
ASUKA...
YOU SAVED ME LOTS OF TIMES BEFORE.
NOW IT'S MY TURN TO SAVE YOU.
PLEASE FOLLOW THE PATH THAT YOU'VE CHOSEN...
...UNTIL THE VERY END.

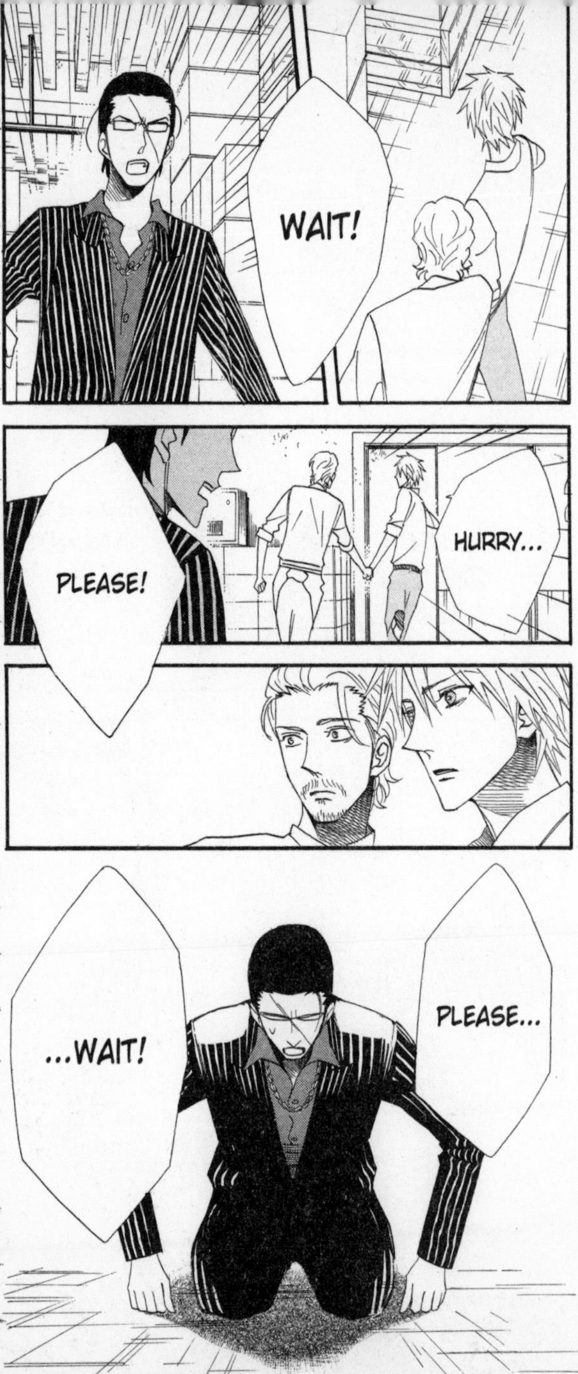
WAIT!
HURRY...
PLEASE!
PLEASE...
...WAIT!

Production Assistance:

Shimada-san
Takowa-san
Kuwana-san
Kaneko-san
Sakurai-san
Nakazawa-san
Tanaka-san
Kawashima-san
Sayaka-san
Yone-yan
Komatsu-san
Ishikawa-san

Special Thanks:

Abe-san
All My Readers
My Family

One-fourth of the volume left to go.

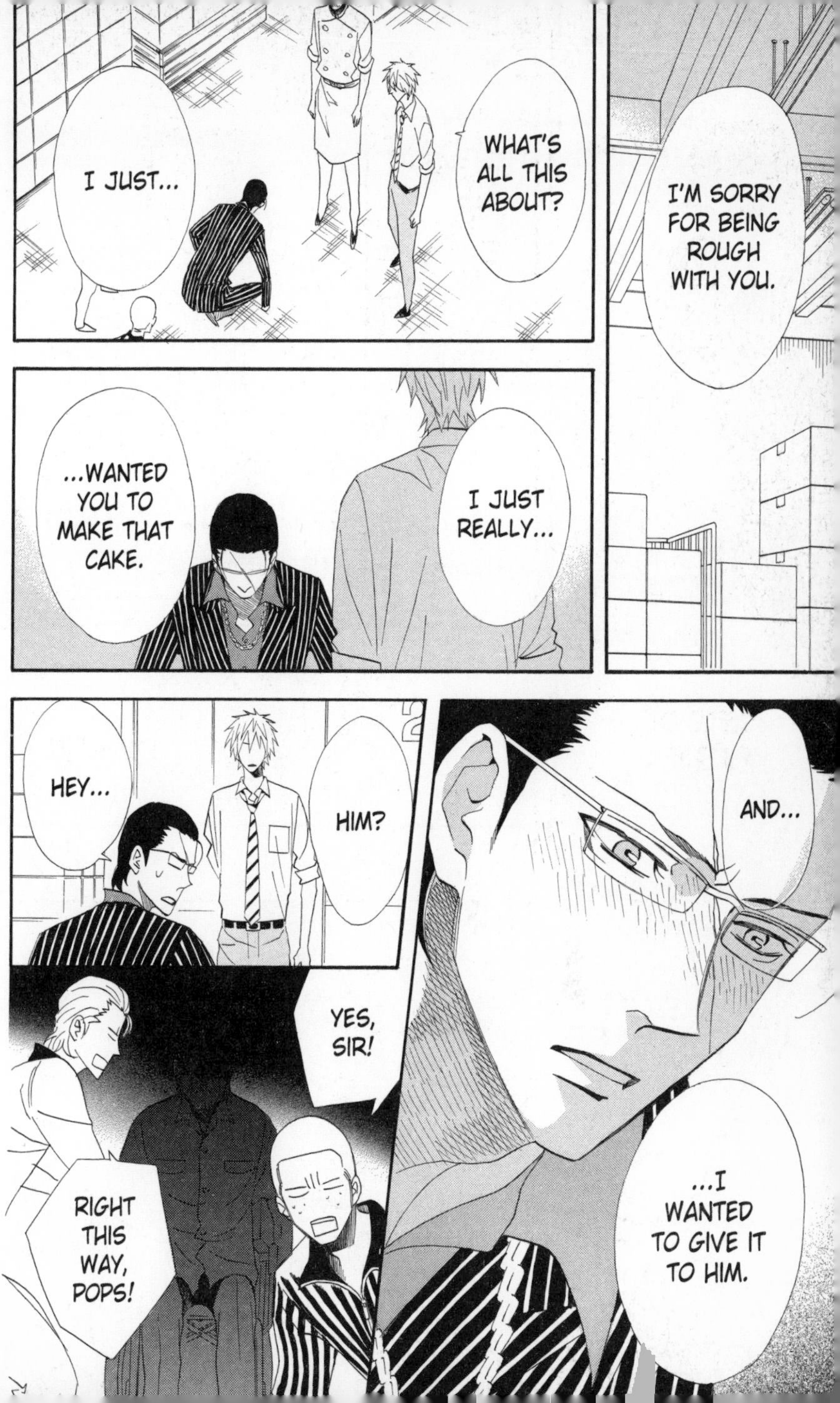
I'M SORRY FOR BEING ROUGH WITH YOU.
WHAT'S ALL THIS ABOUT?
I JUST...
I JUST REALLY...
...WANTED YOU TO MAKE THAT CAKE.
AND...
...I WANTED TO GIVE IT TO HIM.
HIM?
HEY...
YES, SIR!
RIGHT THIS WAY, POPS!

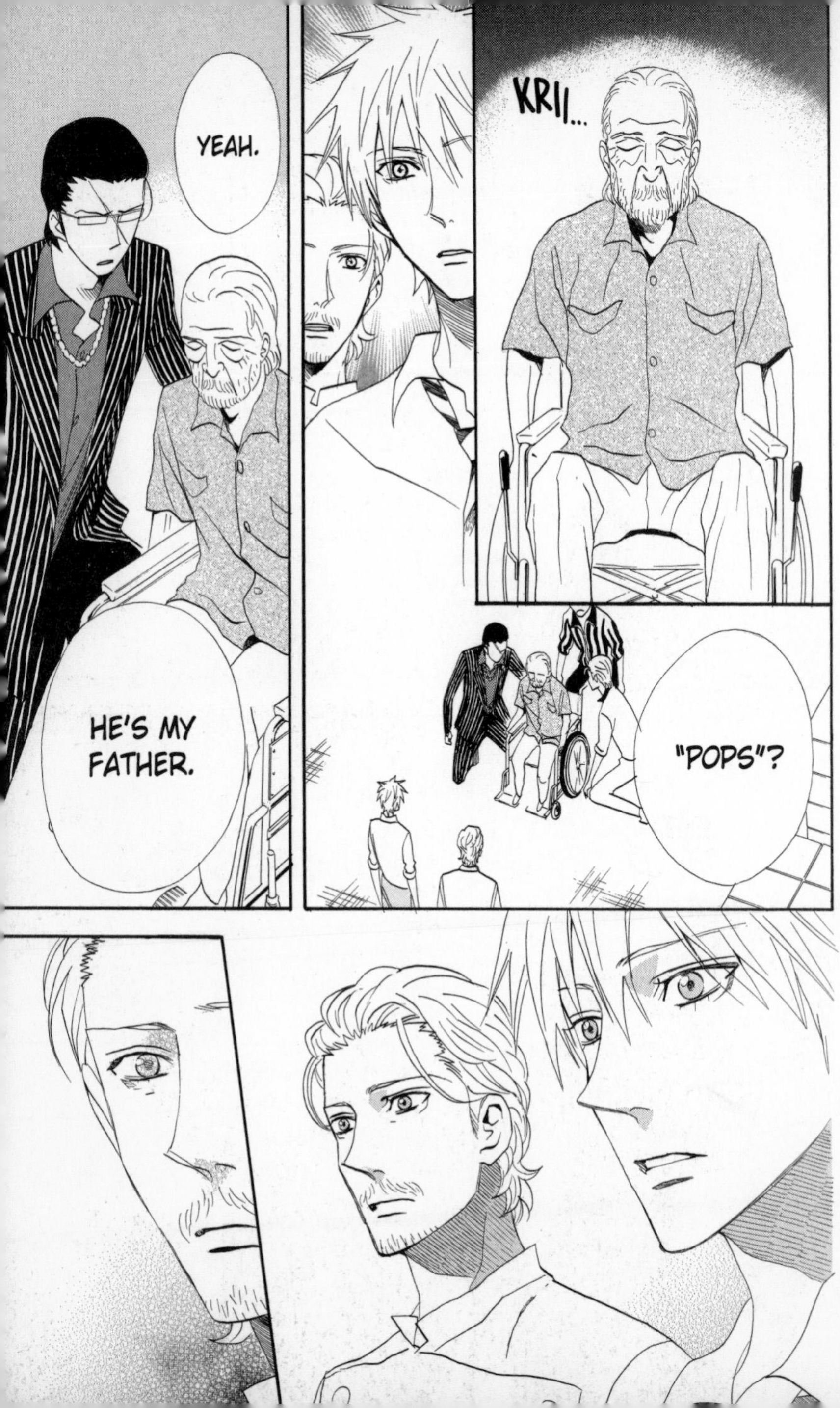
KRII...
"POPS"?
YEAH.
HE'S MY FATHER.

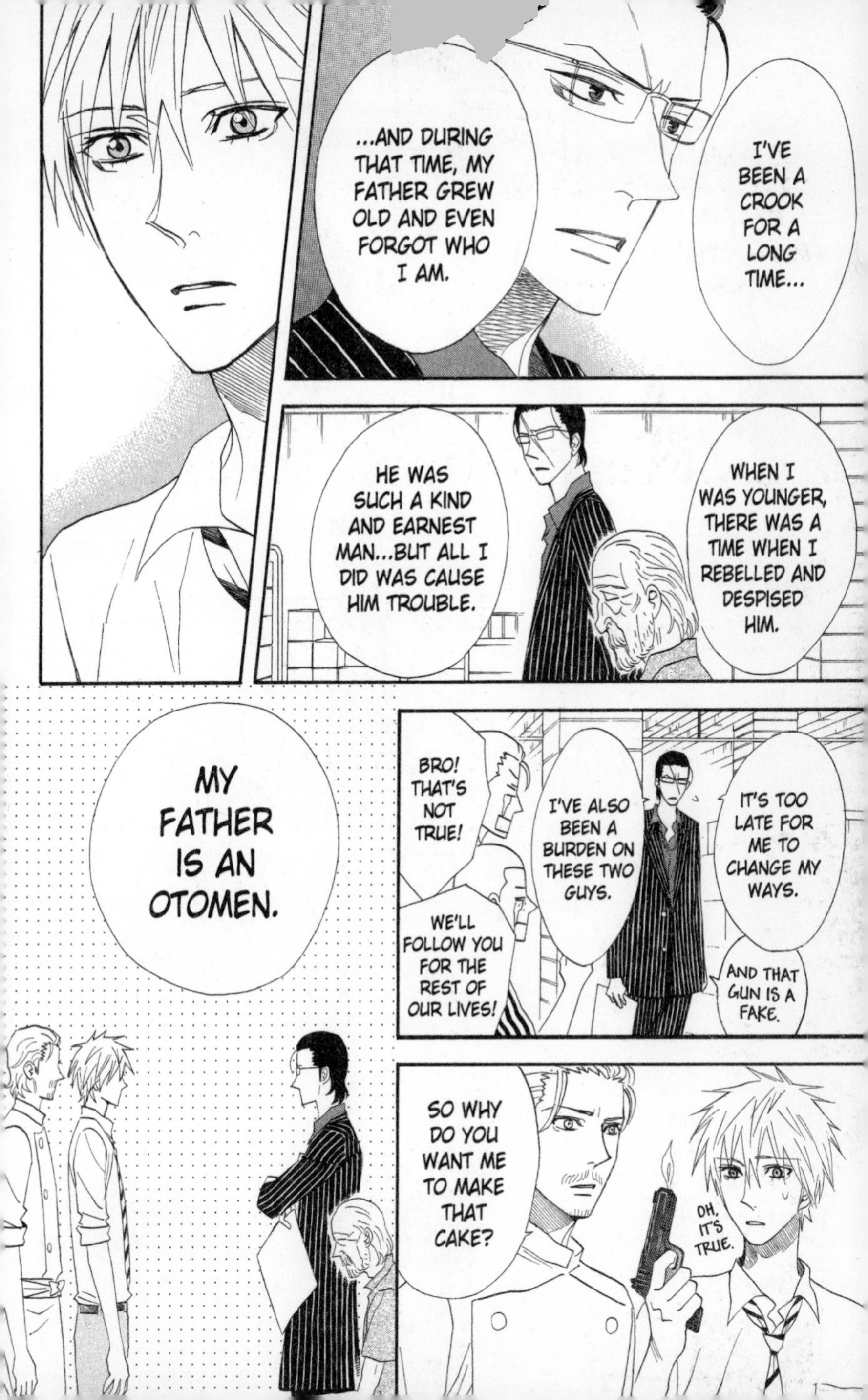
I'VE BEEN A CROOK FOR A LONG TIME...
...AND DURING THAT TIME, MY FATHER GREW OLD AND EVEN FORGOT WHO I AM.
WHEN I WAS YOUNGER, THERE WAS A TIME WHEN I REBELLED AND DESPISED HIM.
HE WAS SUCH A KIND AND EARNEST MAN...BUT ALL I DID WAS CAUSE HIM TROUBLE.
IT'S TOO LATE FOR ME TO CHANGE MY WAYS.
AND THAT GUN IS A FAKE.
I'VE ALSO BEEN A BURDEN ON THESE TWO GUYS.
BRO! THAT'S NOT TRUE!
WE'LL FOLLOW YOU FOR THE REST OF OUR LIVES!
OH, IT'S TRUE.
SO WHY DO YOU WANT ME TO MAKE THAT CAKE?
MY FATHER IS AN OTOMEN.

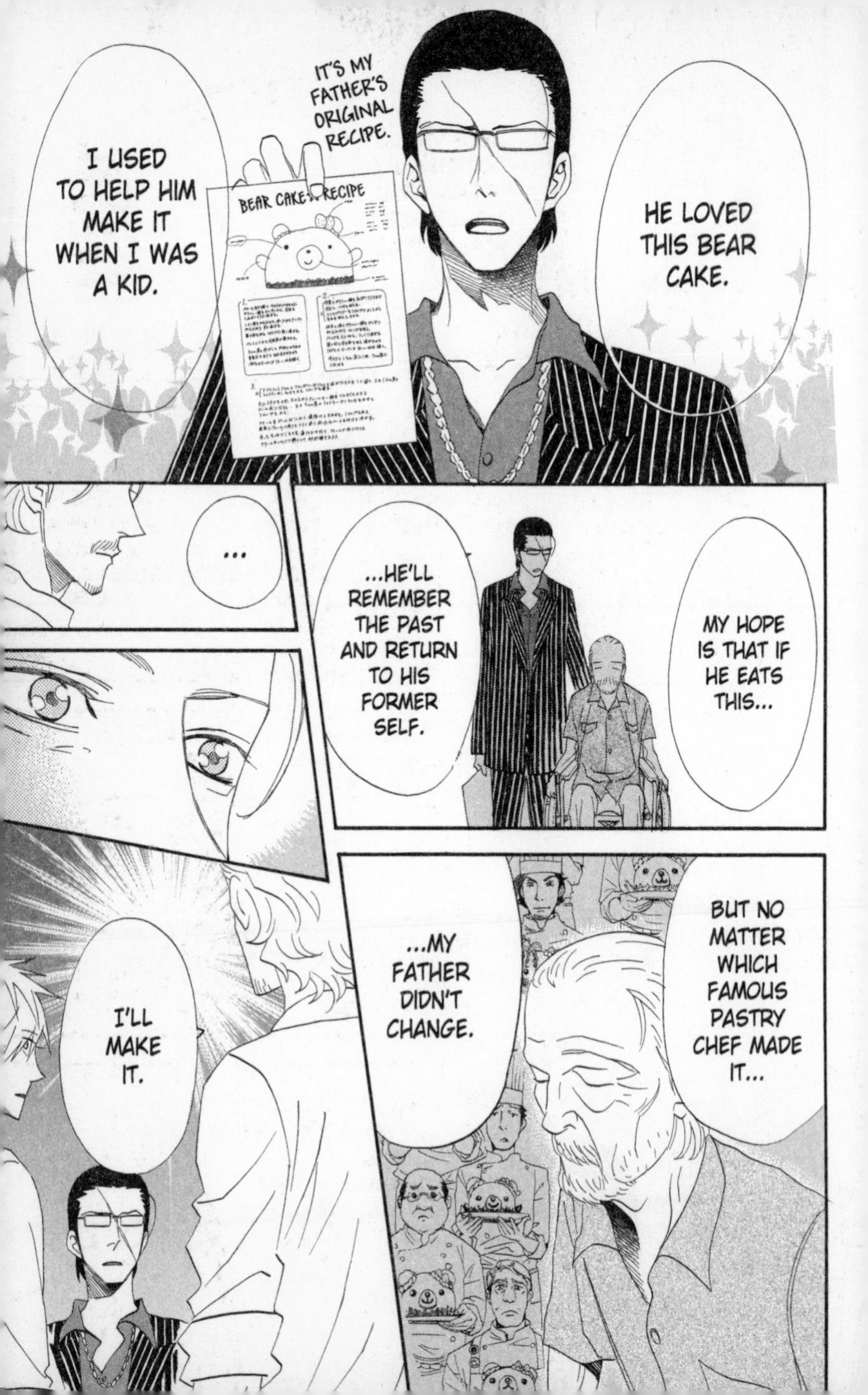
HE LOVED THIS BEAR CAKE.
IT'S MY FATHER'S ORIGINAL RECIPE.
BEAR CAKE RECIPE
I USED TO HELP HIM MAKE IT WHEN I WAS A KID.
MY HOPE IS THAT IF HE EATS THIS...
...HE'LL REMEMBER THE PAST AND RETURN TO HIS FORMER SELF.
...
BUT NO MATTER WHICH FAMOUS PASTRY CHEF MADE IT...
...MY FATHER DIDN'T CHANGE.
I'LL MAKE IT.

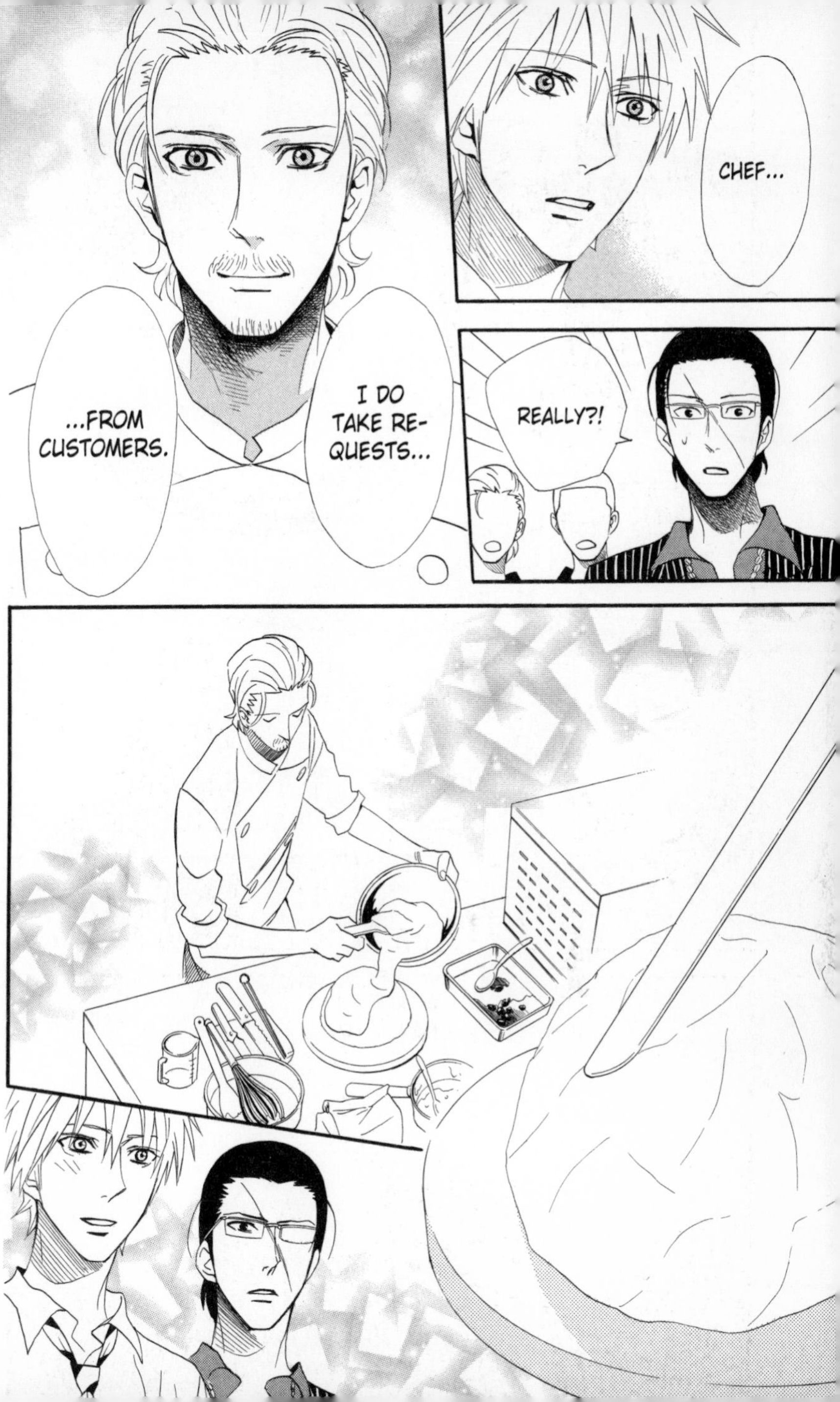
CHEF...
REALLY?!
I DO TAKE RE-QUESTS...
...FROM CUSTOMERS.

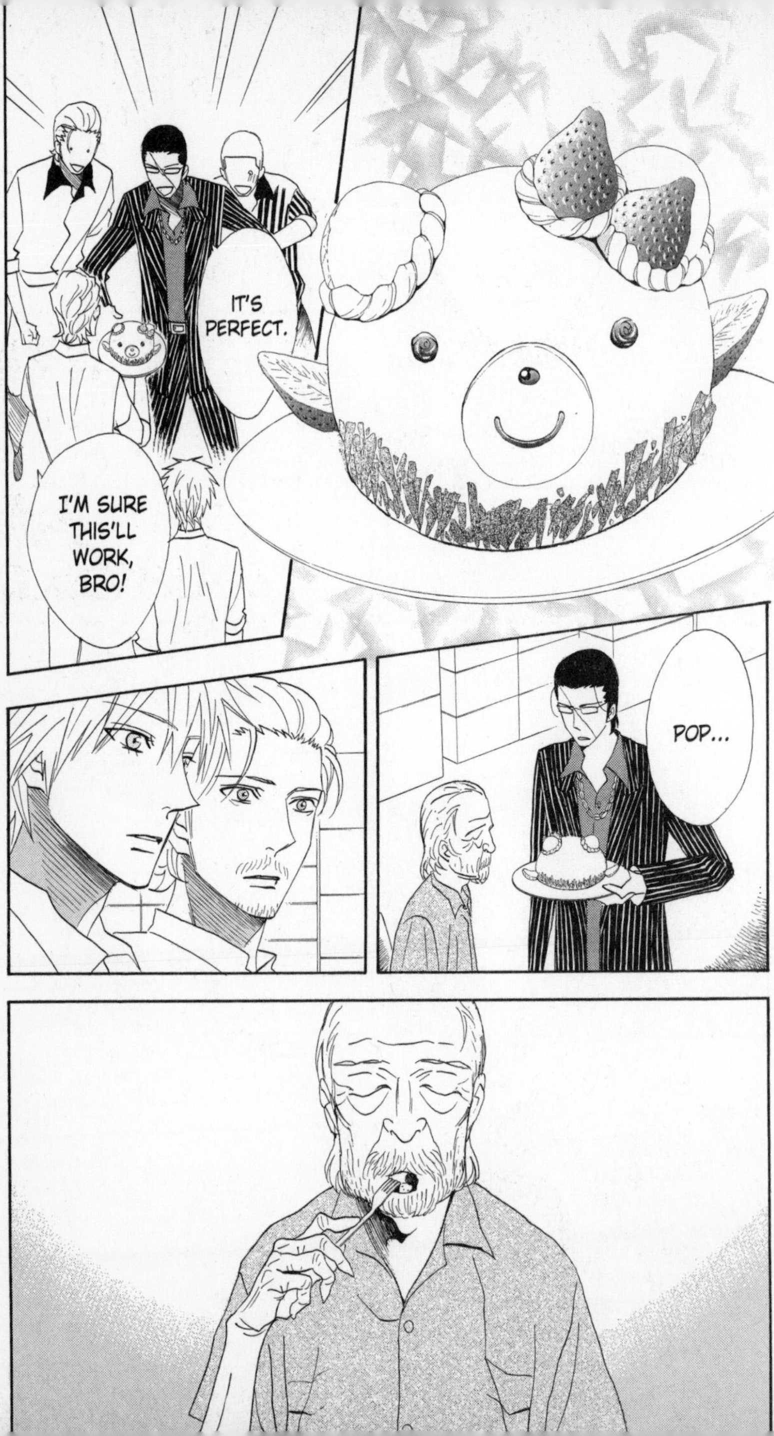
IT'S PERFECT.
I'M SURE THIS'LL WORK, BRO!
POP...

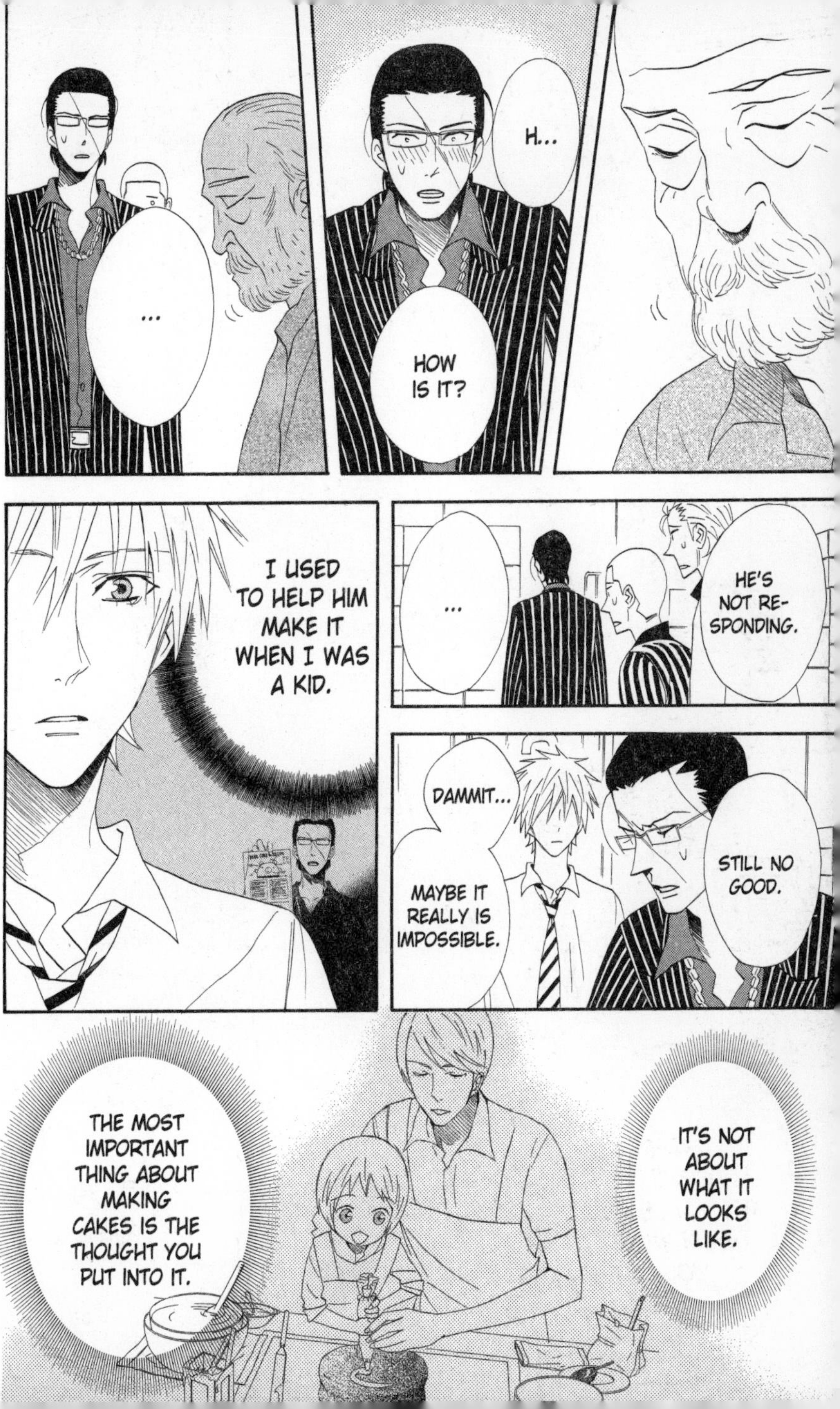
H...
HOW IS IT?
...
HE'S NOT RE-SPONDING.
...
STILL NO GOOD.
DAMMIT...
MAYBE IT REALLY IS IMPOSSIBLE.
I USED TO HELP HIM MAKE IT WHEN I WAS A KID.
IT'S NOT ABOUT WHAT IT LOOKS LIKE.
THE MOST IMPORTANT THING ABOUT MAKING CAKES IS THE THOUGHT YOU PUT INTO IT.

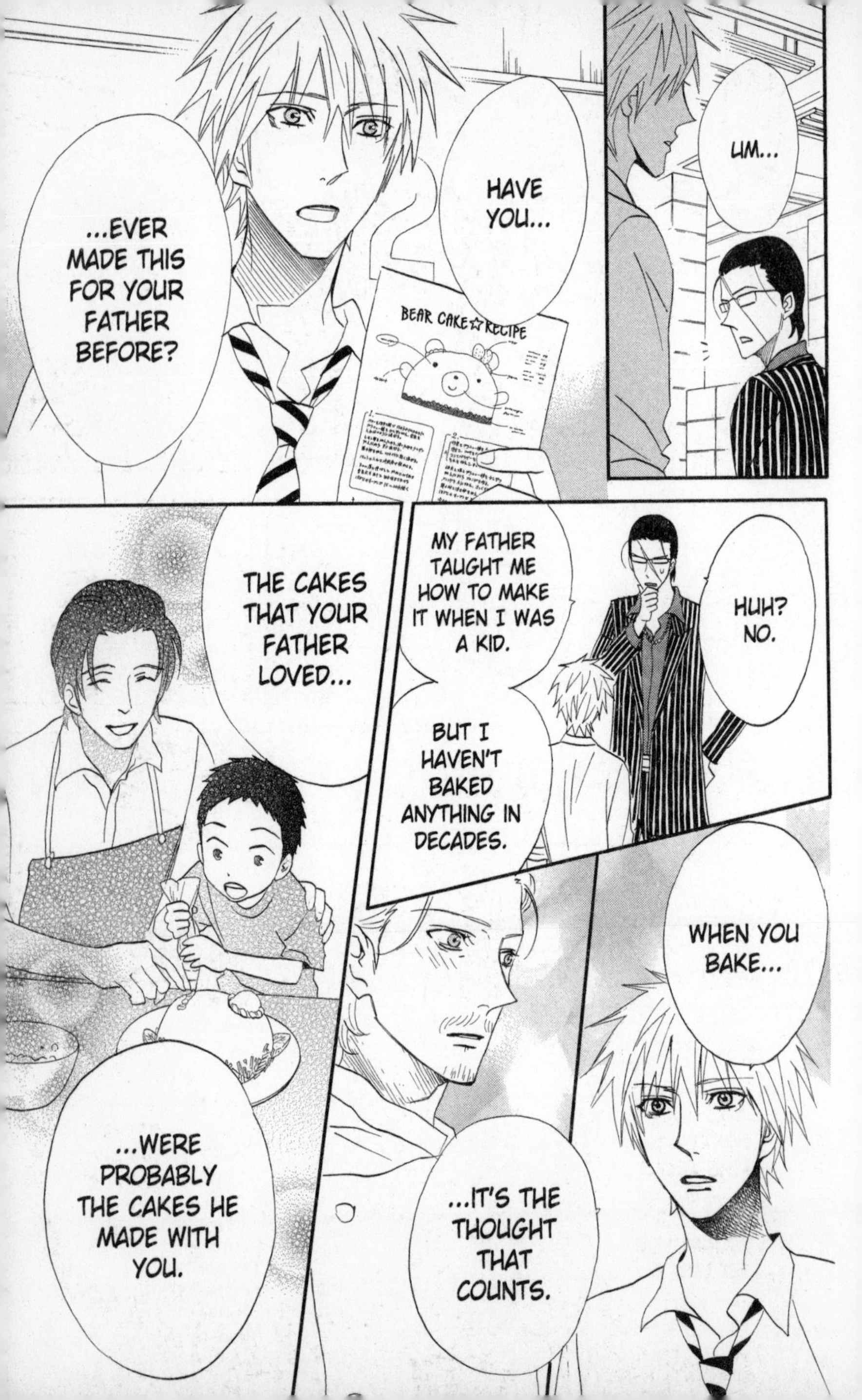
UM...
HAVE YOU...
...EVER MADE THIS FOR YOUR FATHER BEFORE?
BEAR CAKE☆RECIPE
HUH? NO.
MY FATHER TAUGHT ME HOW TO MAKE IT WHEN I WAS A KID.
BUT I HAVEN'T BAKED ANYTHING IN DECADES.
WHEN YOU BAKE...
...IT'S THE THOUGHT THAT COUNTS.
THE CAKES THAT YOUR FATHER LOVED...
...WERE PROBABLY THE CAKES HE MADE WITH YOU.

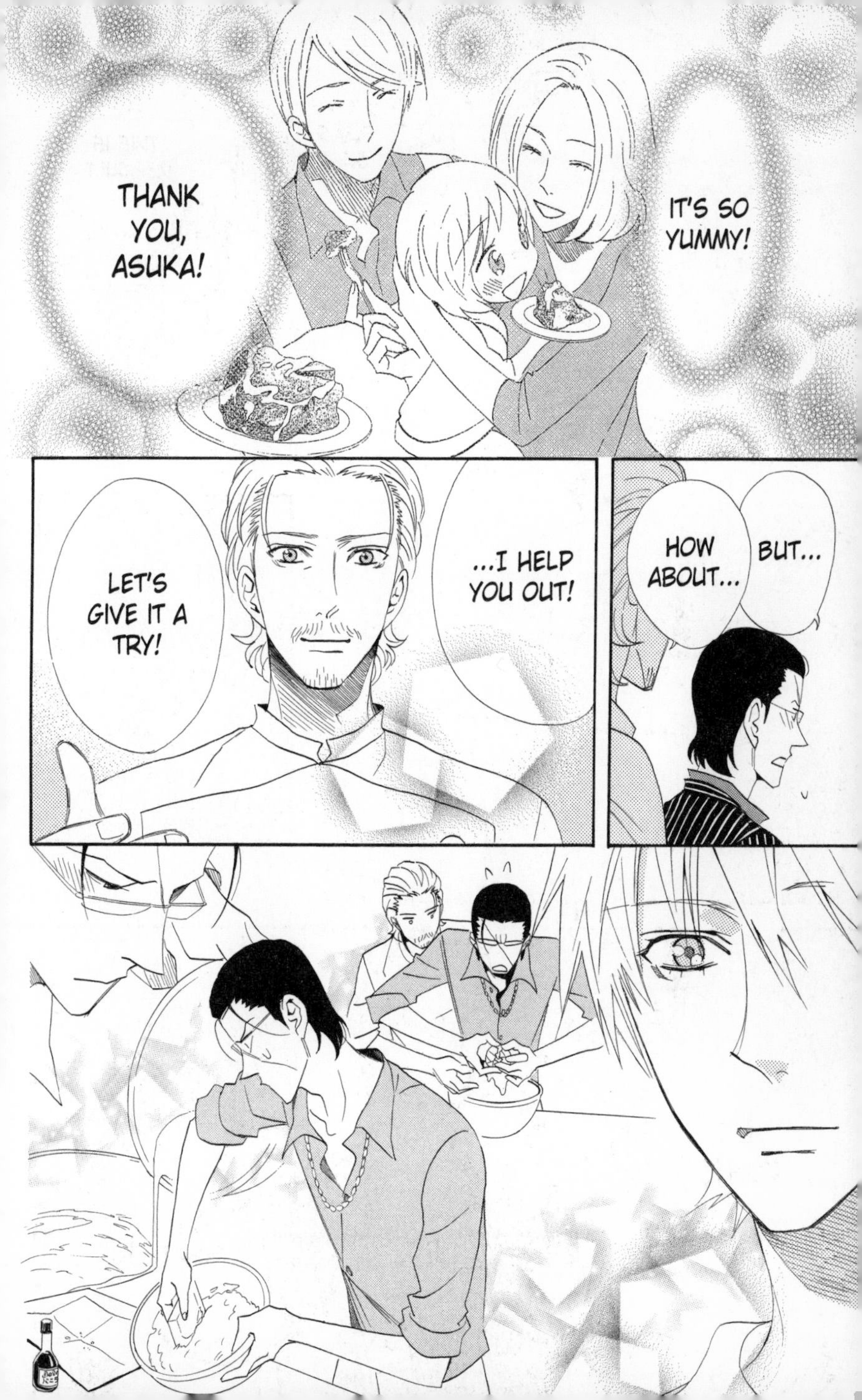
IT'S SO YUMMY!
THANK YOU, ASUKA!
BUT...
HOW ABOUT...
...I HELP YOU OUT!
LET'S GIVE IT A TRY!

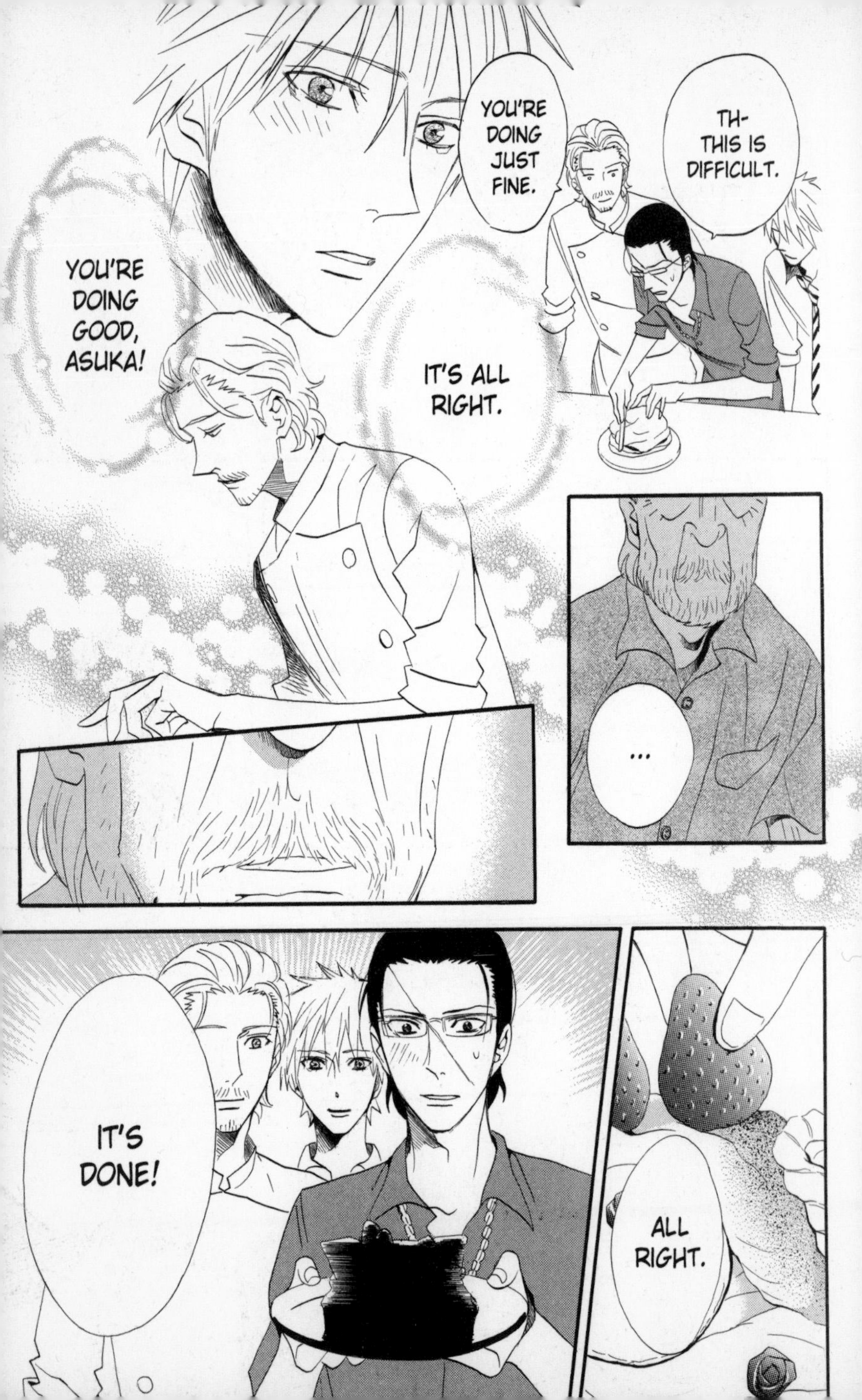
TH- THIS IS DIFFICULT.
YOU'RE DOING JUST FINE.
IT'S ALL RIGHT.
YOU'RE DOING GOOD, ASUKA!
...
ALL RIGHT.
IT'S DONE!

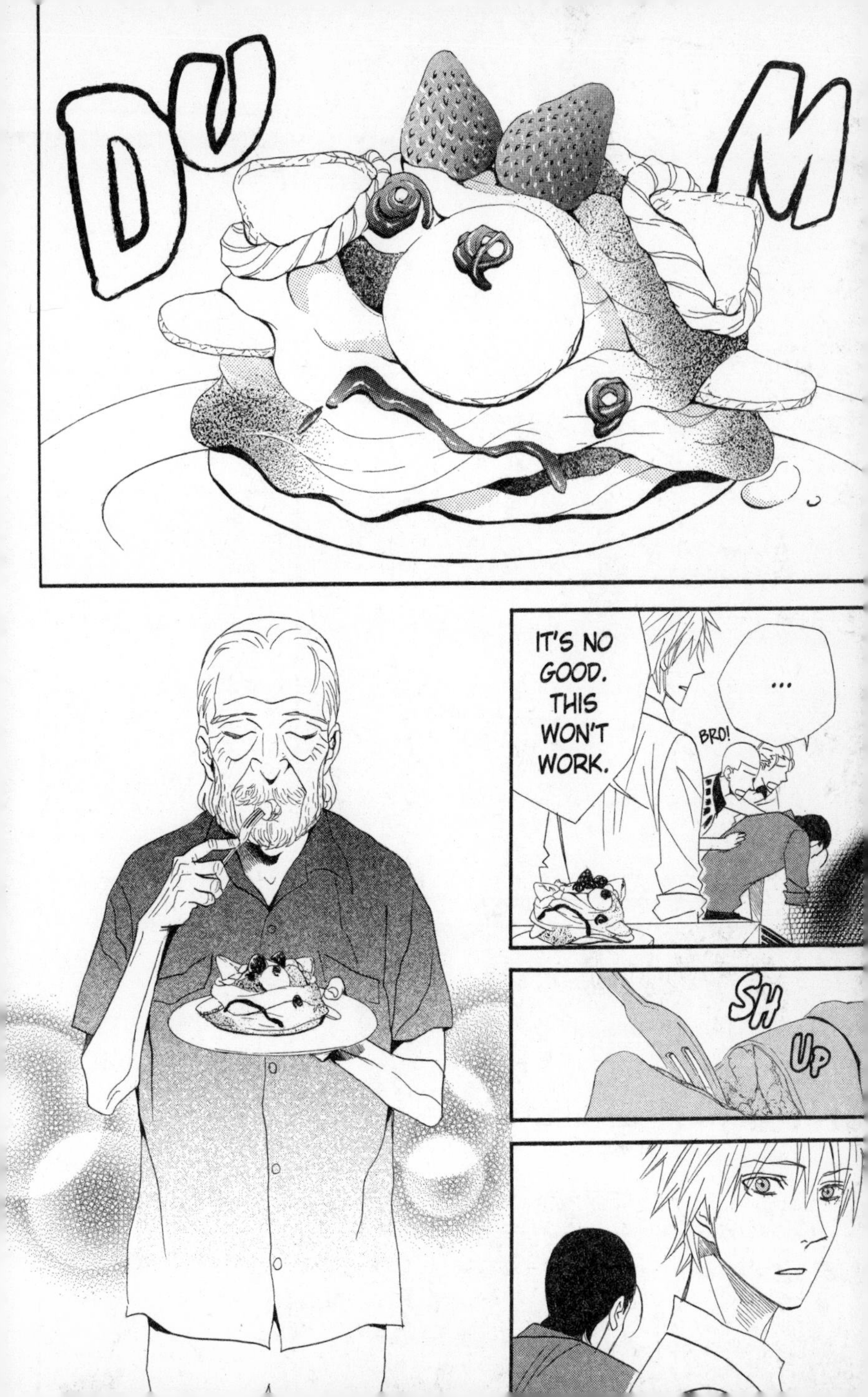
DUM
...
IT'S NO GOOD. THIS WON'T WORK.
BRO!
SHUP

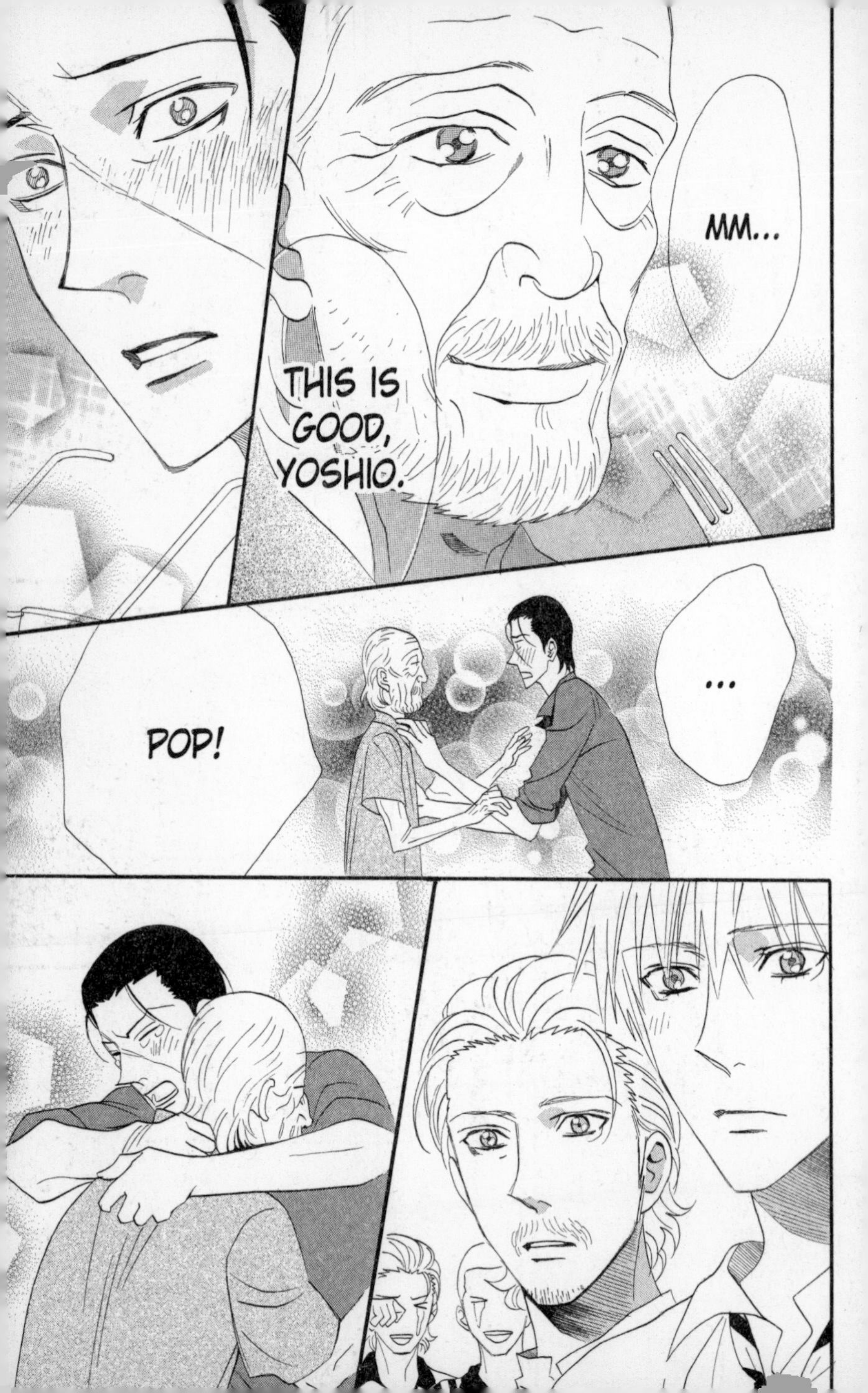
MM...
THIS IS GOOD, YOSHIO.
...
POP!

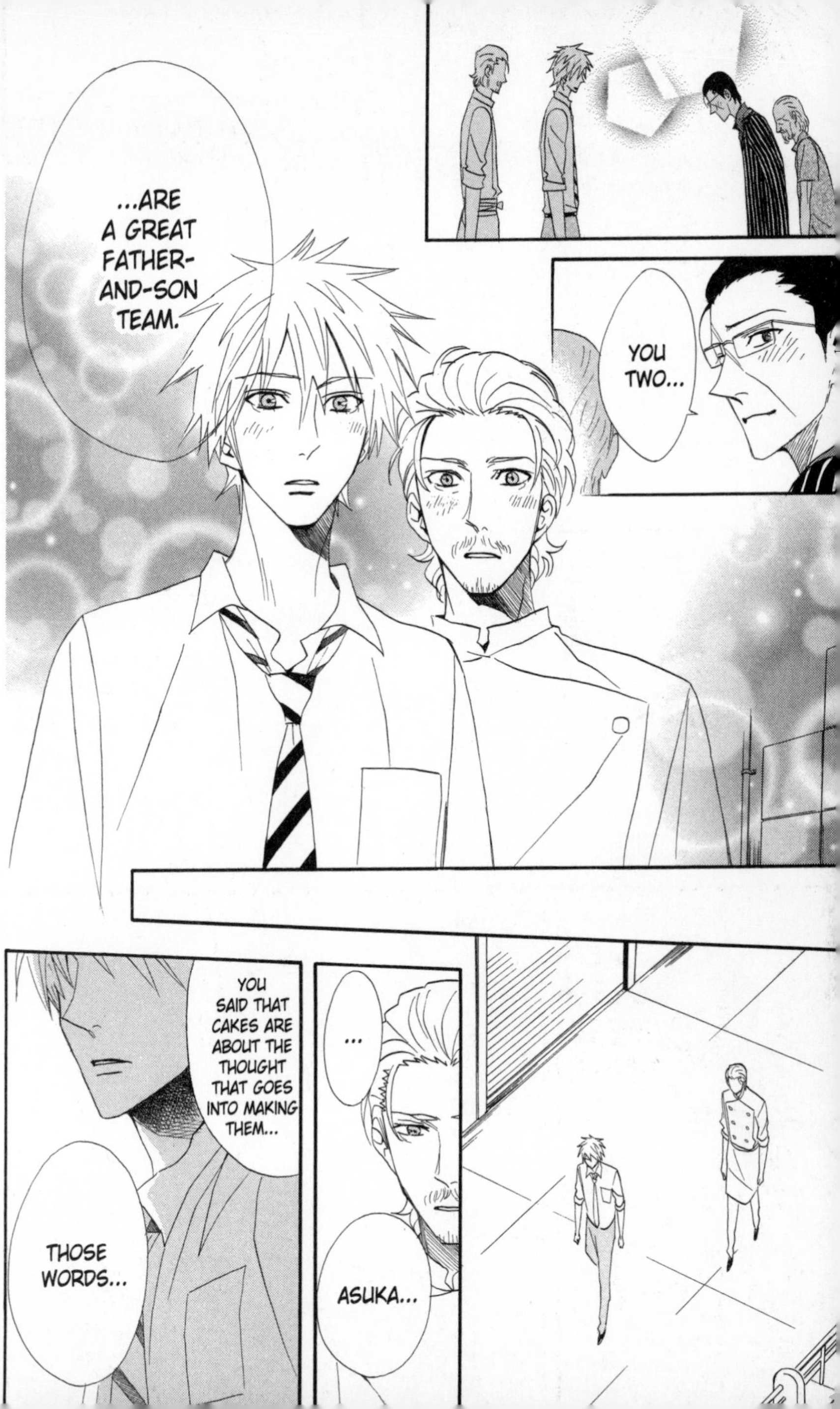
YOU TWO...
...ARE A GREAT FATHER-AND-SON TEAM.
...
ASUKA...
YOU SAID THAT CAKES ARE ABOUT THE THOUGHT THAT GOES INTO MAKING THEM...
THOSE WORDS...

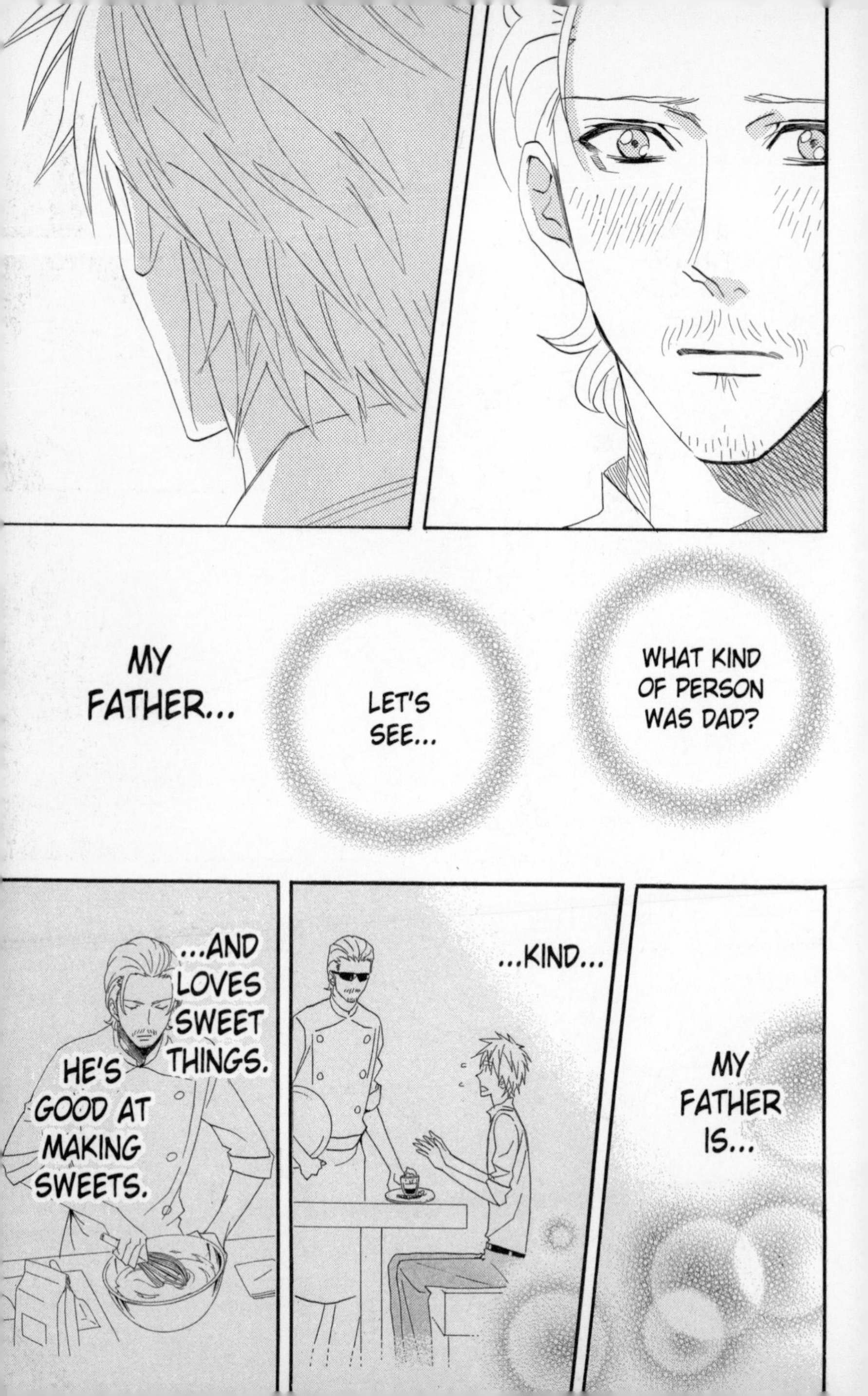
WHAT KIND OF PERSON WAS DAD?
LET'S SEE...
MY FATHER...
MY FATHER IS...
...KIND...
...AND LOVES SWEET THINGS.
HE'S GOOD AT MAKING SWEETS.

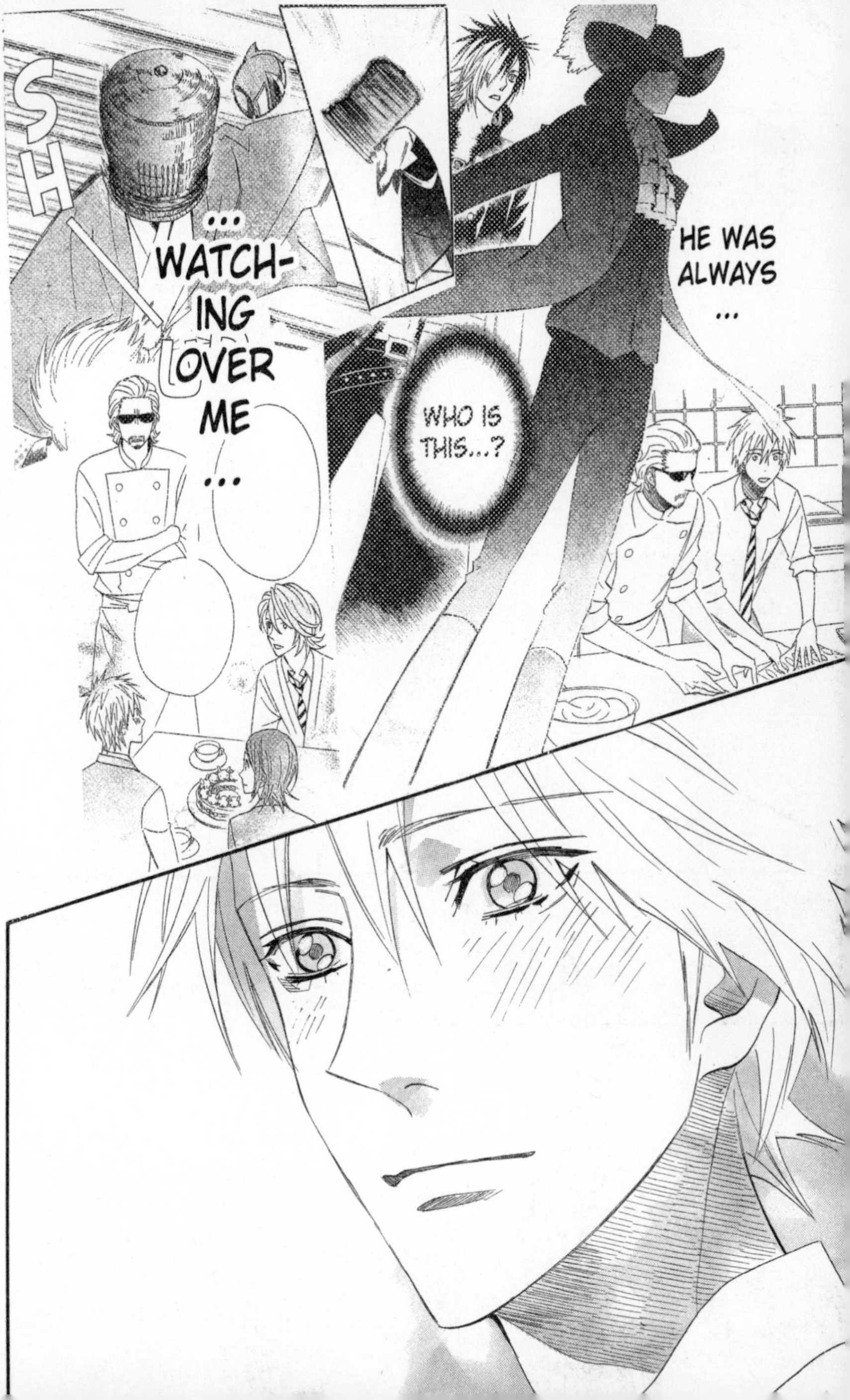
HE WAS ALWAYS ...
WHO IS THIS...?
SH
... WATCHING-ING OVER ME ...

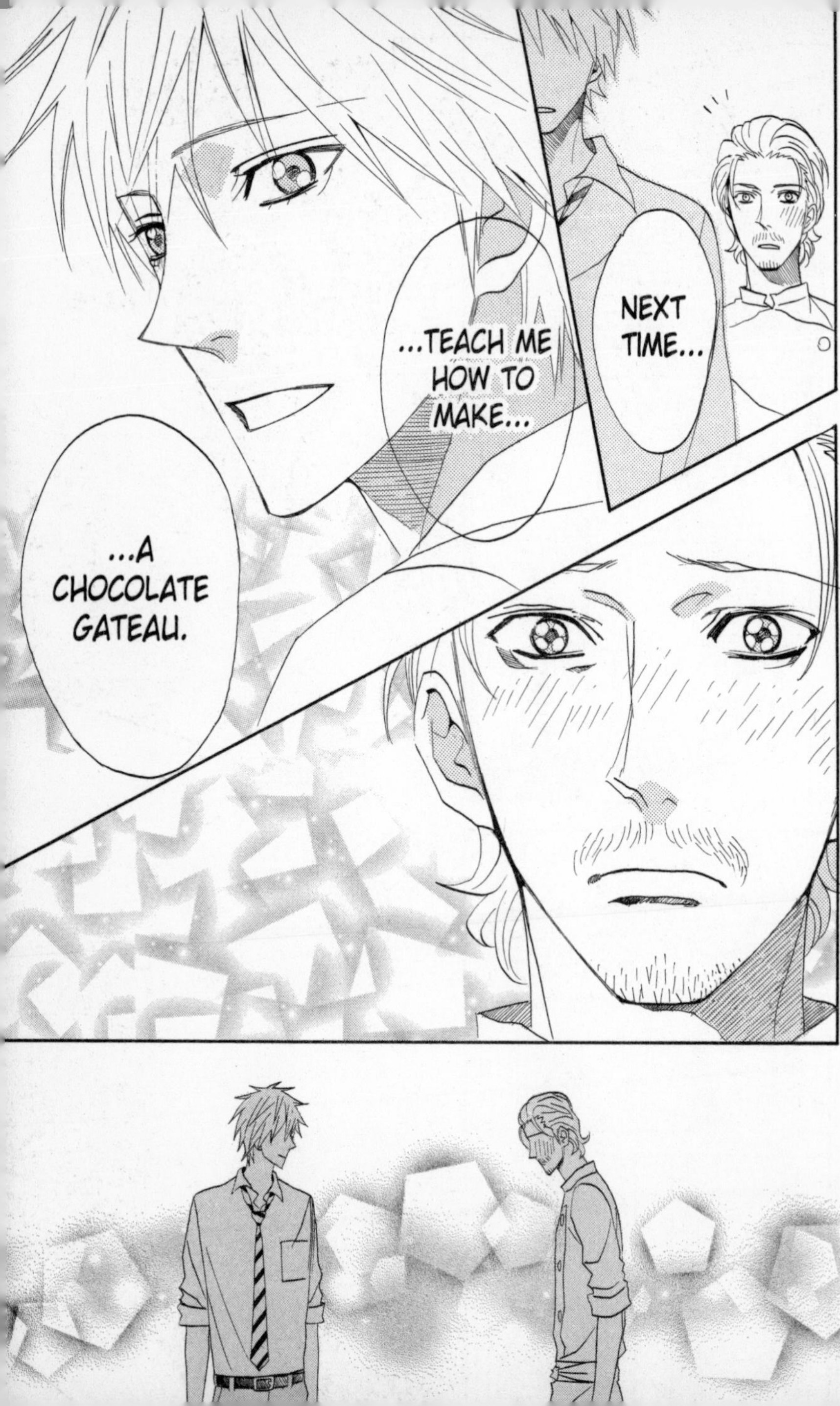
NEXT TIME...
...TEACH ME HOW TO MAKE...
...A CHOCOLATE GATEAU.

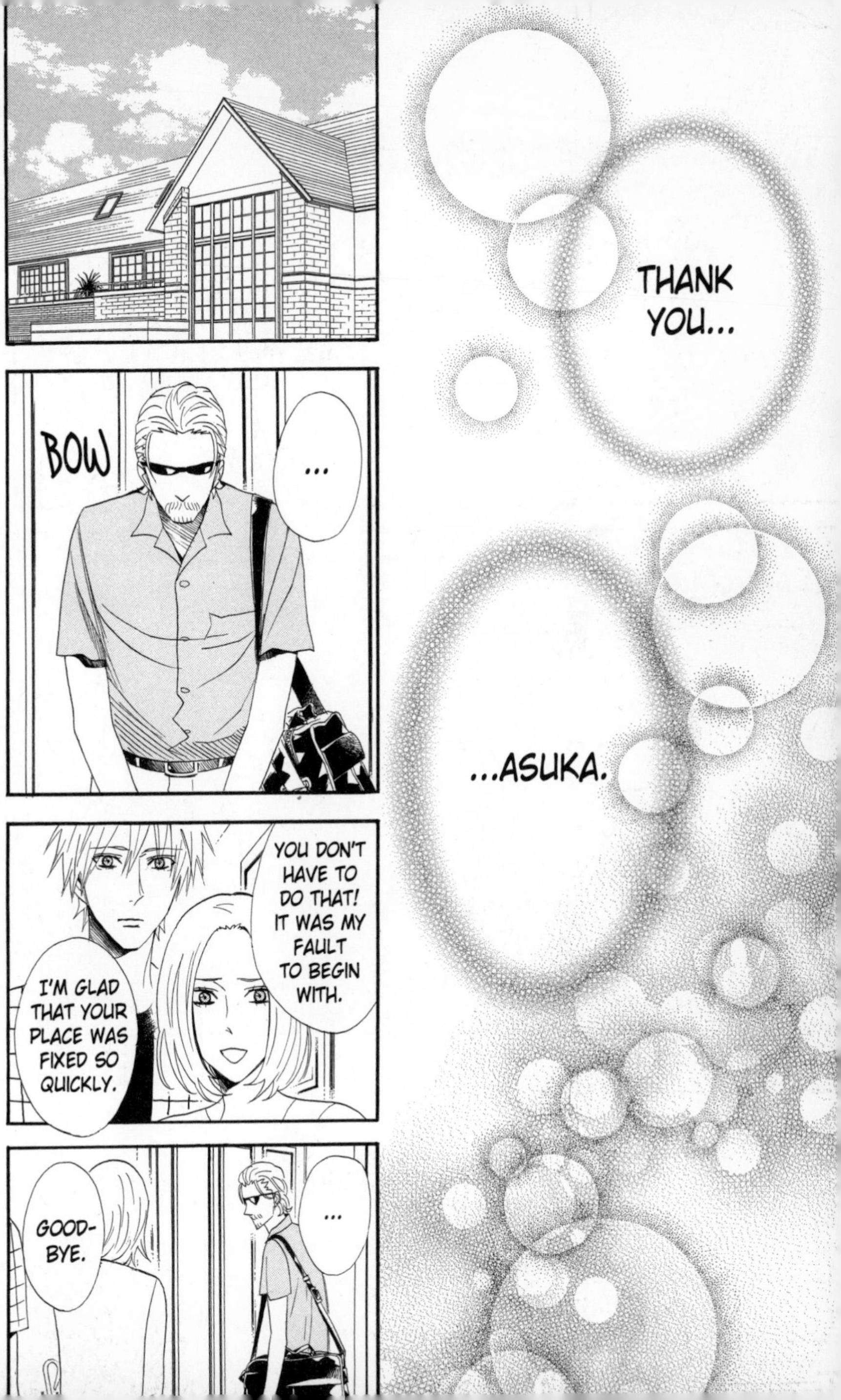
THANK YOU...
...ASUKA.
BOW
...
YOU DON'T HAVE TO DO THAT! IT WAS MY FAULT TO BEGIN WITH.
I'M GLAD THAT YOUR PLACE WAS FIXED SO QUICKLY.
...
GOOD-BYE.

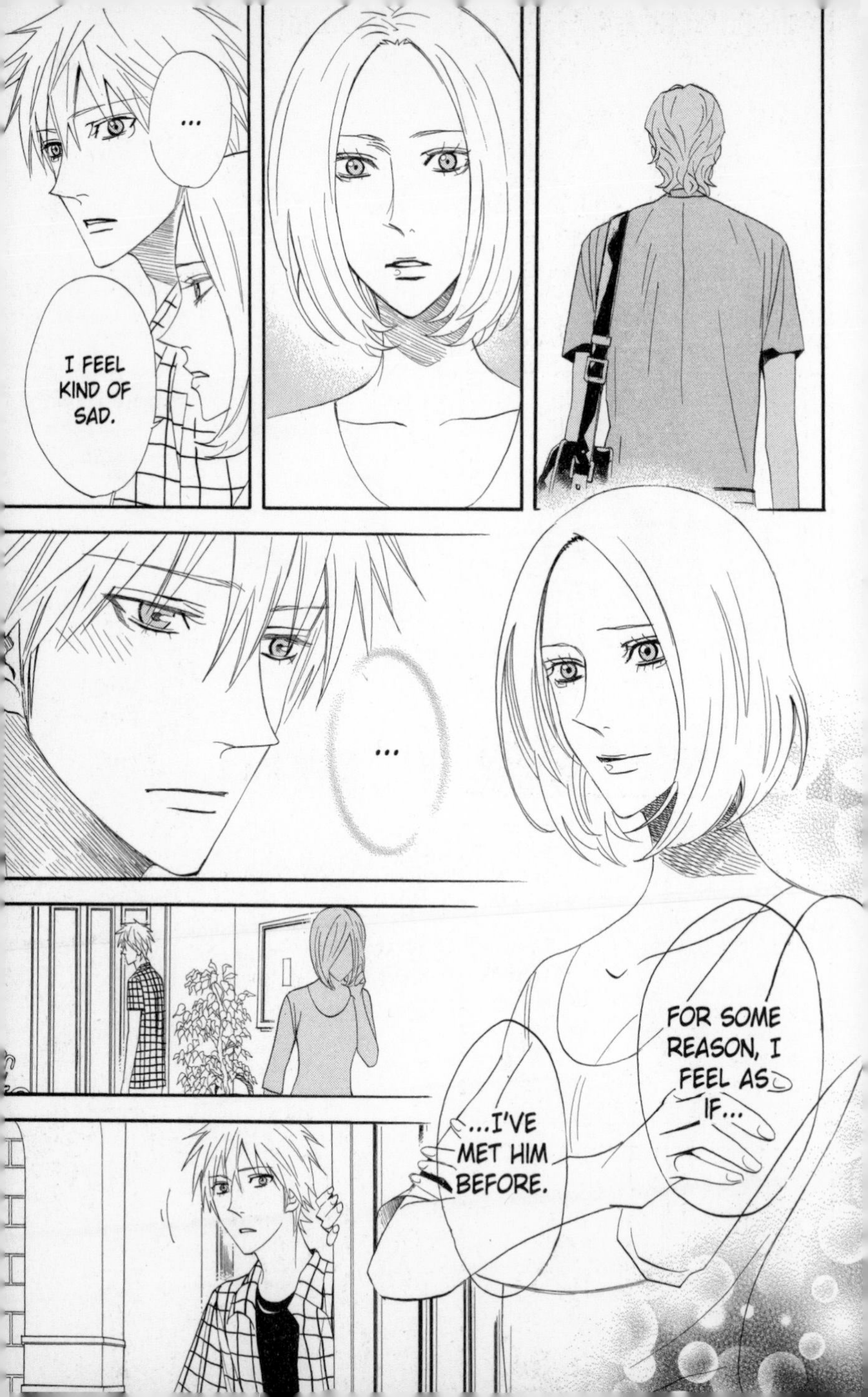
...
I FEEL KIND OF SAD.
FOR SOME REASON, I FEEL AS IF...
...I'VE MET HIM BEFORE.
...

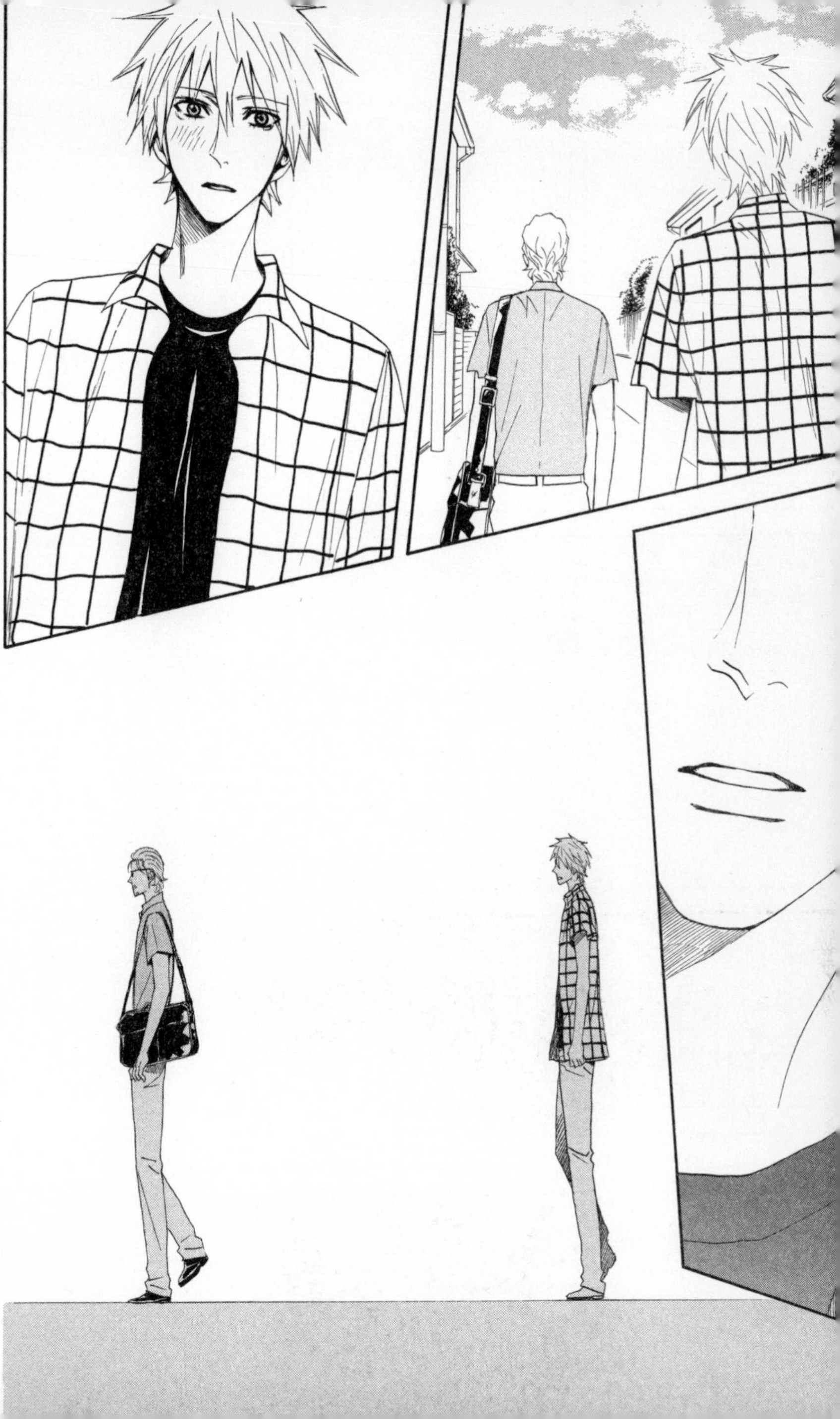

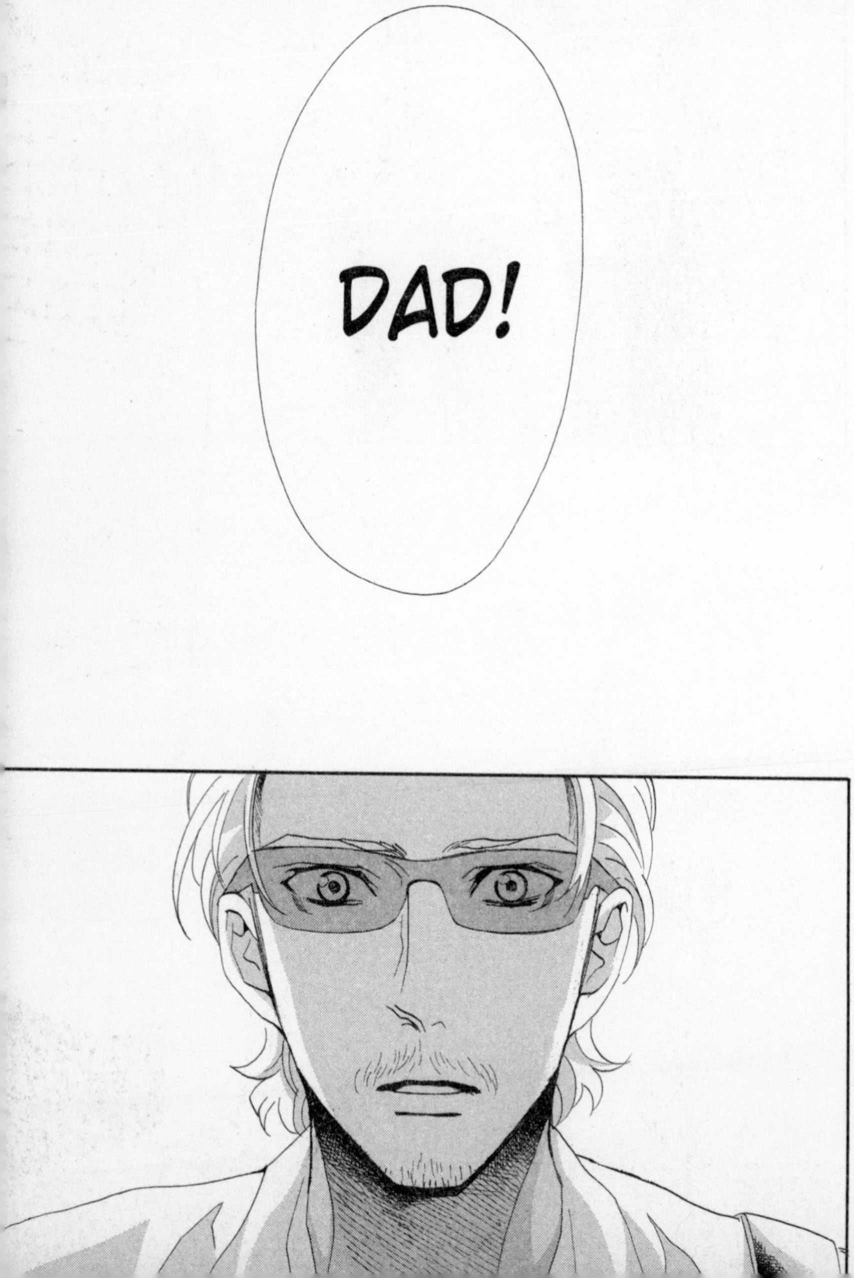
DAD!

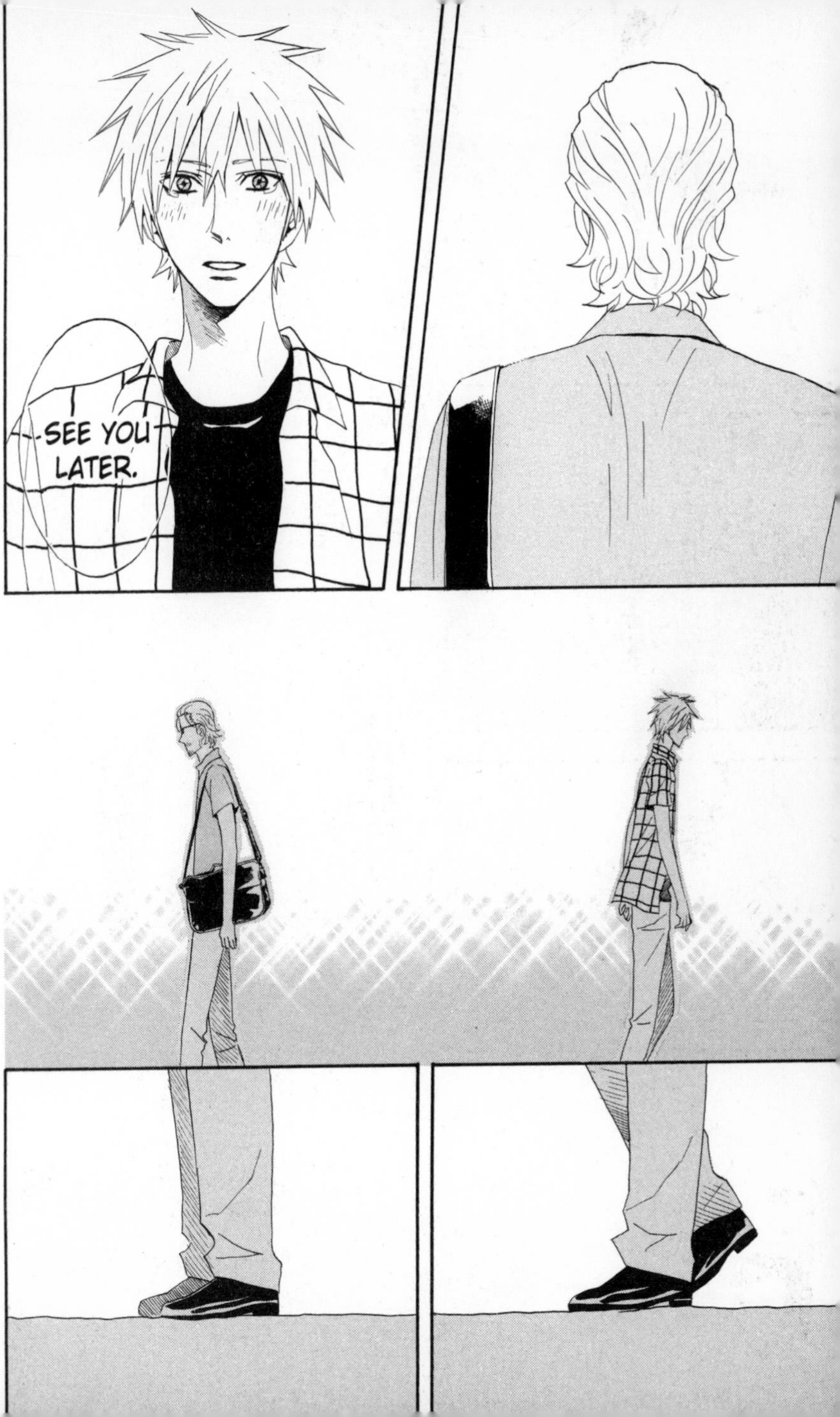
-SEE YOU LATER.

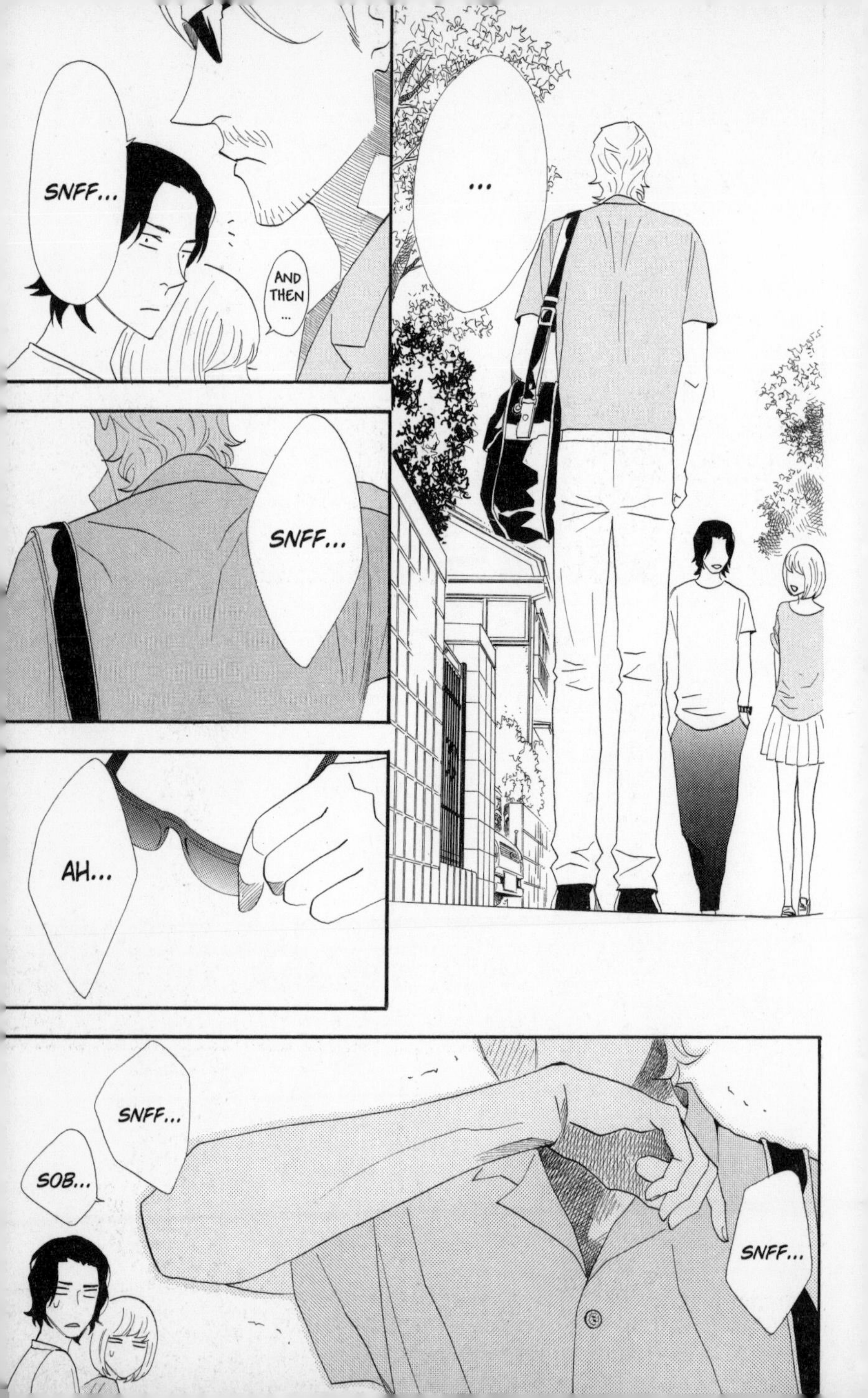
...
AND THEN ...
SNFF...
SNFF...
AH...
SNFF...
SNFF...
SOB...

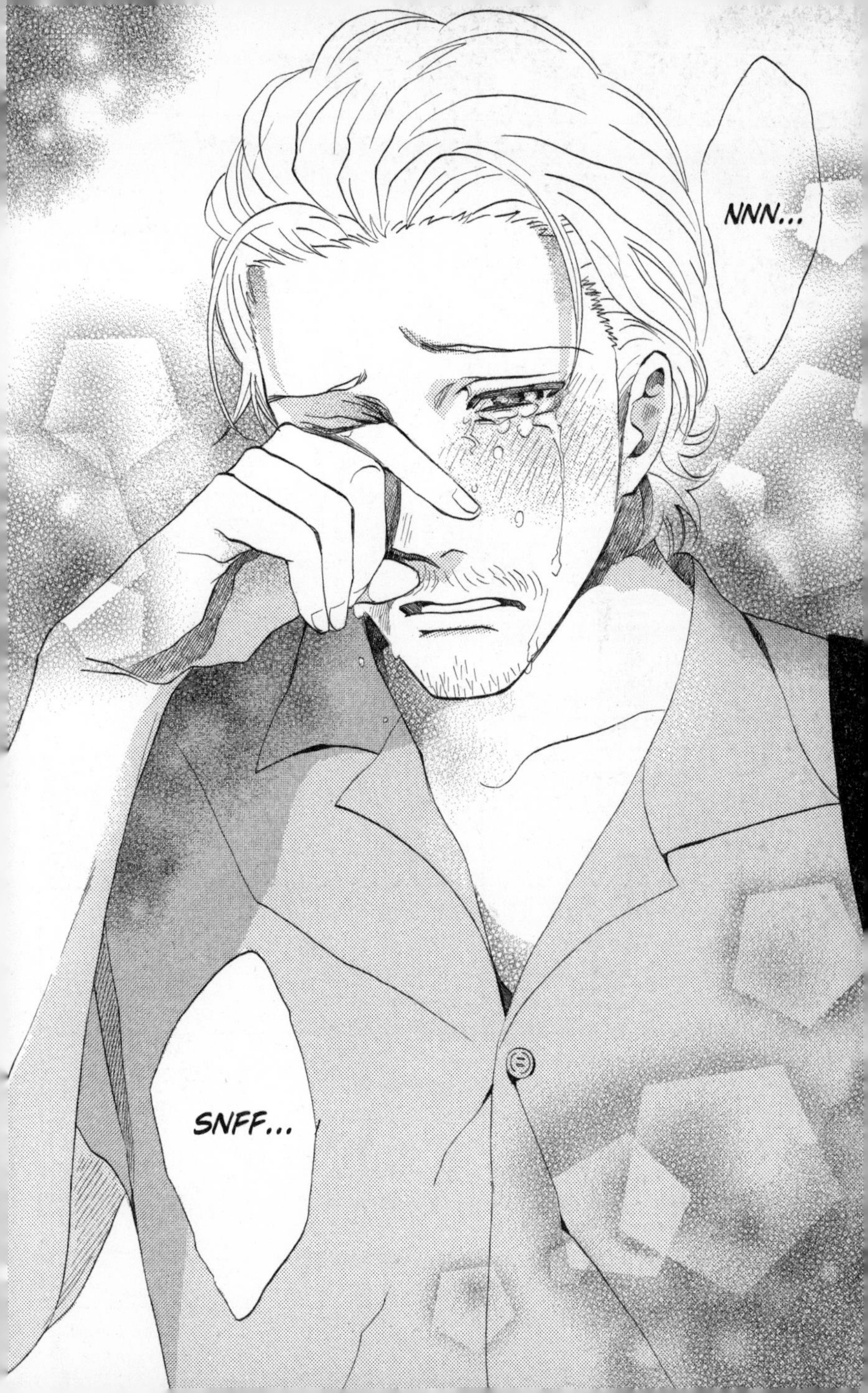
NNN...
SNFF...

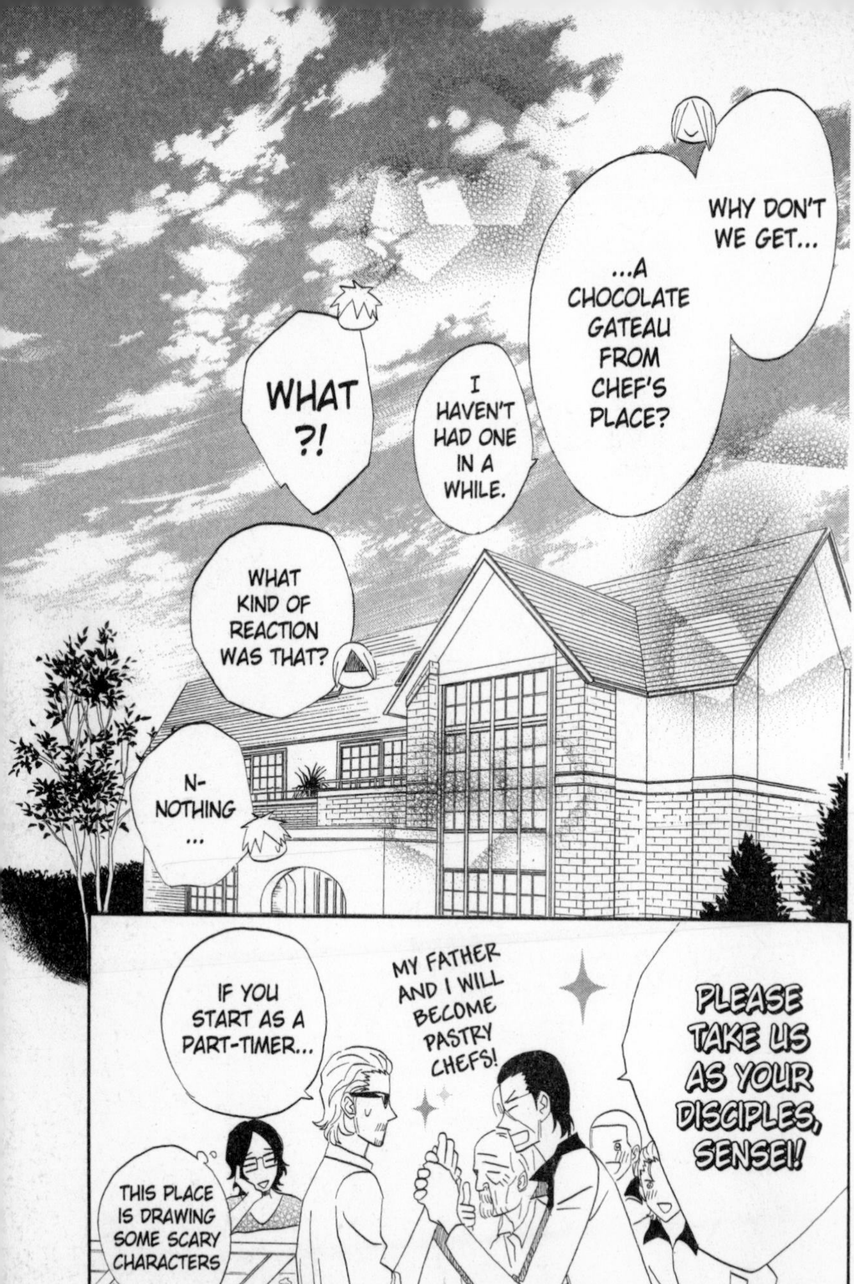
WHY DON'T WE GET...
...A CHOCOLATE GATEAU FROM CHEF'S PLACE?
I HAVEN'T HAD ONE IN A WHILE.
WHAT?!
WHAT KIND OF REACTION WAS THAT?
N-NOTHING...
PLEASE TAKE US AS YOUR DISCIPLES, SENSEI!
MY FATHER AND I WILL BECOME PASTRY CHEFS!
IF YOU START AS A PART-TIMER...
THIS PLACE IS DRAWING SOME SCARY CHARACTERS...

OTOMEN

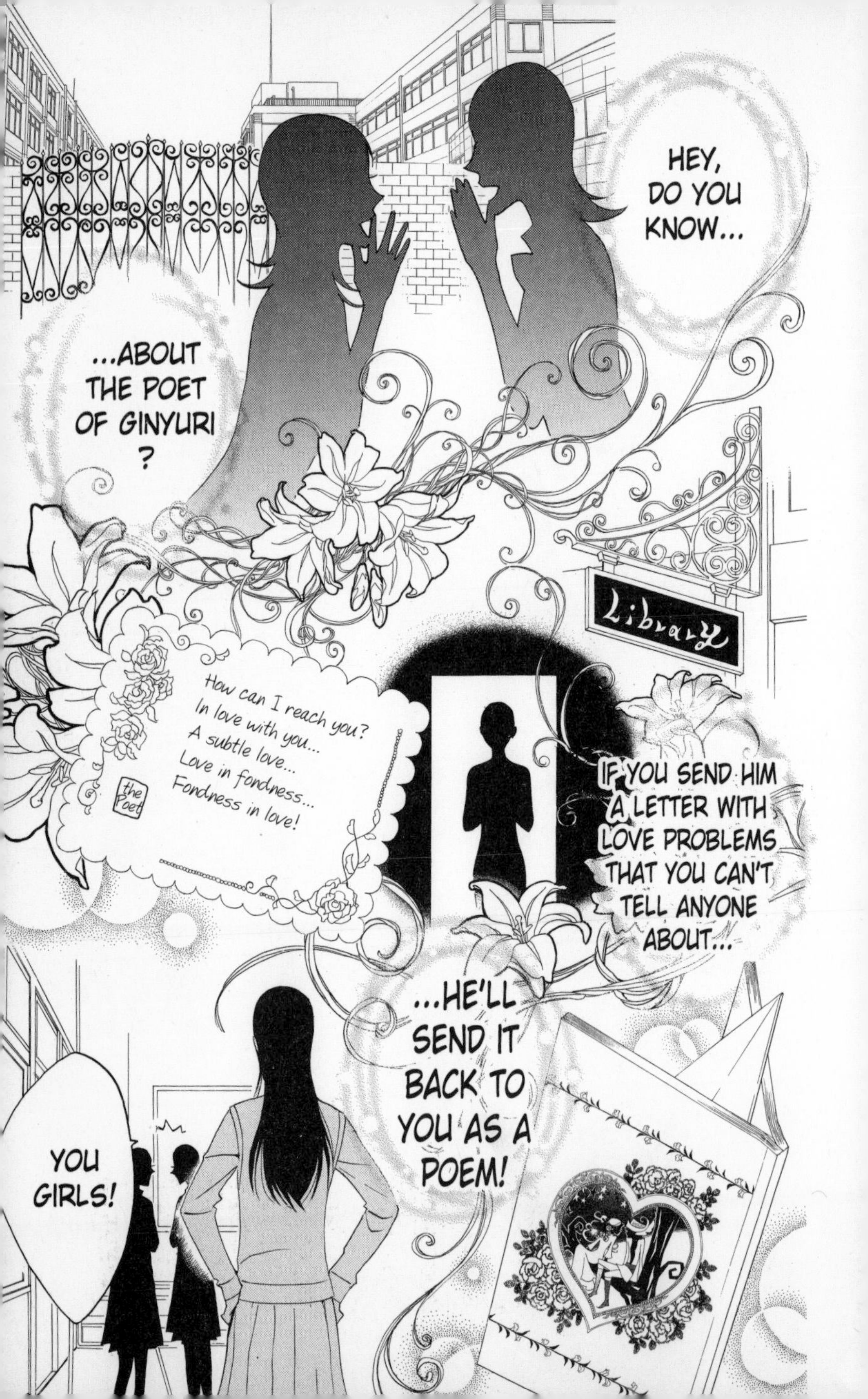
HEY, DO YOU KNOW...
...ABOUT THE POET OF GINYURI ?
Library
IF YOU SEND HIM A LETTER WITH LOVE PROBLEMS THAT YOU CAN'T TELL ANYONE ABOUT...
How can I reach you?
In love with you...
A subtle love...
Love in fondness...
Fondness in love!
the Poet
...HE'LL SEND IT BACK TO YOU AS A POEM!
YOU GIRLS!

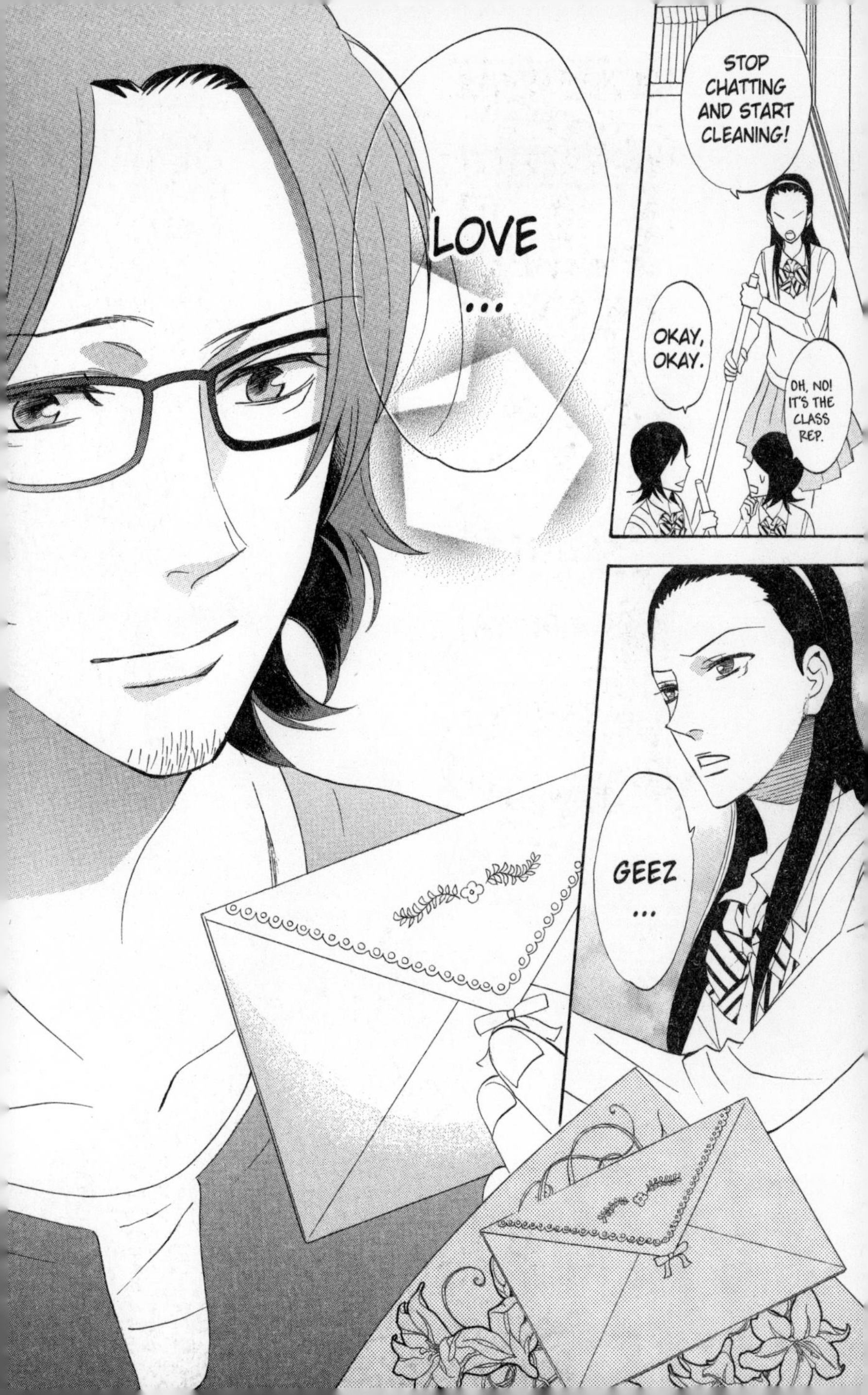
STOP CHATTING AND START CLEANING!
OH, NO! IT'S THE CLASS REP.
OKAY, OKAY.
GEEZ ...
LOVE ...

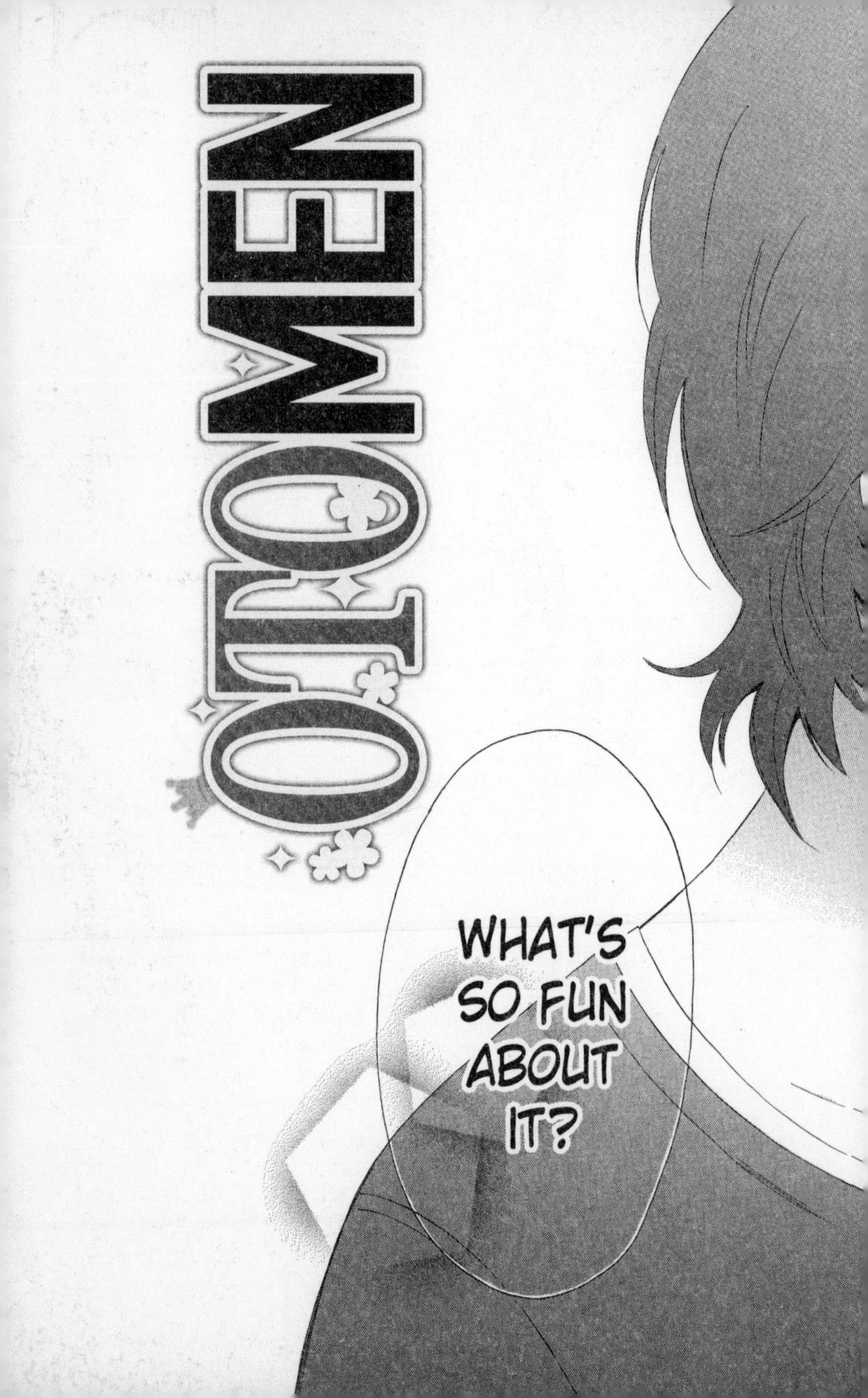
OTOMEN
WHAT'S SO FUN ABOUT IT?

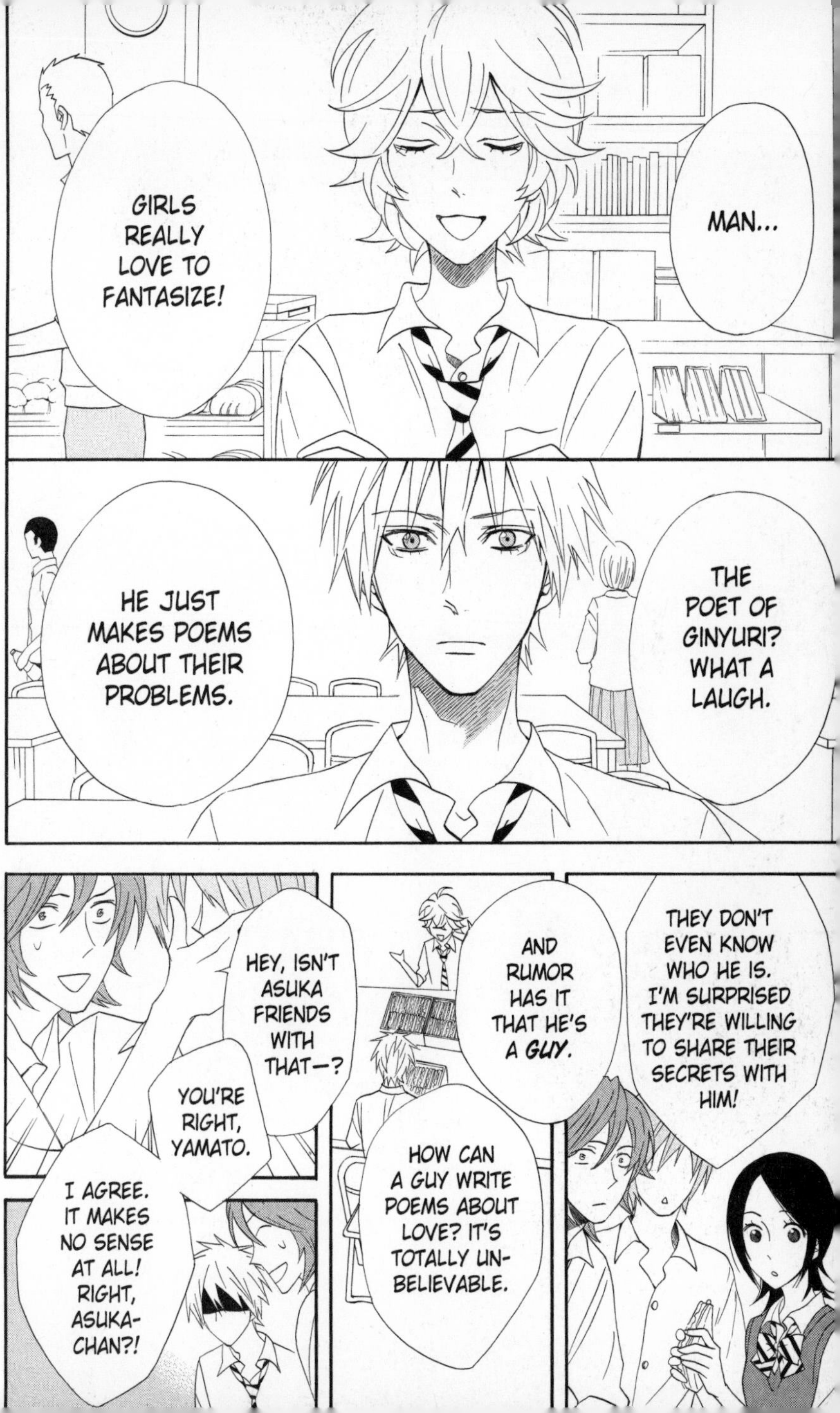
MAN...
GIRLS REALLY LOVE TO FANTASIZE!
THE POET OF GINYURI? WHAT A LAUGH.
HE JUST MAKES POEMS ABOUT THEIR PROBLEMS.
THEY DON'T EVEN KNOW WHO HE IS. I'M SURPRISED THEY'RE WILLING TO SHARE THEIR SECRETS WITH HIM!
AND RUMOR HAS IT THAT HE'S A *GUY*.
HOW CAN A GUY WRITE POEMS ABOUT LOVE? IT'S TOTALLY UN-BELIEVABLE.
HEY, ISN'T ASUKA FRIENDS WITH THAT—?
YOU'RE RIGHT, YAMATO.
I AGREE. IT MAKES NO SENSE AT ALL! RIGHT, ASUKA-CHAN?!

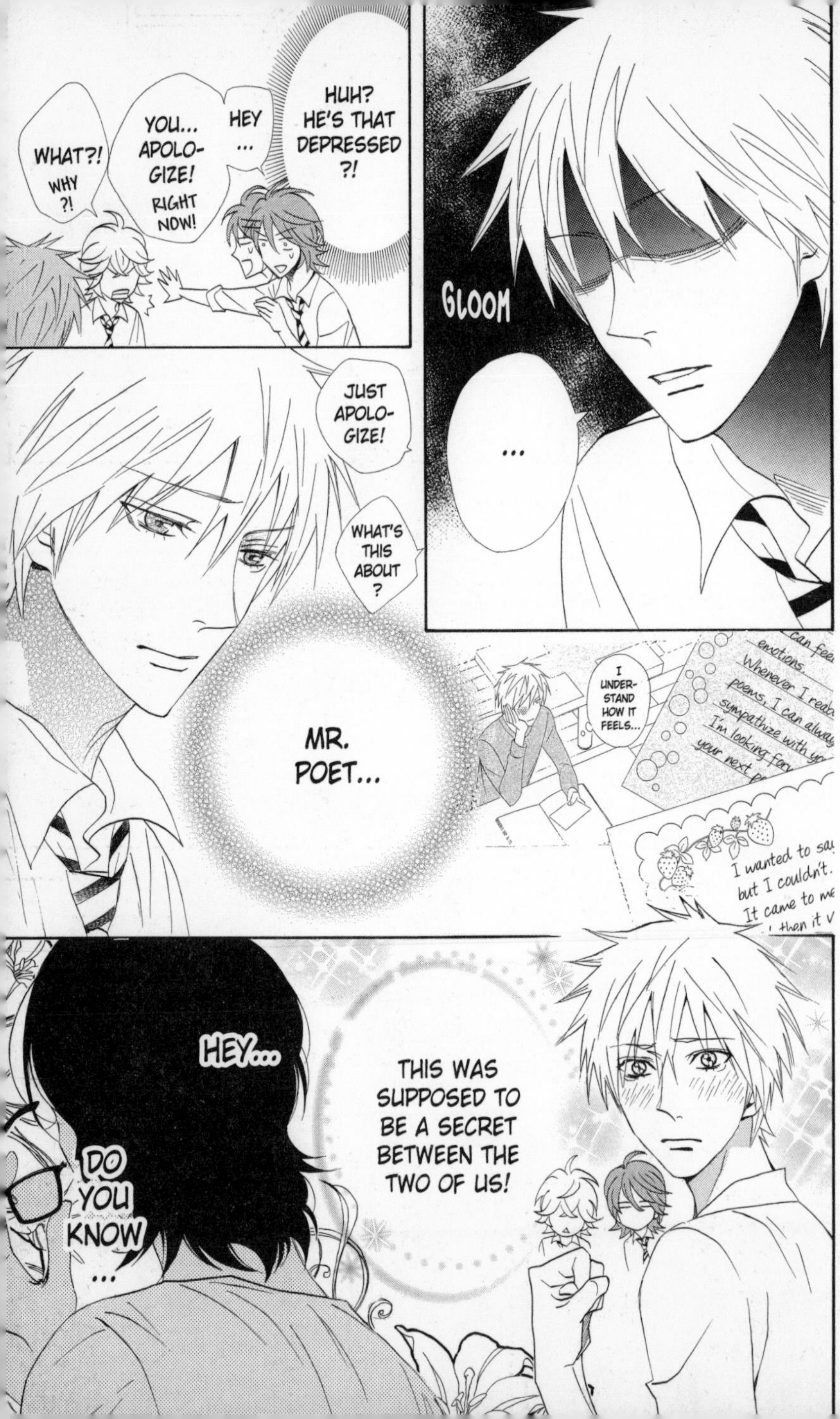
GLOOM
...
HUH? HE'S THAT DEPRESSED?!
HEY...
YOU... APOLOGIZE! RIGHT NOW!
WHAT?! WHY?!
JUST APOLOGIZE!
WHAT'S THIS ABOUT?
I UNDERSTAND HOW IT FEELS...
can fee
emotions.
Whenever I rea
poems, I can alway
sympathzye with yo
I'm looking forw
your next p
I wanted to sa
but I couldn't.
It came to me
than it w
MR. POET...
THIS WAS SUPPOSED TO BE A SECRET BETWEEN THE TWO OF US!
HEY...
DO YOU KNOW...

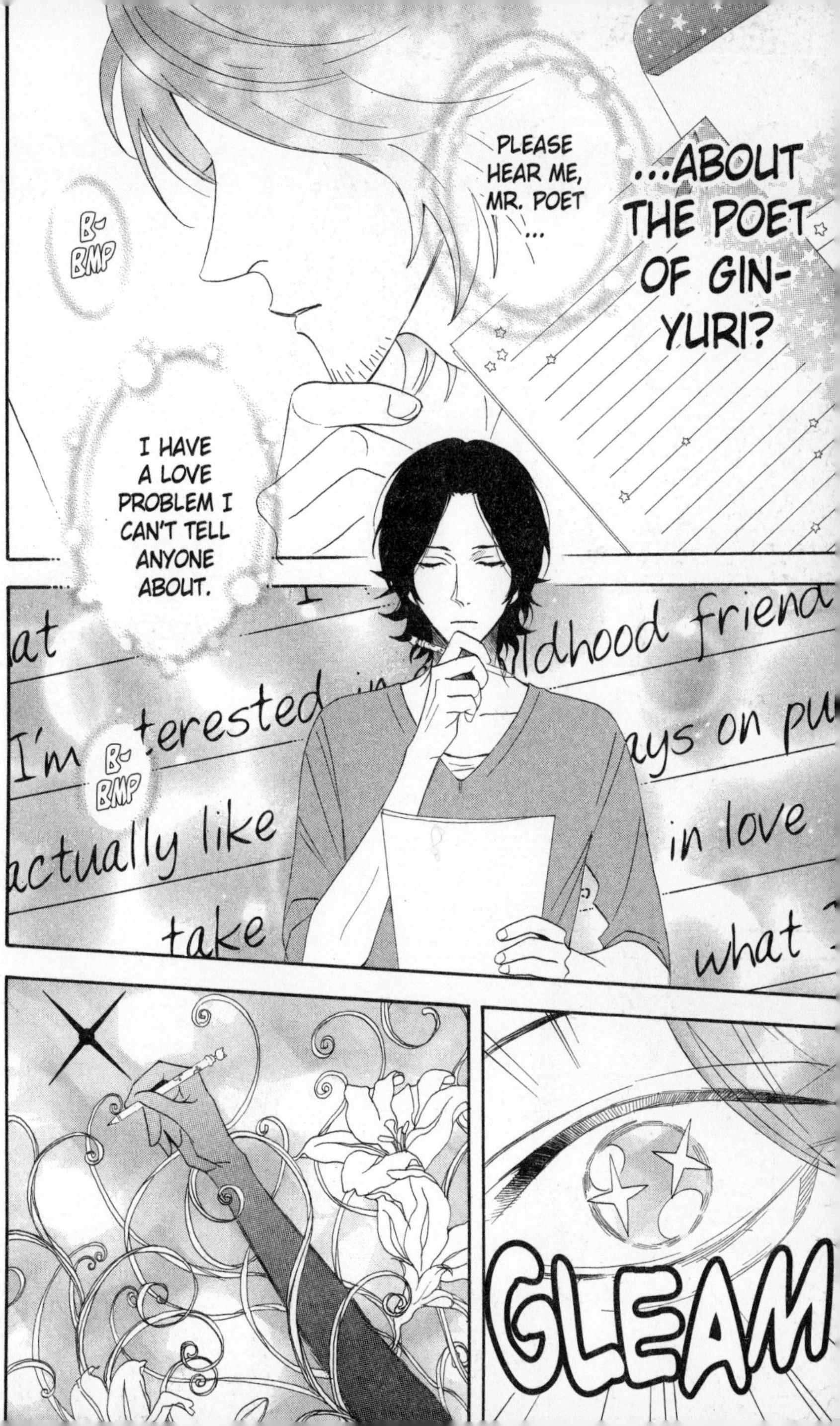
...ABOUT THE POET OF GIN-YURI?
PLEASE HEAR ME, MR. POET...
B-BMP
I HAVE A LOVE PROBLEM I CAN'T TELL ANYONE ABOUT.
B-BMP
at
ldhood friend
I'm terested
ays on pu
actually like
in love
take
what
GLEAM

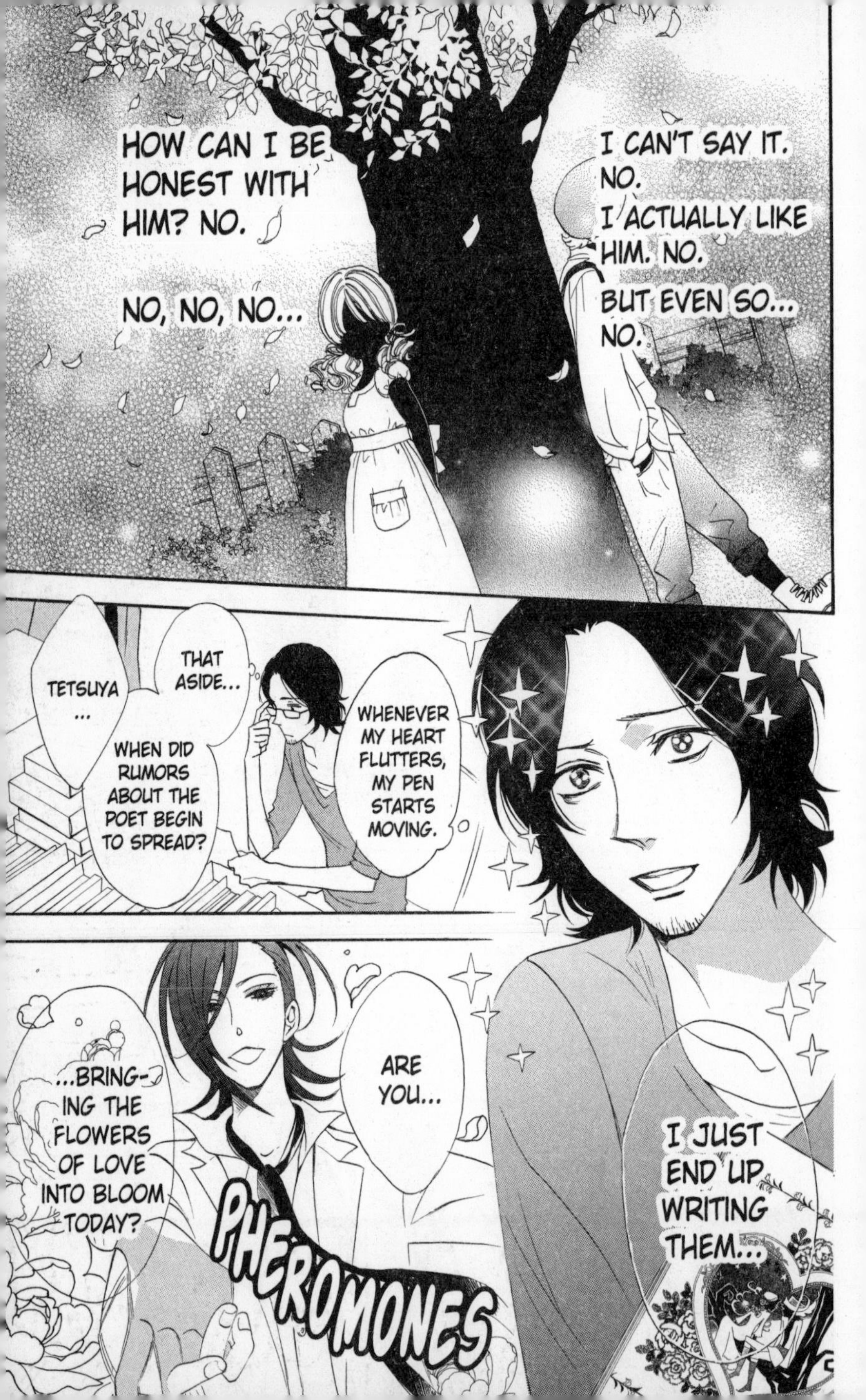
I CAN'T SAY IT. NO. I ACTUALLY LIKE HIM. NO. BUT EVEN SO... NO.
HOW CAN I BE HONEST WITH HIM? NO.
NO, NO, NO...
WHENEVER MY HEART FLUTTERS, MY PEN STARTS MOVING.
I JUST END UP WRITING THEM...
THAT ASIDE...
WHEN DID RUMORS ABOUT THE POET BEGIN TO SPREAD?
TETSUYA...
ARE YOU...
...BRING-ING THE FLOWERS OF LOVE INTO BLOOM TODAY?
PHEROMONES

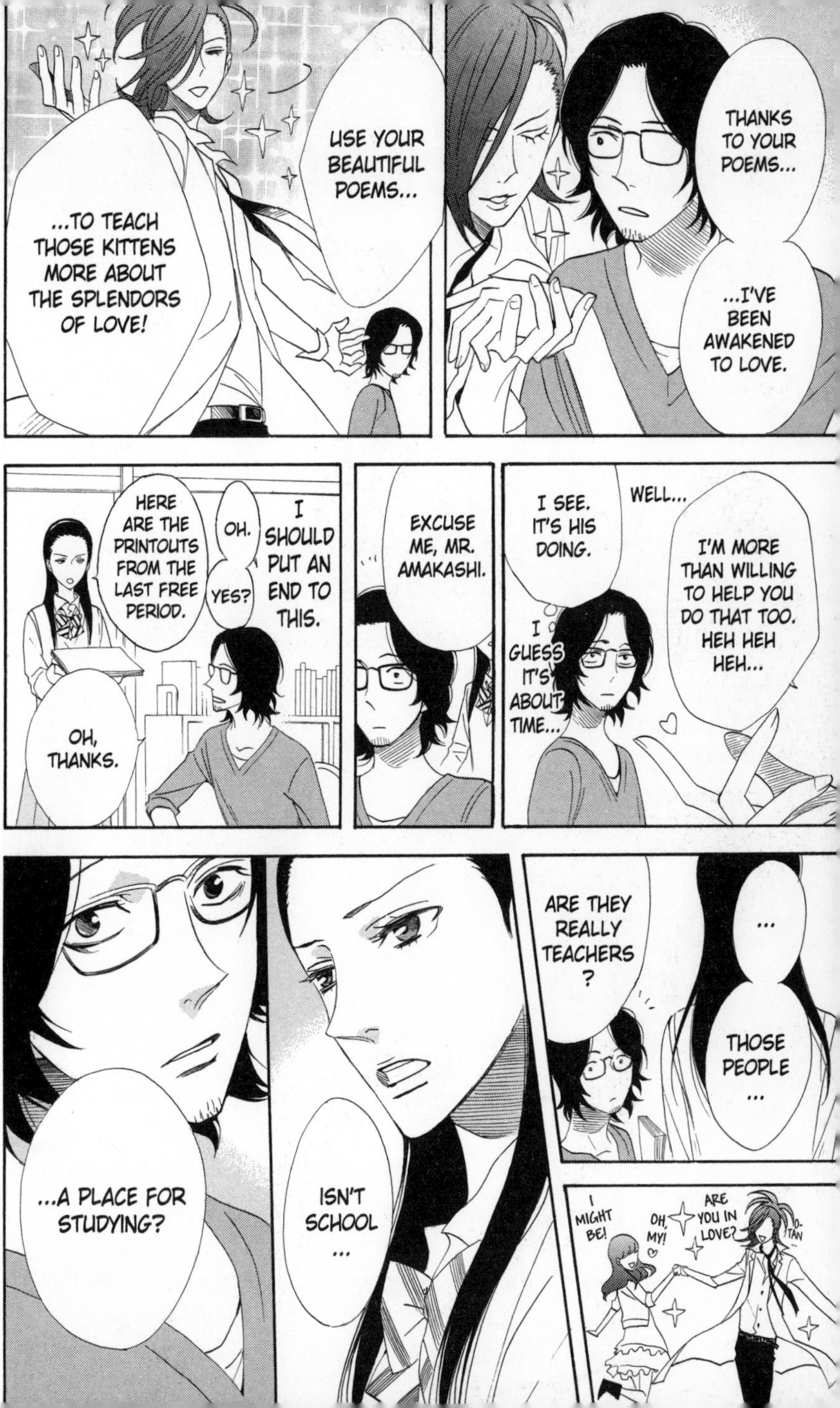
THANKS TO YOUR POEMS...
...I'VE BEEN AWAKENED TO LOVE.
USE YOUR BEAUTIFUL POEMS...
...TO TEACH THOSE KITTENS MORE ABOUT THE SPLENDORS OF LOVE!
WELL...
I'M MORE THAN WILLING TO HELP YOU DO THAT TOO. HEH HEH HEH...
I SEE. IT'S HIS DOING.
I GUESS IT'S ABOUT TIME...
EXCUSE ME, MR. AMAKASHI.
I SHOULD PUT AN END TO THIS.
OH.
YES?
HERE ARE THE PRINTOUTS FROM THE LAST FREE PERIOD.
OH, THANKS.
...
THOSE PEOPLE...
ARE THEY REALLY TEACHERS?
ARE YOU IN LOVE?
O-TAN...
OH, MY!
I MIGHT BE!
ISN'T SCHOOL...
...A PLACE FOR STUDYING?

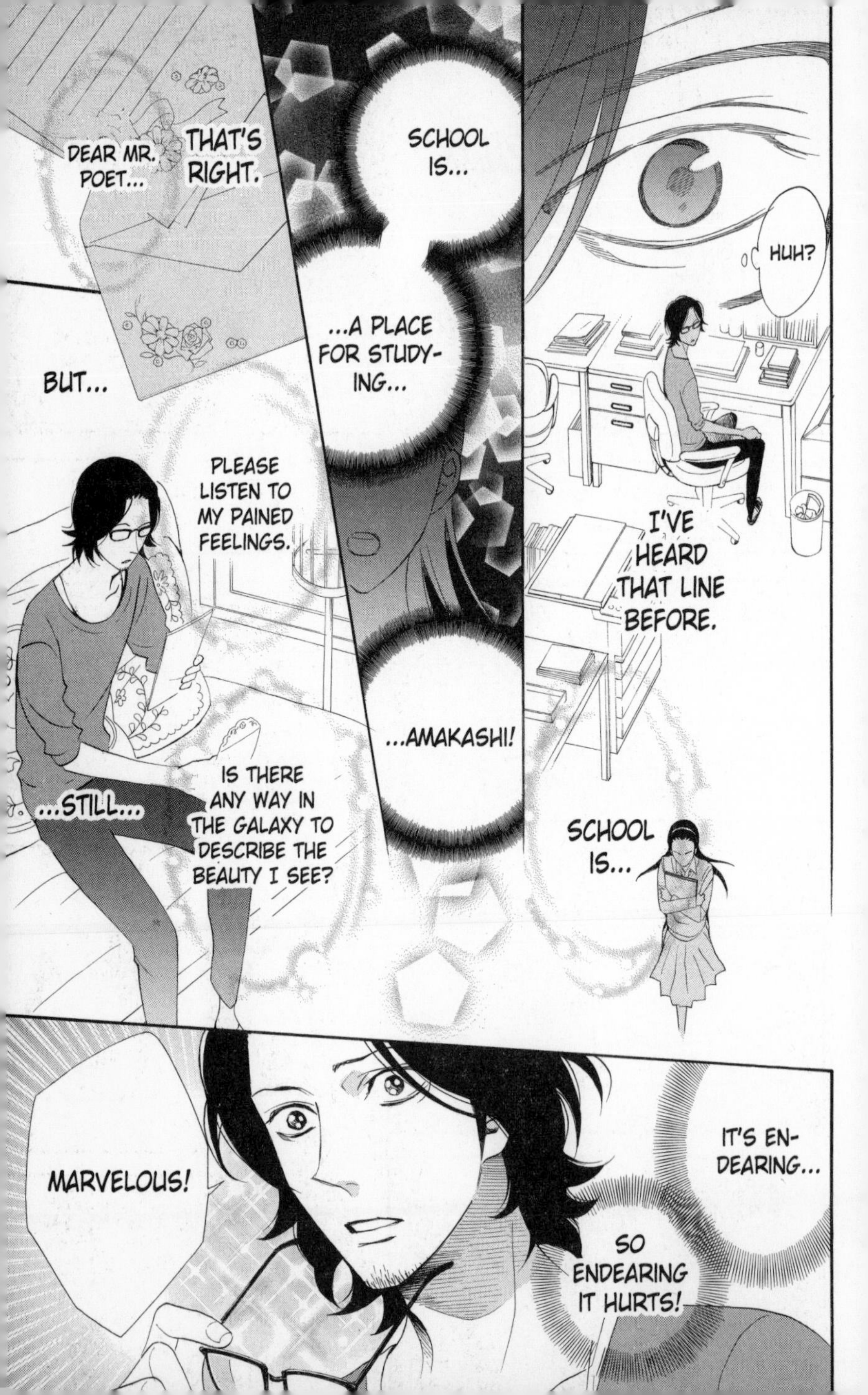
HUH?
I'VE HEARD THAT LINE BEFORE.
SCHOOL IS...
SCHOOL IS...
...A PLACE FOR STUDY-ING...
...AMAKASHI!
THAT'S RIGHT.
DEAR MR. POET...
BUT...
PLEASE LISTEN TO MY PAINED FEELINGS.
IS THERE ANY WAY IN THE GALAXY TO DESCRIBE THE BEAUTY I SEE?
...STILL...
IT'S EN-DEARING...
SO ENDEARING IT HURTS!
MARVELOUS!

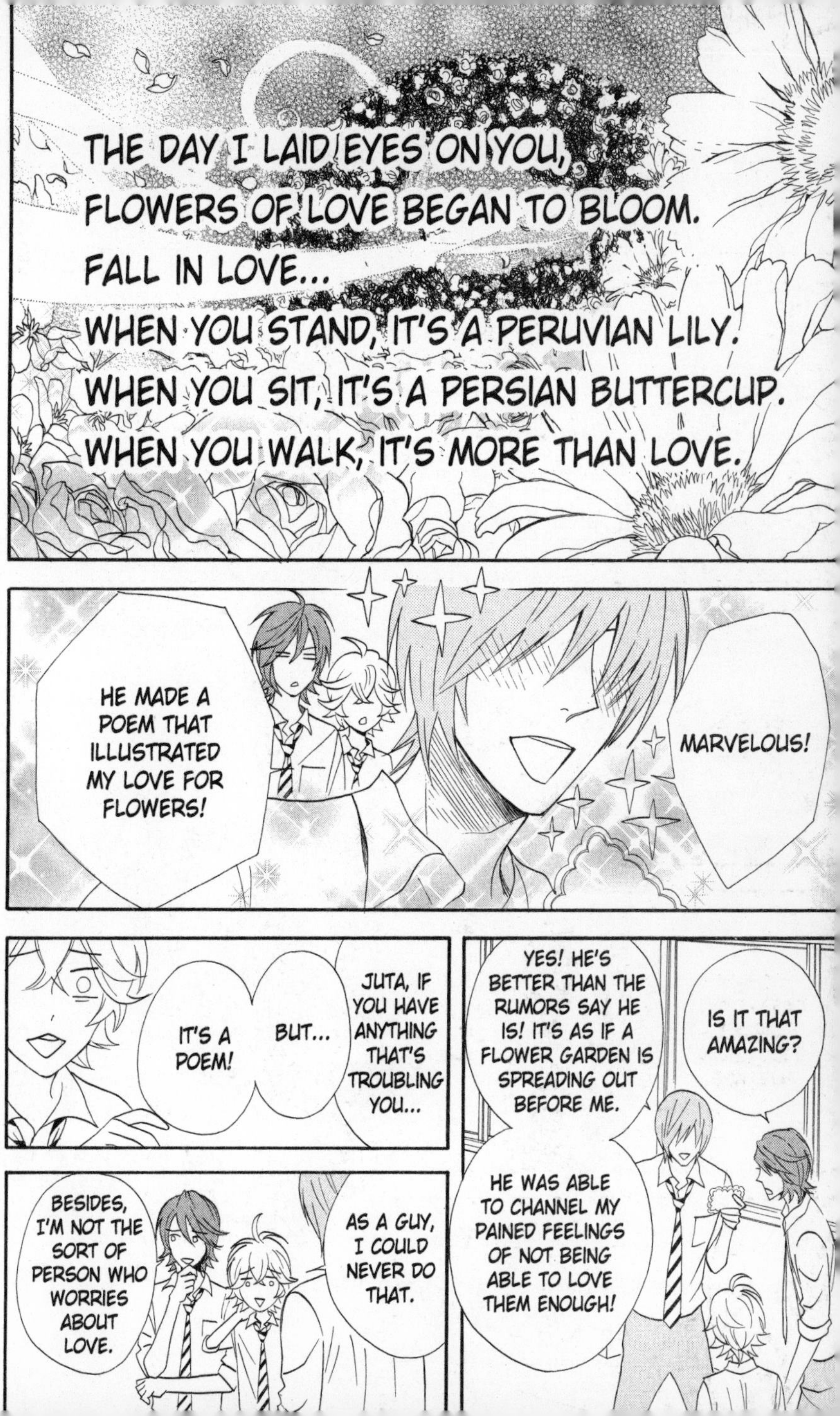
THE DAY I LAID EYES ON YOU,
FLOWERS OF LOVE BEGAN TO BLOOM.
FALL IN LOVE...
WHEN YOU STAND, IT'S A PERUVIAN LILY.
WHEN YOU SIT, IT'S A PERSIAN BUTTERCUP.
WHEN YOU WALK, IT'S MORE THAN LOVE.
MARVELOUS!
HE MADE A POEM THAT ILLUSTRATED MY LOVE FOR FLOWERS!
IS IT THAT AMAZING?
YES! HE'S BETTER THAN THE RUMORS SAY HE IS! IT'S AS IF A FLOWER GARDEN IS SPREADING OUT BEFORE ME.
HE WAS ABLE TO CHANNEL MY PAINED FEELINGS OF NOT BEING ABLE TO LOVE THEM ENOUGH!
JUTA, IF YOU HAVE ANYTHING THAT'S TROUBLING YOU...
BUT...
IT'S A POEM!
AS A GUY, I COULD NEVER DO THAT.
BESIDES, I'M NOT THE SORT OF PERSON WHO WORRIES ABOUT LOVE.

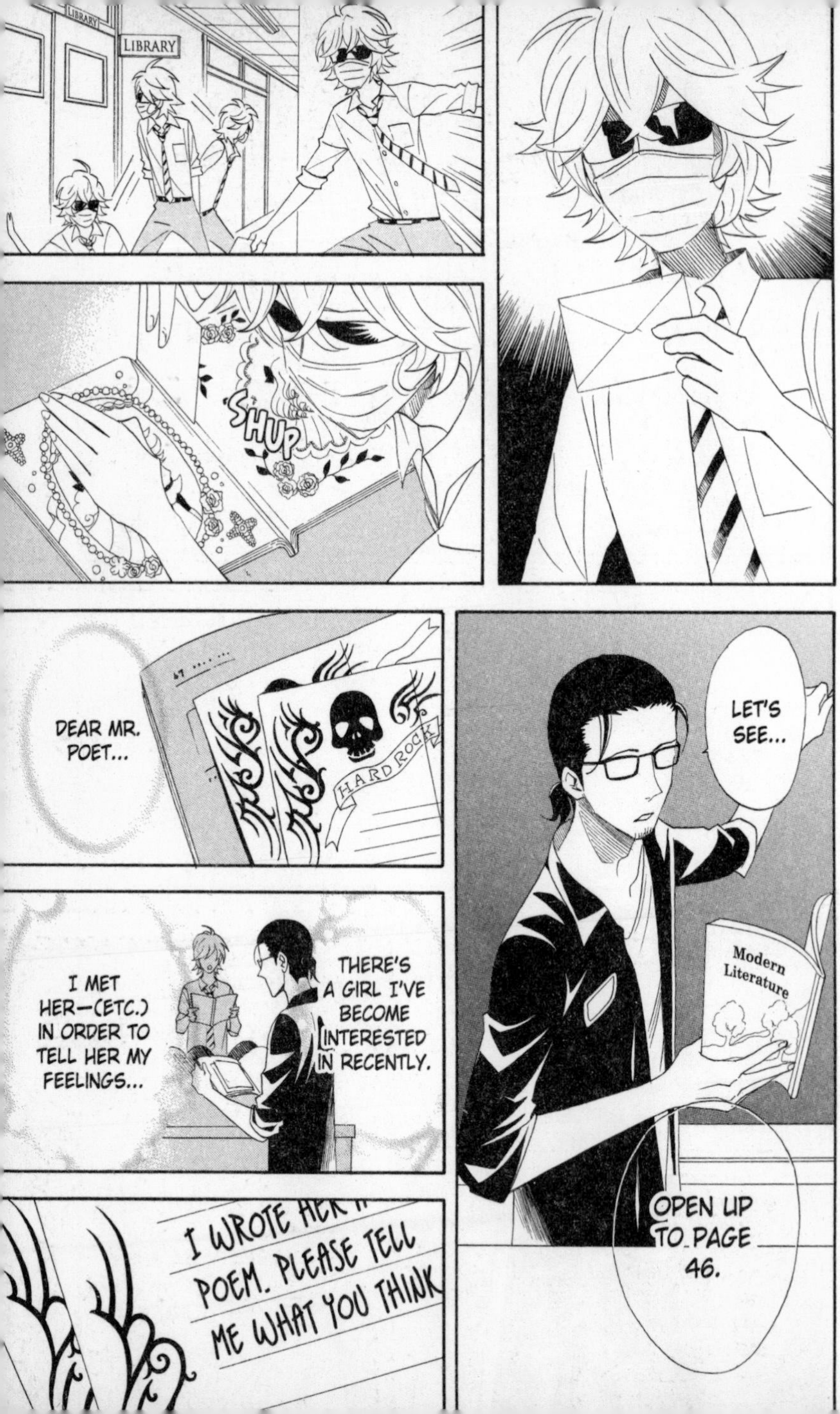
LIBRARY
LIBRARY
SHUP
LET'S SEE...
Modern Literature
OPEN UP TO PAGE 46.
DEAR MR. POET...
HARD ROCK
THERE'S A GIRL I'VE BECOME INTERESTED IN RECENTLY.
I MET HER—(ETC.) IN ORDER TO TELL HER MY FEELINGS...
I WROTE HER
POEM. PLEASE TELL
ME WHAT YOU THINK

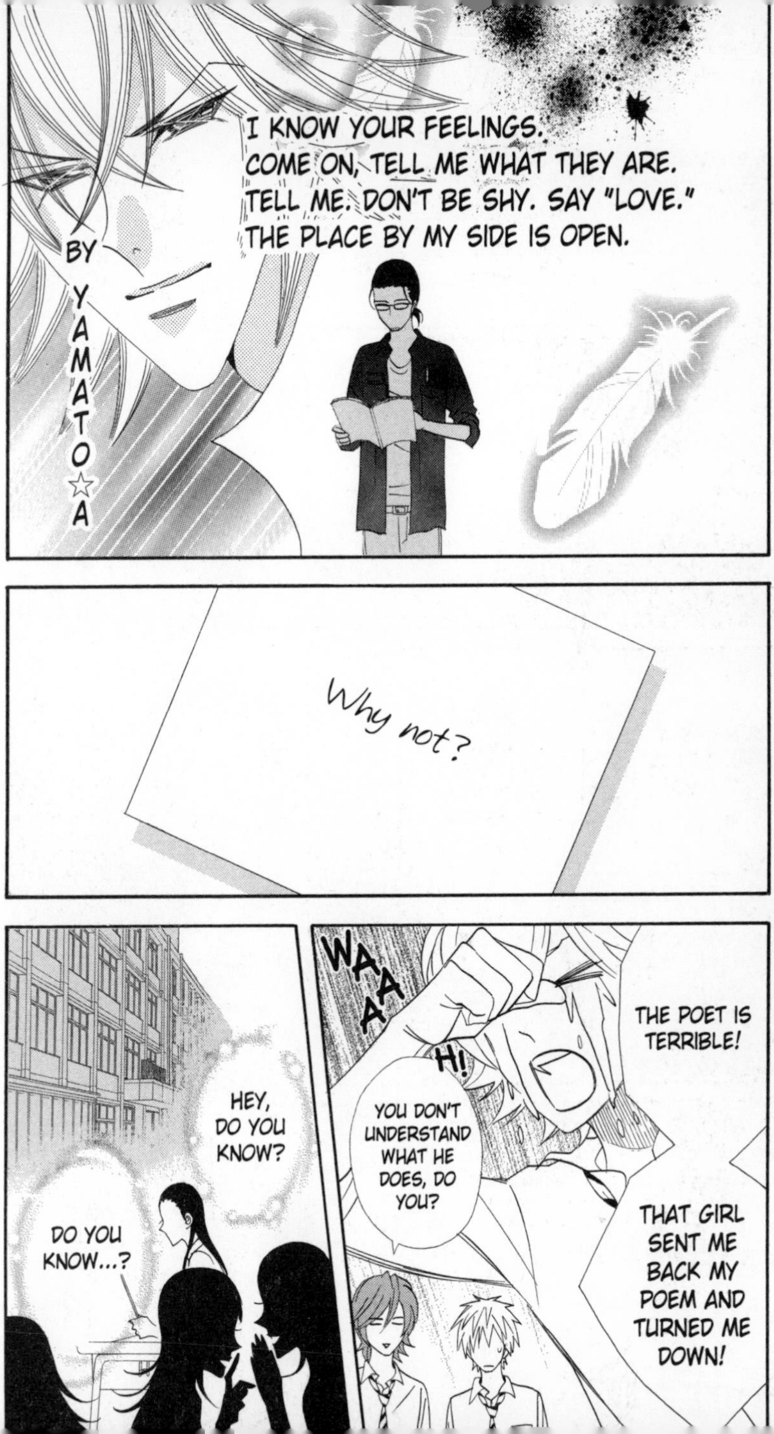
I KNOW YOUR FEELINGS.
COME ON, TELL ME WHAT THEY ARE.
TELL ME. DON'T BE SHY. SAY "LOVE."
THE PLACE BY MY SIDE IS OPEN.
BY YAMATO☆A
Why not?
THE POET IS TERRIBLE!
WAAAAH!
YOU DON'T UNDERSTAND WHAT HE DOES, DO YOU?
THAT GIRL SENT ME BACK MY POEM AND TURNED ME DOWN!
HEY, DO YOU KNOW?
DO YOU KNOW...?

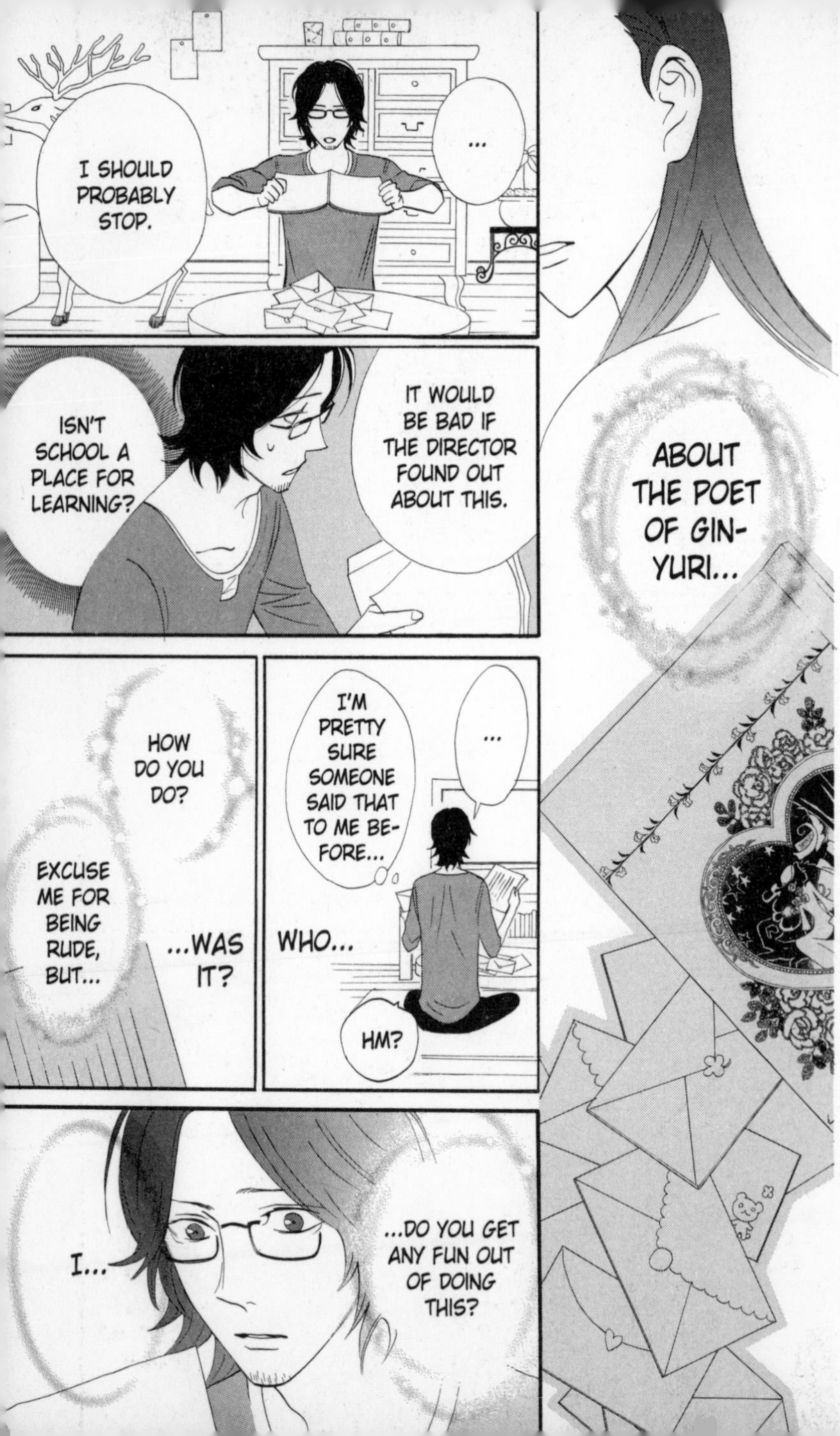
ABOUT THE POET OF GIN-YURI...
...
I SHOULD PROBABLY STOP.
IT WOULD BE BAD IF THE DIRECTOR FOUND OUT ABOUT THIS.
ISN'T SCHOOL A PLACE FOR LEARNING?
...
I'M PRETTY SURE SOMEONE SAID THAT TO ME BEFORE...
WHO...
HM?
HOW DO YOU DO?
...WAS IT?
EXCUSE ME FOR BEING RUDE, BUT...
...DO YOU GET ANY FUN OUT OF DOING THIS?
I...

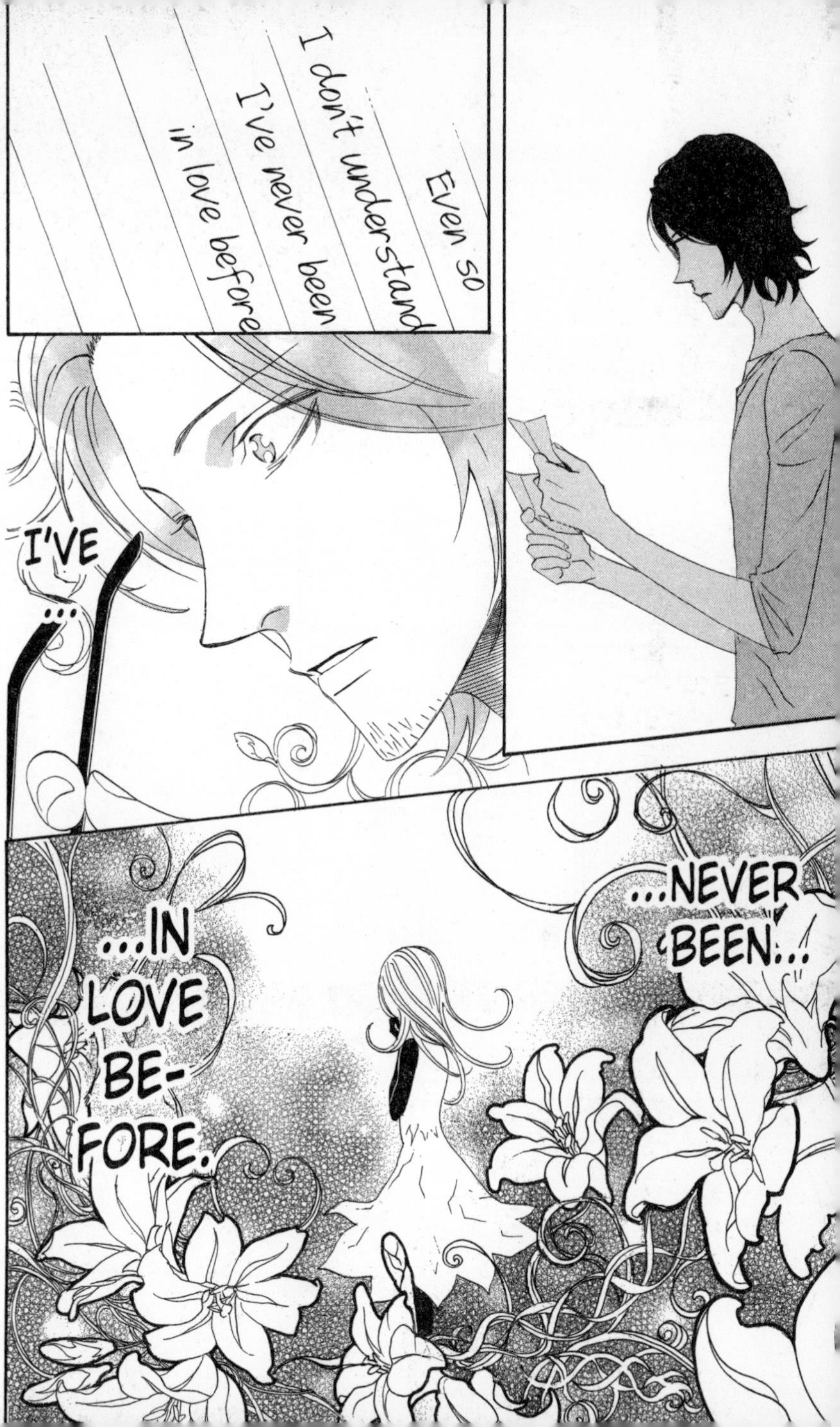
Even so I don't understand I've never been in love before
I'VE ...
...NEVER BEEN...
...IN LOVE BE- FORE.

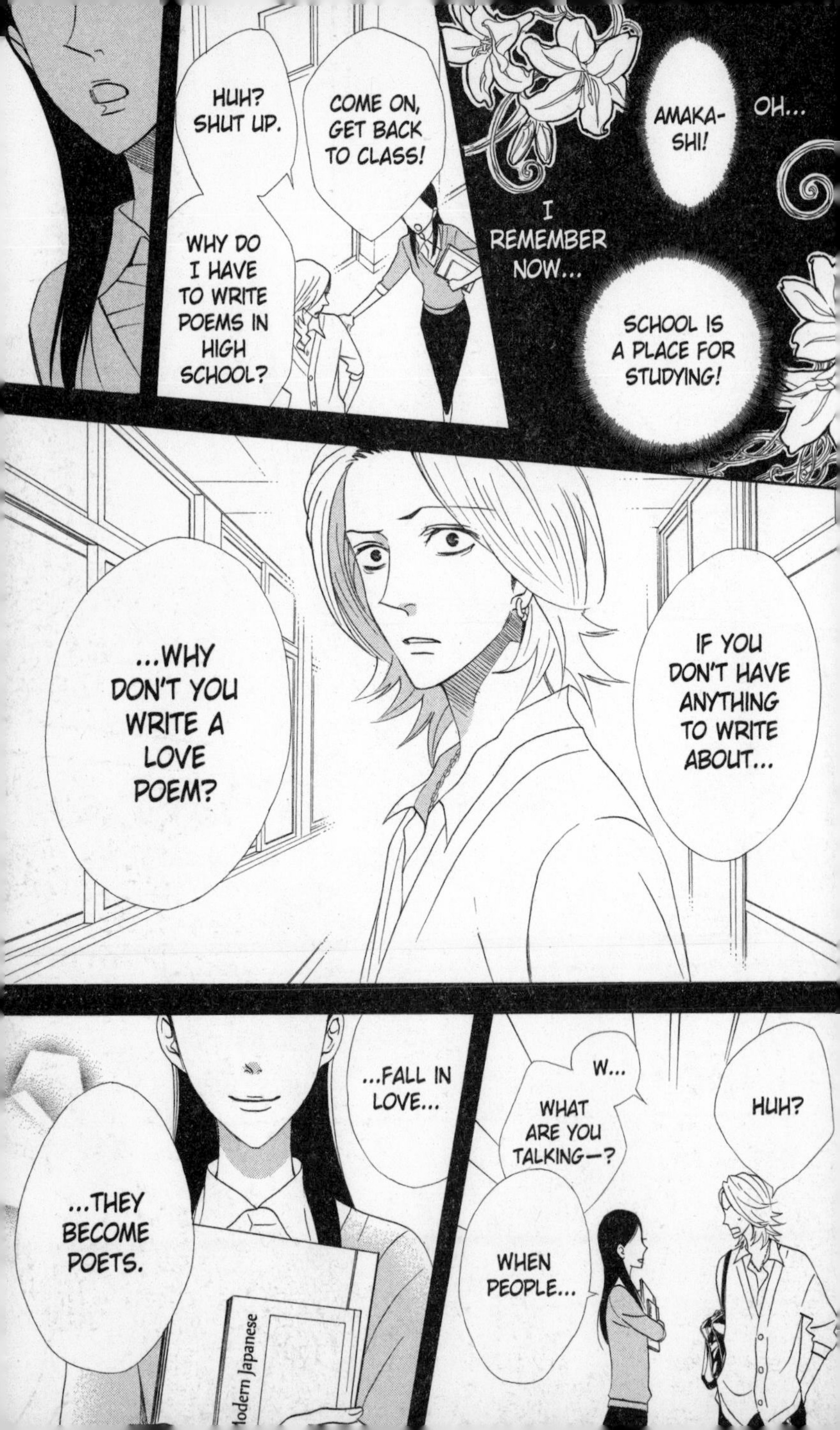
OH...
AMAKA-SHI!
I REMEMBER NOW...
SCHOOL IS A PLACE FOR STUDYING!
COME ON, GET BACK TO CLASS!
HUH? SHUT UP.
WHY DO I HAVE TO WRITE POEMS IN HIGH SCHOOL?
IF YOU DON'T HAVE ANYTHING TO WRITE ABOUT...
...WHY DON'T YOU WRITE A LOVE POEM?
HUH?
W...
WHAT ARE YOU TALKING—?
WHEN PEOPLE...
...FALL IN LOVE...
...THEY BECOME POETS.
Modern Japanese

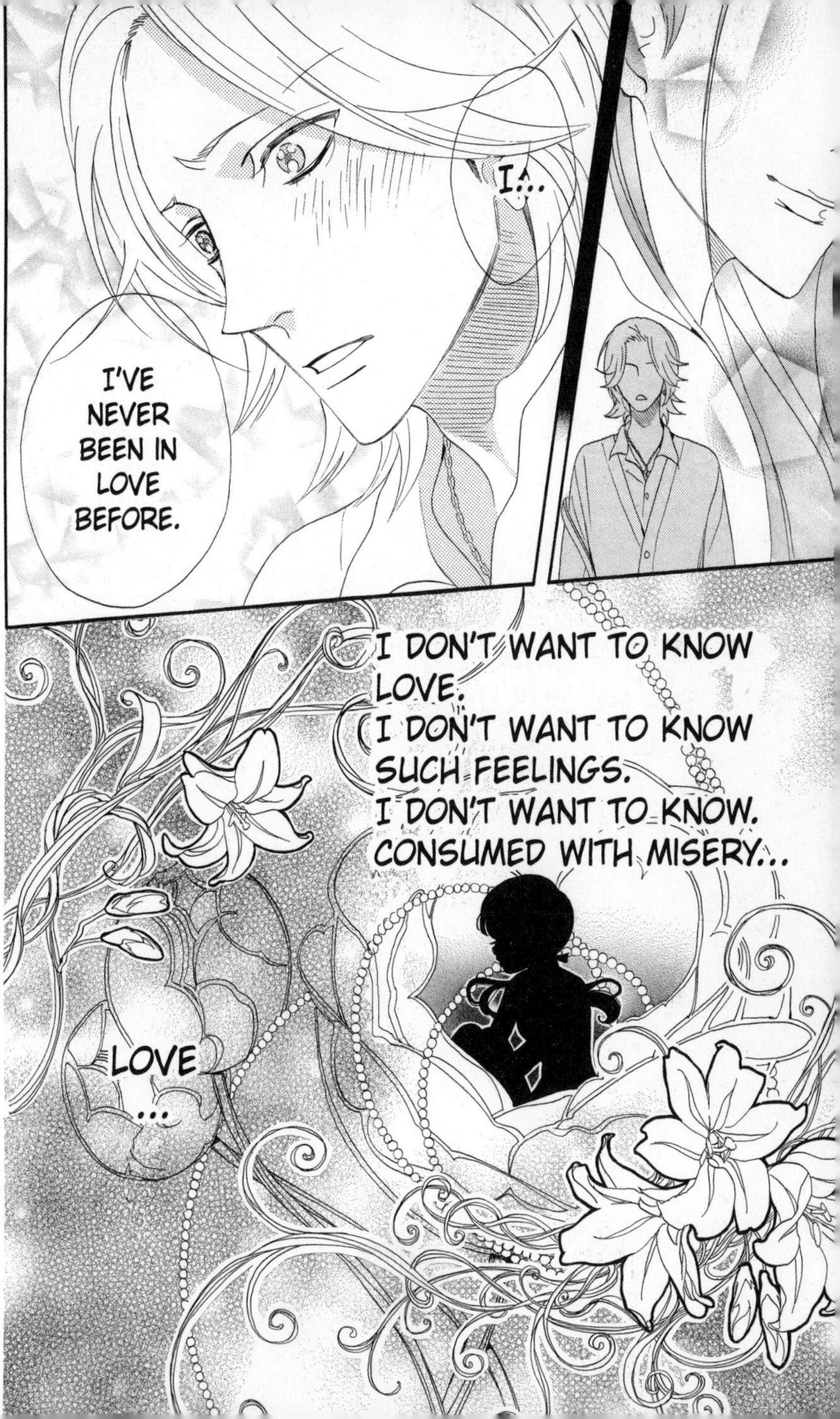
I...
I'VE NEVER BEEN IN LOVE BEFORE.
I DON'T WANT TO KNOW LOVE.
I DON'T WANT TO KNOW SUCH FEELINGS.
I DON'T WANT TO KNOW.
CONSUMED WITH MISERY...
LOVE ...

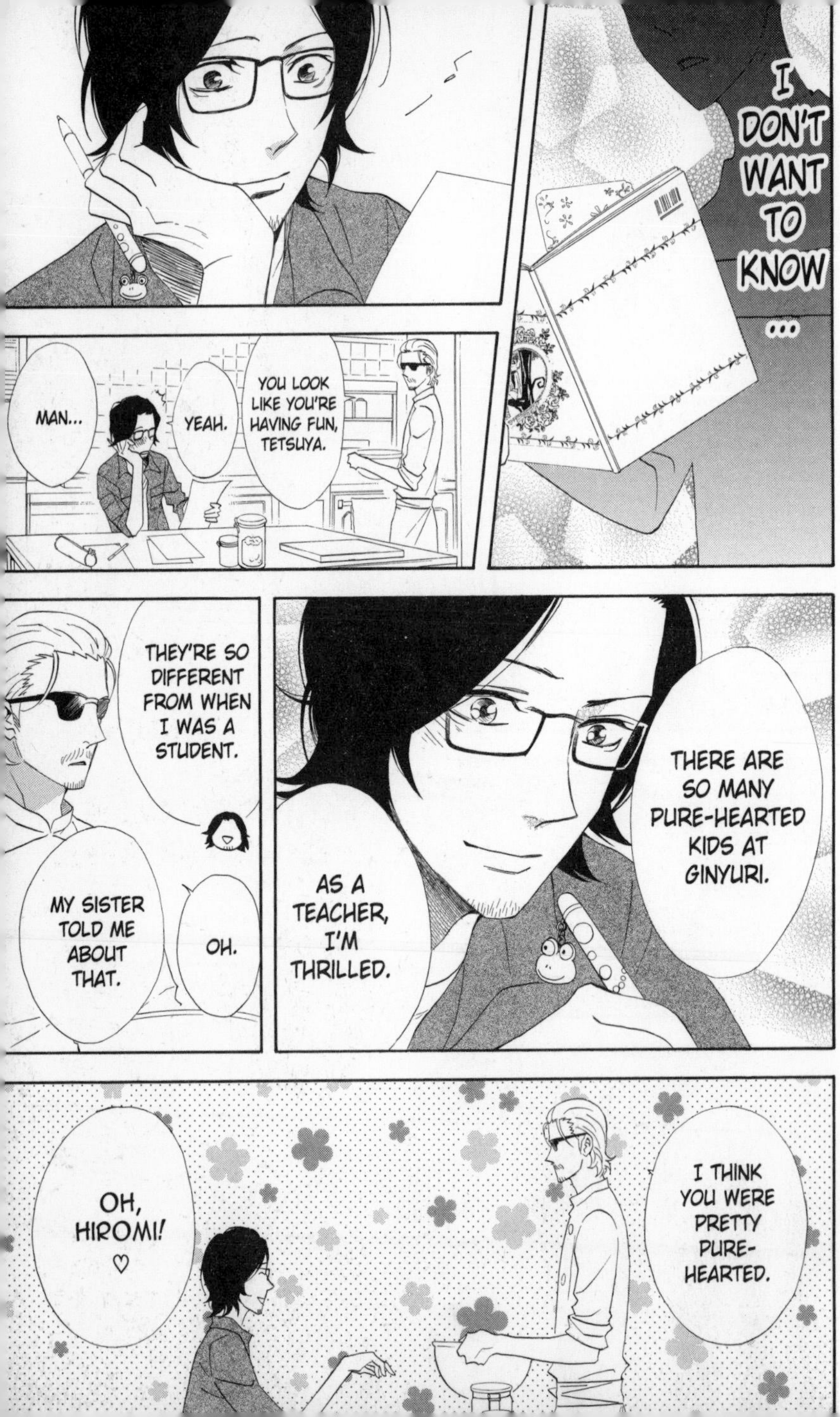
I DON'T WANT TO KNOW...
YOU LOOK LIKE YOU'RE HAVING FUN, TETSUYA.
YEAH.
MAN...
THERE ARE SO MANY PURE-HEARTED KIDS AT GINYURI.
AS A TEACHER, I'M THRILLED.
THEY'RE SO DIFFERENT FROM WHEN I WAS A STUDENT.
OH.
MY SISTER TOLD ME ABOUT THAT.
I THINK YOU WERE PRETTY PURE-HEARTED.
OH, HIROMI! ♡

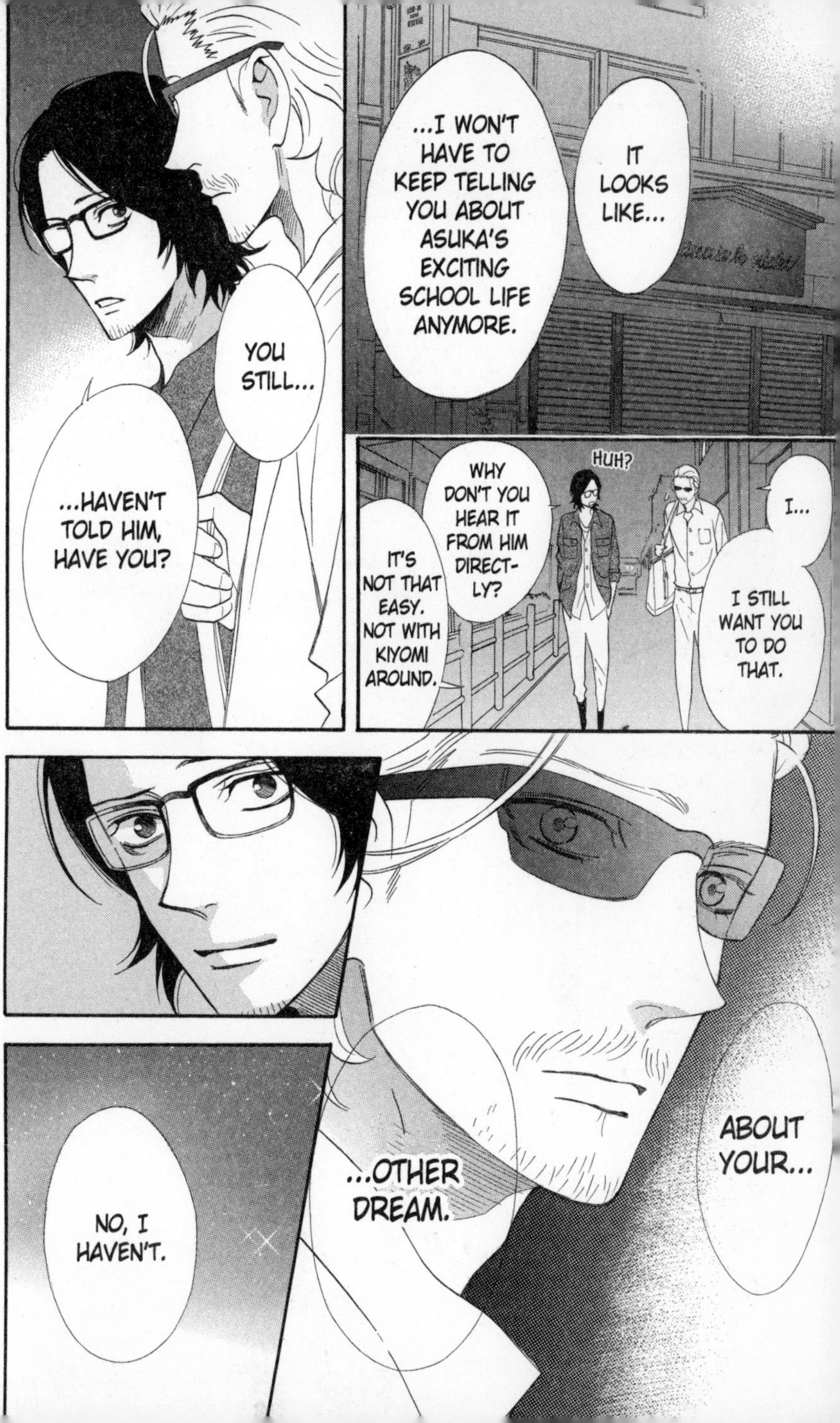
IT LOOKS LIKE...
...I WON'T HAVE TO KEEP TELLING YOU ABOUT ASUKA'S EXCITING SCHOOL LIFE ANYMORE.
I...
I STILL WANT YOU TO DO THAT.
HUH?
WHY DON'T YOU HEAR IT FROM HIM DIRECT-LY?
IT'S NOT THAT EASY. NOT WITH KIYOMI AROUND.
YOU STILL...
...HAVEN'T TOLD HIM, HAVE YOU?
ABOUT YOUR...
...OTHER DREAM.
NO, I HAVEN'T.

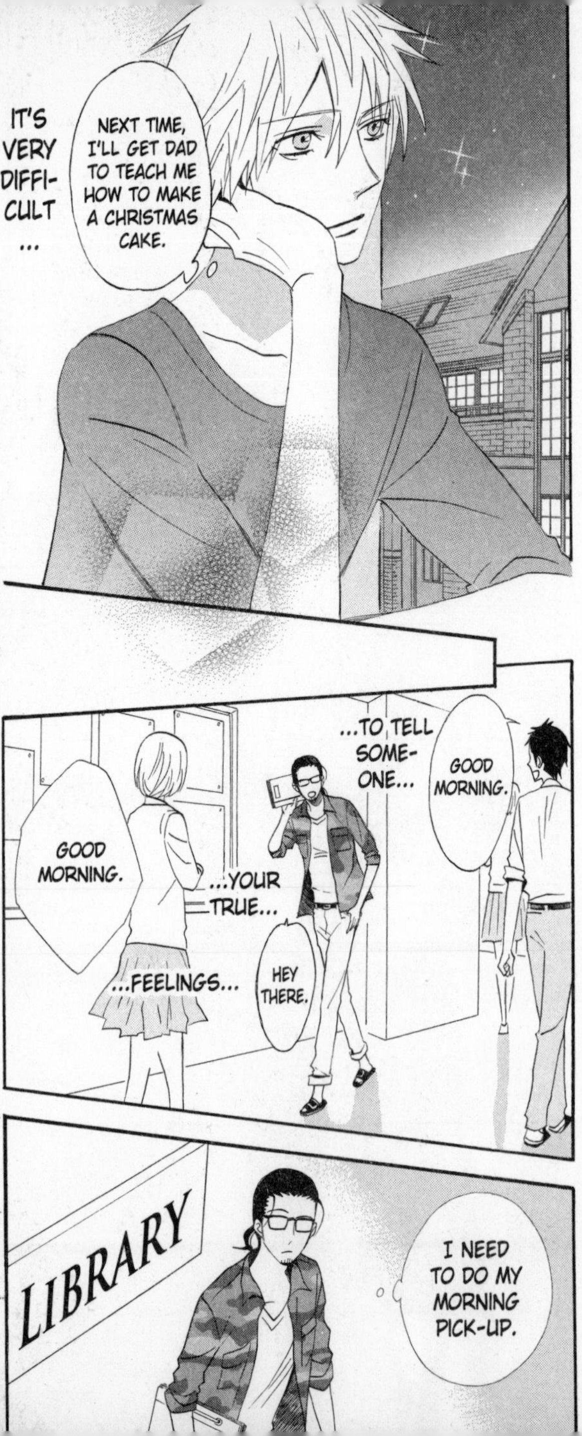
NEXT TIME, I'LL GET DAD TO TEACH ME HOW TO MAKE A CHRISTMAS CAKE.
IT'S VERY DIFFI- CULT...
GOOD MORNING.
...TO TELL SOME- ONE...
HEY THERE.
...YOUR TRUE...
GOOD MORNING.
...FEELINGS...
I NEED TO DO MY MORNING PICK-UP.
LIBRARY

It's an Amakashi chapter.

I've wanted to have a poet show up ever since I started *Otomen*. I ended up making him a teacher as I went along. All of the main otomen in the story have appeared. I'm satisfied.

But surprisingly, or rather, as expected, writing a story about a poet was very difficult.

I made too many jokes involving letters. I know that, but I love letters.
Well, until the next volume!

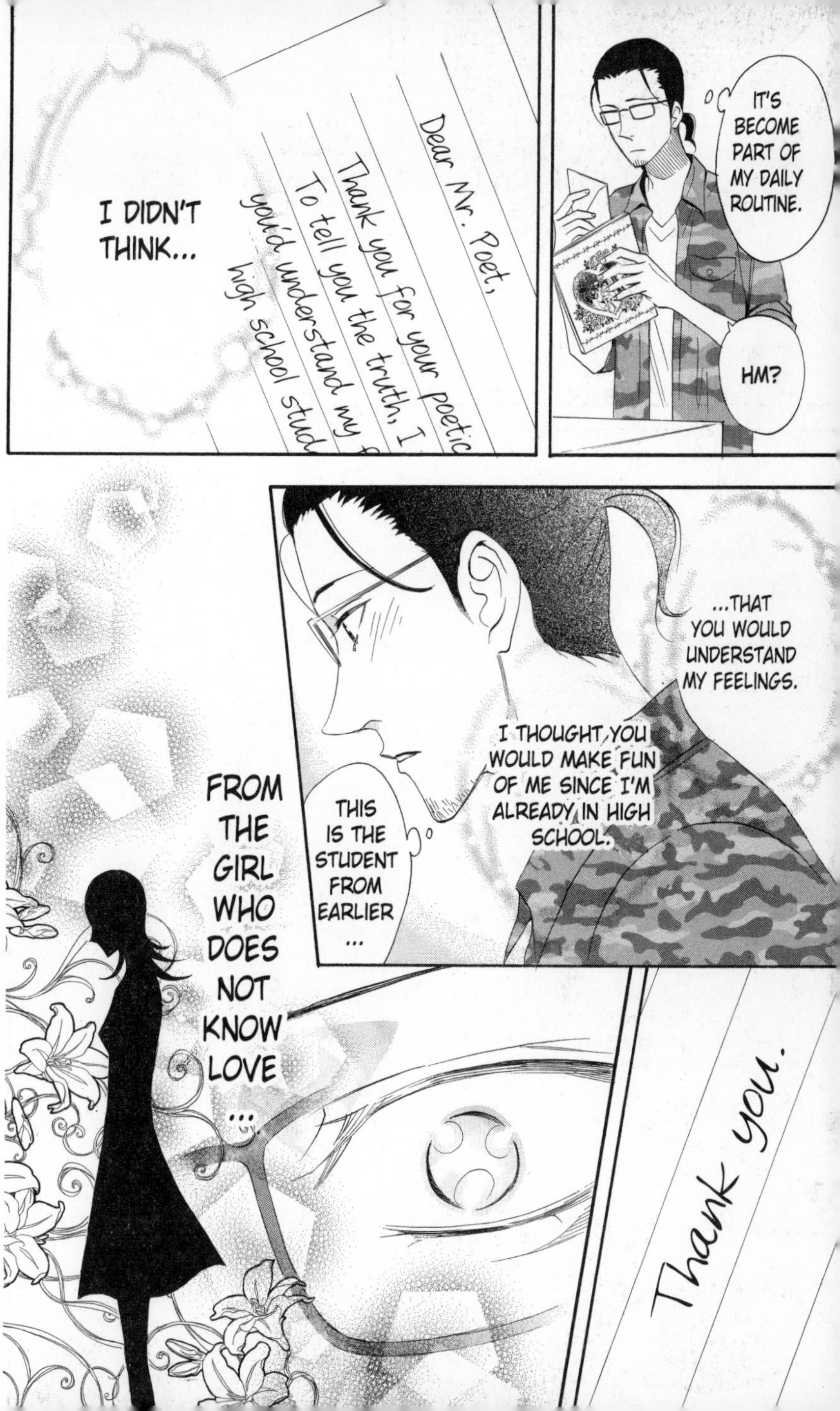
IT'S BECOME PART OF MY DAILY ROUTINE.
HM?
Dear Mr. Poet,
Thank you for your poetic
To tell you the truth, I
you'd understand my
high school
I DIDN'T THINK...
...THAT YOU WOULD UNDERSTAND MY FEELINGS.
I THOUGHT YOU WOULD MAKE FUN OF ME SINCE I'M ALREADY IN HIGH SCHOOL.
THIS IS THE STUDENT FROM EARLIER...
FROM THE GIRL WHO DOES NOT KNOW LOVE...
Thank you.

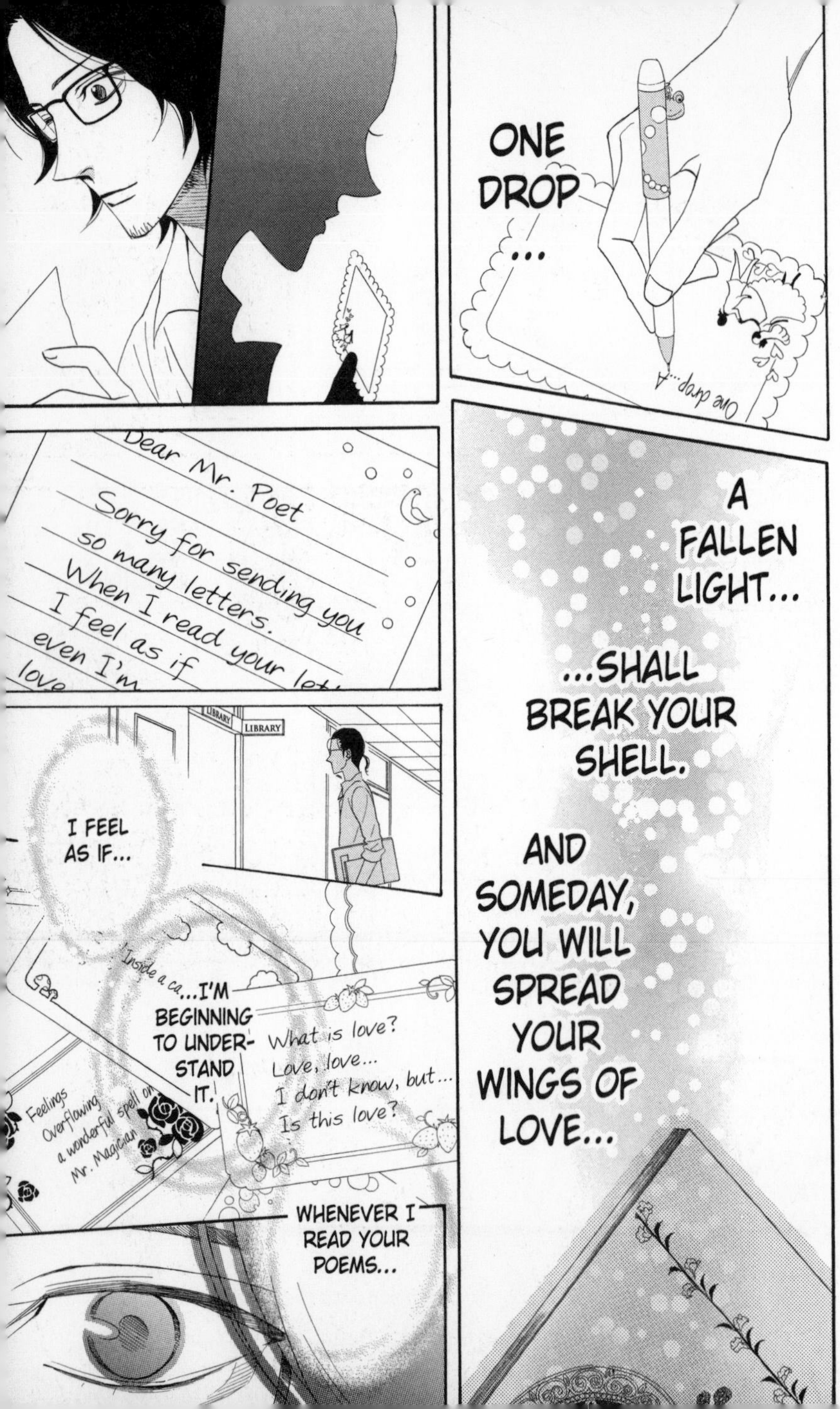
ONE DROP
...
One drop...A
A FALLEN LIGHT...
...SHALL BREAK YOUR SHELL.
AND SOMEDAY, YOU WILL SPREAD YOUR WINGS OF LOVE...
Dear Mr. Poet
Sorry for sending you
so many letters.
When I read your let
I feel as if
even I'm
LIBRARY
LIBRARY
I FEEL AS IF...
Inside a ca
...I'M BEGINNING TO UNDER-STAND IT.
What is love?
Love, love...
I don't know, but...
Is this love?
Feelings
Overflowing
a wonderful spell on
Mr. Magician
WHENEVER I READ YOUR POEMS...

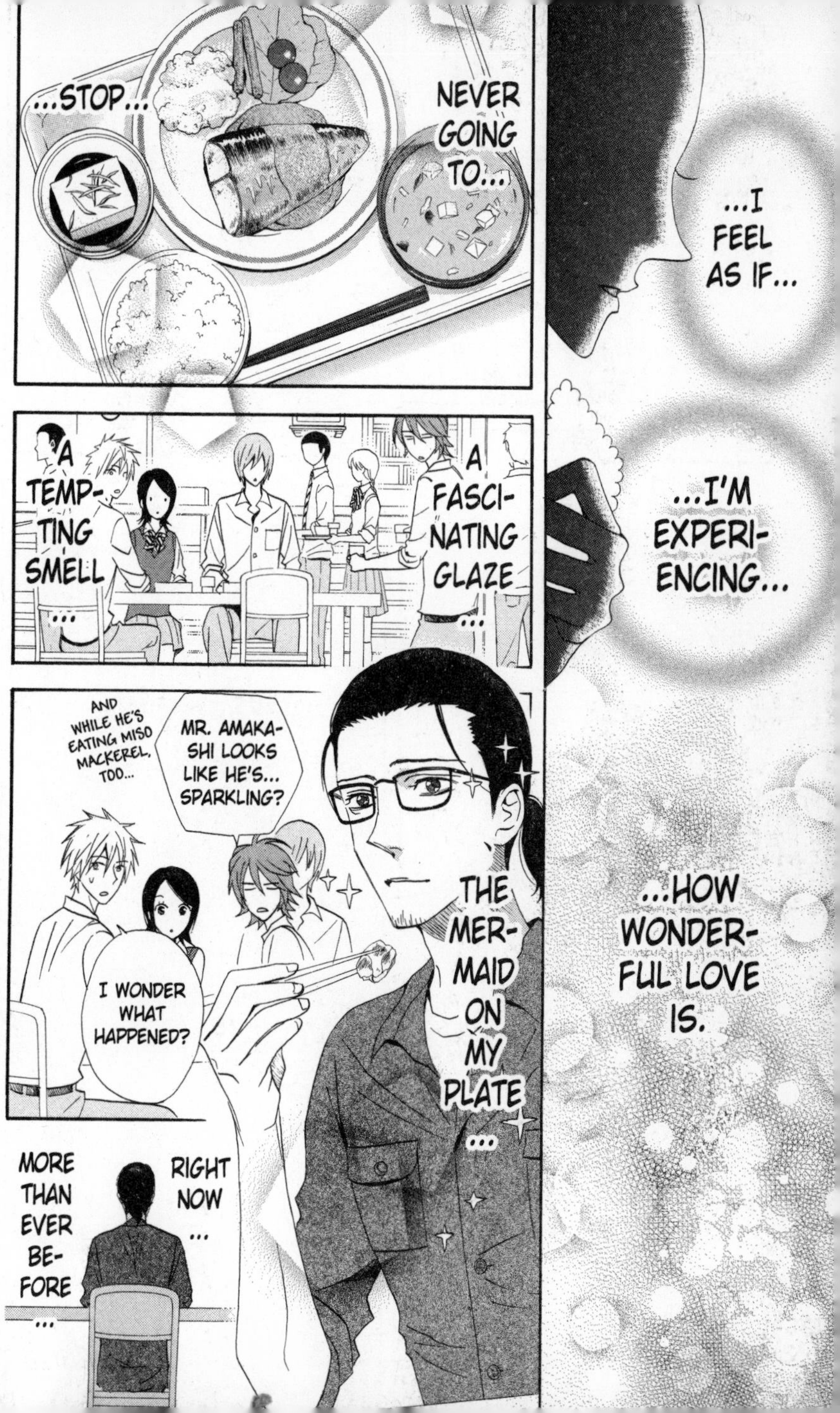
...I FEEL AS IF...
...I'M EXPERIENCING...
...HOW WONDERFUL LOVE IS.
NEVER GOING TO...
...STOP...
A FASCINATING GLAZE...
A TEMPTING SMELL...
THE MERMAID ON MY PLATE...
MR. AMAKASHI LOOKS LIKE HE'S... SPARKLING?
AND WHILE HE'S EATING MISO MACKEREL, TOO...
I WONDER WHAT HAPPENED?
RIGHT NOW...
MORE THAN EVER BEFORE...

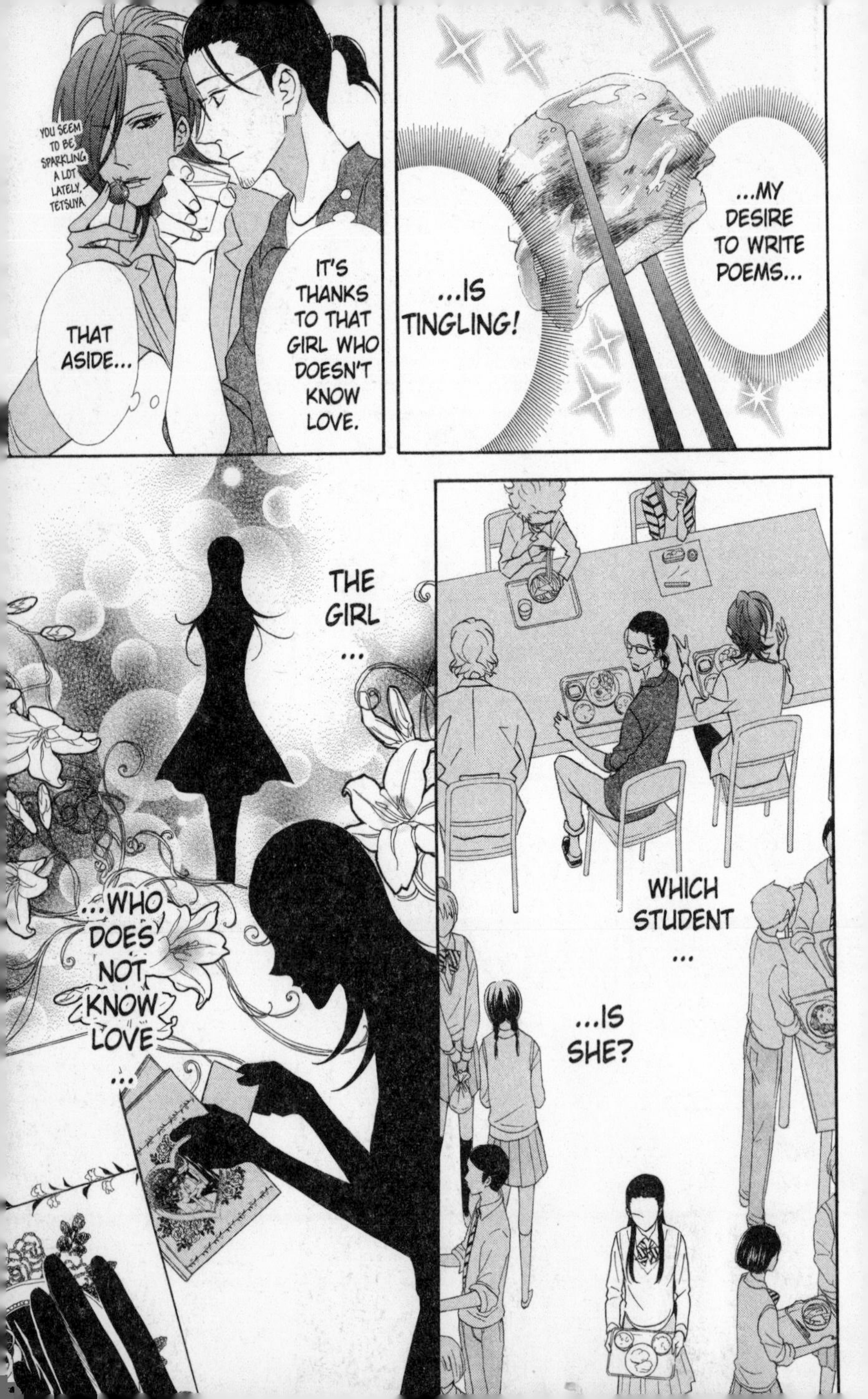
...MY DESIRE TO WRITE POEMS...
...IS TINGLING!
THAT ASIDE...
YOU SEEM TO BE SPARKLING A LOT LATELY, TETSUYA.
IT'S THANKS TO THAT GIRL WHO DOESN'T KNOW LOVE.
WHICH STUDENT ...
...IS SHE?
THE GIRL ...
...WHO DOES NOT KNOW LOVE ...

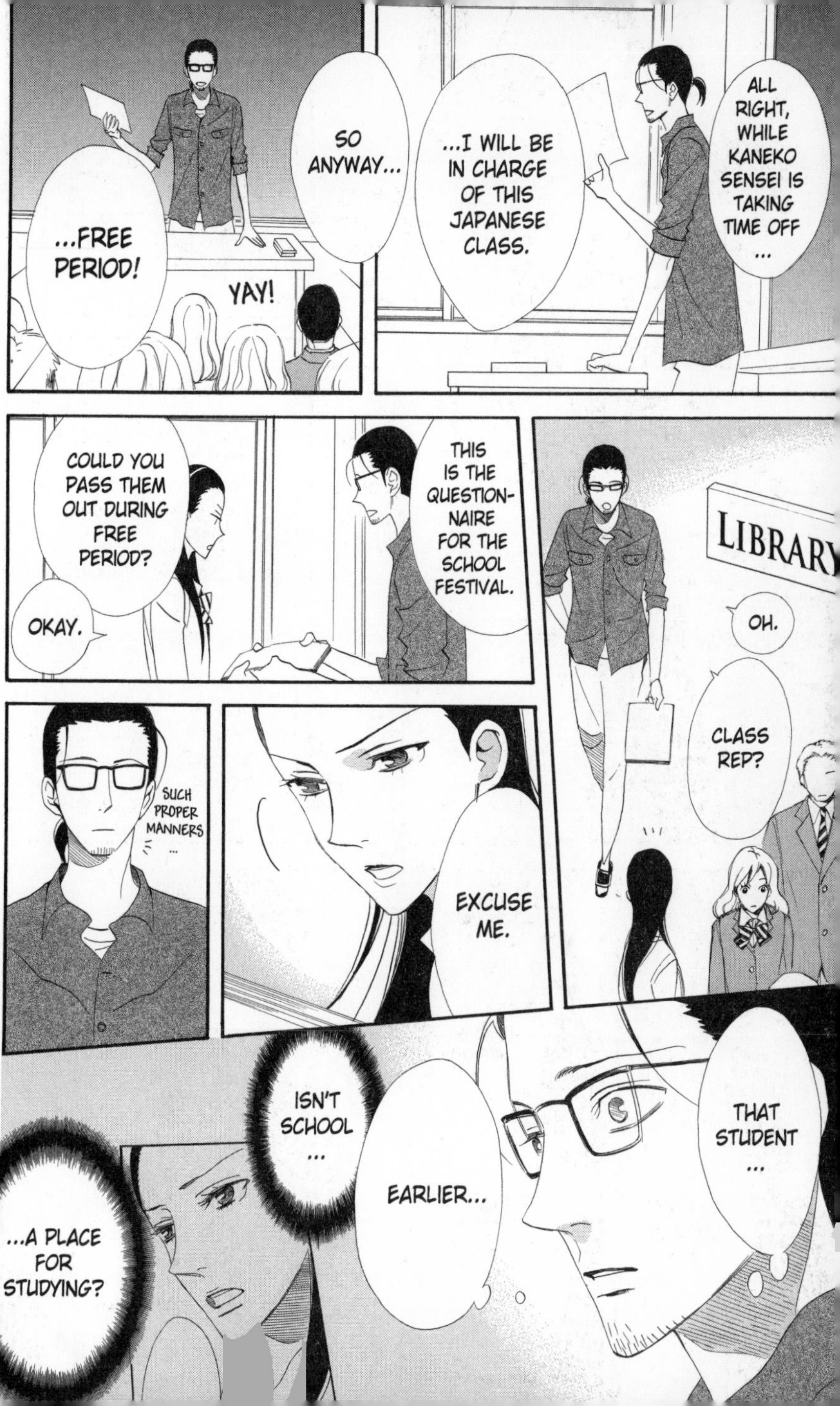

ALL RIGHT, WHILE KANEKO SENSEI IS TAKING TIME OFF ...
...I WILL BE IN CHARGE OF THIS JAPANESE CLASS.
SO ANYWAY...
...FREE PERIOD!
YAY!
LIBRARY
OH.
CLASS REP?
THIS IS THE QUESTION-NAIRE FOR THE SCHOOL FESTIVAL.
COULD YOU PASS THEM OUT DURING FREE PERIOD?
OKAY.
EXCUSE ME.
SUCH PROPER MANNERS ...
THAT STUDENT ...
EARLIER...
ISN'T SCHOOL ...
...A PLACE FOR STUDYING?

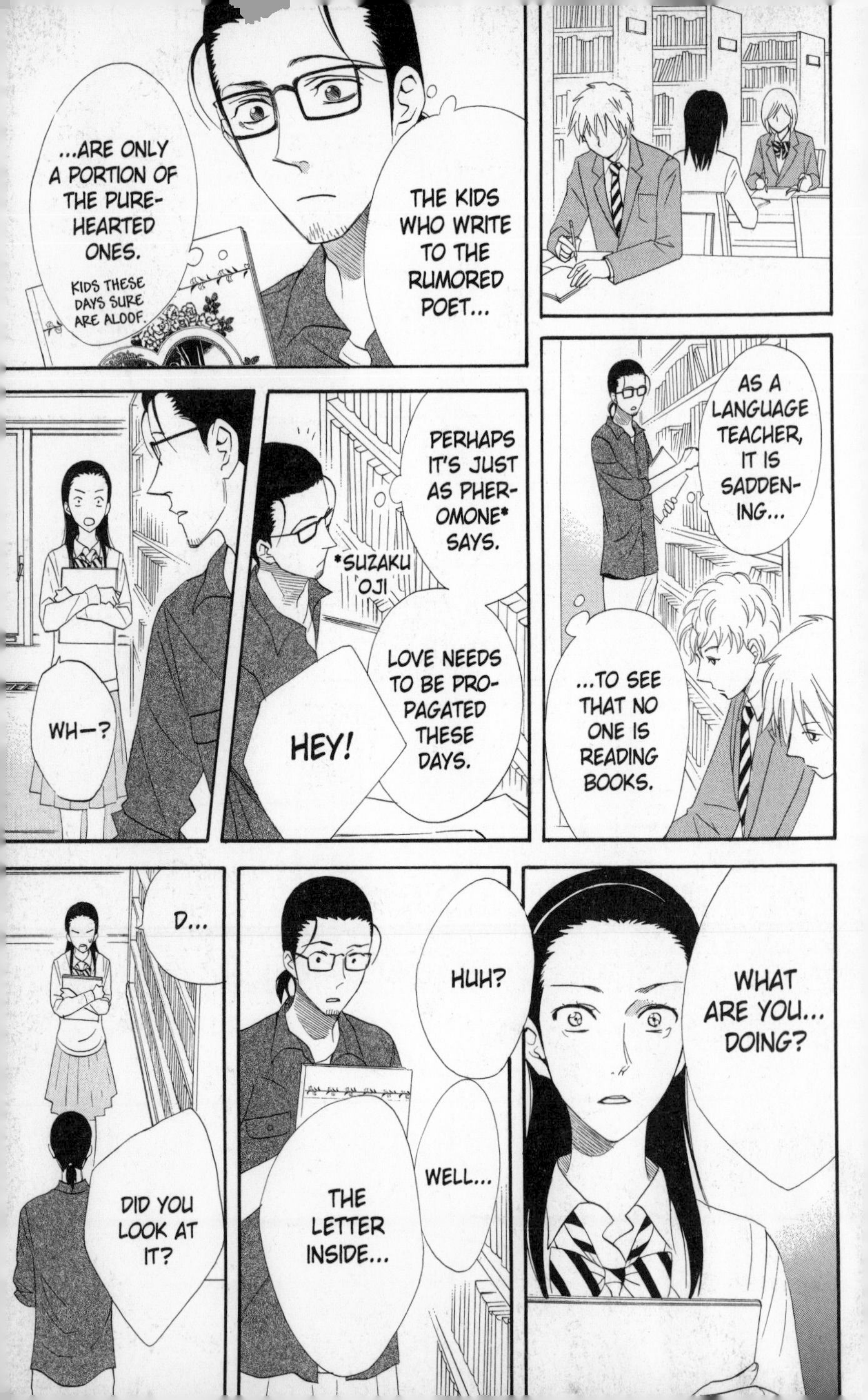
THE KIDS WHO WRITE TO THE RUMORED POET...
...ARE ONLY A PORTION OF THE PURE-HEARTED ONES.
KIDS THESE DAYS SURE ARE ALOOF.
AS A LANGUAGE TEACHER, IT IS SADDENING...
...TO SEE THAT NO ONE IS READING BOOKS.
PERHAPS IT'S JUST AS PHEROMONE* SAYS.
LOVE NEEDS TO BE PROPAGATED THESE DAYS.
*SUZAKU OJI
HEY!
WH—?
WHAT ARE YOU... DOING?
HUH?
WELL...
THE LETTER INSIDE...
D...
DID YOU LOOK AT IT?

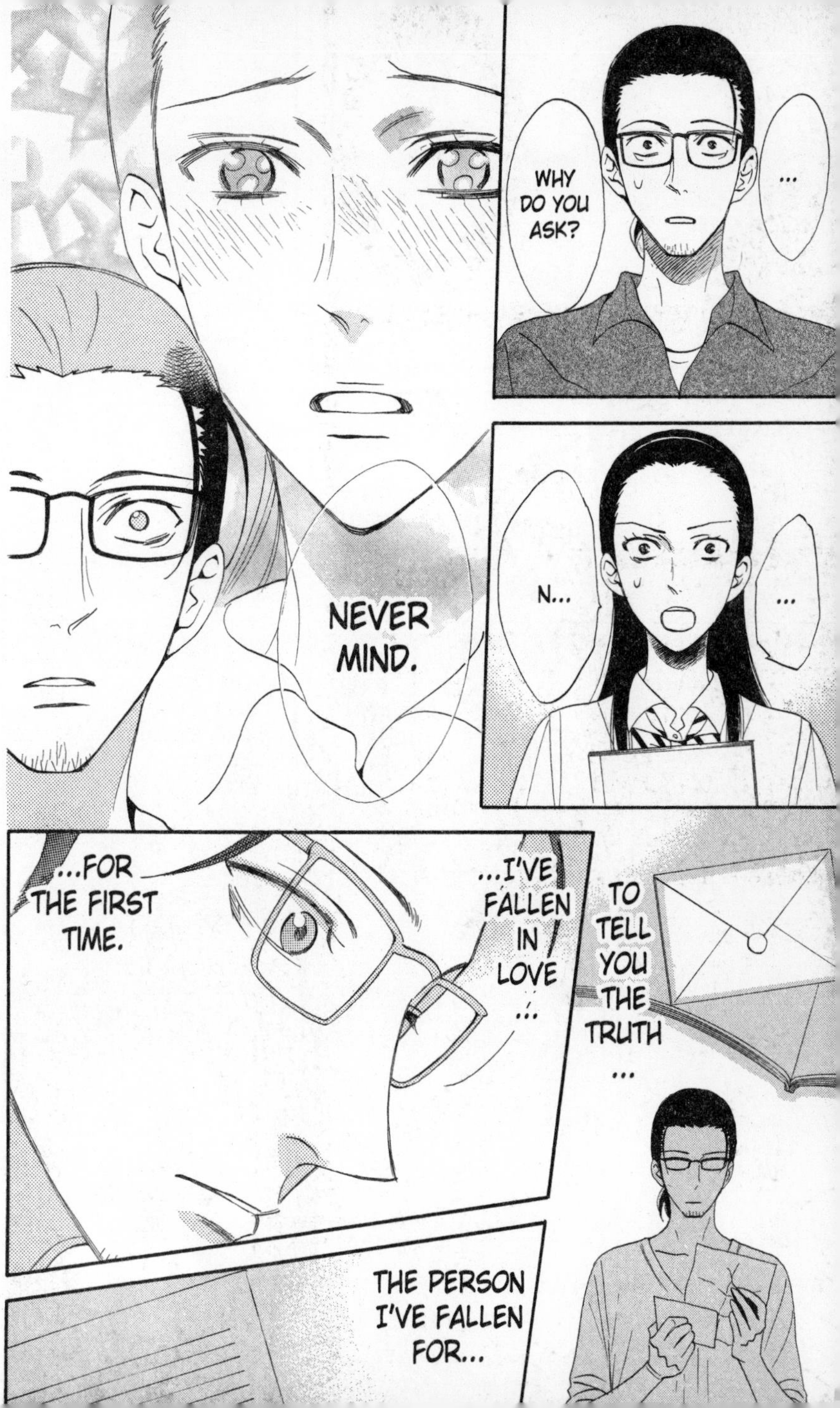
...
WHY DO YOU ASK?
...
N...
NEVER MIND.
TO TELL YOU THE TRUTH...
...I'VE FALLEN IN LOVE...
...FOR THE FIRST TIME.
THE PERSON I'VE FALLEN FOR...

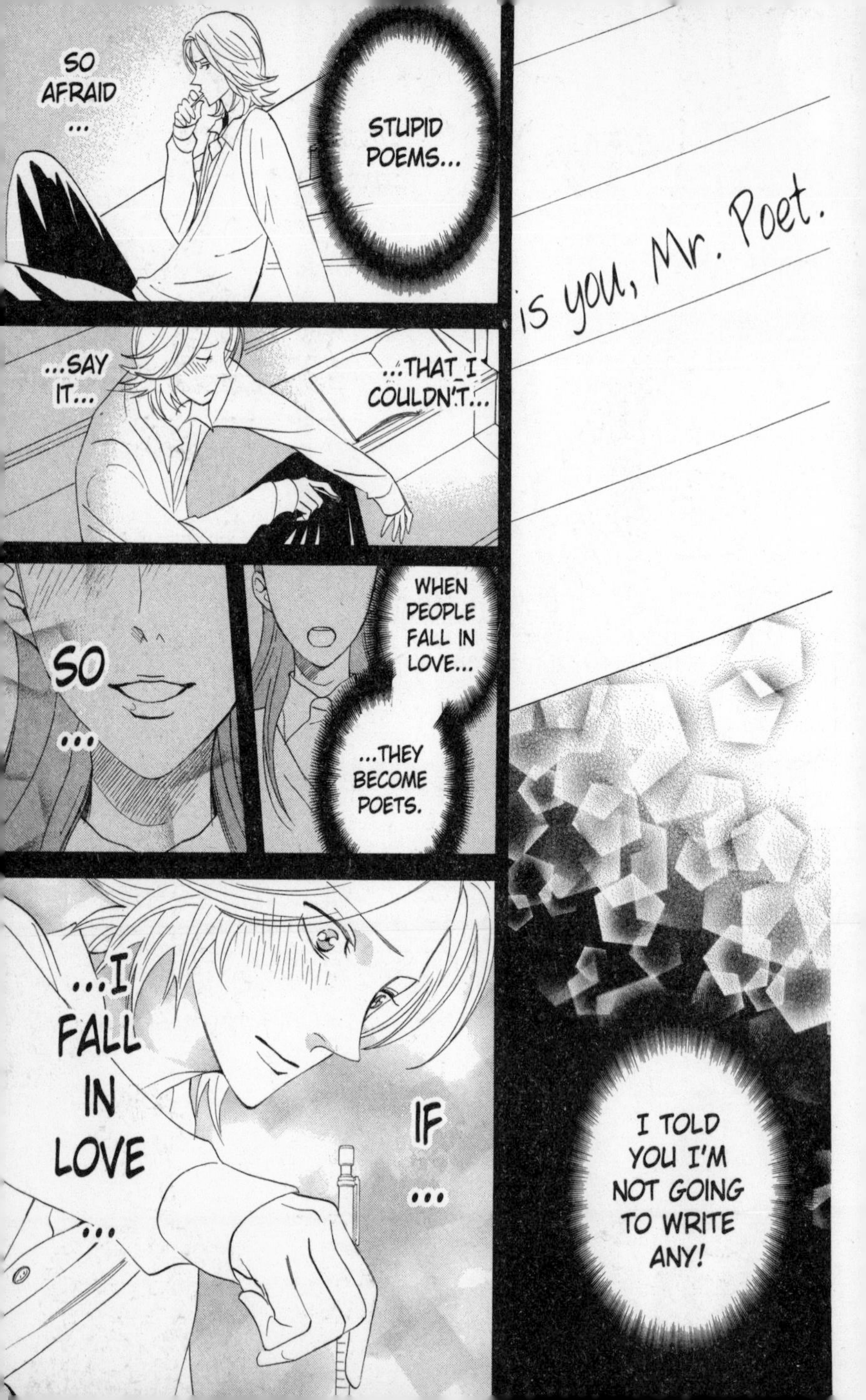
is you, Mr. Poet.
I TOLD YOU I'M NOT GOING TO WRITE ANY!
STUPID POEMS...
SO AFRAID...
...THAT I COULDN'T...
...SAY IT...
WHEN PEOPLE FALL IN LOVE...
...THEY BECOME POETS.
SO...
IF...
...I FALL IN LOVE...

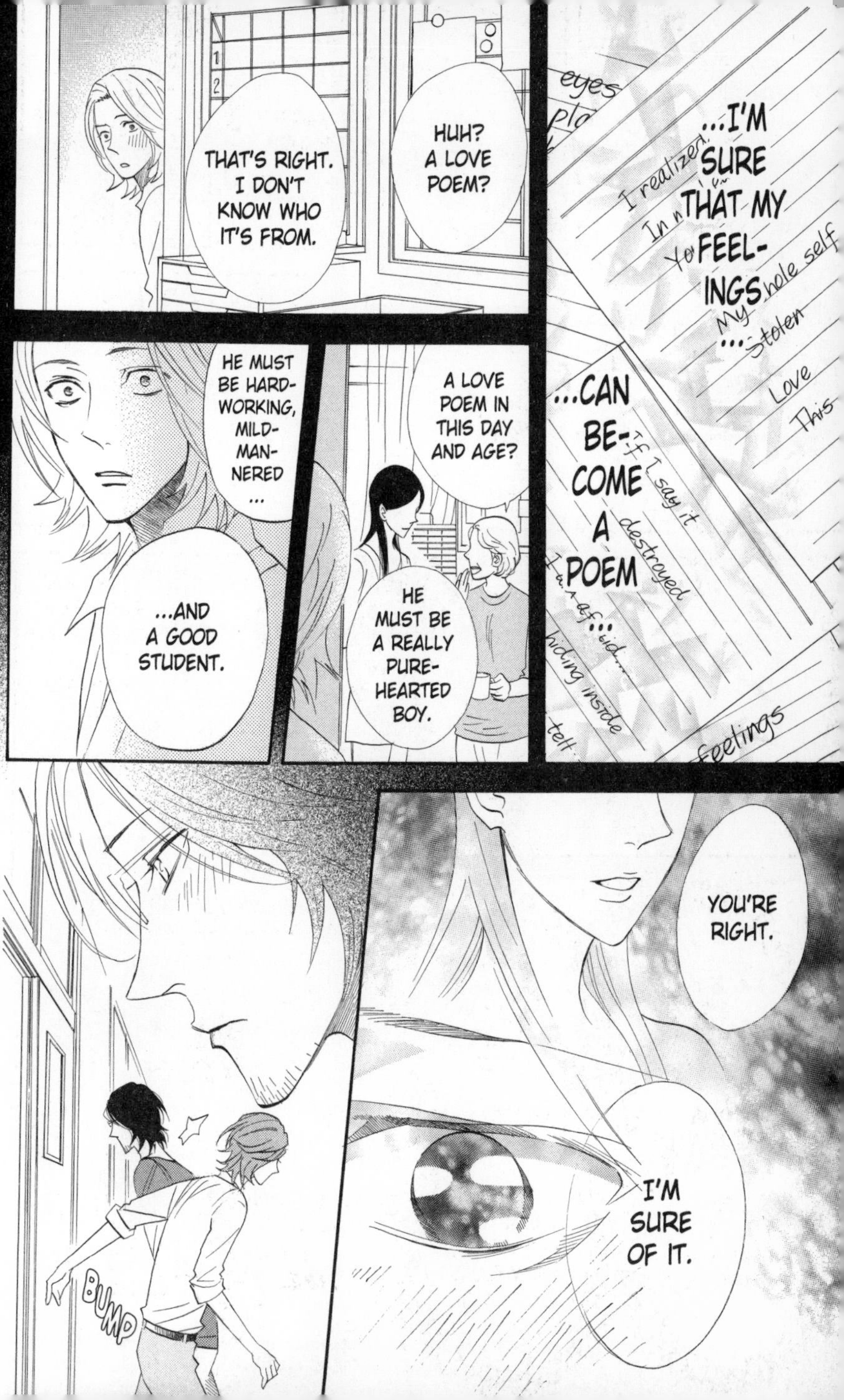
...I'M SURE THAT MY FEELINGS...
...CAN BECOME A POEM
eyes
I realized
My hole self
Stolen
Love
This
If I say it
destroyed
hiding inside
feelings
HUH? A LOVE POEM?
THAT'S RIGHT. I DON'T KNOW WHO IT'S FROM.
A LOVE POEM IN THIS DAY AND AGE?
HE MUST BE A REALLY PURE-HEARTED BOY.
HE MUST BE HARD-WORKING, MILD-MANNERED...
...AND A GOOD STUDENT.
YOU'RE RIGHT.
I'M SURE OF IT.
BUMP

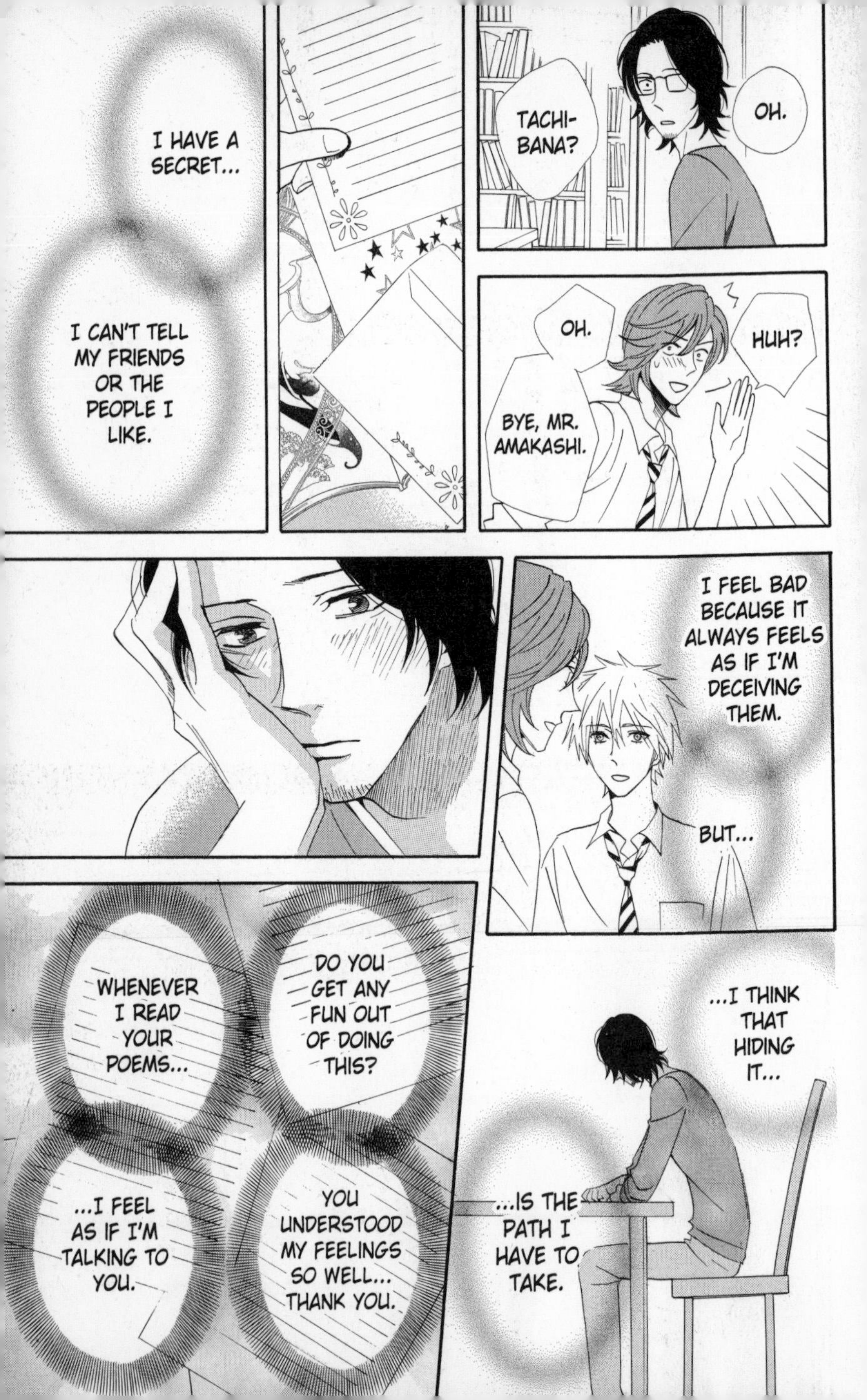
OH.
TACHI-BANA?
HUH?
OH.
BYE, MR. AMAKASHI.
I HAVE A SECRET...
I CAN'T TELL MY FRIENDS OR THE PEOPLE I LIKE.
I FEEL BAD BECAUSE IT ALWAYS FEELS AS IF I'M DECEIVING THEM.
BUT...
...I THINK THAT HIDING IT...
...IS THE PATH I HAVE TO TAKE.
DO YOU GET ANY FUN OUT OF DOING THIS?
WHENEVER I READ YOUR POEMS...
YOU UNDERSTOOD MY FEELINGS SO WELL... THANK YOU.
...I FEEL AS IF I'M TALKING TO YOU.

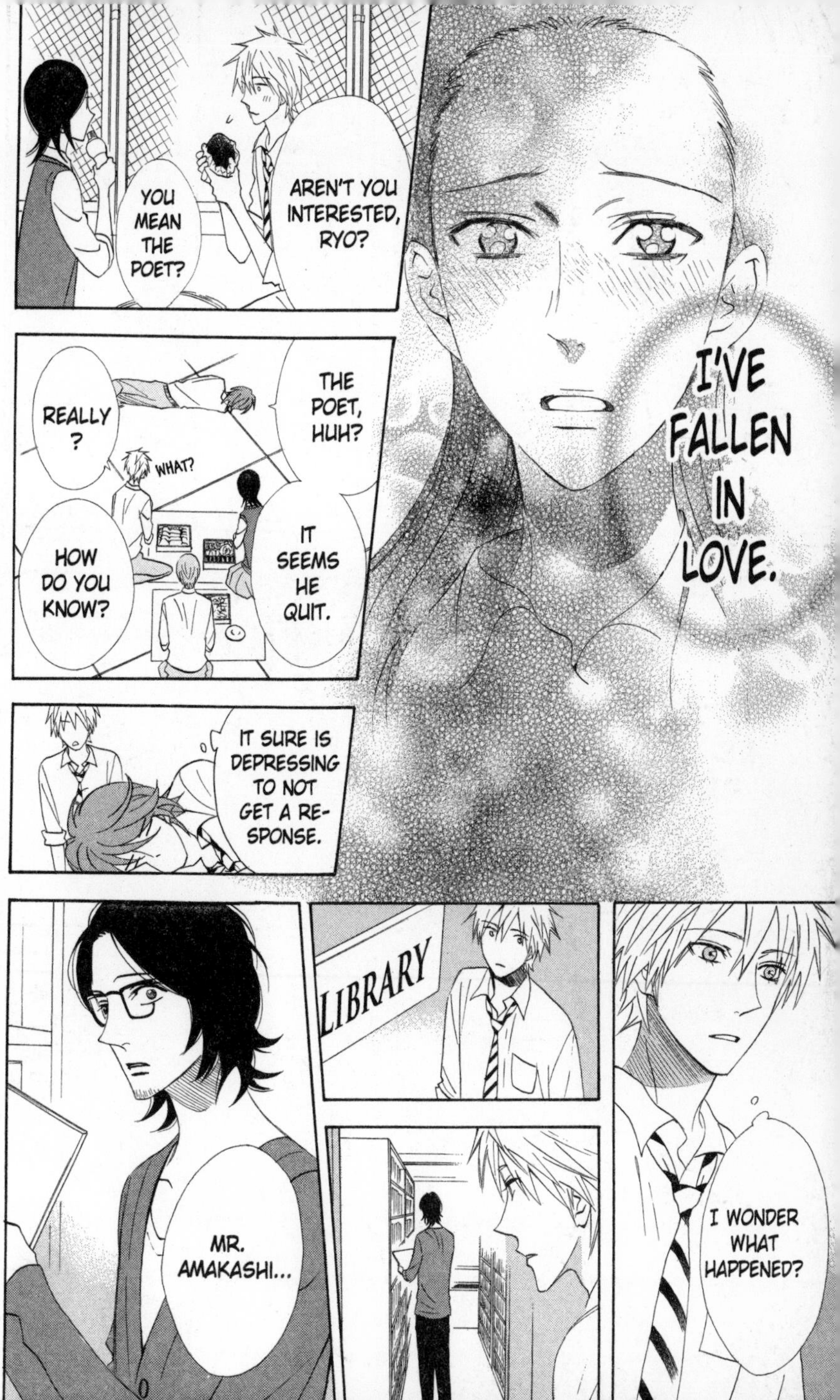
I'VE FALLEN IN LOVE.
AREN'T YOU INTERESTED, RYO?
YOU MEAN THE POET?
THE POET, HUH?
REALLY?
WHAT?
IT SEEMS HE QUIT.
HOW DO YOU KNOW?
IT SURE IS DEPRESSING TO NOT GET A RE-SPONSE.
I WONDER WHAT HAPPENED?
LIBRARY
MR. AMAKASHI...

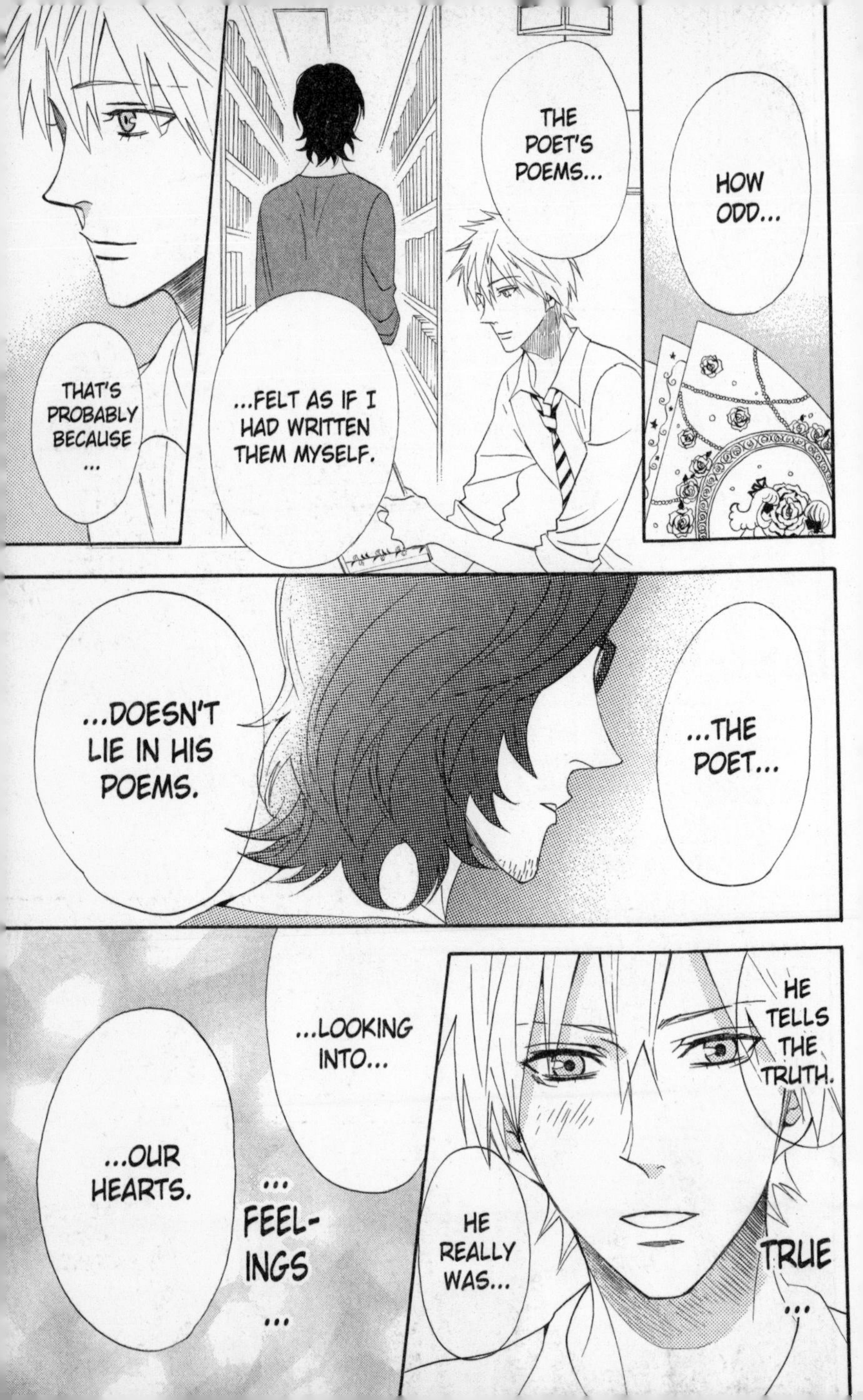
HOW ODD...
THE POET'S POEMS...
...FELT AS IF I HAD WRITTEN THEM MYSELF.
THAT'S PROBABLY BECAUSE ...
...THE POET...
...DOESN'T LIE IN HIS POEMS.
HE TELLS THE TRUTH.
TRUE ...
HE REALLY WAS...
...LOOKING INTO...
... FEEL-INGS ...
...OUR HEARTS.

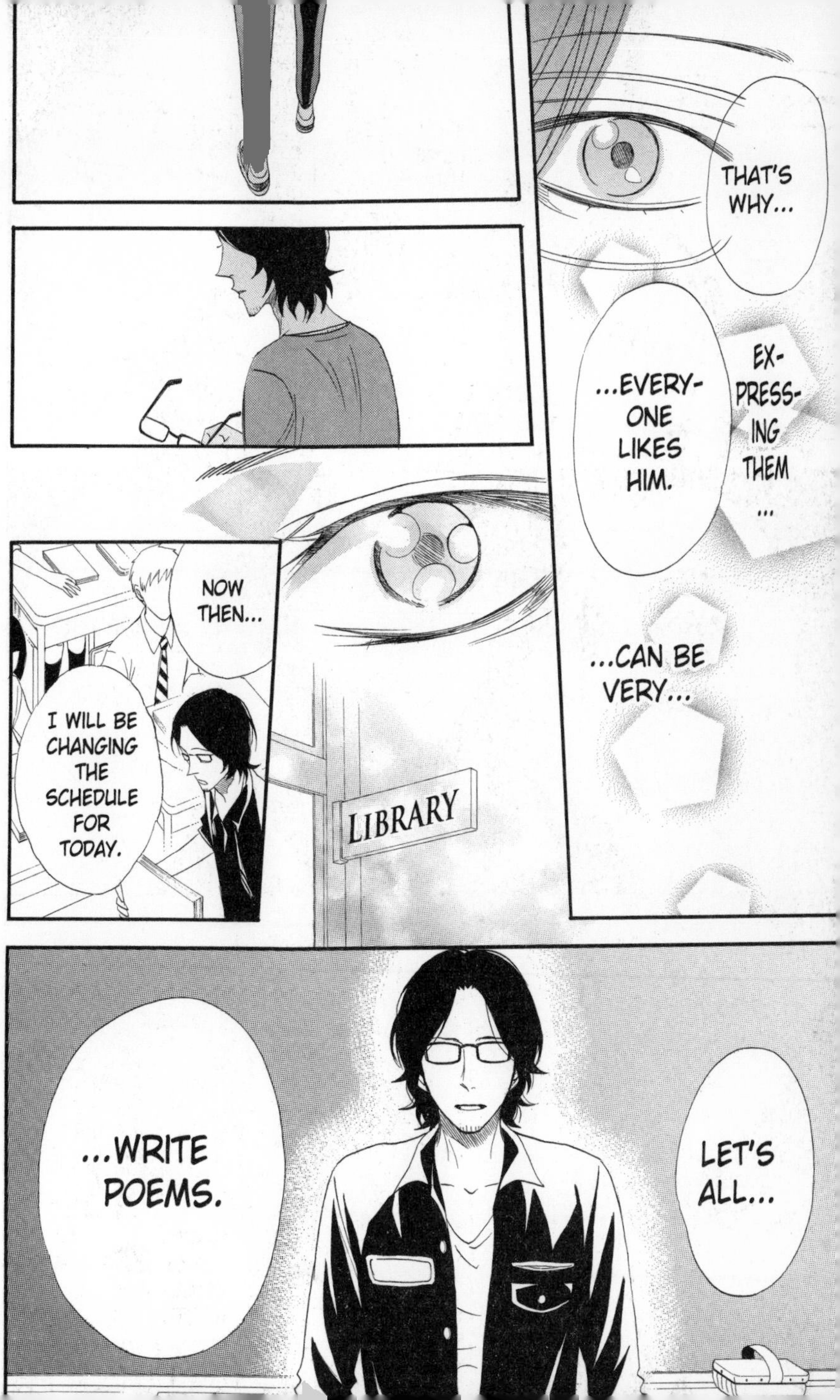
THAT'S WHY...
EX-PRESS-ING THEM...
...EVERY-ONE LIKES HIM.
...CAN BE VERY...
NOW THEN...
I WILL BE CHANGING THE SCHEDULE FOR TODAY.
LIBRARY
LET'S ALL...
...WRITE POEMS.

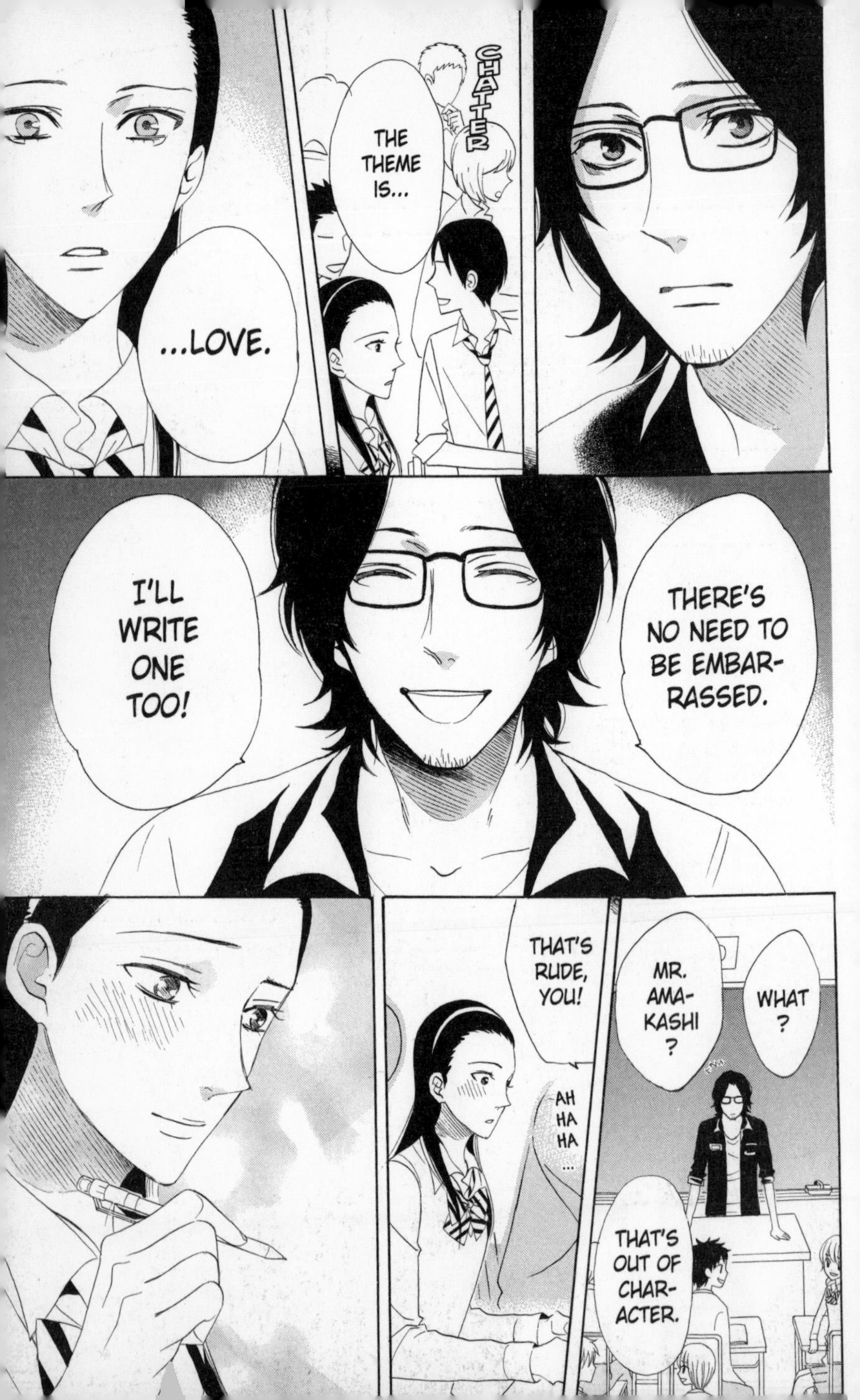
CHATTER
THE THEME IS...
...LOVE.
THERE'S NO NEED TO BE EMBARRASSED.
I'LL WRITE ONE TOO!
WHAT?
MR. AMAKASHI?
THAT'S OUT OF CHARACTER.
THAT'S RUDE, YOU!
AH HA HA...

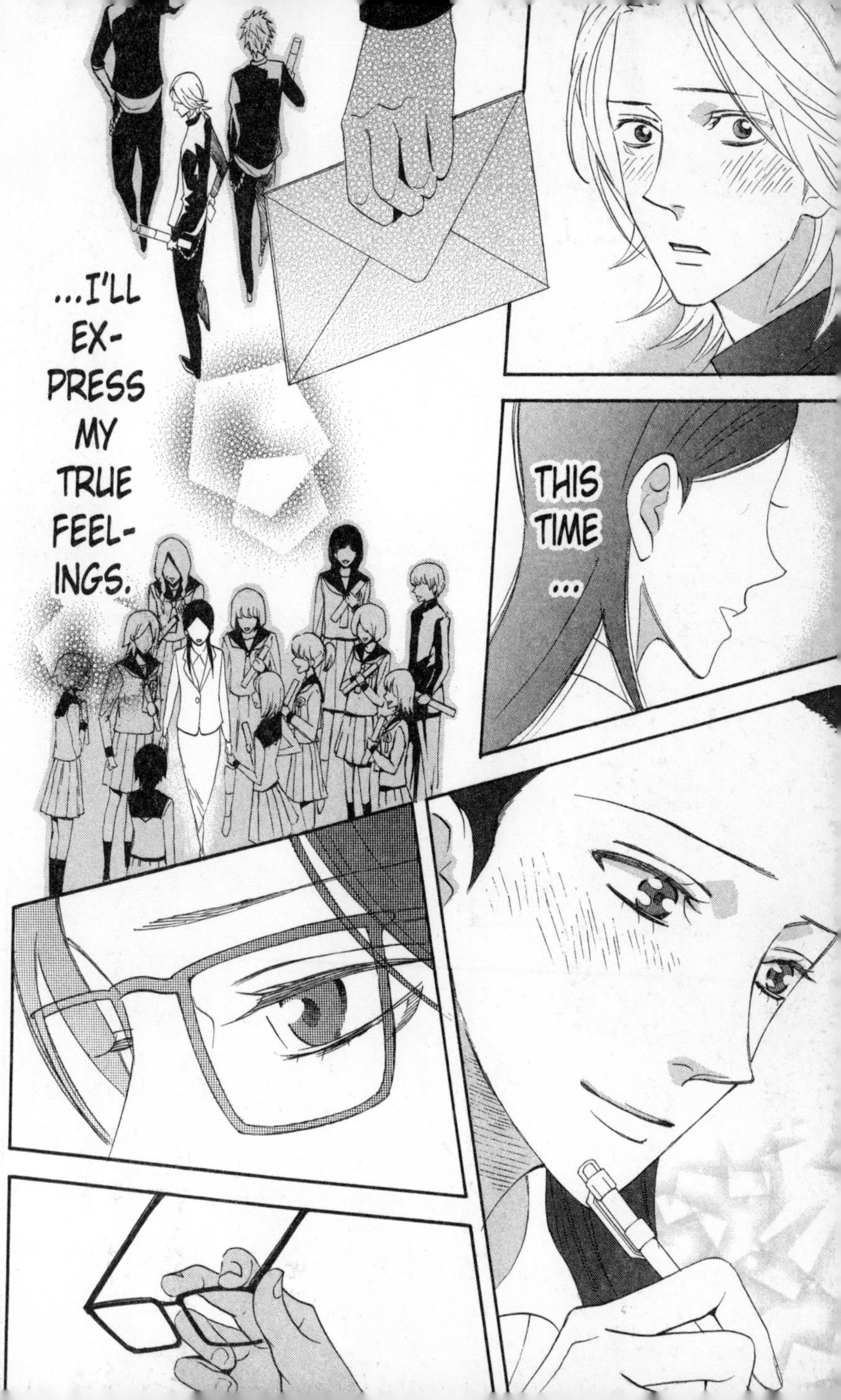
THIS TIME ...
...I'LL EX-PRESS MY TRUE FEEL-INGS.

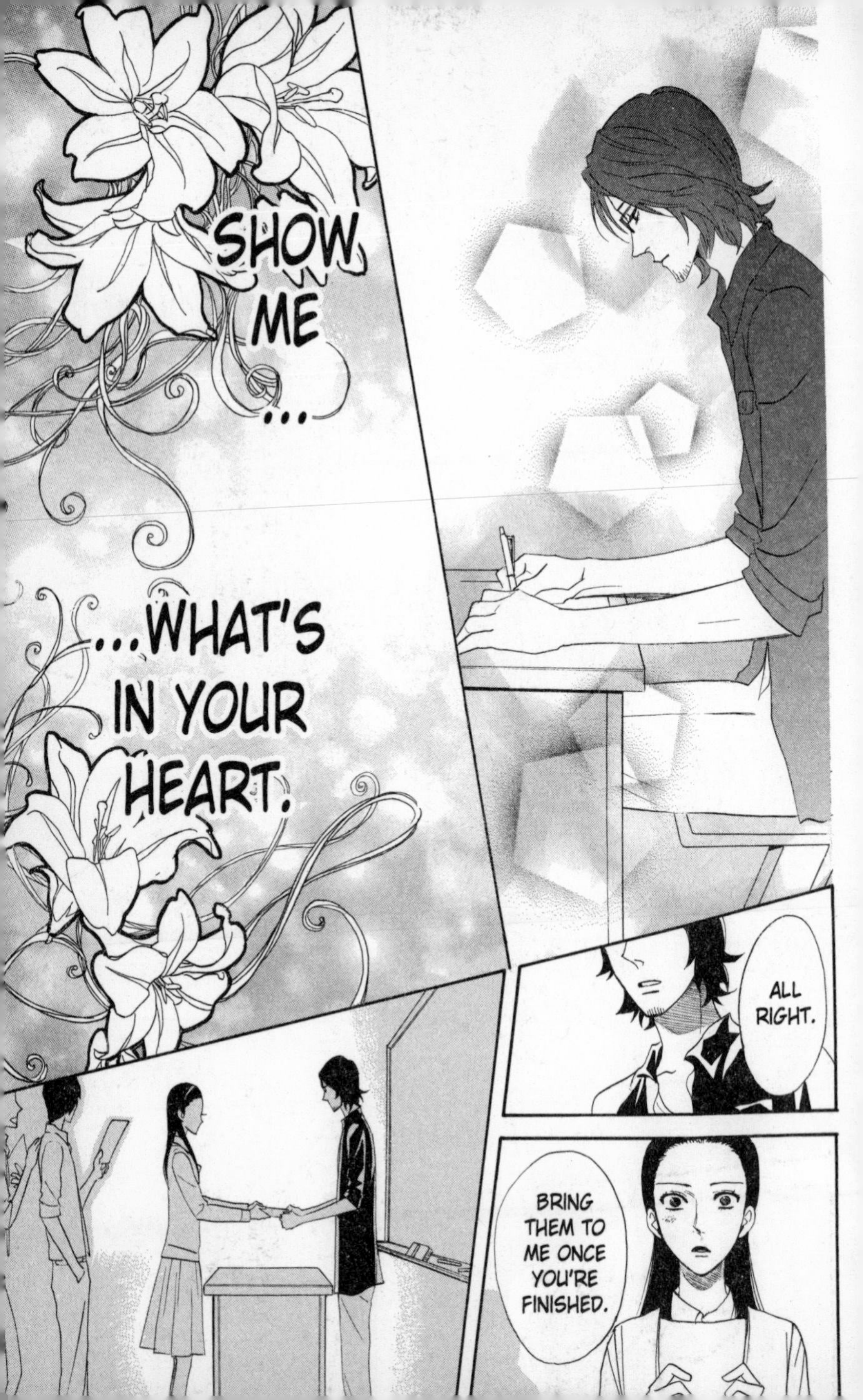
SHOW ME...
...WHAT'S IN YOUR HEART.
ALL RIGHT.
BRING THEM TO ME ONCE YOU'RE FINISHED.

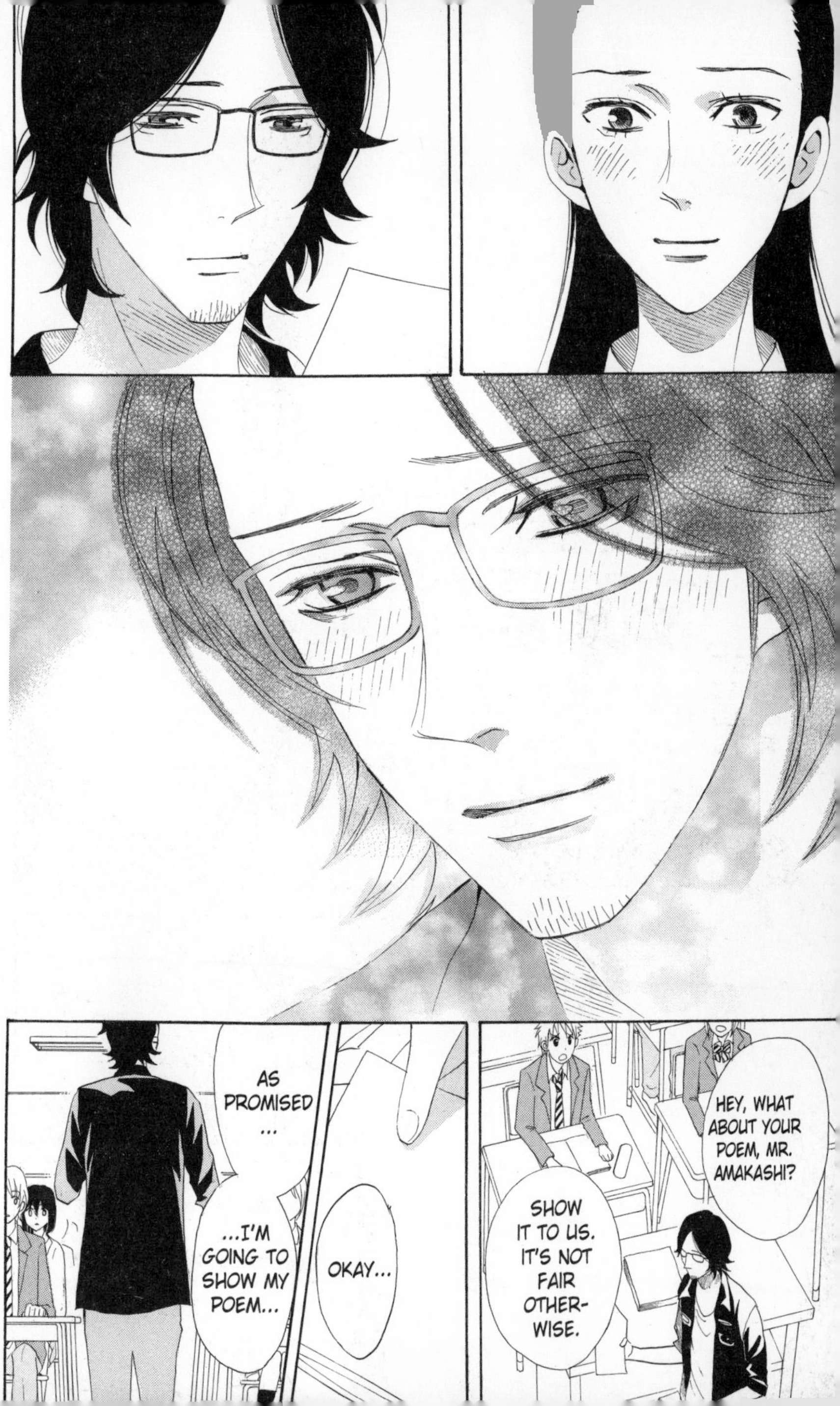
HEY, WHAT ABOUT YOUR POEM, MR. AMAKASHI?
SHOW IT TO US. IT'S NOT FAIR OTHER-WISE.
OKAY...
AS PROMISED ...
...I'M GOING TO SHOW MY POEM...

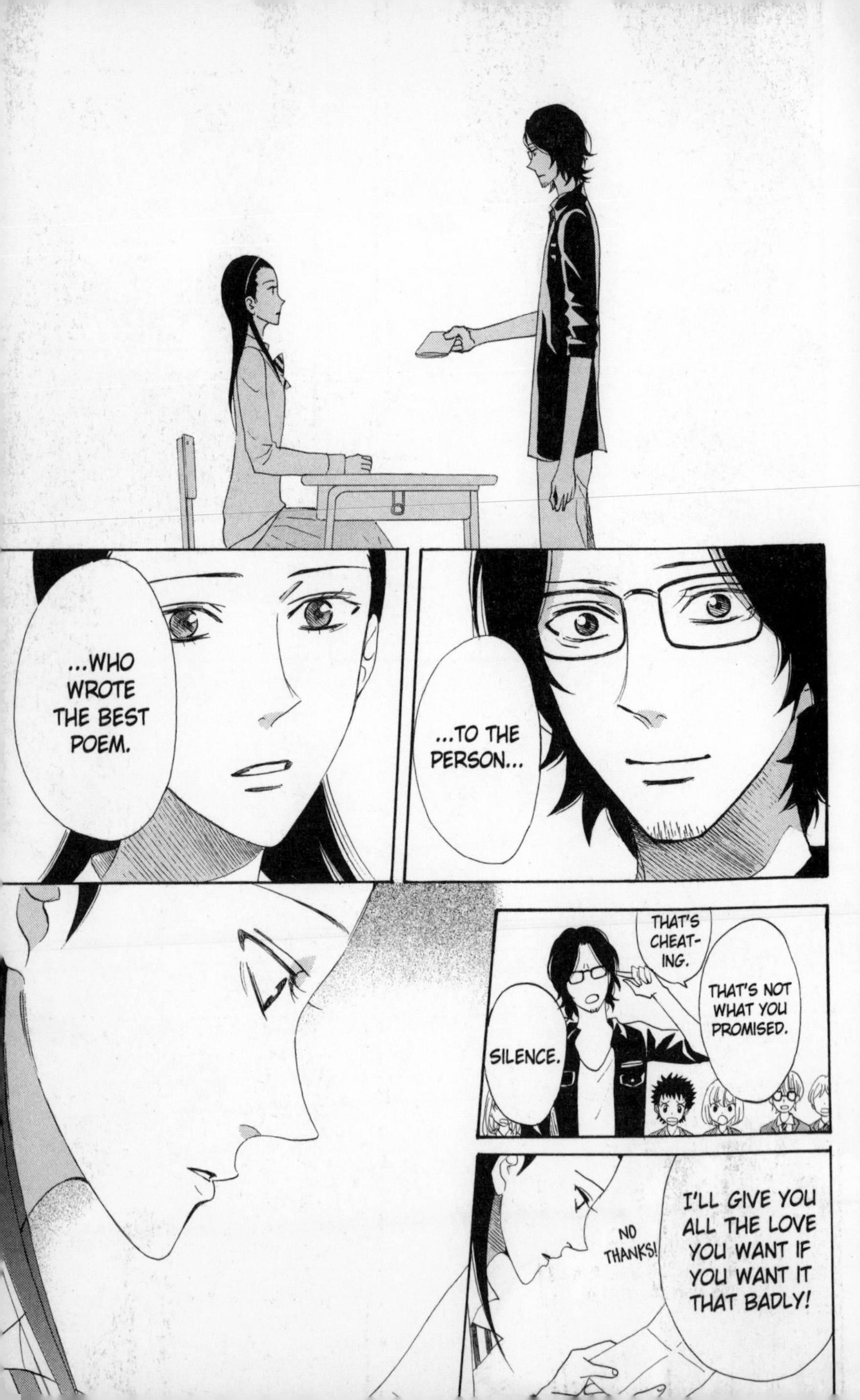
...TO THE PERSON...
...WHO WROTE THE BEST POEM.
THAT'S CHEATING.
THAT'S NOT WHAT YOU PROMISED.
SILENCE.
I'LL GIVE YOU ALL THE LOVE YOU WANT IF YOU WANT IT THAT BADLY!
NO THANKS!

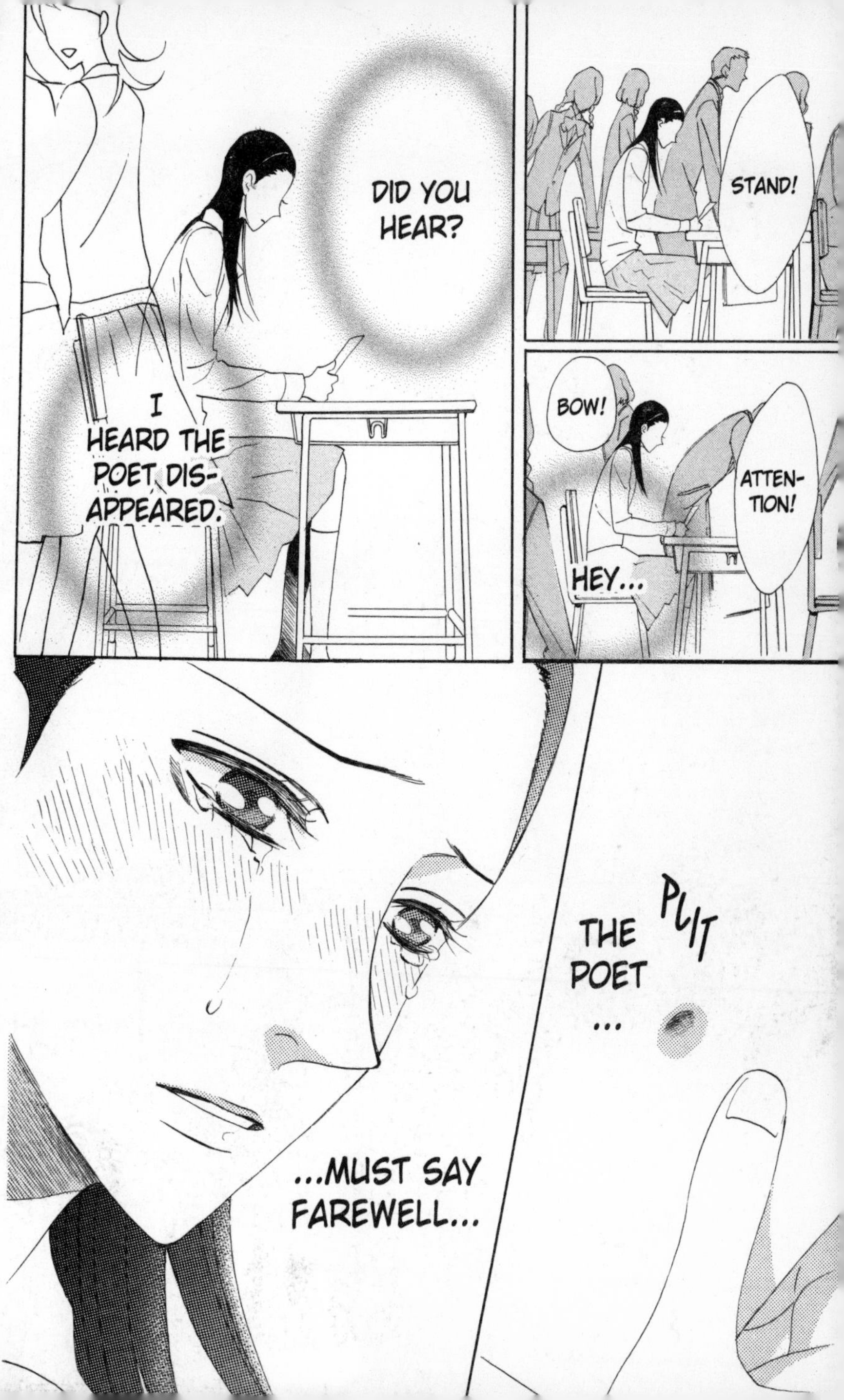
STAND!
ATTENTION!
BOW!
HEY...
DID YOU HEAR?
I HEARD THE POET DIS-APPEARED.
PLIT
THE POET...
...MUST SAY FAREWELL...

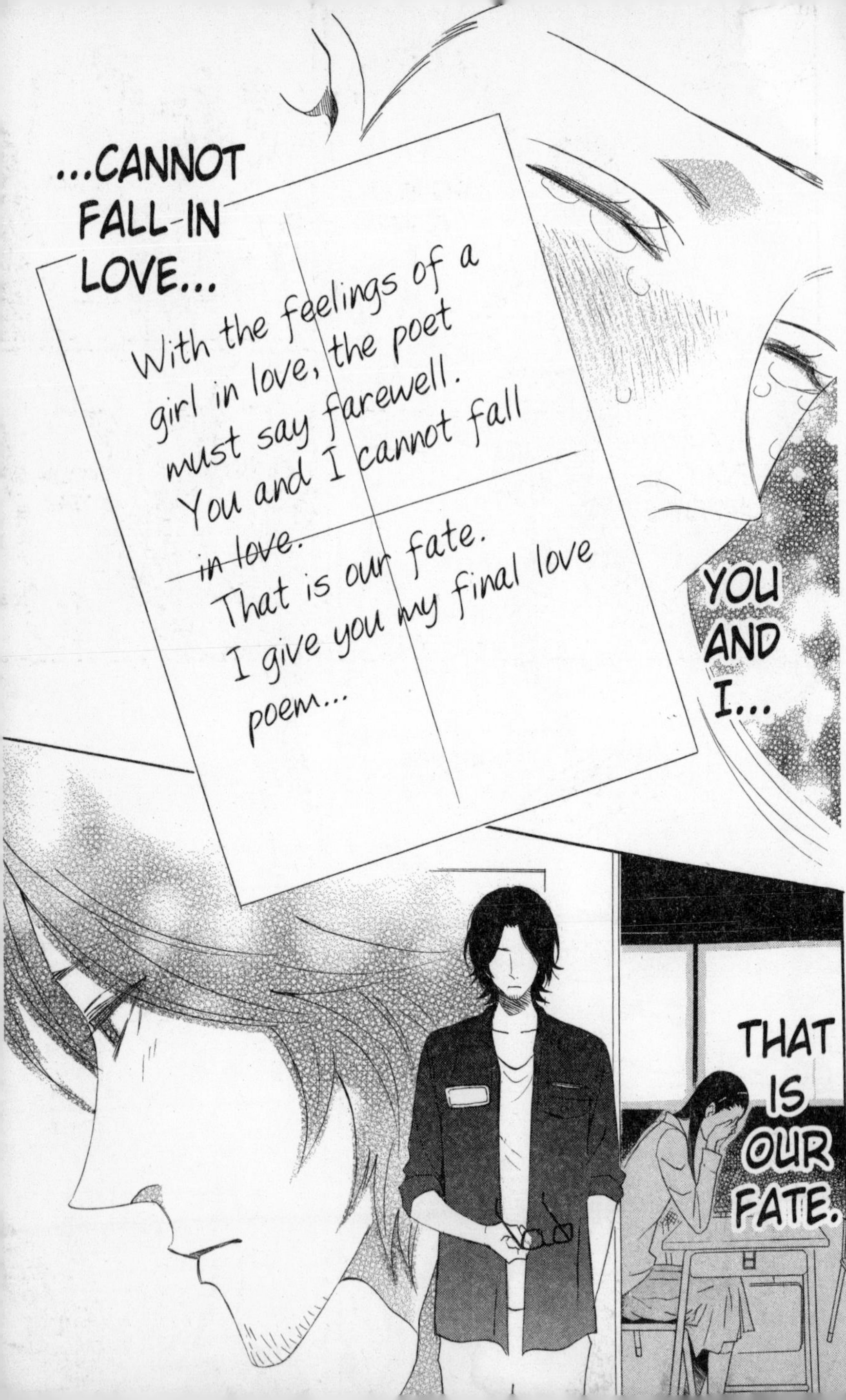
...CANNOT FALL-IN LOVE...
With the feelings of a girl in love, the poet must say farewell. You and I cannot fall ~~in love.~~ That is our fate. I give you my final love poem...
YOU AND I...
THAT IS OUR FATE.

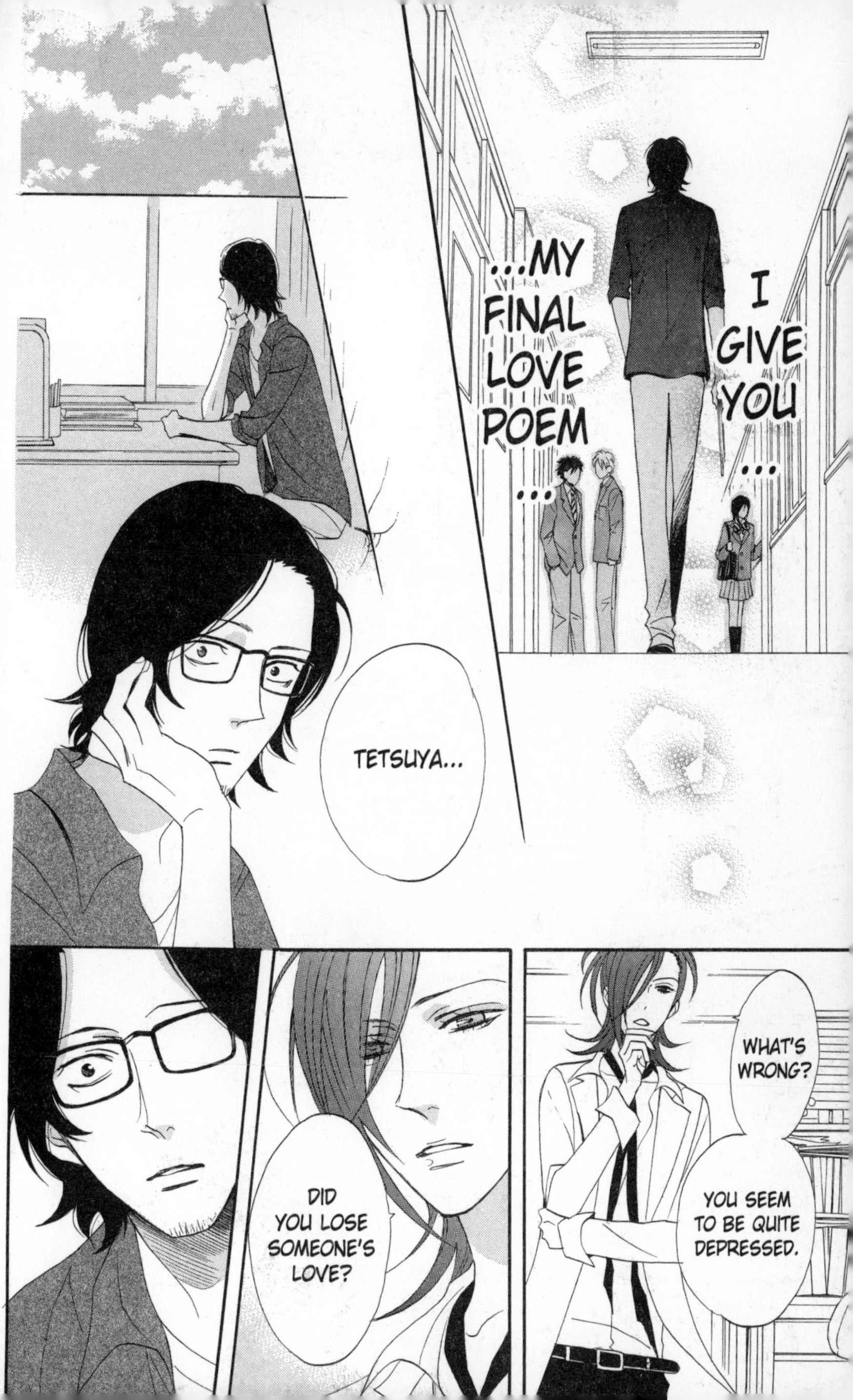
I GIVE YOU...
...MY FINAL LOVE POEM...
TETSUYA...
WHAT'S WRONG?
YOU SEEM TO BE QUITE DEPRESSED.
DID YOU LOSE SOMEONE'S LOVE?

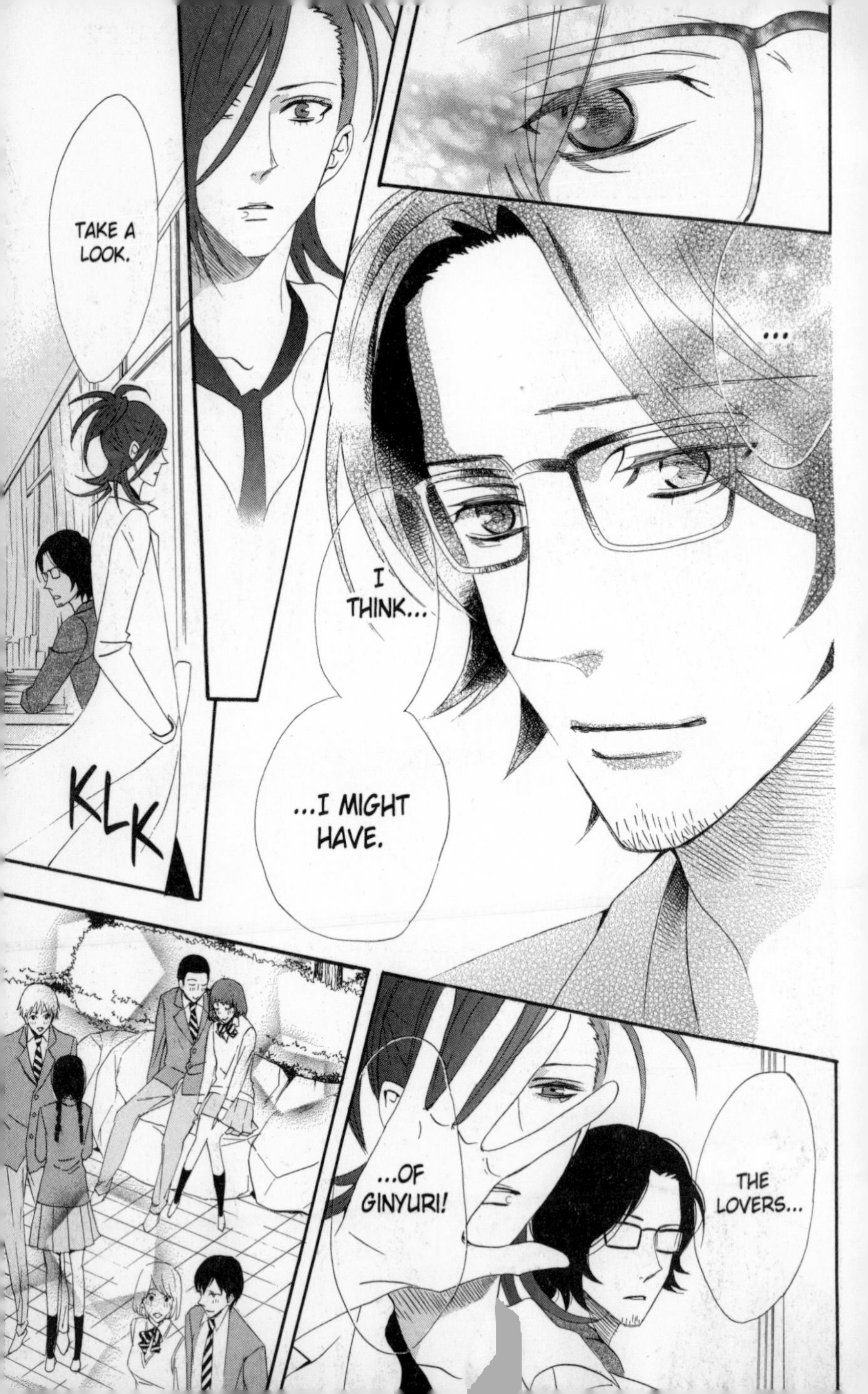
...
I THINK...
...I MIGHT HAVE.
TAKE A LOOK.
KLK
THE LOVERS...
...OF GINYURI!

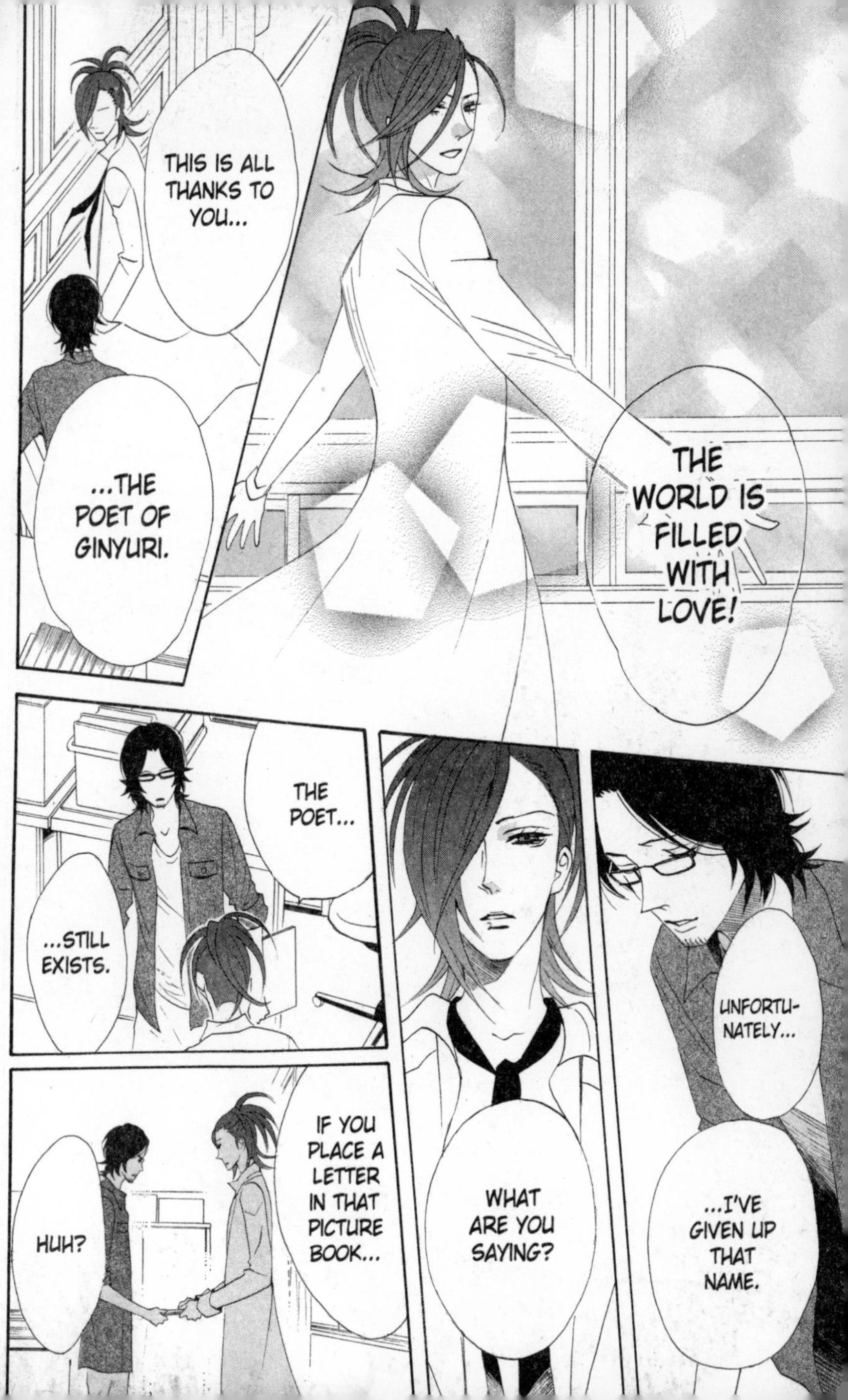
THE WORLD IS FILLED WITH LOVE!
THIS IS ALL THANKS TO YOU...
...THE POET OF GINYURI.
UNFORTUNATELY...
...I'VE GIVEN UP THAT NAME.
WHAT ARE YOU SAYING?
THE POET...
...STILL EXISTS.
IF YOU PLACE A LETTER IN THAT PICTURE BOOK...
HUH?

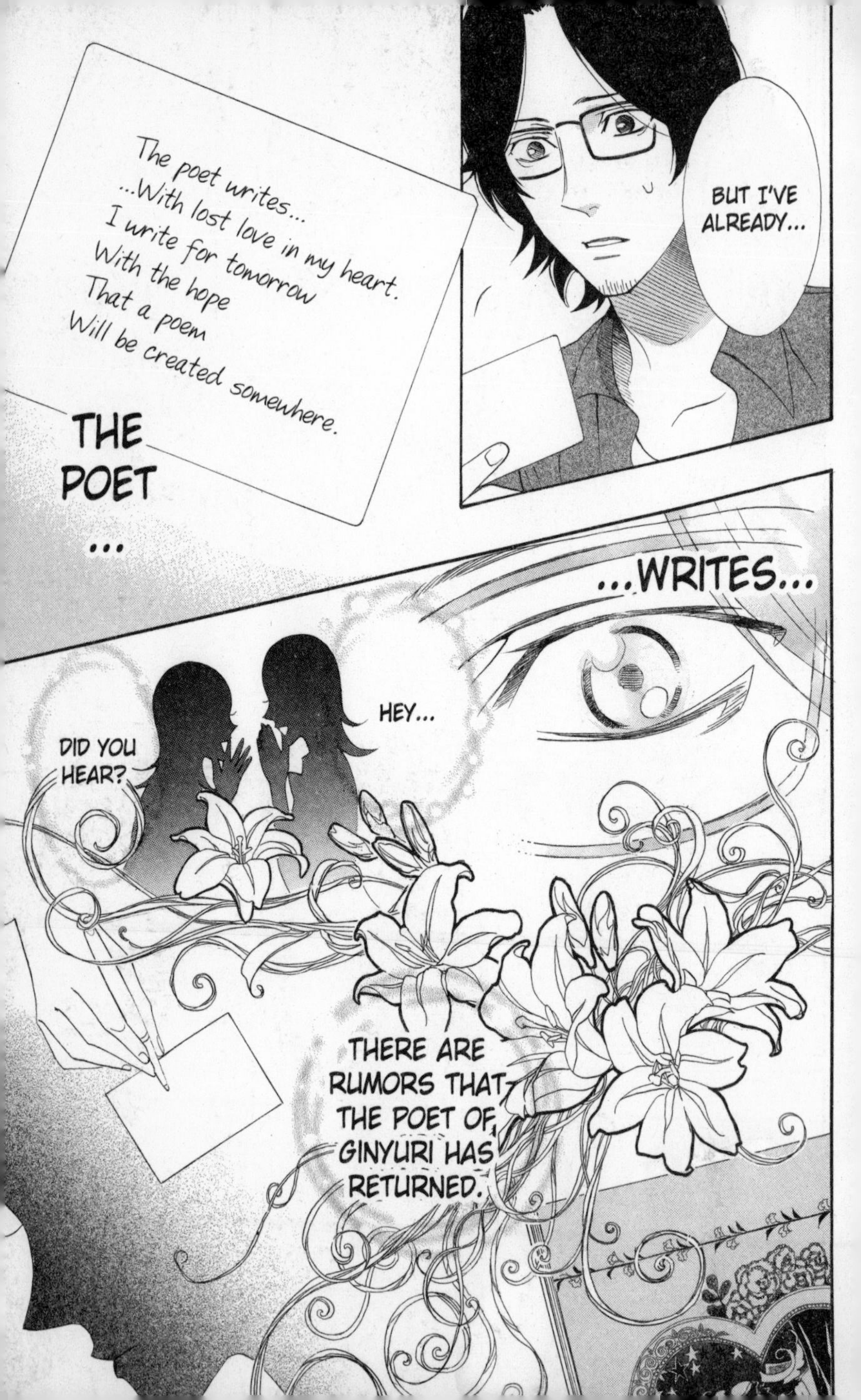
BUT I'VE ALREADY...
The poet writes...
...With lost love in my heart.
I write for tomorrow
With the hope
That a poem
Will be created somewhere.
THE POET ...
...WRITES...
HEY...
DID YOU HEAR?
THERE ARE RUMORS THAT THE POET OF GINYURI HAS RETURNED.

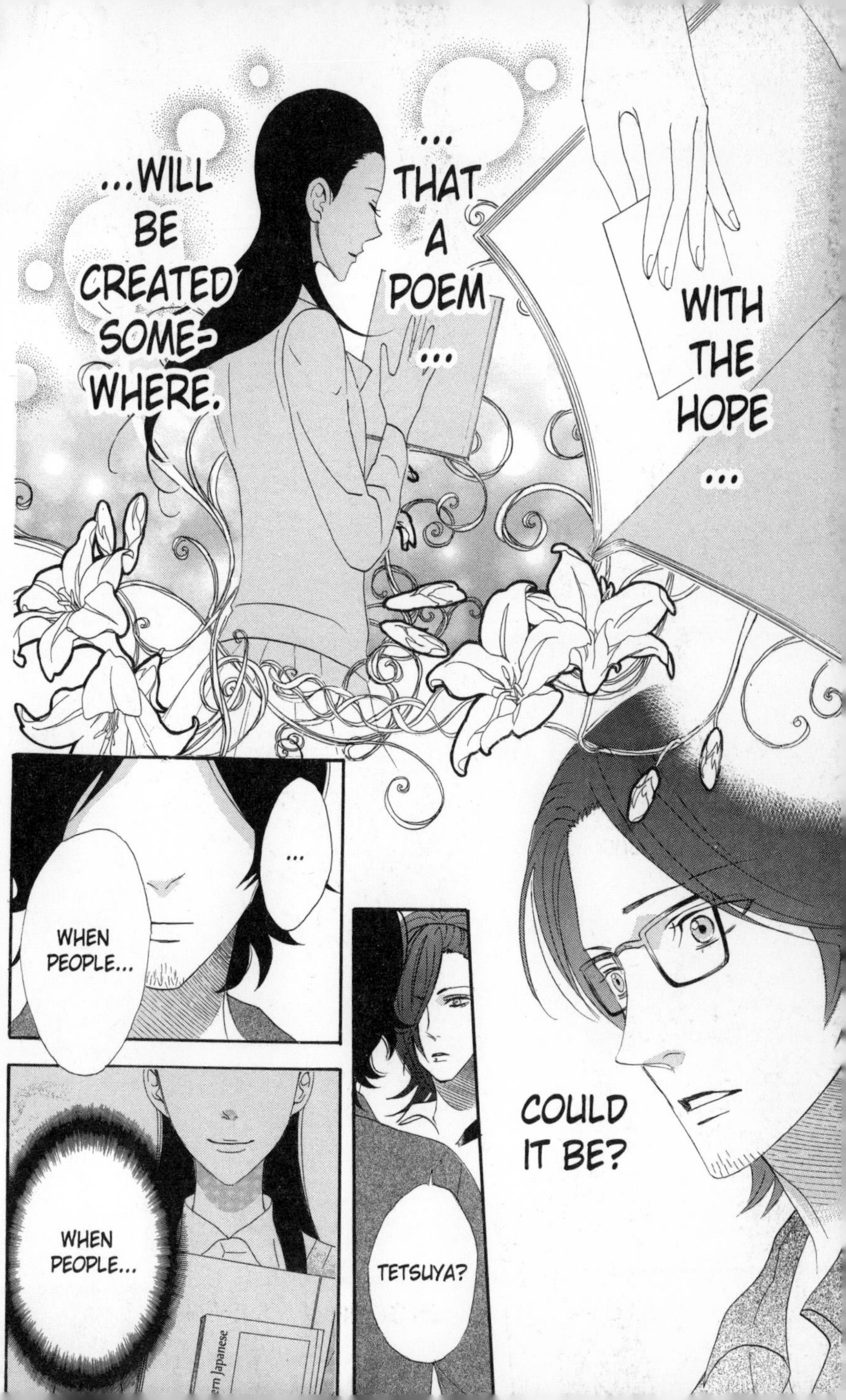
WITH THE HOPE ...
... THAT A POEM ...
...WILL BE CREATED SOME-WHERE.
COULD IT BE?
...
WHEN PEOPLE...
TETSUYA?
WHEN PEOPLE...

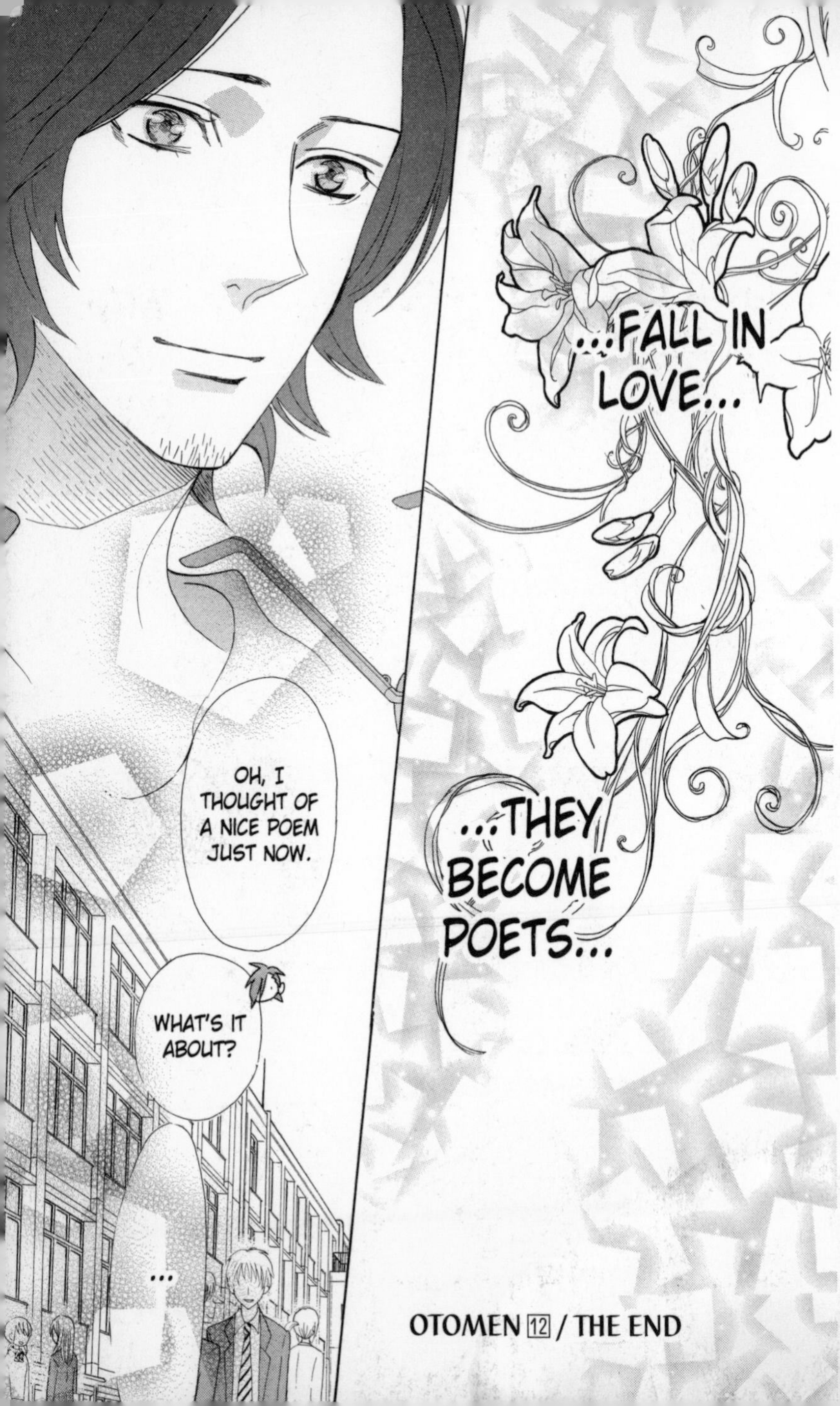
...FALL IN LOVE...
...THEY BECOME POETS...
OH, I THOUGHT OF A NICE POEM JUST NOW.
WHAT'S IT ABOUT?
...
OTOMEN 12 / THE END

OTOMEN

Confused by some of the terms, but too MANLY to ask for help?

Here are some **cultural notes** to assist you!

HONORIFICS

Chan – an informal honorific used to address children and females. *Chan* can also be used toward animals, lovers, intimate friends and people whom one has known since childhood.

Kun – an informal honorific used primarily toward males; it can be used by people of more senior status addressing those junior to them or by anyone addressing male children.

San – the most common honorific title. It is used to address people outside one's immediate family and close circle of friends.

Sensei – honorific title used to address teachers as well as professionals such as doctors, lawyers and artists.

Aya Kanno was born in Tokyo, Japan.
She is the creator of *Soul Rescue* and *Blank Slate*
(originally published as *Akusaga* in Japan's
BetsuHana magazine). Her latest work, *Otomen*,
is currently being serialized in *BetsuHana*.